Corporate Governance

The financial scandals emerging from major corporations from Enron onwards generated an increased interest in governance issues, and emphasized the need for companies to be transparent in their dealings with shareholders and the markets.

Although the issues in Asia are fundamentally similar to those in the rest of the world, there are some crucial differences in the way in which Asian corporations acknowledge and confront these issues, and in the political and legal frameworks under which they operate. Using examples of good and bad governance, this book analyses whether there is a uniquely Asian approach to governance issues.

Corporate Governance in Asia provides a comprehensive overview of both national and international institutions involved in governance, and the organizations which attempt to promote it. It explores compliance issues and the role of directors and boards, and external parties. The book also examines the relationship between governance, value creation and social responsibility, and looks at how Asian firms present their governance.

Business and finance students, as well as executives with an interest in Asian business or corporate governance, will find this an authoritative and insightful guide to this complex and important topic.

Julian Roche is a Corporate Finance trainer based in Singapore and London, and a consultant to various professional bodies, including ICAEW in Europe and Asia. He is also a VP of MHCi, a firm specializing in corporate responsibility issues, where he is responsible for corporate finance issues. He has published various specialist manuals on finance aspects, as well as writing training manuals for executive education. In 1998 he was appointed UN Expert on Commodities, UNCTAD Risk Management Division.

Corporate Governance in Asia

Julian Roche

Routledge
Taylor & Francis Group

LONDON AND NEW YORK

First published 2005
by Routledge
2 Park Square, Milton Park, Abingdon, Oxon OX14 4RN

Simultaneously published in the USA and Canada
by Routledge
270 Madison Ave, New York, NY 10016

Routledge is an imprint of the Taylor & Francis Group

© 2005 Julian Roche

Typeset in Perpetua and Bell Gothic by
Florence Production Ltd, Stoodleigh, Devon
Printed and bound in Great Britain by
TJ International Ltd, Padstow, Cornwall

British Library Cataloguing in Publication Data
A catalogue record for this book is available from
the British Library

Library of Congress Cataloging in Publication Data
A catalog record for this book has been requested

ISBN 0–415–33975–8 (hbk)
ISBN 0–415–33976–6 (pbk)

Contents

Illustrations

FIGURES

TABLES

BOXES

Acknowledgements

Corporate governance is a rapidly moving field of study where all individual efforts must necessarily be imperfect; I owe numerous debts to the other researchers and writers who have made contributions on which I have drawn. Particular thanks must be given to Roger Adams of ACCA, Edgar Fernandez of the Economist Intelligence Unit, Professor Michael Hopkins of Middlesex University, Paul MacKellar of KPMG, James McRitchie of CorpGov.net, Tobias Webb of *Ethical Corporation* magazine, Dr Wei Zhang of Cambridge University and Ghita Alderman of the World Bank. Thanks also to the Hong Kong Stock Exchange for their prompt and informative responses to enquiries – a model for other Exchanges to follow.

My thanks also to my understanding editor Jacqueline Curthoys, and the rest of her team at Routledge.

Final thanks must go to my even more understanding wife Gowri, who watched patiently as an ever-increasing volume of effort and time went into this project.

Acknowledgements

Abbreviations

ACCA	Association of Chartered Certified Accountants
ACGA	Asian Corporate Governance Association
ADB	Asian Development Bank
ADR	American Depository Receipts
ASEAN	Association of South East Asian Nations
BIS	Bank for International Settlements
BLS	Bank-led system (of corporate governance)
CACCI	Confederation of Asia-Pacific Chambers of Commerce and Industry
Calpers	California Public Employees' Retirement System
CAPA	Confederation of Asian Pacific Accountants
CASS	China Academy of Social Sciences
CCGD	Council on Corporate Disclosure and Governance
CEO	Chief Executive Officer
CFO	Chief Financial Officer
CG	Corporate Governance
CGC	Corporate Governance Committee
CGFRC	Corporate Governance and Financial Reporting Centre
CGI	Corporate Governance Index
CGLI	Corporate governance laws and institutions
CLSA	Credit Lyonnais Securities Asia
CPD	Continuous professional development
CSR	Corporate social responsibility
CSRC	China Securities Regulatory Commission
CTI	Corporate Transparency Index
EMS	Equity market-based system (of corporate governance)
EU	European Union
FASB	Financial Accounting Standards Board
FBS	Family-based system (of corporate governance)
FDI	Foreign direct investment
FRRP	Financial Reporting Review Panel
FSC	Financial Services Commission
FSS	Financial Supervisory Service

GAAP	Generally Accepted Accounting Principles
GAAS	Generally Accepted Auditing Standards
GDP	Gross domestic product
GDR	Global Depository Receipts
GTB	Global Trust Bank
HKSA	Hong Kong Society of Accountants
HSI	Hang Seng Index
IAS	International Accounting Standards
IASB	International Accounting Standards Board
IFAC	International Federation of Accountants
IFRS	International Financial Reporting Standards
ILO	International Labour Organization
IOSCO	International Organization of Securities Commissions
IPO	Initial public offering
IRCJ	Industrial Revitalization Corporation of Japan
ISA	International Standards of Audit
KLSE	Kuala Lumpur Stock Exchange
KRW	(South) Korean Won
KSE	Korean Stock Exchange
M&A	Mergers and Acquisitions
MAS	Monetary Authority of Singapore
MESDAQ	Malaysian Exchange of Securities Dealing and Automated Quotation Bhd
MNC	Multinational corporation
NED	Non-executive director
NGO	Non-government organization
NUS	National University of Singapore
NYSE	New York Stock Exchange
OECD	Organisation for Economic Co-operation and Development
P/E Ratio	Price/Earnings Ratio
PERC	Political and Economic Risk Consultancy
PRC	People's Republic of China
ROCE	Return on capital employed
RM	Ringgit Malaysia
RMB	Renminbi (Chinese currency)
SEBI	Securities and Exchange Board of India
SEC	Securities and Exchange Commission
SEHK	Hong Kong Stock Exchange
SFC	Securities and Futures Commission
SID	Singapore Institute of Directors
SME	Small and medium enterprise
SOE	State-owned enterprise
SOX	Sarbanes-Oxley Act
SRO	Self-regulatory organization
WTO	World Trade Organization

Chapter 1

The background

- Introduction
- Huge interest in corporate governance
- Is a definition still useful?
- The cultural and historical perspective
- Institutional prevalence
- What does the study of corporate governance entail?
- The objective of corporate governance
- What corporate governance is *not*
- Systems of corporate governance
- Transition economies
- How to run a corporate governance system
- Examining corporate governance models
- Family-based governance (FBS)
- Corporate governance in the West: a review of the US and UK
  - The United States
  - The United Kingdom
- Corporate governance in Asia
- The lingering effects of socialism
- Is it all good news?

INTRODUCTION

As this book has a practical and regional focus, arguably we should not dwell too much on the theoretical and global background. But it *is* important to understand what is meant by 'corporate governance', and the nature of the economies and corporate structures from which the concept and implementation arose. The original theoretical key was widely dispersed ownership of the corporation, which resulted in the famous idea expressed by Berle and Means, the authors of

1

the most famous book on corporate governance, that 'the owner of industrial wealth is left a mere symbol of ownership'[1] as the control over companies really lies with professional managers. Western[2] literature on corporate governance often starts from this so-called 'principal–agent relationship' and the problems which are alleged to flow from it. This did all stem from Berle and Means who concluded that almost half of large American corporations did not have a single owner who controlled more than 20 per cent of the stock, and argued that the stockholders surrendered 'disposition of use of the enterprise to those in control'[3] by which they meant senior managers and the board. Addressing the future of the US corporation, Berle and Means also said:

> This [corporate] system bids fair to be as all-embracing as was the feudal system of its time. [It] demands that we examine both its conditions and its trends, for an understanding of the structure upon which will rest the economic order of the future.[4]

The concept of corporate governance presumes a fundamental tension between shareholders and corporate managers.[5] In this model, while the objective of a company's shareholders is a positive return on their investment, managers may have other goals, such as the growth and reputation of the company, the security of their employment, the prominence of their division within the company, their own personal financial reward or something else quite unpredictable. Managers have the information and the decision-making power, but the many shareholders take the financial risk. Economists and consultants have suggested many solutions for this *agency problem* between shareholders and managers, focusing on incentive alignment – sometimes through a discipline such as Economic Value Added (EVA$_{tm}$), sometimes through stock options, somewhat discredited now. Monitoring by an independent and engaged board of directors is also supposed to guarantee that managers behave in the best interests of the shareholders.[6] As a last resort, Chief Executive Officers (CEOs) who fail to maximize shareholder interests can be removed by concerned boards of directors, while a firm that neglects shareholder value is disciplined by the market through takeover[7] and ultimately bankruptcy.

But when academics[8] studied the important issue of ultimate control much more recently (i.e. they traced the chain of ownership to find who has the most voting rights), they found ownership is largely concentrated in the hands of families and the state even in Western countries; moreover, the concentration of ownership is enhanced through the use of pyramid structures, deviations from one-share-one-vote rules, cross-holdings and the appointment of managers and directors who are related to the controlling family. Think Parmalat, and it is clear that even in the twenty-first century the Berle and Means paradigm is far from universality even in the West, especially outside the US and the UK. Nor, with the risen power of private equity in the US and Europe, does it look likely to be.

What does flow from this alleged divergence between the interests of owner and manager? Does it matter? At root is an argument about *legitimacy*: the extent of congruence between what the firm does and what society as a whole expects it to do – which is why the 'stakeholder' debate is so closely linked to corporate governance and why the shape, ownership and management of a firm is relevant to its legitimacy, which is at root a *political* question. And about *legitimation*, the way in which a firm, and the financial system in general, seeks to achieve that legitimacy. Both, of course, change over time, and perhaps nowhere more so than in Asia in the coming decade where political opinion is being expressed more freely than hitherto and more demands are being placed on corporations to be *legitimate*, in this sense.

HUGE INTEREST IN CORPORATE GOVERNANCE

Since Berle and Means wrote their pathbreaking book, the concept has gone much, much further than the separation of ownership and control that led to the first widely accepted meaning of corporate governance. Corporate governance has become – *to such an extent that it is reasonable to ask in whose interests all this analysis really is* – a dominant concern among academics, practitioners, lawmakers and companies' stakeholders. No surprise: it is because corporate governance has to do with the perennially interesting and important questions of ownership, accountability and control, incomplete contracts and agency problems, performance and incentive design. Cynically, we can also observe that it has become a feeding frenzy for academics in particular, but also for policy-makers and journalists alike. Authors, too. It was after research carried out in the 1960s and 1970s by academics at Harvard and elsewhere – Jensen, Fama, Williamson and Hart, among others – that the subject established itself as an individual field in its own right. The initial focus on comparative financial performance and the compensation packages of CEOs and senior managers broadened throughout the 1990s to include *inter alia* the performance of boards, the way directors were appointed and their functions, the role of independent and non-executive directors, efforts to create more diverse and inclusive boards of directors; the way executive pay in general was determined, audit practices, and a wider range of corporate social responsibility (CSR) concerns, including such issues as workplace diversity, glass ceilings for women, human rights abuses, allegations of sweatshop conditions in domestic and overseas factories, pollution and other environmental issues, the overseas sales of military hardware, the legal status of tobacco and employee codes of conduct. Reflecting public concern, in 2001 for example – which may admittedly have been close to the high water mark for shareholder activism in the US – shareholder motions were introduced to force corporate action on *inter alia* clean

3

energy, genetically engineered agricultural products, products containing the PVC compound, equal opportunities, drilling for oil in the Arctic National Wildlife Refuge in Alaska, predatory lending by financial institutions, mandatory reporting on greenhouse gas emissions, overseas contractor employment (for example, slave, prison and child labour, and pay scales), and workplace discrimination, health and safety, and violence. Also, of course, the big one: revelations about accounting irregularities in the United States and elsewhere galvanized the US Administration to improve the effectiveness of corporate governance mechanisms to prevent and detect material accounting irregularities, accurate accounting now being included within the corporate governance framework. Shareholder activism in the US has become interwoven with political correctness and a profound awkwardness in the public consciousness about the role, methods and achievements of US corporations, the standard-bearers of the American way of life. *It is hard to resist the temptation to observe that it has all become a political game.* All this is vitally important when we come to examine corporate governance in Asia because of its *alien* quality.

IS A DEFINITION STILL USEFUL?

As a result of the perpetually expanding borders of the subject matter, it is not easy to define 'corporate governance'. Moreover, depending on their perspective, different authors define corporate governance in different ways, so that a single precise or universally accepted definition does not exist. That said, it is usually worth under such circumstances trying to put some boundaries on the subject matter, especially if it threatens to engulf nearby disciplines such as CSR and the pursuit of shareholder value, so as to avoid such neologisms as *The Business Roundtable Calls On Boards Of Directors To Make Security A Key Part Of Corporate Governance.*[9] We now also face the prospect of 'enterprise governance', which is [naturally] 'the framework that covers both corporate governance and business governance'. Some definitions then . . .

A useful and still widely accepted definition of corporate governance is that set out in the Principles of Corporate Governance developed by the Organisation for Economic Co-operation and Development (OECD) in 1999:

> Corporate governance is the system by which business corporations are directed and controlled. The corporate governance structure specifies the distribution of rights and responsibilities among different participants in the corporation . . . and spells out the rules and procedures for making decisions on corporate affairs. By doing this it provides the structure through which the company objectives are set, and the means of attaining those objectives and monitoring performance.

(OECD, 1999)

4

Later, as the previous definition gained widespread acceptance, the OECD offered a broader definition instead:

> . . . corporate governance refers to the private and public institutions, including laws, regulations and accepted business practices, which together govern the relationship, in a market economy, between corporate managers and entrepreneurs ('corporate insiders') on one hand, and those who invest resources in corporations, on the other.
>
> (OECD, 2001)

In its narrowest sense, corporate governance can be viewed as a set of arrangements internal to the corporation that define the relationship between the owners and managers of the corporation. An example is the definition by key shareholder activists that corporate governance:

> . . . is the relationship among various participants in determining the direction and performance of corporations. The primary participants are (1) the shareholders, (2) the management, and (3) the board of directors.
>
> (Monks and Minow, 2001)

Corporate governance, according to one of its most famous Western practitioners and analysts, Sir Adrian Cadbury, is:

> . . . holding the balance between economic and social goals and between individual and communal goals. The governance framework is there to encourage the efficient use of resources and equally to require accountability for the stewardship of those resources. The aim is to align as nearly as possible the interests of individuals, corporations and society. The incentive to corporations is to achieve their corporate aims and to attract investment. The incentive for states is to strengthen their economics and discourage fraud and mismanagement.
>
> (1992)

A US lawyer offered this definition:

> In its most comprehensive sense, 'corporate governance' includes every force that bears on the decision-making of the firm. That would encompass not only the control rights of stockholders, but also the contractual covenants and insolvency powers of debt holders, the commitments entered into with employees and customers and suppliers, the regulations issued by governmental agencies, and the statutes enacted by parliamentary bodies. In addition,

5

the firm's decisions are powerfully affected by competitive conditions in the various markets in which it operates. One could go still further, to bring in the social and cultural norms of the society. All are relevant, but the analysis would become so diffuse that it risks becoming unhelpful as well as unbounded.

(Professor Kenneth Scott of Stanford
Law School, March 1999)

The World Bank defined corporate governance from the two different perspectives:

From the standpoint of a corporation, the emphasis is put on the relations between the owners, management board and other stakeholders (the employees, customers, suppliers, investors and communities). Major significance in corporate governance is given to the board of directors and its ability to attain long-term sustained value by balancing these interests. From a public policy perspective, corporate governance refers to providing for the survival, growth and development of the company and at the same time its accountability in the exercise of power and control over companies. The role of public policy is to discipline companies and, at the same time, to stimulate them to minimize differences between private and social interests.

(World Bank, 1999)

According to the World Bank, within the governance framework there are internal and external forces facing one another and affecting the behaviour and activities of existing corporations. We may ask whether it is really necessary to make such an arbitrary distinction, but according to the World Bank, internal forces define the relationship among the key players in the corporation, whereas external forces are used as amplification for disciplining the behaviour of insiders. In developed market economies, these forces are institutions and policies that insure greater transparency, monitoring and discipline for corporations. Specific examples of external forces include the international and national legal frameworks for competition policy, legal machinery for enforcing shareholders' rights, however frail and faulty, the system of accounting and auditing, a well-regulated financial system, the market for corporate control, and the bankruptcy system. These internal and external elements have come together in different ways to create a range of corporate governance systems that reflect market structures, legal systems, traditions, regulations and cultural and social values.

For sheer succinctness, this definition is hard to surpass:

Corporate governance refers to the processes and structures by which the business and affairs of an Institution are directed, managed and controlled.

(MAS, 2003)

Not to be outdone, a recent Asia-Pacific meeting of Directors came up with this ringing declaration:

Statement on Corporate Governance by the Confederation of Asia-Pacific Chambers of Commerce and Industry (CACCI)

1. *Good corporate governance is a fundamental pillar of the competitive, liberal market economy.*

2. *CACCI and its member organisations consider good corporate governance to be a virtue of itself, an asset to business, and essential to the credibility of commerce and industry in the communities, societies and nations in which they operate.*

3. *By corporate governance we mean the structures through which the objectives of the company are set, the means by which those objectives are attained, the monitoring of performance and the ways it can be improved. Good corporate governance is the responsibility of the board of directors and management in the pursuit of the long-term interests [of the] company.*

4. *The absence of good corporate governance is likely to result in diminished consumer, investor and public confidence in business, less competitive and efficient firms, weaker national and international economic performances, and add to pressure for greater government regulation of the affairs of commerce and industry.*

Good Corporate Governance

5. *Good corporate governance policies, practices and processes are essential to ensure efficient and well-functioning markets. They enhance the integrity of capital markets, whether for equity or debt instruments. They are essential to promote interests of shareholders, employees, customers, suppliers and the community in which the company operates, within the framework of law.*

6. *Deficient or poor corporate governance policies and practices compromise the capacities of capital markets, diminish the confidence of savers and investors, and provide comfort for those advocating greater government regulatory interventions in the conduct of commerce and industry.*

7. *Good corporate governance practices are also essential to ensure necessary disciplines over management, by providing an efficient means of assessing and benchmarking the performance of existing management and identifying others who may do better.*

8. *In this context, continuing disclosure of material information to markets, and its dissemination and evaluation by analysts, shareholders and investors, acts as a discipline on boards and management to act in the best interests of shareholders*

and other interested parties. Where necessary, industry self-regulation, mediation and arbitration are to be preferred to government intervention in corporate governance practices.

9. Effective systems of corporate governance are also essential to ensuring robust markets for corporate control.

10. The potential for a takeover places real commercial pressure on existing directors and management to continually improve corporate performance, both against past practice, relevant competitors and industry benchmarks.

11. If equity and financial markets, and those for corporate control, are not well-informed, such that poorly performing businesses are not exposed to the potential for takeover, then market pressures are diminished, resulting in less competitive and efficient firms, and economies.

Corporate Failures

12. Commerce and industry recognises public confidence in business has had setbacks due to recent high-profile corporate failures around the Asia Pacific region, and elsewhere in the world.

13. However, CACCI and its member organisations do not automatically accept that all corporate failures are evidence of deficiencies in corporate governance.

14. Companies can fail despite the best corporate governance standards and practices, for example changing market conditions, poor economic and regulatory policy settings by government, and the vagaries of the world economy.

Characteristics of Good Corporate Governance

15. CACCI and its member organisations recognise there is no single, uniform model of corporate governance which can be applied around the Asia Pacific region, or indeed the world, reflecting the different commercial and economic histories and cultures of countries, and their standards of corporate, economic and legal development.

16. Nevertheless, CACCI and its member organisations have identified a number of important characteristics of good corporate governance that warrant careful consideration by those championing competitive and efficient market economies. These characteristics are:

    a. a preference for self-regulatory approaches to corporate governance matters, ahead of heavy-handed government-mandated intervention;

    b. transparency in corporate governance arrangements, including ongoing disclosure of material information, especially financial information, to markets and to shareholders;

8

   c. *clear statements of the rights and responsibilities of shareholders and other
       interested parties, and independent corporate regulatory agencies, operating
       within a rule of law, to ensure the necessary enforcement of corporate law
       including effective penalties for substantive breaches of corporate governance
       laws;*

   d. *effective Boards and senior management teams, committed to grow-
       ing the enterprise for the long-term benefit of shareholders and other inter-
       ested parties, while giving due consideration to the interests of employees,
       customers and suppliers, and showing leadership within their businesses, and
       integrity in their business conduct;*

   e. *commitment to sustainable corporate development and continuing high ethical
       standards and corporate and social values in business and society and in the
       broader context of the communities in which they operate.*

In Conclusion

17. *CACCI and its member organisations reiterate our fundamental support for competi-
    tive market systems as the best way to generate economic development and growth,
    and raise standards of living for populations as a whole.*

18. *Ethical, sound and transparent corporate governance arrangements, both for the
    private and public sectors, are an essential pillar of healthy market economies.*

19. *Business has the primary responsibility of identifying, reaching and then main-
    taining these high standards. Where they fall short, governments can legitimately
    intervene through well-designed and proportionate corporate law and regulation.*

Mr. Yussuf Abdullah Harun
President
The Federation of Bangladesh Chambers
   of Commerce and Industry

Sheikh Abas Sheikh Mohamad
President
National Chamber of Commerce and
   Industry Brunei Darussalam

Oknha Sok Kong
President
Phnom Penh Chamber of Commerce

Mr. Tong, Kwok Wah
Chairman
Kowloon Chamber of Commerce

9

Shri R. S. Lodha
President
Federation of Indian Chambers of
  Commerce and Industry

Mr. Aburizal Bakrie *
General Chairman
Indonesian Chamber of Commerce
  and Industry

Amb. Micho Mizoguchi
Special Adviser
The Japan Chamber of Commerce
  and Industry

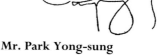

Mr. Park Yong-sung
Chairman
The Korea Chamber of Commerce
  and Industry

Mr. Sambuu Demberel
Chairman & CEO
Mongolian National Chamber of
  Commerce and Industry

Mr. Ravi Bhakta Shrestha
President
Federation of Nepalese Chambers of
  Commerce and Industry

Mr. Nigel Gould
Chairman
The New Zealand Chamber of
  Commerce and Industry, Inc.

Mr. Michael Mayberry
President
Papua New Guinea Chamber of
  Commerce and Industry

Mr. Sergio Ortiz-Luis, Jr.
President
Philippine Chamber of Commerce
  and Industry

Mr. Primakov Evgeny Maximovich
President
Chamber of Commerce and Industry
  of the Russian Federation

Mr. Stephen Lee
Chairman
Singapore Business Federation

Mr. Tilak de Zoysa
Chairman
Ceylon Chamber of Commerce

Mr. Theodore M. H. Huang
Chairman
Chinese National Association of
   Industry and Commerce

Amb. Jeffrey L. S. Koo
Chairman
Chinese International Economic
   Cooperation Association

Mr. Doan Duy Thanh
President
Vietnam Chamber of Commerce and Industry

Issued at the end of the 19th CACCI Conference held on 29–31 October
2003 in Jeju, Korea

---

* Interestingly, the declaration also threw up another yet another definition of corporate governance, from Mr Bakrie, who suggested the revision of paragraph 3 to read as follows:

---

3. *By corporate governance we mean the structures through which the objectives of the company are set, the means by which those objectives are attained, the monitoring of performance and the ways it can be improved.*

Good corporate governance principles are:
  a. *To maximize corporate and shareholder value by enhancing transparency, accountability, reliability, responsibility, and fairness in order to strengthen the company's competitive position both domestically and within the Asia Pacific region, and to create a sound environment to support investment.*
  b. *To encourage the management of the company to behave in a professional, transparent, and efficient manner, as well as optimizing the use of and*

enhancing the independence of the board of directors, the executing manage-
ment and the general meeting of shareholders.

c. *And to encourage shareholder[s], members of the board of directors and the*
executing management to make decisions and to act with the strict adherence
to morality, in compliance with the prevailing regulations in the country of
the member of the Confederation of Asia-Pacific Chambers of Commerce and
Industry (CACCI), and in accordance with their social responsibility towards
the various stakeholders and the protection of the environment.

In the pursuit of the long-term interests of the company, the board of
directors and the executing management shall be responsible to carry out the
above principles.

The hinge on shareholder value is especially interesting because, as Chapter 10 demonstrates, although there is now an almost indisputable positive correlation between good corporate governance and superior delivery of long-term shareholder value by comparison to less well-governed competitors, it is by no means certain that there will never be conflicts between the two. Professionalism and transparency are already two terms indissolubly linked with corporate governance, but the introduction of the term 'ethics' raises still more issues.

Here is a definition, or check-list at least, from Argentinian scholar Dr Rodolfo Apreda:[10]

By Corporate Governance it is meant the field of learning and practice related with [sic] the following subject matter:

- Ownership structure
- Company's Charter and bylaws
- Board of Directors, Trustees, and the allocation of control rights
- Managers' fiduciary duties towards owners, and the allocation of decision rights
- Creditors' protective covenants
- Changes in the capital structure
- Conflicts of interest between managers, creditors and owners
- Accountability to stakeholders
- Tight budget constraints and short-termism
- Managers' performance and incentives
- Information production and disclosure to markets and stakeholders
- The role of gatekeepers
- National and international corporate law, regulations and law enforcement.

Apreda makes some further remarks about the players in the corporate govern-ance game: that everybody who is able to hold a claim on the company becomes a stakeholder: owners and creditors are the main stakeholders, followed by managers, employees, government (taxes and complaints), suppliers (bonding and trust), customers (quality and conveniences) and communities (labour devel-opment and environmental damages). Second, he refers to 'gatekeepers' as distinctive organizations that safeguard the interests and rights of different stake-holders. Such organizations include auditing and accountancy firms, investment banks, law firms, market regulators, institutional investors, creditors' trustees, NGOs (non-government organizations acting as watchdogs of corporations, markets, regulators) and credit-rating firms.

From the perspective of a work on Asian corporate governance, the import-ance of these definitions is not whether they are comprehensive, inclusive or in any sense 'accurate'. What matters is how facts and opinions are marshalled among the huge amount of available material to provide information that is compatible with these definitions, which is where Apreda's checklist is useful. An understanding of corporate governance based on these definitions has informed the contents of the chapters which follow. So, for example, the governance of public entities – a subject in its own right – has been excluded. Corporate dividend policy, on the other hand, has been included.

THE CULTURAL AND HISTORICAL PERSPECTIVE

Marxism is deeply out of fashion, and with good reason. Yet there is much to be said for the more persuasive and obvious aspects of cultural and historical deter-minism, whether it is called 'path dependence', 'historical relativism' or simply a theory of difference – and convergence. Clearly, when it comes to corporate governance, just as much as personal ethics or cuisine, Asia does not start where the US does, nor indeed anywhere else. In the past, the result of cultural differ-ences, timing differences, differences in political process and international affilia-tions, treaty responsibilities, etc. has been a massive range of disparities between countries. The subject of international objectives for corporate governance is rarely discussed. There are various systems for defining jurisdiction:

a that of the State in which the transnational has requested legal identity;
b that of the headquarters of the company or the place where decisions are taken;
c that of the State in which the company is registered.

There is also an idea of control: when a company controls 100 per cent of all the shares of another company it must answer for its actions or for crimes committed by the branch. States can exercise jurisdiction on multinational corporations (MNCs) but they do not wish to do so.

13

This objection, however, is diminishing over time and may be seen as a legacy of the previous century. It can now be argued, in fact, that quite the reverse is the case: that legislation is in advance of corporate practice, especially in Asia, and that therefore the introduction of legislation, as opposed to reliance on self-regulation, will accelerate convergence and the achievement of best practices. This is certainly a view supported by regulators and governments in Asia – although it is clearly in their interests to hold such a view. Asian countries embrace very considerable legal and economic diversity, in many cases the legacy of European colonialism; for example, Hong Kong, India, Pakistan and Malaysia have common law frameworks, Thailand and the Philippines have frameworks based on French civil law, while China, Chinese Taipei and South Korea draw upon German civil law traditions. That is without introducing all the differences that two billion people can create among themselves culturally, linguistically and religiously. Even the mitigation of agency costs, if that is what corporate governance is about, can result in the evolution of a purely national, let alone regional, system of corporate governance which can exploit the advantages of the corporate form of organization while mitigating concomitant agency costs in a manner consistent with a country's history and legal, political and social traditions.[11] If you want to envisage it as a model, a nation's system of corporate governance can be seen as an institutional matrix producing, analysing and changing relations between corporate owners, boards and top managers. Is it important? Some believe so – that the nature of this institutional matrix is one of the principal determinants of the economic vitality of a society.[12] More than that, advocates of corporate governance believe that there is a global dynamic working in its favour: it is important to note that the drive of corporate governance, while recognizing that 'national conditions may determine how corporate governance aspirations should be fulfilled',[13] argues that these conditions 'do not excuse jurisdictions from having to fulfil them'. The political game of corporate governance is becoming, like the rules of the World Trade Organization (WTO), part of the new global governance regime.[14] Some have concluded that globalization is a decisive factor in making a case for more extensive global governance: one noted protagonist argues that:

> There should be one set of rules for everyone who operates in the United States. If a foreign company operates here, then the same rules should apply to it as apply to a U.S. firm. There's talk about changing this, but I don't see anything happening right away. There's a lot of anxiety about it.[15]

One day, it will happen. The only question is, by then how much pain it will cause at the other end. Markets have already started to apply sanctions that cross borders far more effectively than any nationally based code or legislation. The decision by the California Public Employees' Retirement System (Calpers) to pull out of several Asian markets is a case in point. Perceived inadequate standards of transparency and investor protection in the subject countries contributed to this decision by one of America's largest and most influential institutional investors, and the reverberations were felt throughout Asia as governments, companies and investors took notice.

INSTITUTIONAL PREVALENCE

The new regime to which Calpers so ostentatiously subscribes is heavily institutional. A key example is the World Bank Group and OECD Global Corporate Governance Forum. The forum guided transition economies on corporate governance. It has three functions: to broaden the dialogue on corporate governance; to exchange experience and good practices; to coordinate activities and identify and fill gaps in provision of technical expertise. By convening governance conferences and roundtables at national and regional levels, the forum has provided a means to bring together the players from all sides to debate the issues, identify priorities for reform, develop an action plan and spearhead initiatives. Regional roundtables have been organized in Russia and Latin America as well as Asia between 1999 and 2003; Africa is also now in view. The Asia Roundtable is of especial interest to us as its June 2003 White Paper represented 'state of the art' collective thinking on corporate governance in Asia, building on the OECD Principles of Corporate Governance, and providing region-specific guidance and suggestions to assist policy-makers, regulators (including stock exchanges) and other standards-setting bodies.

WHAT DOES THE STUDY OF CORPORATE GOVERNANCE ENTAIL?

Apreda provides more useful suggestions as to what is needed to get to grips, as he says, with the facts and indications which bear on the major corporate governance issues for major firms. For example:

1   What can be said about the ownership and control structure of the firm, its chart and bylaws?
2   Are there multiple voting rights schemes? What is the structure of the Board of Directors?
3   How the firm is to be financed and what are the warranties for financiers to be paid eventually?
4   To what extent does the firm's capital structure mirror the institutions of the country where the company runs its businesses? What kinds of conflicts of interest arise among stakeholders and how should they be relieved?

15

5 Does the firm belong to the common law (Anglo-Saxon countries) or the civil law (continental European) tradition? How are the property rights of creditors and stockholders protected? How enforceable are contracts?

6 To what extent is the information provided by the firm to owners and third parties accurate and reliable? What about the way such production of information is influenced by current accountancy and auditing practices?

7 What are the incentives fostered by formal and informal institutions so that companies become more efficient and reputable?

8 To what extent managers are prevented from plundering owners or creditors?

9 How good are the covenants that the company pledges on behalf of creditors, owners and other stakeholders?

10 To what extent a legal framework holding in a country can be regarded as a competitive advantage for companies willing to invest in that country?

11 Which is the way capital-flows move around within and between national boundaries? What about the regulations in capital markets and the money markets across boundaries? Is there a fiduciary capitalism?

12 How to prevent companies and managers from creative accounting, money laundering and self-dealing?

13 Which corporate governance procedures and practices should be enacted so as to avoid rogue states, crony firms, mafia-partnerships and terrorism linkages, from investing in corporations and banks through special purpose vehicles like those that Enron, and so many companies, set up eventually all over the world?

14 Do good practices in corporate governance pay off? Do they enhance the companies' value? If so, how important is communication? Or are they just a regulatory burden?

15 What is the relationship between corporate governance and public governance? What about international linkages?

It is a tall order to do all this for each Asian country, even for the OECD. Also, Apreda's approach is essentially a 'micro' one, examining a particular firm. Whereas it is true that corporate governance focuses on the firm, at the level of an international analysis individual firms can serve only as examples of particular legislation, codes, scandals, trends or other points. No one can presume to be able to compare the extent *overall* to which the covenants in Thai companies, for instance, compare to those in Taiwan. Even their respective governments do not possess information at that level of detail, no more than do Western governments. As a result, many of the points he cited are judgemental, or require speculative analysis, for example, on the best policies to enact in Asia against money laundering, or for accurate accounting, so these have been eschewed in favour of a largely empirical approach: even the future can be viewed as a consensus view of likely change rather than a wish list.

THE OBJECTIVE OF CORPORATE GOVERNANCE

Just as definitions of corporate governance differ, so opinions on what it is *for* wander. A Japanese academic suggests:

> It is my opinion that the fundamental objective of corporate governance should not only be the protection of stockholder interests but also the promotion of effective management. To promote effective management, a company's leaders must have the intelligence to judge the worthiness of each appeal made by share-holders and other vested entities. However, this type of judgment is possible only when a company's management has some degree of independence from its shareholders. As stockholders boost their clout, not only management's responsibilities, but their own responsibilities as well are required to be taken into account. Unfortunately, commercial law scholars have not presented theories on stockholder responsibility. As far as theories go, about all we have seen pertains to the protection of small shareholders' rights achieved through limitations imposed on major shareholders' rights. What we need is some serious debate on the subject of stockholder rights and to what extent they can be limited to promote successful corporate management.[16]

Coming at the problem from a different perspective, a Chinese academic argues that:

> Policy-makers around the world have another important reason to be concerned with corporate governance: low corporate governance standards also breed corruption. Corruption, defined here as the misuse of public office for private gain (Rose-Ackerman, 1978), has both the demand and supply sides to it. While much attention of the global anti-corruption campaign has been directed towards the demand side of corruption, that is, the corrupted govern-ment officials, the supply side of corruption is just as important, and the impacts of the governance of corporations – the main contributors of bribe payment – on the level of corruption should not be underestimated. Rules of corporate governance, such as accountability, transparency and fairness, have profound impacts on the motives and constraints for both the corrupted and the corruptors involved in corrupt practices.[17]

17

The OECD, at the time it issued its original definition of corporate governance, also issued fundamental principles, that the corporate governance framework should:

- protect shareholders' rights;
- ensure the equitable treatment of all shareholders;
- recognize the rights of stakeholders as established by law and promote the concept of good corporate citizenship;
- ensure that timely and accurate disclosure is made on all material matters regarding the corporation, including the financial situation, performance, ownership, and governance of the company;
- ensure the strategic guidance of the company, the effective monitoring of management by the board, and the board's accountability to the company and the shareholders.

It is a noticeable feature of the OECD analysis that no contradictions are presumed between these different objectives. The process is seamless, worthwhile and praiseworthy. Nor for that matter is there any question about the relative allocation of resources between corporate governance and other government objectives.

WHAT CORPORATE GOVERNANCE IS *NOT*

What is noticeable about the functional aspects of corporate governance cited above is what they leave out as much as what they include. *Distributional justice and the nature of production are both specifically excluded.* This is especially important in the Asian context where a widespread shareholder democracy, except in advanced countries such as Singapore, does not exist. Legislating in favour of minority shareholder rights is one thing in the US, where shareholdings are widely distributed and have been for decades, and where lower-income and wealth groups may be the shareholders in a company with affluent managers; it is quite another in an Asian, especially Chinese or Indonesian, context, where it is highly likely that the average income or wealth of the shareholders in a listed company will be significantly higher than the workers in it. Where within corporate governance theory, even, let alone practice, is the comparative analysis of shareholder and employee wealth? Not there, is the answer. Such critics would rather have a secretive company run benevolently than one run openly, but sacrificing everything for the pursuit of shareholder value. Those concerned with distributional justice might well argue that, like the proverbial gun, *corporate governance is only morally good if aimed true.*

As has been well said, 'The debate about social regulation bears little resemblance to the traditional interest-group concerns over the division of the pie, relevant to economic regulation, but rather is concerned with the recipe for making it.'[18] As a result, although there has been much debate in the closely related subject of ethical investment, a cigarette company making huge profits can have exemplary corporate governance: but what does this say about the significance and morality of corporate governance? Corporate governance may or may not involve ethics or morality in the way ordinary people use the term: it is perhaps, therefore, a red herring to introduce it in a definition of corporate governance as Mr Bakrie tried to do. It is no accident, one feels, that he should have been the delegate from Indonesia, where there has been so much criticism of the moral consequences of the actions of such *well-governed* Western corporations.

The alternative perspective has not gone entirely neglected, at least at the national and NGO level. Both the Indian and Chinese governments have argued for enforceable codes of conduct for foreign investors to check their abuse of economic power in host countries, double standards illustrated by the Bhopal tragedy in India. They have also argued for greater transparency in accounting disclosures by MNCs, besides obligations from home countries like prohibiting corrupt foreign practices by their corporations. A paper on investor and home country obligations drafted by India and submitted to the World Trade Organization's working group on trade and investment, for example, called upon the group to consider incorporating legally binding measures to ensure corporate responsibility and accountability on the part of MNCs. The paper encountered predictably stiff opposition from Western countries, who argued that such measures would put a brake on investments in developing countries.

The existence of an international court has also been suggested as a way of forcing MNCs to use their prerogatives. Probably not a workable idea, because legislation and enforcement is usually required, and this remains a power retained largely by national governments and related agencies. On the other hand, in the case of both the environment and labour rights, critics argue that the most important issues are not national but global and require a global policy. The anti-multinational campaign has been seen as a new form of participatory democracy, given voice by the fact that the gap between the rich and poor countries has been widening over the past three decades. And this trend could even increase, since, as the World Bank has stressed, the knowledge gap between rich and poor countries is far greater than the income gap. But the important point to concern us is that *none* of this comes within the usual remit of corporate governance, except at the periphery of ethical investment and corporate social responsibility.

What seems certain, however, is that:

Academics may speculate on the scope and objectives of corporate govern-ance, politicians on its merits, and marketing experts twist it to serve as advertising copy, . . . without an understanding of what it is for, widespread acceptance of the principles and practice, proper enforcement of whatever regulations are put in place, it makes little sense to discuss further. An ounce of enforcement is worth a pound of unenforced regulations.

Although Dr Apreda was thinking specifically of Latin America, this plaintive cry is perhaps even more appropriate to consider in an Asian context, where we will frequently have cause to ask (and be open-minded about it) whether the passing of regulations has in any way stood in for practical enforcement of corporate governance.

SYSTEMS OF CORPORATE GOVERNANCE

At present, each system of corporate governance is still essentially a national one. In the US, of course, it is a federal one, and likewise in Australia. China's munici-palities and regions also have considerable authority. The powers of the European Union (EU) seem to encroach ever more on European national authority in this area. But for the majority of Asian countries, in the absence yet of an Association of South East Asian Nations (ASEAN) with legislative clout, national systems are the subject of analysis. Most legislative measures to improve corporate govern-ance are still being taken everywhere on an ad hoc, national basis, usually in response to a crisis or specific corporate scandals. Thus, the UK's Cadbury Report in 1992 took as its starting point the excesses of the 1980s. Enacted in the wake of Enron, Tyco and other debacles, America's Sarbanes-Oxley legislation of 2002 followed the same pattern. What *is* changing, as Chapters 2 and 3 demonstrate, is the gap between different national systems, legislation and rules: it's dimin-ishing. This in turn has important implications for relative national competitiveness.

In the traditional conflict of interest model, the system of corporate govern-ance varies significantly depending on the mechanisms that the owners of a com-pany use to influence the managers.[19] The authors of this model identify three different ways that owners maintain control over the work of management:

1 the owners directly influence the corporate strategy and selection of the top management team;
2 the owners delegate their rights to the board but ensure that compensation and other incentives are aligned with share price maximization;
3 the owners rely on the market mechanisms of corporate control, such as a takeover, when due to a decreasing share price new owners take over a company and change to management in order to rehabilitate the company and increase its market value.

In other words, the corporate governance mechanisms can be both internal and external. The internal mechanisms of corporate governance include owner-ship concentration, the board of directors, ways of rewarding managers and a multidivisional organizational structure. The external mechanism of corporate governance refers to the market for corporate control, i.e. a group of potential owners attacking the undervalued companies in order to change the ineffective top management team and improve the competitive position of the company.[20]

It is simply not so straightforward and unitary in practice. The most commonly invoked paradigms of corporate governance are the US equity system of corporate governance, which boasts strong capital markets but possibly weak institutional constraints on management, and the German bank model, where strong institutional (bank) controls on management may compensate for weak capital markets. But it has been argued that:

> Within the EU, many different national systems of corporate governance prevail, but both European integration and globalisation are creating pressures toward convergence to an 'ideal' corporate governance system. An understanding of the relation between corporate governance and economic performance is therefore of profound importance to the evolution of the EU.[21]

Now it is one of Europe and the US's best kept secrets that the majority of their wealth comes from family businesses. Nor is it surprising to find that small and medium enterprises (SMEs) are the engine of economic growth in the US and UK, the best performing Western economies recently. Asia differs little: 'Prominent features of the Asian business landscape include the predominance of family-run firms, the informal nature of stakeholder relations and the legal and economic diversity of the region.'[22] In Asia, where approximately two-thirds of listed companies, and substantially all private companies, are family-run,[23] their prestige is at its highest where it is perceived that there is an issue at stake. Academics[24] investigated ultimate control patterns in 2,980 publicly traded companies in nine East Asian countries (Hong Kong, Indonesia, Japan, Korea (South), Malaysia, the Philippines, Singapore, Taiwan and Thailand), and predictably found large family control in more than half of East Asian corporations. This study used a 20 per cent ownership threshold for control. Another study suggested that in 1996, the five largest family groups in the Philippines, Indonesia, Thailand and Malaysia controlled 42.8 per cent, 40.7 per cent, 32.2 per cent and 17.3 per cent respectively of their countries' corporate sector in terms of market capitalization.[25] The fact that these surveys exclude companies where the ownership cannot be traced because of nominee holdings suggests the actual degree of family control may be even higher than two-thirds. An Association of Chartered Certified Accountants (ACCA) study in 2003 quoted David Webb, powerful protagonist for corporate governance standards in Hong Kong and founder of Hong Kong's Association for Minority Shareholders, to the effect that single shareholders control over 90 per cent of Hong Kong listed companies. Significant cross-country differences do exist, however. Corporations in Japan, for example, are generally widely held, while corporations in Indonesia and

Thailand are mainly family-controlled. And state control is still significant in Indonesia, Korea, Malaysia, Singapore and Thailand. Because in Asia shareholder groups frequently control management, the region's companies as a result rarely employ management entrenchment devices such as shareholders' rights plans (poison pills) which have been trenchantly opposed by shareholders' rights groups in Western jurisdictions.[26]

The OECD generously concedes that: 'Over the last several decades, the collective talents and efforts of these family-business owners have resulted in strong economic growth and substantial increases in living standards.'[27] Research on corporate governance, however, cannot be expected to dwell on living standards. The OECD observes that those who run Asian companies tend to set up, with the participation of their families, large interlocking networks of subsidiaries and sister companies (see Figures 1.1 and 1.2) that include partially owned, publicly listed companies (not at all like the UK's Virgin Group or the Easy Group, or Italy's Ferruzzi Group or Parmalat, to name just four very public examples, you understand).

It follows from family ownership that the legal documentation of such firms rarely covers all the bases. Informal stakeholder relationships, sometimes dovetailed with government itself, possess great strength. Major investors in even the biggest companies are often family members or friends. Either pressed by Asian governments or simply recognizing the truth, the OECD again concedes that: 'The informal nature of Asian stakeholder/company interaction can produce real and lasting benefits for stakeholders that equal or exceed those offered through more formalistic approaches based on "rights".'[28] Such a statement runs counter to the instinct of most Western corporate governance protagonists – they just do not believe this. Whatever the benefits of such structures, corporate governance theory suggests that they can – indeed *should* – lead to the great evil of corporate governance, 'severely inequitable treatment of shareholders'.[29] The underlying reason why this may occur is because of informational asymmetry: the subsidiary company structure allows controlling shareholders control of operations and/or cash flows much larger than their equity stake in individual companies. The OECD observes disapprovingly that the extent of this control is frequently opaque to outsiders and undisclosed by insiders. However, it is worth observing that Parmalat and the Ferruzzi Group, to name Italy's two most famous private company bankruptcies, were also companies run on exactly these lines. These structures, and to be fair the problems encountered with them, especially when companies fail, are definitely not confined to Asia. But what is certain is that analysing corporate governance in an Asian context ought to take into consideration the facts of how business is done, how corporations are owned and how resources are allocated. Because of its Western – and in fact Anglo-Saxon – origin and development, with a heavy focus on public (quoted) companies, where information is more plentiful and foreign investment more prevalent, this is not achieved in practice.

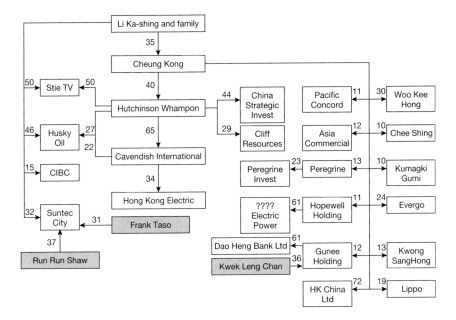

Figure 1.1 *Spot the difference: Li Ka-shing Group table*

Source: World Bank

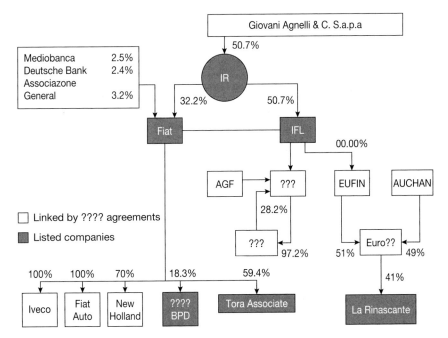

Figure 1.2 *Agnelli Group table*

Source: World Bank

TRANSITION ECONOMIES

It is worth stating now that there are few economies left in Asia that come under this heading. A significant sized state sector does *not* necessarily demonstrate an economy in transition, rather it is a reflection of national priorities and perspectives. Many Scandinavian countries still have a large state sector and they are not in transition to anything different. Rather, relatively low GDP per head[30] and difficulties in creating effective corporate governance are the tell-tale signs in our context. There are two key problems connected with the corporate governance problem in transition economies. First, is it possible to have more or less the same system that has evolved over centuries in developed market economies for the emerging markets, or is it better to try to fit corporate governance to the specific circumstances of a transition economy? The second problem relates to whether the usual paraphernalia of external governance mechanisms – accounting transparency to improve the accuracy of stock market valuations, regulatory pursuit of fraud, the role of the shareholders' general meeting, 'disciplinary' takeovers, legal requirements for the appointment of 'external' directors, etc., – can be applied to a transition economy.[31]

At the same time, in transition economies, the internal mechanisms as identified by the World Bank – owners, board of directors and managers – differ significantly in comparison to the internal mechanisms of the developed market economies. First, the concept of ownership itself is problematic. Ownership of post-socialist enterprises was often shared between the state, public corporate bodies, banks, municipal bodies, managers, employees, other state or private companies, private individuals and foreign individuals and corporations. The absence of 'real owners' led to neglect of the interests of capital itself and thus to degradation in the quality of the capital, damaging the long-term interests of the firm.[32] In that sense it was little improvement on the socialism it replaced.

Second, the boards of directors failed to exercise a true monitoring role. Because the state was the key stockholder, there was an imbalance of power among the various stockholders. The members of the board of directors were usually the representatives of the state, the ruling party, public corporate bodies or even the banks. For individual board members, therefore, any motivation to question, let alone act, was inhibited by their dependence on management for benefits such as lucrative appointments to boards of directors. Even if they had the inclination to exercise direct control over managers, they lacked the knowledge to make managerial decisions. Even if one director breaks ranks, 'divide and rule' will mean that others are unlikely to follow. As a consequence, the role of the board of directors was reduced to financial control, which assumes maximization of the short-term results and evaluation of the managers' performance retroactively.

Third, the upper 'echelon' of managers in transition economies acquired their knowledge and skills in a business environment which did not require the development of the skills of transformational or strategic leadership. So, transition countries still have an archaic cadre of managers who do not possess a capacity for strategic thinking, vision creation, team work, risk taking and change management. Potentially new managers and leaders are facing a new challenge which comes from the Western countries in the form of ready-made solutions provided largely by consultants, which they surmount mainly because of its high cost, but they are also facing a challenge to respond to specific requirements of the business environment encountered in particular countries. Another problem is related to the non-existence of a market for management talent and the difficulty of evaluating managers in an impartial manner.

In summary, therefore, corporate governance is especially hard to achieve in the context of a transition economy. The experience of Eastern Europe, however, suggests that these problems gradually but inevitably do resolve themselves with the combination of economic growth and political democracy. Asia certainly has one, but can effective transition be made without effective democracy? China seems to be demonstrating that it *can*.

HOW TO RUN A CORPORATE GOVERNANCE SYSTEM

The key is the extent of regulation.

> This trade-off between institutional and market controls has received a considerable research interest. [Researchers in the past] identified a trade-off in corporate governance between the characteristic of liquidity, which provides investors with a ready exit option in case their investment goes sour, and the characteristic of voice, which gives investors the ability to affect the performance of the firms in which they have invested if they become dissatisfied. The latter is reminiscent of institutional controls, the former points at the role of capital markets.[33]

Corporate dynamics:

- De facto standards set through competitive dynamics usually develop faster than formal standards. Therefore, they may better reflect current requirements. However, market-based standards may be inefficient (e.g. VHS standard, safety standards in India). Moreover, some companies apparently still face little competition in setting low standards (e.g. health and safety on Asian construction sites).
- Coordinating mechanisms such as hierarchies or standardization committees are supposed to ensure that the standard set is widely accepted and of high quality. At the same time, such development mechanisms underlie a political decision-making process and may be subject to corruption.

25

- Standardization committees may be preferable to hierarchies due to the involvement of all market participants in the development process.

Advantages of laissez-faire:

- No pressure is asserted concerning the development of control and governance structures. Therefore, any such development is purely market-based.
- Standards (best practices) are developed by representatives of all types of market participants involved. Thus, self-regulation in corporate governance is a form of standardization committee. Sometimes this can go badly wrong, however, when companies freeze out their competitors via the use of standards (e.g. in the software industry). Courts are then the regulator of last resort, and this works well in the US context where there is a long tradition of court independence. Asia has not.
- Codification set through hierarchical power (i.e. government bodies and international agencies).

Shortcomings of the laissez-faire approach:

- Many investors may not have the knowledge to distinguish between 'well' and 'badly' governed enterprises – in Asia as yet there is insufficient 'interrogative' media to help investors to do this.
- Insufficient reporting on corporate governance activities.
- Limited contact with company representatives.
- Danger of individual dominance (especially combined CEO/Chairman functions) which may be felt to be especially important in Asia where there is a tradition along these lines anyway.
- Boards often neglect their control function.
- No ongoing involvement in company (free-rider problem).
- Ad hoc activism in case of emergencies.

Ultimately, the most devastating criticism of laissez-faire is therefore that it can be inefficient in the allocation of resources.

Development of corporate governance structures through competition:

- Under efficient market circumstances, shareholders and other stakeholders will honour better governance structures through the market mechanism or face capital starvation.
- Equity and debt investors increase demand (pay premiums).

- Employees increase supply (accept discounts).
- Best practices develop concerning the executive and control (non-executive) functions of boards as well as other governance mechanisms.
- Committees may formalize these best practices between themselves into standards or rely on multiple opinions to create new standards.
- Therefore, an optimal combination of board, shareholder and auditor responsibilities is supposed to develop (other stakeholders, e.g. employees, also play a part).
- The board members are expected to develop their own objectives and policies (such as meeting schedules, agendas, etc.).

Advantages of self-regulation:

- Expertise of all parties can be incorporated into standard.
- Involvement of market participants hopefully insures later acceptance of standard.

Shortcomings of self-regulation:

- The success of self-regulation hinges on the compliance by all parties involved. Thus, effective enforcement mechanisms need to be implemented.
- Pressure groups (e.g. shareholders, customers, suppliers, political parties).
- Track record as a signal of commitment, etc.
- Standard-setting process becomes political. If parties involved collude, standard set may be sub-optimal.

Types of statutory regulation:

- Securities market regulations.
- Fiduciary responsibilities of directors and officers.
- Laws governing mergers and acquisitions.
- Rules governing shareholder voice.

Shortcomings of statutory control:

- Relying on statutory control requires perfect information of the standard setting body and timeliness of regulation – in reality, neither of these two conditions is fulfilled.
- Enforcement mechanism needs to be effective.
- Legal standards may only be used as minimum requirements.

- Risk of companies complying only with the explicit requirements, not with the intentions behind them.
- Incentive to circumvent requirements exists as long as market does not penalize.

Advantages of legal standards:

- Statutory control may not be easily compromised due to threat of legal sanctions integrated with the statute.
- Statutory control may be best used for making governance regulations that are common to all types of companies and do not change significantly over time or bear minute interpretation by corporate lawyers.
- Self-regulation can be seen as the extension of statutory control onto specific governance needs for some types of companies or applications.
- A laissez-faire approach can be taken, once the existing governance needs have been met. The best achieving companies may set new de facto standards, which can later be transformed into formal standards, if they prove effective.

EXAMINING CORPORATE GOVERNANCE MODELS

The countries with developed economies apply two different systems of corporate governance: the group-based system and the market-based one,[34] or, as they are referred to more often, the insider and outsider systems. They have both grown from different institutional, regulatory and political surroundings, but with an internally consistent governance system and a unique mixture of corporate control.

Most of continental Europe still deviates from the outsider model in important ways:

1 Corporate ownership remains more concentrated in the hands of large shareholders. Family ownership has survived to a greater extent. Likewise, state ownership, cooperative networks among industrial corporations and strong ties between banks and industry are important to varying degrees in different countries. In concentrated ownership structures, ownership and/or control is concentrated in the hands of a small number of individuals, families, managers, directors, holding companies, banks and/or other non-financial corporations. Most countries, especially those governed by civil law, have concentrated ownership structures. Insiders exercise control over companies in several ways, frequently owning the majority of the company shares and voting rights or alternatively owning a minority of shares but still with the majority of the voting rights, usually because of multiple classes of shares, some enjoying more voting rights than others. It also

occurs if there are proxy votes and voting trusts. If a few owners own shares with significant voting rights, they can effectively control a company even though they did not provide the majority of the capital.

2 Balancing this, employee participation is an institutionalized part of corporate governance, although the extent of such rights differs widely across countries. Germany, for example, has the most extensive codetermination rights, both through employee representation within the board, and works councils having wide ranging rights to information, consultation and co-determination.

3 More broadly, different conceptions of the public interest play a role in defining good corporate governance. Whereas the Anglo-American tradition sees the firm as a private association, Germany and Japan historically developed a different approach where the role of shareholders and employees each became 'constitutionalized' within law.[35] Hence, the insider model, characteristic of continental Europe and Japan, has a less developed stock market with a large concentration of owners. The control over the company is executed by a small number of significant shareholders structured in relatively closed networks and committees through planning and industrial policy mechanisms. In realizing long-term economic goals, special attention was paid to the relationship between the state and industry.

Companies that are controlled by insiders do enjoy certain advantages. Insiders have the power and the incentive to monitor management closely, thereby minimizing the potential for mismanagement and fraud. Moreover, because of their significant ownership and control rights, insiders tend to keep their investment in a firm for long periods of time. As a result, insiders tend to support decisions that will enhance a firm's long-term performance as opposed to decisions designed to maximize short-term gains. However, insider systems are said to predispose a company to certain corporate governance failures. One is that dominant owners and/or vote holders can bully or collude with management to expropriate firm assets at the expense of minority shareholders. This is a significant risk when minority shareholders do not enjoy legal rights. Similarly, when managers control a large number of shares or votes they may use their power to influence board decisions that may directly benefit them at the company's expense. In short, insiders who wield their power irresponsibly waste resources and drain company productivity levels; they also foster investor reluctance and fail to generate liquid capital markets. Illiquid capital markets, in turn, deprive companies of capital and prevent investors from diversifying their risks.

Dispersed ownership is the other type of ownership structure, the outsider model of the US and UK. Here, a large number of owners each hold a small number of company shares. Small shareholders have little incentive to closely monitor a company's activities and tend not to be involved in management decisions or policies. Hence, they are called outsiders, and dispersed ownership structures are referred to as outsider systems. Common law countries such as the UK and the US tend to have dispersed ownership structures. The outsider system or Anglo-American, market-based model is characterized by the ideology of corporate individualism and private ownership, a well-developed and liquid capital market, with a large number of shareholders and a small concentration of investors. The corporate control is realized through the market and outside investors.

In contrast to insider systems, owners in outsider systems are supposed to rely on independent board members to monitor managerial behaviour and keep it in check. As a result, outsider systems are considered more accountable and less corrupt and they tend to foster liquid capital markets. Despite these advantages, dispersed ownership structures have certain weaknesses. Dispersed owners tend to be interested in short-term profit maximization. And they tend to approve policies and strategies that will yield short-term gains, but that may not necessarily promote long-term company performance. At times, this can lead to conflicts between directors and owners, and to frequent ownership changes because shareholders may divest in the hopes of reaping higher profits elsewhere, both of which weaken company stability. Small-scale investors have less financial incentive to vigilantly monitor boardroom decisions and to hold directors accountable. As a result, directors who support unsound decisions may remain on the board when it is in the company's interest that they be removed.[36]

In the outsider model, the discussions about corporate governance are focused on the responsibility of corporate managers, the lack of control and direct supervision from the owners' part, and the imperfection of existing control and compensation mechanisms. In the current Anglo-American version of stock market capitalism, the criterion of success is shareholder value, as expressed by a company's share price. The problem of corporate governance contemplated in this way bore the concept of creating shareholder value, which was originally promoted for the purpose of obtaining the quantitative indicators of managers' responsibility to maximize the shareholders' value. Hence, while the approach to value in the US means that weaker owners should try to 'tame' strong managers, in Europe it means that managers and minor holders should show resistance to powerful blockholders. It has been suggested[37] that the success of the European managers in showing resistance (and succeeding in relating the dispersed ownership to dispersed right to vote) could be counterproductive due to an absence of developed market mechanisms of discipline which exist in the Anglo-American model.

Can this divergence last? Back in 1999 the OECD principles were somewhat general and both the Anglo-American system and the continental European (or German) systems were quite consistent with them. But the globalization of the entire economy, including the financial and investment market, in the 1990s led to a growing convergence of initially separated initiatives in the field of corporate governance. Comparative studies about corporate governance systems began to point to the possibility of their gradual convergence thanks to the influence of global corporate standards and business practice. The convergence of the two corporate governance models would mean the coexistence of the active market of corporate control and direct control of blockholders. The outsider model includes two groups of changes which point to the convergence: one group includes the changes in the market control from the hostile takeover to a slow, gradual restructuring, while the second group refers to the more active role of institutional investors in the direct control of the company. In the insider model, the changes refer to the development of financial markets, the increasing market control of corporations and the emphasis on the concept of creating shareholder value.

The influence of international investors and capital markets contributed to the convergence of different practices of corporate governance and to setting up the standards, but so far only the direct actors of this process have applied them. The extent to which the corporations use the basic principles of good corporate governance is a relative factor for making investment decisions. International capital flows enable companies to find sources of financing from a wider circle of potential investors. Even when corporations do not primarily use foreign sources of capital, the application of good corporate governance practices will help them to gain the trust of domestic investors, reduce their capital costs and induce more stable financial sources (Holly, Weil, 1999). However, the dynamics of today's changes are such that potential fields for investors quickly lose their attractiveness. Therefore, new standards of corporate governance should not be introduced through a slow process of economic osmosis. It is necessary to have a coordinated initiative at the global level which will promote good corporate governance standards.

To summarize, although there are considerable differences between the Anglo-American, German and Japanese corporate governance systems, they all share the luxury of defining the subject of corporate governance within the context of functioning market systems and highly developed legal institutions. However, many developing and emerging economies lack or are in the process of developing the most basic market institutions. That is the main reason why corporate governance problems in the context of transition economies require a much wider range of issues. But where does Asia stand in this?

FAMILY-BASED GOVERNANCE (FBS)

There is in Asia discussion of yet another alternative framework for the analysis of corporate governance, aptly and tactfully called the family-based corporate governance system (FBS), and distinguished, according to Haider Khan who coined the term,[38] by the fact that 'under FBS, neither the banks nor the equity markets ultimately control the family business groups. This can give rise to serious agency problems necessitating reforms'. Khan believes that FBS *can* work, but only if there are proper monitoring capabilities of the financial system, managerial expertise and market competition. At an early stage of development, Khan explains, family firms are financed internally, but even when external finance is introduced into such companies, the family group continues to control the governance aspects, for example the hiring and firing of management, or the selection of members of the board. No takeover threat or potential bank action can deter this. Whether, as Khan says, this can be defined as a problem of asymmetric information, or whether it is simply a question of what control money should buy, the possibility clearly exists from the standpoint of a conventional model that such 'slack governance' may result in inefficient production and the mismanagement of assets. Hong Kong, Khan's example par excellence, has a predominance of the family-based system (FBS) of corporate governance. The main difference between FBS as a governance system and others such as bank-led systems (BLS) or equity market-based systems (EMS) of corporate governance is that ultimate control of the firm resides with the family groups rather than the banks or the equity markets. As the share of external finance rises with the growth of the firm, agency costs increase due to problems of asymmetric information between management and external financiers. FBS can be a workable form of governance under such conditions only with proper monitoring capabilities of the financial system, managerial expertise and market competition. Particularly important for reforming the FBS is the need for recruiting and training competent professionals so that the financial institutions can gather and analyse the relevant information about the firms they finance.

CORPORATE GOVERNANCE IN THE WEST: A REVIEW OF THE US AND UK

The United States

With an increasing number of Asian companies seeking to raise capital in Western markets, including on public exchanges in the US, the importance of changes in US corporate governance rules is more than just as a pointer to the future for Asian jurisdictions. Indeed, as Chapter 2 will show, none of the changes outlined below now represent great differences or a threat to the majority of Asian corporations' capital raising abilities – in theory, at least. Various congressional committees, the Justice Department and the Securities and Exchange Commission (SEC) conducted investigations in the wake of the collapse of Enron in December 2001. Significant changes in regulations and structures and practices of companies, the extent of compliance with a corporate governance code, and the role of share-holders in fixing directors' remuneration all came within the US Congress' wide purview. Other proposals on corporate governance include strengthening share-holders' rights, minority protection, and the right to vote by 'special investigation' procedures as well as holding directors accountable for letting the company continue to do business when it can no longer pay its debts.

Most of the current US provisions that affect board structure and function have now been implemented through federal legislation and SEC rule-making and a series of new and proposed regulations and stock market listing require-ments, some of which have still not yet been completed in detail, although in broad terms the new regime is now in place. While some of the provisions have been implemented and enforced directly by the SEC,[39] other provisions have been administered through the self-regulatory process of the stock markets under new 'national market system' provisions which were added to Section 10A of the Securities Exchange Act of 1934, as amended (the 'Exchange Act').

To a certain extent, the current US minimum standards embody what up to now have been non-binding best practices:

- populating boards with a majority of independent directors;
- strict standards for determining director independence;
- instituting wholly independent audit, compensation and nominating/governance committees and allocating specific responsibilities to these committees;
- establishing the responsibility of audit committees for the annual independent audit of the corporation and over the corporation's satisfaction of its other financial reporting, disclosure and legal and regulatory compliance obligations;
- regular meetings of non-management directors;
- regular board and committee self-evaluations and publication of company-specific governance guidelines and codes of conduct, all with the goal of enhancing the effectiveness of board oversight of corporate affairs.

None of this now seems very controversial or difficult for a company to achieve. The current standards do involve a greater degree of formality and rigour than used to be involved in these matters when they were addressed in the past. The new standards also apply to both foreign and domestic companies whose securities trade in the US, although the requirements applicable to publicly owned domestic companies are more far-reaching. Legislation and rule-making continues. For example, US Exchange Nasdaq on 11 March 2003 and the New York Stock Exchange (NYSE) on 12 March 2003 filed with the SEC a revision of its previ-ously submitted corporate governance listing standard proposals. The SEC on

10 January 2003 publicly released the text of its rule proposal under Section 301 of the Sarbanes-Oxley Act (SOX), discussed below.

Congress has also mandated numerous changes to financial reporting:

- real time disclosures
- officer certification
- increasing transparency
- independence – now a law, not a virtue
- mandated SEC review
- final rules for pro forma statements due by 26 January 2003
- new audit committee requirements – 26 April 2003 deadline
- loans and certain trades prohibited.

Finally, Congress has given new powers to the SEC:

- criminal penalties for 'white collar' crimes strengthened
- statutes of limitations changed
- new Public Company Accounting Oversight Board
- a set of analyst conflicts of interest rules
- attorney professional responsibility rules
- protection for whistleblowers.

The devil in the detail: an overview of major points in SOX

On 30 July 2002, President Bush signed into law the Sarbanes-Oxley Act. The most dramatic change to federal securities laws since the 1930s, the Act radically redesigned federal regulation of public company corporate governance and reporting obligations. It also significantly tightened accountability standards for directors and officers, auditors, securities analysts and legal counsel. SOX included several corporate governance related provisions, along with new corporate disclosure requirements and auditor regulatory and securities law enforcement measures, all of which are now in effect. While these new corporate governance standards did not alter the basic fiduciary duties of care and loyalty of corporate directors and officers, they did provide detailed mandates that have implications for, and should be considered carefully when assessing, what directors should do in order to satisfy their fiduciary duties to the corporation and its shareholders.

Among the key changes:

- By 26 April 2003, the SEC had directed the NYSE and Nasdaq to prohibit listing any public company whose audit committee does not comply with a revised list of requirements affecting auditor appointment, compensation and oversight. The audit committee must consist solely of independent directors.

- CEOs and Chief Financial Officer (CFO) must certify in each periodic report containing financial statements that the report fully complies with Sections 13(a) and 15(d) of the Securities Exchange Act of 1934 and that the information fairly presents the company's financial condition and results of operations. Certifying officers will face penalties for false certification of $1,000,000 and/or up to 10 years' imprisonment for 'knowing' violation (twice the previous level) and $5,000,000 and/or up to 20 years' imprisonment for 'willing' violation.
- No public company may make, extend, modify or renew any personal loan to its executive officers or directors, with limited exceptions.
- SOX changed the deadline for insiders to report any trading in their companies' securities to within two business days after the execution date of the transaction.
- Each company must disclose 'on a rapid and current basis' additional information about the company's financial condition or operations as the SEC determines is necessary or useful to investors or in the public interest.
- All annual reports filed with the SEC containing financial statements must include all material corrections identified by a public accounting firm.

SOX created several new crimes for securities violations, including: destroying, altering or falsifying records with the intent to impede or influence any federal investigation or bankruptcy proceeding; knowing and wilful failure by an accountant to maintain all audit or workpapers for five years; and knowingly executing a scheme to defraud investors in connection with any security.

Exchanges have raised their game, too. The NYSE now designates the audit committee as the 'sole authority' to retain and terminate the external auditor, requires the audit committee to approve all independent auditor fees and terms, including significant non-audit engagements, demands that NYSE-listed companies are expected to have an internal audit function, limits audit committee member compensation to board-service fees only, and requires an annual performance evaluation of the audit committee.

The United Kingdom

Corporate governance in the UK seems, typically, to be defined by a series of official inquiries and reports. The 1992 Cadbury Report was the first, possibly the best and certainly the most influential. It was the first to put corporate govern-ance firmly on the business agenda. It recommended the general desirability of separating the chairman and CEO roles, the importance of effective non-executive directors, the forming of board committees (audit, remuneration and nomina-tion) mainly of non-executives, the rotation of audit partners, and generally

35

encouraged investment institutions to take an interest in board appointments. The acceptance of splitting the top two roles and tougher accounting standards saved the UK from the type of scandals that happened in America – a remarkable achievement. (Or was it just good fortune?) The 1995 Greenbury Report addressed the then widespread public and government concerns over alleged excessive executive remuneration. It was a sound and hard-hitting report covering the most pertinent points but its effect on the inexorable rise of remuneration was sadly negligible. It insisted on transparency in the high cost of senior management pensions but the revealed costs were largely ignored by the investment institutions. Transparency alone, without fundamental reforms, was demonstrated to be quite insufficient in achieving change. The 1998 Hampel Report saw its role as primarily consolidatory because it believed that '. . . public companies are now amongst the most accountable organisations in society' – a sideswipe at the public sector. It recognized few conflicts of interest and felt that shareholders had sufficient power for any needed reforms. The extensive government-sponsored Company Law Review of 2001 argued that the role of investment institutions was a matter of major public interest and that they should be active and responsible in the exercise of shareholder power. It also accepted the need for better regulation. The other major report was the Myners Report on institutional investment, also in 2001. It recognized that corporate managements should be held properly accountable to shareholders and that investment institutions should be prepared to look after beneficiaries' interests despite conflicts of interest. The final key Higgs Review investigated the role and effectiveness of non-executive directors in the United Kingdom – who they are, how they are appointed, and how they can be drawn from a wider pool of talent, their independence and effectiveness, the actual and potential relationship between non-executive directors and institutional investors, and how the quality, independence and effectiveness of UK non-executive directors could be strengthened. By the mid years of the first decade of the twenty-first century the feeling was widespread among both legislators and business communities that the UK was facing the legislative buffers: no more could Parliament really do.

CORPORATE GOVERNANCE IN ASIA

From the definitions and discussion above, we can appreciate that so far as Asia is concerned, corporate governance is an *import*. For example, the concept itself was virtually unknown in China even a decade ago. This is not surprising given how little understood it was in the rest of Asia at that time and the fact that China's securities market was then only a few years old itself. But in China a series of significant financial and market-manipulation scandals, inspired by a stock market boom in the late 1990s, caused officials and regulators (and to a lesser degree, investors) to look to improved corporate governance regulation as the solution.

The OECD's take on the history is that the 1997 crisis exposed severe and urgent capacity-building and enforcement challenges for securities regulators and stock exchanges across the Asian region. With a few exceptions, Asian regulatory regimes lacked the institutional capacity and authority necessary to ensure company compliance. As in some other regions, regulators may also have lacked the institutional capacity or authority to ensure proper performance by self-regulatory organizations in the accounting and auditing professions. In some cases, adoption of disclosure-based regulation also added substantially to monitoring and enforcement burdens. Lastly, in more than a few cases where regulators had evidence of law-breaking, bias, political influence and corruption permitted wrongdoers to escape punishment.

In practice, as observed by Jamie Allen, Secretary-General of the excellent Asian Corporate Governance Association[40] (ACGA), a non-profit investor pressure group with its finger on the pulse of corporate governance in Asia, like the apocryphal curate's egg, Asian corporate governance now is a case of good in parts and rotten in others. Providing a five-year 'interim assessment' on the rise of corporate governance in Asia in 2003, he suggested on the positive side of the balance that 'awareness has risen, governance is firmly part of policy, reform is underway in all major economies, there are higher standards (in theory) and emerging shareholder activism. On the negative side, he believed that the depth of change had been shallow, that governance was seen as a compliance issue, not a competitive one, that regulatory will vacillated, and that significant disincentives to shareholder activism continued to exist.' A recent Credit Lyonnais Securities Asia (CLSA) report, produced jointly by the ACGA, measuring corporate governance in Asia, highlights the point (see Chapter 10). The report reviewed ten Asian markets and found that in almost all countries efforts are being made to improve the legal and regulatory systems that underpin good corporate governance. For example, Korea is planning to implement class action legislation and continues its purge of family-controlled conglomerates. Indonesia now requires audit committees and independent directors. Malaysia has implemented a code of corporate governance, as have Taiwan, the Philippines and Thailand. So far, so encouraging. But the report also scored individual Asian companies on seven key categories, such as discipline, transparency and accountability. The results show a vast disparity in quality, underlining just how far many Asian companies have to go before they approach generally accepted international standards. Top of the country class, as might be expected, is Singapore, followed by Hong Kong and, somewhat surprisingly, India, where overall disclosure standards have improved dramatically, accounting differences between local and US standards have been progressively reduced and the number of companies with a majority of independent directors has risen significantly. A satisfactory but could-do-better report card is returned by companies in Taiwan, Korea and Malaysia, while in need of significant improvement are firms in Thailand, the Philippines and 'the perennial laggard', Indonesia. In these countries in particular, corporate governance is more a matter of form over substance, with enforcement of legislation raising doubts as to how serious these governments really are about raising governance standards. From the standpoint of many analysts, Japan has the most to do to improve governance, in the view of our survey group. It is also the worst performer in the new transparency research carried out for this report.

China is a special and overwhelmingly important case. On the basis of any regional or international comparison, the quality of corporate governance in China is still low – on a par with underperformers such as Indonesia and the Philippines. What is encouraging, however, is the direction and pace of change: most Chinese regulatory authorities have been energetic reformers in recent years, well aware that better corporate governance is critical to the stability and growth of the country's securities market, hence to state-enterprise reform and overall economic development as well. Clearly there is an interrelationship between different national economic objectives. For example, the Commonwealth Business Forum 1999 confirmed the recipe required to attract foreign direct investment (FDI) as a combination of political stability together with the rule of law and enforceability of contracts.

But these beliefs might not be quite accurate: China attracted more FDI in 2002 than any other country, and although it may have the former it certainly doesn't have the latter. There is little evidence, either, that improvements in corporate governance in China after 2002 have brought in more foreign investors. It could only really be argued that they were necessary to keep the flow of money going, and even that is contentious.

Another consequence of the growing supremacy of economic power is the attempt to replace the normative function of the State in Asia with private rules and regulations, voluntary codes of conduct, and so on. Chapter 3 looks at these efforts in detail.

THE LINGERING EFFECTS OF SOCIALISM

The OECD observed that: 'Where the state is a major or controlling shareholder, as is often the case in Asia, stakeholder interests are often given considerable weight although enforcement can also be complicated by the state having, in effect, to police itself.'[41] The role of the state in the transition economies is ambiguous. On the one hand the role of the state in post-socialism should be limited. On the other hand, strong state power is needed to carry through the political programmes required by economic transformation. Weak governments have proved to be incapable of economic transformation.[42] In reality, the state still has a great role in both the industrial and financial sectors. State authorities and company managers are tightly related, so that the line between the 'controllers' and the 'controlled' is unclear. In practice, informal constraints, such as relational ties and family and government contacts play a greater role, leading to different outcomes. The state gives subsidies to companies directly or indirectly while on the other hand, companies enable state representatives to have a certain amount of control over the process of making decisions and cash flow. Behaving in such a way, managers are constantly searching for new subsidies instead of looking for existing or potential strategic partners.

The creation of networks of linked enterprises, rather than of autonomous independent firms, is a relationship characteristic of transition economies. Transactions between privatized enterprises become linked to each other, to banks and to the state through complex structures of cross-shareholding and corporate interlocks. Relationships between enterprises and banks are especially crucial in view of the shortage of capital and credit, and continue to be influenced by personal and institutional connections. Where credit is not available from banks, barter relationships among organizations known to and trusted by each other provide an alternative means of financing. So, the relationships between firms in post socialism are based on networks rather than markets or hierarchies.[43]

In transition economies the most important firms, such as public sector companies that contribute more to the nation's gross national product, employment, income, and capital use than private sector firms, are controlled by the state. Moreover, public sector companies often shape public policies. From a governance perspective, state-owned firms are controlled by bureaucrats with control rights but with no formal ownership. Although all citizens of a country own the firms, in practice control rights rest with powerful ministries. As a result, citizens subsidize state firms and end up as 'minority shareholders' with practically no voice.

The 'missing ingredient' in the context of corporate governance development in transition economies is the lack of institutions associated with successful market economies. In the market economies there is a standard set of institutions that have been successful as the tools used to control corporations. Institutions are the 'rules of the game' in a society.[44] They are the rules that society established to reduce the uncertainty of human interactions. The institutional framework has three components: formal rules, informal rules and enforcement mechanisms. While both the formal legal environment and the informal institutional constraints affect corporate governance, institutional theory and common sense both suggest that when formal institutions are weak, informal constraints play a larger role in shaping firm behaviour. But is it possible to reproduce all at once the institutions from developed market economies in transition economies? The standard institutional portfolio has evolved gradually in different circumstances and under significant pressure from the media, competition and academic institutions, as

39

Table 1.1 *Examples of risks from poor corporate governance*

The table below provides examples of some of the common risks to minority share-holders in companies that have poor corporate governance standards. Many of these issues do not matter when the company has a single shareholder or group of related shareholders (such as a family-owned business), but they become significant areas of risk when independent shareholders invest in the company.

Risk factor	Negative impact
Loans to related parties – The company makes a significant loan to a shareholder or senior executive, at interest rates lower than market rates, or on terms which do not sufficiently take into account the level of risk.	The company generates a return on those loans which does not sufficiently compensate for the level of risk. Also if the company borrows to finance this loan, it increases its own risk levels.
Loans from related parties – A share-holder makes a loan to the company at interest rates higher than market rates.	The company's borrowing costs are higher than they would be if the company borrowed from an independent third party.
Guarantees – The company issues guarantees for the benefit of a shareholder.	This increases the company's risks levels, with insufficient compensation to the company for incurring that risk.
Asset sales to shareholders – The company sells assets to a shareholder at lower than fair market value.	This has a negative impact on the net asset value of the company.
Asset purchases from shareholders – The company purchases assets from a shareholder at higher than fair market value.	The company generates a lower return on its assets than it could otherwise achieve.
Contracts with related parties – The company buys raw materials or services from related parties or sells finished products to related parties, at prices which are beneficial to the related party.	This often leads to transfer pricing, whereby profit is transferred to the related party at the expense of the company.
Share sales to shareholders – The company sells shares to a shareholder at prices lower than the fair market value.	This lowers the value per share for those shareholders who did not participate in the purchase of new shares.[1]
Share purchases from shareholders – The company purchases shares from a shareholder at prices higher than fair market value.	This is an inefficient use of the company's cash, which has a negative impact on the net asset value per share.
Fraudulent asset transfers – Senior managers improperly transfer the company's cash or assets outside of the company.	This is theft of the company's assets and therefore lowers the value of the company for the shareholders.

◼ **Table 1.1** *continued*

Risk factor	Negative impact
Commissions – Managers or a share-holder receive undisclosed commissions on the company's contracts, purchases or share sales.	This is theft of the company's assets and therefore lowers the value of the company for the shareholders.[2]
Poor transparency – Investors do not have sufficient information about a company's financial condition.	Shareholders are unable to make well informed decisions about how to value the company's shares, or how to vote on major decisions. This also leads to poor accountability by the management team.
Unclear procedures – Procedures for making major decisions within the company are unclear.	This can lead to a slow decision-making process and poor accountability, due to a general uncertainty as to what are the rights and responsibilities of the various participants.

1 This should be distinguished from a legitimate employee share bonus or option programme, which is part of the remuneration package of employees, and which has been properly approved by the board of directors or shareholders.

2 This should be distinguished from a legitimate compensation or bonus plan, which is designed to incentivize the sales team and/or management team, and which has been properly approved by the board of directors or shareholders.

Recommendations on Good Corporate Practice in Vietnam.

Source: Mekong Capital

well as internal pressures within fund management organizations themselves. Merely transplanting these institutions is not possible because there are new conditions and many cultural differences. On the other hand, to develop entirely new institutions would be an unpredictable adventure. The transition economies cannot afford the luxury of searching for new third way between socialism and capitalism. Instead, they have to find a way to accept the existing institutional portfolio and to make it work in the specific cultural, historical and economic environment. Each region is in a different stage of establishing a democratic, market-based economy and a corporate governance system. Hence, each nation has its own particular set of challenges.

Future researchers in governance issues in transition economies will be aware of these research areas. Solutions derived from a principal-agent perspective – while applicable to developed economies (especially the US and UK) – may fail to address the corporate governance problems in a different institutional setting. Analytically, integration with the stakeholder-agency theory may be helpful. The

41 ◼

stakeholder-agency theory puts less emphasis on the rights of shareholders and instead recognizes several groups which have an arguably legitimate claim on the firm. Therefore, current work for transitions economies focuses in more detail how organizations influence institutions, shedding light on how these two evolve together.

Corporate governance is directly related to financing and investments. Making managers disciplined by means of corporate governance mechanisms results in an efficient allocation of resources. For countries in transition it is doubly important: the scarcity of domestic savings demands that capital be directed towards the most profitable companies, which is possible only if principles of corporate governance are given publicity, transparency and monitoring; in addition, due to the imperfection of market mechanisms (underdeveloped stock and bond markets and an ineffective banking system), corporate governance presents an additional mechanism for discipline and effective management control in corporations. We can deduce that good corporate governance is an important factor for the functioning of a financial market in a transition economy, which in turn leads to efficient allocation of financial resources and is the key to economic growth. The efficient financial market itself should promote better practice of corporate governance, reinforcing market discipline for corporate managers.

International capital flows enable companies to tap sources of financing from a great number of investors. If countries want to take full advantage of global capital markets, which in Asia they all do, and if they want to attract long-term capital, they must follow clear standards of corporate governance at the international level. The degree to which corporations use basic principles for good corporate governance is a relevant factor for investment decisions as well. It is especially important in considering foreign direct investment (FDI), which is highly significant for countries in transition because it means not only capital, but the transfer of skills, technology and know-how. Although foreign direct investors exercise a lot of control, they also pay considerable attention to the framework of corporate governance. Many request adapting to the global corporate governance standards, in order not to be caught in the trap where local companies undercut them by means of corruption and hidden government subsidies.

Finally, it is important to point out that division of the world into two different camps, namely, 'emerging' versus 'developed' economies, risks over-generalization. National and regional cultures also generate idiosyncratic differences in governance across countries, but as a group, transition economies tend to exhibit governance characteristics that cluster around relatively similar dimensions. This is precisely why Asia should no longer be analysed in this way. Transition theory and practice may have provided many useful insights, although perhaps most of them could be identified by common sense. What is important to recognize for Asia is that these insights no longer apply to the majority of Asian countries. They are playing in the big league now.

IS IT ALL GOOD NEWS?

Advocates for better corporate governance claim a great deal for their charge. The OECD believes that good corporate governance promotes national competitiveness, economic/financial stability, growth, job creation, poverty alleviation and higher living standards for the country as a whole, while concurrently facilitating better corporate performance, management succession (particularly intergenerational succession within family-run firms), access to (and lower cost of) capital, diversification of wealth and informed entrepreneurial risk-taking. It ought on such an assessment be relatively easy to convince everyone of its benefit, and implement it.

We all remember the free rider problem: we all want something, but I'll benefit just as much as you if you (and others) do all the work. Once it is done I will of course benefit just as much, if not more, than you do. Insufficient attention in the West has perhaps been paid to the fact that this applies particularly well to the world of corporate governance as it is often perceived in Asia. What may be in my interests as a company director is for everyone else to be well governed, but for my company to avoid the costs involved, at least so long as I can persuade outside investors and – increasingly – internal regulators aiming at a level playing field that it is. At the national level, however, this is harder to argue: countries as a whole do not benefit from poor corporate governance in terms of their international competitiveness. This is generating a most interesting tension between regulators and central government in Asia on the one hand, and some – by no means all – companies on the other.

Chapter 2

Catching up and copying

- What's meant here
- The motivation
- From there to here
- Hong Kong
- China: rapidly demystifying itself
- The newcomers
- It means something
- Effects of the process
- Problems with the process
- *Plus ça change*: the scandals continue
- Winners and losers

WHAT'S MEANT HERE

The examples of whole cultures – or segments of them such as industries – adopting a policy of *copying* is hardly new. Examples abound from a whole range of activities. Famously the Soviet Union used to copy Western military designs, with results ranging from the very successful to the mundane; the Japanese 'economic miracle' of the middle years of the last century was based on copying *and eventually superseding* US and European industrial designs. Asian manufacturing in particular was distinguished by initiating competition through copying, especially by producing a cut-price version, and going on to produce highly engineered competitors with a distinctive brand, like Lexus – even if perhaps Europe retains a lead in style and the US in cutting-edge technology. Few doubt that there is a lesson to be learned here for services, and now that regulation and governance is also a competitive arena, it would not be surprising if Asia began with copying. That is what is happening. Even Vietnam is now alive to most of the major issues and is implementing regulations.[1] The time lag between a new corporate governance regulation or principle being promulgated in the West and its adoption in

Asia is, moreover, getting shorter. As Matt Linsey, head of emerging-market investment at Deutsche Asset Management, said: 'No-one has a monopoly on good corporate governance any more.'

THE MOTIVATION

It is time to move on from visualizing corporate governance in Asia as largely a response to the Asian financial crisis of 1997–8, although this response did play a major part in encouraging Asian governments, and the Asian Development Bank (ADB), to take corporate governance more seriously: many companies were held to have opened themselves up to bankruptcy by the combination of high gearing, lack of internal controls, poor management and overexpansion. In fact the extent to which blame for the financial crisis can be attributed, as Krugman suggested,[2] to poor governance, has now been disputed. And likewise the effects of Enron, WorldCom and others in Asia have been limited.[3] Challenges in Asia are heightened by the prevalence of family control among many of the largest publicly traded companies. Such companies may hesitate to disclose problems and setbacks because managers and controlling shareholders have much of their personal wealth tied up in shares and also because they fear reputational harm and loss of face from disclosure of poor results.

Although the international organizations, especially the ADB and the OECD claim to be 'leading the charge to implement rapid improvements in corporate governance across Asia', as Kang[4] has pointed out, the reform of corporate governance is a domestic matter, intricately limited to democratic reform and institutional and legal change at the widest level. Corporate governance *matters* for countries in Asia for several reasons. One is because their governments want firms in the region to compete for financial capital. China's Ministry of Finance has encouraged Chinese banks to clean up their balance sheets and reputations so that they can raise money by selling shares on international stock markets. 'Foreign institutional investors have legitimate concerns about governance,' said China Securities Regulatory Commission Vice-Director Tong Daochi in 2002. 'We want to get across the message that we are working to protect shareholder rights.' Equally important are the potential benefits of improved corporate governance for overcoming barriers to achieving sustained productivity growth, such as the actions of vested interest groups. The second reason is globalization. Academic study results show that integrating corporate governance into an Asian firm's strategy is not yet a competitive necessity as companies rank profitability as the least important incentive to implement corporate governance. But Asian governments recognize that in the future good corporate governance may become a competitive necessity for companies issuing debt or an implicit consideration for firms borrowing money from banks. Former OECD Corporate Governance director Stilpon Nestor commented:

45

This might become the Trojan horse through which corporate governance will assume a direct role in the ex ante pricing of corporate cost of capital, especially in markets where equity corporate finance is still relatively under-developed and bank finance preponderant.[5]

The Corporate Governance Forum of Japan, a group of business executives, academics, investors and journalists, which was one of the earliest proponents of corporate governance reform, began its Corporate Governance Principles with a statement emphasizing global compatibility of corporate governance:

> The globalization of the marketplace has ushered in an era in which the quality of corporate governance has become a crucial component of corporate survival. The compatibility of corporate governance practices in an international context has also become an important element of corporate success. The practice of good corporate governance has been a necessary prerequisite for any corporation to manage effectively in the globalized market.[6]

By 'shining a bright spotlight on dodgy business practices', as Malaysian Minority Shareholder Watch Group Chairman Yusof Abu Othman was quoted, he was hoping to remove what might be called the 'Malaysian discount', a phenomenon whereby international markets still value companies in Malaysia lower for equivalent revenues than those in Singapore and Hong Kong. Jamie Allen of the ACGA agrees: 'If perceived as generally low on corporate governance and relatively high risk, markets in the region will be seen to deserve being at discounts.' An academic survey found that Taiwanese directors 'clearly want international harmonisation of corporate governance standards and view corporate governance reform as a means of attracting foreign funds into Taiwan'.[7]

> In Hong Kong, as elsewhere, the standards of corporate disclosures and practices affect the interests of all shareholders. It also has a direct impact on the degree of confidence with which existing and potential investors, both retail and institutional, view investing with Hong Kong securities market as a long-term investment prospect.[8]

It is the same refrain everywhere in Asia:

> Poor corporate governance practices followed by corporate India in the past has led the primary market into its present state where there is not a single issue pending for clearance. The only remedy to revive the sentiment and bring back small investors to the initial public offering (IPO) market is for the corporate sector to follow and implement best practices in corporate governance.[9]

46

The motivation should not be thought of as exclusively from government: many Asian executives themselves have said they are looking for other ways to improve efficiency and transparency in management through such measures as the appointment of outside directors and auditors, and the establishment of advisory panels.

FROM THERE TO HERE

The OECD recognizes that:

> Since the 1997 financial crisis, Asian regimes have made considerable progress in raising awareness of the value of good corporate governance. Over the past several years, most Asian jurisdictions have substantially revamped their laws, regulations and other formal corporate-governance norms. In many [surely most] cases, Asian rules now reflect the most developed thinking of established corporate-governance systems.[10]

Perhaps the easiest way to see how the copying process has moved quickly and effectively since the late 1990s is by comparing Tables 2.1 and 2.2. Reforms since the late 1990s in Asian countries have included campaign finance limits, laws against nepotism, mandates for greater corporate transparency and codes of corporate governance.

Progress has not been uniform. Viewing Western corporate governance regimes from different angles, and responding to different domestic political and economic pressures, each Asian country has made a different copy. So for example in South Korea, the Monopoly Regulation and Fair Trade Act (MRFTA) prohibited direct cross-shareholdings between any two subsidiaries of the each of the 30 largest conglomerates, and also mutual debt payment guarantees among chaebol subsidiaries. Conglomerates were also required to designate three core companies and divest extraneous units. The MRFTA also introduced fiduciary responsibilities of corporate directors, making de facto directors, including controlling shareholders, accountable and liable as normal directors. In Thailand, the central bank was given greater power to intervene in bank operations in cases of mismanagement and fraud, while limits on foreign ownership were removed. In Malaysia, the government tightened rules on insider trading and the Exchange has clamped down on trading while insolvent: the number of so-called PN4 (Practice Note 4/2001) companies has been drastically reduced. As of 18 December 2003, there were only 61 PN4 companies – although arguably that's still 61 too many. The Philippines formed the Presidential Commission on Governance, and an Institute for Corporate Directors, although in both Indonesia and the Philippines the view held by the World Bank and institutional investors alike is that corporate governance is still relatively weak. The Chandra committee

47

Table 2.1 *What they had then: January 1997*

Country	Official code of best practice?	Mandatory independent directors?	Mandatory audit committees?
China			
Hong Kong	Yes	Yes	
India			
Indonesia			
Japan			
Korea			
Malaysia		Yes	Yes
Philippines			
Singapore		Yes	Yes
Taiwan			
Thailand			

Source: ACGA Ltd

Table 2.2 *What they had later: January 2003*

Country	Official code of best practice?	Mandatory independent directors?	Mandatory audit committees?
China	Yes	Yes	Yes
Hong Kong	Yes	Yes	(No)
India	Yes	Yes	Yes
Indonesia	Yes	Yes	Yes
Japan	in 2003?	Optional	Optional
Korea	Yes	Yes	(Yes)
Malaysia	Yes	Yes	Yes
Philippines	Yes	Yes	Yes
Singapore	Yes	Yes	Yes
Taiwan	Yes	Yes	(No)
Thailand	Yes	Yes	Yes

Source: ACGA Ltd

on corporate governance in India researched topics ranging from defining the role of chartered accountants, the quality of certified audited work, pinning down responsibility of financial information shared by companies, and many other issues concerning corporate governance.

HONG KONG

Since 1991 Hong Kong's corporate governance reforms have included a clearer understanding of the directors' duties, especially their fiduciary responsibilities, and the requirement for the board of directors of a listed company to have at least two independent non-executive directors. A Code of Best Practice was introduced in 1993 and since 31 December 1995 all listed companies have been required to include in their reports a statement affirming compliance with the Code. In May 1998, two additional guidelines were added to the Code of Best Practice. The first emphasized that the directors should keep abreast of their responsibilities. The second advised the listed companies regarding the establishment of audit committees. It was suggested that the audit committees' scope should be extended in order to include a report on companies' wider obligations to community and business ethics. The Listing Agreement in effect now also outlines clearly the responsibilities of companies for information disclosure. These responsibilities include the requirements for disclosing the public details of a wide variety of transactions including connected transactions which must be approved in a general shareholders' meeting. Interested parties must refrain from voting at these meetings. The Hong Kong Stock Exchange (SEHK) itself is supervised and monitored by the Securities and Futures Commission (SFC). Under the existing institutional setting the SFC can play a variety of roles from providing advice to directly suspending trading under Rule 9 of the Securities Rules. The SFC can also start an investigation or recommend to the Financial Secretary that an inspector be appointed. Furthermore, the SFC has been given powers to handle and monitor all matters connected to merger and takeover transactions of listed companies. In effect, this makes the SFC responsible for seeing that the takeover codes are applied properly.

The process is continuous. In the 2003–4 period, the Exchange finalized a fresh Code on Corporate Governance Practices. The Exchange set up a working group to express views on the practical aspects of the draft Code provisions 'having regard to Hong Kong's own circumstances'. Senior officials are absolutely *explicit* about the derivative nature of this work.

> In drafting the Code the Exchange drew on the revised UK Combined Code and the proposals set out in the consultation paper issued by the Standing Committee on Company Law Reform in June 2003. The draft Code holds up well to international comparison and is a worthy benchmark to which listed companies in Hong Kong should aspire.[11]

49

UK regulators have not failed to notice: 'It is notable that many emerging countries are looking to the UK model of corporate governance for their own markets. This is certainly true in Asia.'[12] The only reason that detailed comparative analyses have not been done showing the way in which Asian jurisdictions such as Hong Kong have introduced Western practices is that the process is so well known that it does not need scrutiny.

One man, David Webb, has launched a crusade for better corporate governance in Hong Kong. Rarely can one person be said to have achieved so much single-handedly. He campaigns for better rules governing initial public offerings; for shareholder democracy, and an improved system for voting stocks; for the Exchange to lose its status as a frontline regulator, promoting the election of independent directors to company boards; reforming rubber-stamp shareholder voting procedures; and the legalization of class actions against mismanaged companies. As it is now, the families that control most Hong Kong companies simply appoint directors and put through their formal elections at shareholder meetings. To force real votes, Webb launched Project Poll in time for 2003's chain of annual meetings. After buying shares in each of the 33 Hang Seng index companies, he attended meetings and demanded formal votes on all proposals. Another Webb initiative, dubbed Project Vampire, seeks to thwart companies trying to push through resolutions that allow for massive share dilutions. In April 2003 he was elected to the board of Hong Kong Exchanges and Clearing Ltd, the publicly listed company that runs the Stock Exchange of Hong Kong. The election of Webb and the CEO of BOC-Prudential Asset Management Ltd broke the exclusive election of Hong Kong's brokers to the Exchange's board. His website, www.webb-site.com, is one of the most important websites for the detailed, practical study of corporate governance in action in Asia and is highly recommended.

CHINA: RAPIDLY DEMYSTIFYING ITSELF

Chinese officials have been enthusiastic about corporate governance ever since the Shanghai and Shenzhen stock exchanges started trading in December 1990 and April 1991 respectively. The China Securities Regulatory Commission (CSRC) says that more than 1,100 companies have listed on the exchanges. Officials hoped the stock markets would put household savings to use as financing for listed companies, most of which were – and still are – profitable parts of state-owned enterprise (SOE) companies. They were also interested in separating SOE management from government. Largely these objectives were achieved, but major institutional investment has been lacking. As China's capital market developed and SOE reform progressed, a string of SOEs were restructured into what were termed 'shareholding' firms in the early 1990s, some of which then listed on the Shanghai and Shenzhen exchanges, and numerous unlisted SOEs have turned into shareholding or limited liability entities. The CSRC hoped the existence of capital markets would facilitate the introduction of a modern enterprise management system based on efficiency and transparency, and help overhaul ailing state-owned businesses without the social turbulence that they feared would result from massive bankruptcy in the SOE segment of the economy. But they wanted, and to some extent still want, to achieve all this without forgoing the control over private firms that is taken for granted in Western jurisdictions. The government is well aware of this problem.

Both officials and academics were disappointed when most of these 'modernized' enterprises failed to start earning profits, although it is important to recognize that failures of corporate governance were only contributory factors to their failure to do so. Worse, from 2001 onwards there were a series of scandals (see p. 53). Both the lack of profitability and the corruption scandals stemmed from the prevalence of structural distortions among China's listed companies, which have obstructed the development of a healthy corporate management system in China and have created an untrustworthy setting for long-term investors. CSRC responded by issuing a raft of new regulations and decrees, but the effect thus far on China's stock market has been only gradual: share prices have not risen significantly since the decline of mid-2001.

Meanwhile, external supervision by government industry regulators, and the media, remained a uphill struggle. Since most listed firms emerged out of state-owned entities, the government in many cases still owns more than half, and in some cases up to 80 per cent, of a company's shares. Typically, however, the state does not exercise its rights as a shareholder to influence management effectively. In fact, majority government control of listed companies can make it difficult for systems managers to build working corporate governance systems and enhance profitability; the government is certainly aware of this problem. Even when Chinese regulations governing the relationship between the state and company management are adequate, they are not yet always implemented, in part because of inadequate resources. Unfortunately, China's lack of an accounting culture, coupled with the widespread practice of reporting only good news to higher-ups, make the organic development of a fair incentive mechanism unlikely in the near future. Many analysts have highlighted the distortion caused by the government's role in selecting companies for listing. There is also a perception problem: the prevalent mindset among SOE managers has usually been that capital raised from the financial markets is free money that can be squandered with relative impunity. This attitude derives from the era of the planned economy, when SOE managers would receive loans from state-owned banks with no serious sanctions on not repaying them.

In many cases in the past, share prices in China have not reflected corporate performance or operational cycles because institutional investors, insiders and the listed companies themselves work with artificial figures. As a result, investor psychology is fixatedly short term. Until relatively recently, when the inutility of the strategy became obvious, Chinese investors typically focused less on a company's fundamental, let alone sustainable, performance when making investment decisions than on the names of the company's key institutional investors. Thus, managers in a Chinese listed company, unlike their Western counterparts, are under little pressure to improve performance and self-discipline. Listed companies in China still report to multiple government institutions, with each institution exerting considerable influence over the companies' management. Most listed companies in China still lack an incentive mechanism that ties the management team's performance to its compensation. In addition, the absence in past years of reliable accounting and adequate disclosure increased management's autonomy. Unfortunately, China's lack of an accounting culture, coupled with the widespread practice of reporting only good news to higher-ups, made the development of a fair incentive mechanism hard to achieve. Poor corporate governance in China has tended to begin before a company is approved for listing. Many analysts have highlighted the distortion caused by the government's role in taking the lead in choosing companies for listing. In order to increase their chances to be selected for listing, companies have an incentive to inflate their figures and produce deceptive financial reports. Collusion with local governments and interest groups facilitated the circumvention of accounting rules. But it is changing: the CSRC reported in mid-2003 that, in its opinion at least, Chinese listed companies were now keen to prevent practices such as IPO proceeds being held in the parent company's bank account, as well as abusive related party transactions. The CSRC admitted that the worst culprits had often been the state-owned enterprises owned by central ministries, which had siphoned cash out of the listed company for their own use.

Corporate governance in China is moreover now well buttressed with legislation. The current legal framework for corporate governance is based primarily on the Certified Accountant Law (issued in 1993), Audit Law (1994), Company Law (1994), People's Bank of China Law (1995), Commercial Bank Law (1995), Securities Law (1998) and Accounting Law (1999). The key regulatory bodies involved in the lawmaking process are the CSRC, the State Economic and Trade Commission, the Ministry of Finance and the People's Bank of China, but the regulatory scene is changing rapidly with the introduction of new regulators, for example for the banking sector. The problem does not lie with the drafting or extent of regulations governing the relationship between the state and company management, but rather that they are not always implemented, in part because of inadequate resources. Authorities did patiently focus on how to allocate controlling rights among corporate leaders and prevent excessive control by management; how to ensure that management maximized investors' interests; and how to design and implement incentive mechanisms. CSRC worked out a scheme to sell off some state-owned shares, but the proposal caused turbulence in the market and drove individual investors – fearing a crash in stock prices from a massive sale of state shares – out of stocks when the government raised the possibility of flooding the market with a sell-off of its large shareholdings. To maintain market stability, CSRC announced in mid-2002 that it would put the plan on hold.

According to Chinese Company Law, there are three tiers of control over a company's operations: the shareholders' general meeting, the boards of directors and supervisors, and management. The general shareholders' meeting has the final say over the key issues of the company, such as approval of the senior management strategy, the financial budget and key investment plans, and the nomination of the boards of directors and supervisors. The board of directors makes key investment plans and the board of supervisors oversees the decision-making process and performance of senior management and directors. And management is responsible for day-to-day operations and for implementing the decisions of the board of directors. But in many companies, the problem has been that key managers have sometimes gained control over the shareholders' general meeting, rendering its voice merely an echo of decisions already made by senior management. Insiders have also occasionally won dominant positions on the boards of directors and supervisors and proceeded to multiply. In such cases, the boards of directors and supervisors merely serve the demands of controlling parties and their representatives. Blatant corruption has also been a problem: in some instances, managers have simply diverted money from state and company accounts into their own pockets. Critics commented that government and company efforts to build a corporate governance system during the 1990s, though well-intentioned at the senior level, thus frankly existed largely on paper and ultimately contributed little toward an effective system.

Attention has also been focused on the banking system, which is dominated by four state-owned commercial banks: ICBC, Bank of China, Construction Bank and the Agriculture Bank of China. Together, the big four employ over 1 million people and account for almost 70 per cent of total bank lending. These banks are caught between government and social pressures to prevent the bankruptcy of state firms, and the economic pressure of the market for them to make a profit, especially as China's World Trade Organization commitments include opening up banking to full competition by 2007. Part of the reluctance may be because helping the banks is likely to prove immensely expensive, following a cash injection into the four biggest commercial banks of RMB270 billion ($33 billion) in 1998. By 2003 Beijing has already taken ¥1.4 trillion in bad loans off the banks' books, but there is still more to come. Xinhua news agency quoted an official from the People's Bank of China (PBOC) as saying in 2003 that the Bank had yet even to do a feasibility study on how to go about cleaning up the non-performing loans. Foreign banks have the ability to help strengthen Chinese banking by bringing in independence, managerial and technical expertise and international best practices, but their impact in the medium term can only ever

53

be relatively insignificant: China's banking problems will have to be solved at home. The new breed of second-tier banks[13] may point the way forward. In the past decade, these banks have put increasing pressure on the big four.

THE NEWCOMERS

This new breed now controls 15 per cent of the market and their performance is far superior to that of large state banks. In 2001, these second-tier banks posted returns of 0.46 per cent on assets and 10.18 per cent on equity, compared with 0.16 per cent and 3.13 per cent, respectively, for the big four. This yawning gap is only partly explained by the new banks' focus on more affluent urban areas. Importantly, it is also a result of better corporate governance. Unlike the big four, which are fully owned by the state, the fast-growing banks have multiple shareholders or a diversified ownership that often includes public and private sector bodies. The key is multiple versus single ownership. Banks with diversified owners must respond to varied interests, which makes it easier to resist state interference. Further growth of banks with diversified ownership is needed to help the government evolve from its role of owner and player in a centrally planned economy to that of rule-setter and regulator in a market economy. Increasing competition from the second-tier banks will also provide a stimulus to reform the big four banks. Good corporate governance in the second-tier banks hinges on the diversity of shareholder interests, and to ensure that its benefits are realized, minority interests must be protected. The new Banking Regulatory Commission now takes responsibility for supervising the financial services industry away from PBOC.

IT MEANS SOMETHING

The scope of the change throughout most of Asia has been emphasized by many organizations, and perhaps what Tables 2.1 and 2.2 do not indicate is the extent of the change in approach required. Institutions have been heavily involved. Between March 1999 and March 2003, the OECD and the World Bank Group, in partnership with the government of Japan, the Global Corporate Governance Forum and the Asian Development Bank, and in cooperation with regional and local partners, organized no fewer than five roundtable meetings to discuss improving corporate governance in the Asian region – using the original Western OECD corporate governance principles as a basis.

These meetings and others fed through into action: legislatures in Asia have had to turn their attention to completely fresh subjects, as have regulatory bodies, courts and self-regulating professional organizations. The local driver of corporate governance reform varies: for example, in Hong Kong the main initiator of

Corporate Governance rules is the Exchange. In Singapore it is the Monetary Authority of Singapore (MAS) and the government.

> The rules of governance (including disclosure rules) are set by the Monetary Authority of Singapore (MAS) and Stock Exchange of Singapore (if the financial services firm is listed). The MAS, in particular, sets stringent standards for regulating the financial services sector. Thus the governance structure of the financial firms is in general consistent with the goals of restraining risky lending and speculative deals. In terms of the capital adequacy ratio, for instance, the 12% requirement set by MAS is not only met but is exceeded in many cases.[14]

Khan says that analysts from Daiwa and JP Morgan put it on average at 17 per cent. The government set up the Council on Corporate Disclosure and Governance (CCDG) in 2002, to monitor the developments in regulatory standards, both locally and, tellingly, abroad too. Its remit was acceptance and implementation of corporate law reforms to support new business structures and models, and proposed enhanced corporate governance standards for MAS-regulated financial institutions. Established in August 2002, the CCDG comprises members from businesses, professional organizations, academic institutions and the government. Its primary role is to: prescribe accounting standards in Singapore in consultation with the Institute of Certified Public Accountants of Singapore; strengthen the framework of disclosure practices and reporting standards, taking into account trends in corporate regulatory issues and international best practices; and review and enhance the framework on corporate governance and promote good corporate governance in Singapore, taking into account international best practice.

Similarly, countries have instituted awards for well-managed companies – for example the annual Singapore Corporate Governance Awards, which are endorsed by the Corporate Governance and Financial Reporting Centre (CGFRC) in association with leading organizations like Standard & Poor's, Pricewaterhouse-Coopers, the Singapore Exchange, Singapore Institute of Directors (SID), Institute of Certified Public Accountants of Singapore (ICPAS) and *Business Times*. There are also Transparency Awards issued by the *Business Times*/Securities Investors Association of Singapore. The Hong Kong Society of Accountants (HKSA) has made its Best Corporate Governance Disclosure Awards (BCGD Awards) since 1999. 'The entrants' latest annual reports are assessed in terms of the breadth and depth of disclosures and the quality of presentation of corporate governance information, as well as the standard of the underlying governance practices'. Awards are presented in three different categories: Hang Seng Index (HSI) constituent companies, other (non-HIS constituent) listed companies and public sector/not-for-profit organizations. The focus is said to be on the clarity and

55

extent of corporate governance information disclosed in each entrant's annual report as well as the practices reflected by this disclosure. In 2002, 120 companies and organizations participated in the awards. As the aim of the awards is not only to establish absolute benchmarks but also to encourage improvements, the Significant Improvement Award, added for the first time in 2002, was extended in 2003 to cover each of the three categories.

Meanwhile, when they are not covering Corporate Governance Award ceremonies, the media in Asian countries have enjoyed fresh freedoms to investigate companies. With respect to China in particular, mention should be made of magazines like *Caijing* and the *Far Eastern Economic Review*. The extent of even-handedness expected of regulators and courts, especially where state institutions are involved, has rapidly become a major issue for debate. A plethora of codes of conduct, as the succeeding chapter shows, has emerged as a result.

Asian universities have likewise had a field day creating centres to study corporate governance. For example in January 2003, the National University of Singapore (NUS) Business School set up the Corporate Governance and Financial Reporting Centre. 'The Centre will contribute to the research and the promotion of best practices in corporate governance and financial reporting, and will hopefully help entrench high standards among our companies.'[15] The stated objectives of the Centre are to:

1 Conduct high-quality academic research in the areas of corporate governance and financial reporting.
2 Undertake applied projects in corporate governance and financial reporting that are relevant to practice and policy-making, either independently or in collaboration with industry and governmental organisations.
3 Disseminate the results and practical implications of academic and applied research to practitioners and policy-makers.
4 Organise industry conferences and seminars in corporate governance and financial reporting, either independently or in collaboration with relevant organisations.
5 Produce case studies that illustrate relevant corporate governance and financial reporting issues.

In China, the Chinese Centre for Corporate Governance was established in 2000 as a non-profit research organization under CASS, with the functions of: organizing information exchange forums; conducting research projects; organizing training programmes; providing a policy consulting service and building an international network with counterparts worldwide. In Malaysia, the Malaysian Institute of Corporate Governance (MICG) was set up in 1998. The MICG has since organized public awareness campaigns to promote good corporate governance with emphasis on the Malaysian Code of Corporate Governance.

EFFECTS OF THE PROCESS

This combination of legislation and quasi-legislative initiatives has not been without effect. Throughout Asia, expectations of the standard of behaviour expected
from company directors, especially of public companies, have risen. China is also
making progress in tackling the influence of 'guanxi', or relationships that keep
the wheels of business greased and were traditionally just as important to doing
deals as good business practices. 'Guanxi still exists, but to a lot less extent now',
according to Anthony Wu, chairman of Ernst & Young's China practice, as early
as 2002. Commenting on corporate governance in Asia, *Euromoney* said: 'Investors
suspect companies are paying no more than lip service [to corporate governance].'
'However, a few Asian companies have been quietly setting their own standards,
and reaping significant gains.'

PROBLEMS WITH THE PROCESS

A copying process is not without its effects, or its perils. On such a large canvas
as corporate governance, drawing in government departments, legislatures, regulators, courts, exchanges, private business and numerous other bodies, as well
as shareholders and their representatives, it cannot but cause major effects. As
the OECD points out,

> many Asian business leaders and controlling shareholders are thus being
> challenged to re-think their relationships with their companies and with the
> minority shareholders who lay claim to partial ownership in them. Such
> re-orientation in thinking requires not only a strong national commitment to
> corporate governance, but one that is also broad-based.[16]

However, Asian governments on the whole are well capable of national resolve.
More than that, many of them possess a high degree of political and economic
cohesion.

The problems that can arise from the process are outlined below:

1 *What has been described by Jamie Allen as 'regulatory activism'* – where a regulator
goes beyond enforcing the law and galvanizes public activism – has driven much
corporate governance reform. He suggests that:

> The paternalistic styles of government in Malaysia, Singapore and China have
> spilled over to the corporate arena. Governments are actively taking the
> lead in pushing for transparency by introducing new disclosure requirements
> for companies. In one poll, CFOs polled 'believe that government will
> bring to bear more pressure for change over the next five years': many of the

respondents evidently expect more legislation of the kind recently introduced in the US.

Regulatory activism is widespread in Asia: for example in Malaysia, the Minority Shareholder Watchdog Group formed in 2001 was led by the Employees Provident Fund; in Thailand in May 2002 the SEC and SET helped to form the Shareholders Association, a retail body, while the Government Pension Fund together with other funds and insurance companies created the Institutional Investors Club in July 2002; in Taiwan the Securities and Futures Institute has facilitated 'quasi' class-action law suits involving retail investors. Allen asks whether regulators should seed such activism, and asks whether these groups can ever act independently. Perhaps the former question is otiose: this is the best it is going to get, the issue is whether it works as well as a multi-player corporate governance environment.

2 *Problems also come, as we shall see, when corporate governance comes knocking at the door of the very institutions and people setting out to implement it*, like Temasek in Singapore. Singapore regulators may be all in favour of corporate governance, but no doubt irritated when it leads to difficult problems of conflict of interest among senior figures in the government: but then this paradox is yet to be resolved in Western countries either. Is it OK in the new global governance regime for Rupert Murdoch's son to become CEO of BskyB, or not? What criteria should we use: is it the shareholder vote, or a more general principle?

3 *Another important issue is convergence.* Singapore and Hong Kong have for decades enjoyed a comparative advantage in the region with respect to corporate govern- ance standards. Their governments continue to argue publicly that: 'We should keep up the momentum of improved disclosure and corporate governance practices in Singapore. It will continue to be a competitive differentiator, for our companies and for Singapore,' but the political leadership of both countries as well as the boards of their home-grown companies are increasingly recognizing that this comparative advantage is slipping away. The Hong Kong Exchange refers to 'the UK Listing Rules on which our Rules are principally based' but these are no secret, and they are open to being copied by every jurisdiction. Two-speed Asia, with Singapore and Hong Kong differentiated from the pack, is beginning to be replaced, in corporate governance as in so much of business and enterprise, by a two-speed ASEAN in which the Philippines and Indonesia are perceived as lag- gards but the rest of the pack is increasingly close together. Then there is Japan.

Debate on the prospects of corporate governance reform tends to be framed around two extremes of convergence and inertia. Those who predict con- vergence argue that global capital and product markets will inevitably drive

Japanese firms to a 'global standard' – or more specifically, American practice. Some proponents of the opposite viewpoint argue optimistically that existing Japanese governance institutions are effective and do not require dramatic reform. Others argue pessimistically that inertia and fear of upsetting the status quo make change impossible.[17]

Analysts have argued that convergence of legislation, codes, standards and above all behaviour is happening not just between Asian countries, but between Asia as a whole and Western countries: for example, *Sarbanes-Oxley for the legislation, the UK Combined Code for the code.*

4 *A key problem with the copying process, though, is its potential two-dimensionality.* The process of copying notoriously brings with it difficulties of comprehension. We are all familiar with the copy of a branded product which fails on point of detail, in the absence of a plausible accompanying guarantee, sometimes rendering it immediately obvious as a copy. There is some evidence that this problem is real. In 2002, ACCA commissioned a study, polling 200 Asian CFOs from the top 300 companies in China, Malaysia and Singapore for their opinions on corporate governance. The picture that emerged from the findings indicates that Asian corporate governance still focuses more on disclosure and compliance, rather than enhancing transparency. As late as 2003, the CLSA commented in its Annual Asian Corporate Governance Report,

> Much of the improvement is in form: making publicly stated commitments to good corporate governance, setting up of board committees, appointing nominally independent directors, etc. . . . The commitment to corporate governance is not yet clear. In all the markets, cases abound of egregious transgressions.

There is still no natural feel for openness and disclosure: but is there in US or European corporations either?

5 *Another related problem is timing.* Asian corporate governance will never be anything other than in arrears so long as there is nothing but aspirational, derivative thinking, which is why even the suggestion that accountancy reform anticipated US action on the subject is so pathbreaking and meritorious. Asian corporate governance legislation and rules will really have come of age when a revision of the UK Code, or a piece of US legislation, explicitly draws on an Asian precedent. For that, we will have to wait decades.

6 *Finally, everyone agrees that improved corporate governance cannot be considered in isolation.* In the financial sector, attention must also be given to measures to

strengthen the banking sector, and a country's financial institutions as a whole. In the 'real' sector, close attention must be given to competition policy and sector-specific regulatory reform (OECD, 2001).

So, the final test. Corporate governance reform has certainly had an *impact*. But has it made a *difference* or has it merely been 'sound and fury, signifying nothing'?

PLUS ÇA CHANGE: THE SCANDALS CONTINUE

The improvement of corporate governance, on which countries have been judged in the preceding section, has as one of its main objectives a reduction in corporate scandals of various sorts, and a resultant increase in public confidence in the way that large companies in particular are managed. The series of corporate scandals that have beset Asia in the 1990s and on into the new millennium are ample proof that whatever else corporate governance has changed, this objective is very far from being achieved. There are so many different examples of corporate scandals in Asia that it is completely impossible to list them all. What is interesting is to compare the scandals with the advances in corporate governance since the mid-1990s and speculate on whether any of them would have been avoided by such improvements.

In **Brunei,** the small size of the country and the strength of the royal family in corporate finance mean that it is hard to disentangle improving corporate governance from threatening political change: the sultanate's accounts are not made public. Prince Jefri, the younger brother of the sultan, was Brunei's finance minister from 1986 to 1997, as well as the head of the Brunei Investment Agency (BIA), which managed the country's overseas investments once valued at more than $110 billion. Prince Jefri was dismissed from BIA in 1998 after the conglomerate he headed, Amedeo, collapsed with $6 billion in debts. Subsequently, it was also found that under Prince Jefri's tutelage BIA had squandered more than $40 billion in state funds in a variety of dubious investments. In 2003, the sultan took his brother and 70 others to court to recover some of these state funds. The court case exposed the lavish lifestyle of the royal family and how its members used state funds as virtually their private money. It was the first time that the financial dealings of the BIA were made public, and so far from transparency it is even a criminal offence to divulge or report on the country's finances.

China has had its fair share of scandals, most of which came to light accidentally; of great interest is the fact that many of them do indeed seem to have had a great deal to do with the poor governance of the firms in question. These scandals not only put the buzz-words 'corporate governance' (*gongsi zhili*) in newspaper headlines, but also prompted disillusioned investors to demand reform of the country's corporate governance structure for listed companies, hoping that greater confidence in the numbers produced by companies would help revive the declining values of companies on Chinese stock markets. The regulators are now hoping that reforms introduced over the past decade will have a significant and lasting effect in reducing the level of such scandals and boost company values permanently.

The corporate sector scandals have revolved around the state sector on the one hand and corruption, especially surrounding IPOs, on the other. State sector scandals have often been about huge unrectified errors. For example, the '12.23' gas blowout caused by the negligence of the Chuandong Oil Exploration Drilling Company under China National Petroleum Corporation led to the death of several hundred innocent people and made many thousands homeless. 'State-owned monopoly enterprises gained so much power *while the government is not able to supervise them.*' Why? The argument was put that one-third of the RMB250-billion profit realized by China's 510 key enterprises in 2002 is from the petroleum and petrochemical industries to which China National Petroleum Corporation is a major contributor. China National Petroleum Corporation earned RMB379.2 billion of sales income, RMB64.4 billion of tax payment, and RMB53.6 billion of profits, thus making it top the list of all domestic enterprises.[18] One small crumb of comfort from the disaster was the active, not to say militant, attitude of the Chinese media: no Chernobyl-style cover-up here, but precise and apparently accurate reporting together with a great deal of finger-pointing. Examples multiply. The CEO of Brilliance China Automotive Holdings and reportedly one of China's wealthiest individuals, Yang Rong, was dismissed from the company after rumours of financial irregularities. Shanghai property developer Zhou Zhengyi, reputed as Shanghai's richest man with a personal wealth of US$320 million according to the 2002 Forbes ranking, was arrested by Chinese authorities investigating allegations he lied to borrow $80 million for his businesses. One of Mr Zhou's land development projects brought protesters onto the streets of Shanghai claiming that they had not been adequately compensated for the loss of their homes, demolished to make way for new developments.

Some scandals have become famous:

China's newest popular hero is a bookish professor, a woman who endured death threats and intimidation in a courageous campaign to expose financial wrongdoing at a high-flying corporation. Liu Shuwei was an unknown academic when she began poring over the financial reports of a government-linked company that boasted of dramatic revenue growth. For 16 days she studied every line in Hubei Lantian's public statements, analyzing the profit claims that had fuelled its surge on the Shanghai stock exchange. She concluded that it was an empty shell that could not even afford to repay its bank loans. Her findings were restricted to a tiny newsletter with only 180 subscribers but Ms. Liu still got anonymous death threats by e-mail. Her probe triggered an

61

avalanche: The company lost its bank loans, a legal battle ensued, and eventually the police arrested 10 of its top executives. The case has been called 'China's Enron'.

Part of the problem was that CSRC shared authority over Lantian with the Ministry of Agriculture and Hubei local authorities. The Ministry of Agriculture, as a supervisory agency of Lantian Co. Ltd, was either unable or unwilling to point out the company's financial misconduct before it became public. Companies such as Lantian and Zhengzhou Baiwen Co. Ltd were, in effect, scandals in the making even before their IPOs. Yet government officials showered praise on the companies even after the IPOs, obscuring the companies' faults. Another bad case involved Yinguangxia, a biochemical firm that reported a net profit of RMB417 million (US$50 million) in 2000, but was later found to have made a loss of RMB150 million. Laura Cha, Vice Chairman, CSRC, put it bluntly when she said in late 2001: 'Some recent cases in China show that some controlling shareholders have all along used their listed companies as their own little ATM machines. When this is discovered, they say they cannot repay, so it is the listed company that suffers.'[19]

The financial sector itself has also been hit by scandals. According to Fred Hu of Goldman Sachs: 'Chinese banks have neither a functioning system of internal controls, nor effective eternal oversight.' In 1999 the audit office found RMB400 billion ($48.3 billion) in 'misused funds' at 4,600 branches of the Industrial and Commercial Bank of China (ICBC) and 1,700 branches of the China Construction Bank (CCB). Five Bank of China (BoC) officials in the small southern Chinese city of Kaiping stole at least $483m, and up to $725m through the local BoC branch over a period of a decade and then laundered the money in gambling centres such as Las Vegas and Macau. This was the largest financial scandal since the founding of the People's Republic of China. The alleged theft followed the BoC's agreement to pay a $20m fine for loan irregularities at its New York branch. The former head of the BoC has been jailed as a result of the scandals. On top of this, it has been suggested for years that China's big four state-owned banks, the ICBC, the BoC (with an estimated bad loan percentage of 27 per cent), the Agricultural Bank and the CCB, are technically insolvent. The State Council has pumped US$22.5 billion into the CCB in an effort to increase its capital, using the nation's foreign currency reserve, and the bank has said that as part of the effort to strengthen corporate governance, it will set clear business strategies and targets, seek to effectively supervise daily operations, and enhance the ability of risk mitigation and internal control. About time, many commented.

What repays careful study is the interplay between the dates of these scandals and the introduction of successive corporate governance legislation and rules. It is certainly true that the period from the beginning of 2003 has seen fewer corporate and financial scandals in China: but it has always been the case in America and Europe that such scandals have gone in phases, and it is surely far too early to be congratulating the CSRC and the other Chinese regulators for a job well done – any more than SOX can be guaranteed to have prevented recurrences of Enron-style events in the US.

Hong Kong's scandals are more difficult to fathom, although David Webb does a great job of tracking them. Hong Kong-based Gay Giano International Group Ltd was claimed to have rehired chairman Cheung Sing-chi as a consultant, two days after he resigned following his arrest for what police said was conspiring to manipulate the retailer's shares, but if this is the most serious abuse of corporate governance that can be found since the Peregrine Investments scandal, Hong Kong is doing well. However, there is always the mainland to worry about. In mid-2003 the SFC was forced to confirm media reports of an ongoing investigation into a mainland enterprise, China Rare Earth Holdings, under Section 179 of the Securities and Futures Ordinance because the company had refused a request from the Stock Exchange to make the disclosure itself. The SFC enquiry arose from certain anonymous allegations made in the mainland Chinese press that Rare Earth had deliberately inflated its sales in its listing prospectus and accounts. The company denied the allegations: interestingly its new auditors were appointed in April 2003 after two previous auditing firms resigned. Problems like this for the regulators in Hong Kong are expected to continue.

India is scarcely immune to corporate scandals either. An example was that barely months after the actions of Tata in the wake of its takeover of Videsh Sanchar Nigam Ltd (VSNL) which themselves raised a controversy, the role of its non-banking finance company (NBFC), Tata Finance Ltd (TFL) was brought into question along with the reputation of one of the oldest audit firms in India, when A. F. Ferguson (AFF), withdrew a special report prepared for the Tatas and dismissed one of its senior partners. Officials of the Registrar of Companies (RoC) in Mumbai, acting on behalf of the Department of Company Affairs (DCA) in Delhi, began an investigation into shredded documents. TFL, by the Tatas' own admission, is believed to have run up losses amounting to nearly Rs 500 crore by 30 June 2001, allegedly to protect its other group entities. This is what lies at the centre of the controversy. The question to ask here is whether new accounting regulations on subsidiaries would have made a difference.

In **Japan**, some of the most well-known companies have been involved in a string of scandals. Sloppy health and safety practices at Snow Brand Milk Products Co. led to mass food poisoning. Mitsubishi Motors Corp. tried to conceal a recall. Tokyo Electric Power Co. (TEPCO) concealed problems at nuclear energy plants for years by falsifying inspection data. Although this scandal cost the jobs of top management, it was a pervasive *operational* problem at mid-management level. It is at least by no means certain that even the most independent director could reasonably have known what was going on, and of course changes to

63

accountancy, audit and other financial practices were irrelevant. Mitsui was revealed to have engaged in unfair bidding for a power-generation plant on Kunashiri Island and allegedly to have bribed a senior official in the Mongolian government in connection with an official development assistance project. Again, there were high-level casualties among the board, but we are left asking how corporate governance reform would have helped – perhaps effective internal audit might have discovered and stopped any bribe, but unfair bidding is notoriously difficult to identify before the event. The relevant authorities did not prosecute in either case. Auditors had found Mitsui Mining was burdened with much larger losses than it had reported to the Industrial Revitalization Corporation of Japan (IRCJ) which was planning a rescue in a $1.5 billion bail-out. Also well known is the case of Snow Brand Foods and Nippon Meat Packers, which evaded the government's countermeasures against bovine spongiform encephalopathy (BSE, commonly known as mad cow disease). The Japanese media vigorously attacked the corporate culture which allowed all these evasions of responsibility.

The link to improving corporate governance, at least according to the Ministry of Economy, Trade and Industry, was failure to act on the part of senior management and the role of whistleblowers. Defending the position of whistleblowers is an important part of running an ethical corporation, but it does not feature very highly in the list of improvements in corporate governance enacted by Asian governments over the past decade. In Japan, companies have responded by expanding their internal inspection setups, formulating behaviour guidelines for employees, and claiming, at least, to have strengthened compliance. There is also an increasing number of companies, such as Matsushita Electric Industrial Co. and Eisai Co., that not only offer counselling for legal and ethical violations but also have set up departments for the reception of whistleblowing information. Furthermore, the Japan Business Federation has revised its Charter on Good Corporate Behavior and announced a policy calling for the strengthening of arrangements to prevent scandals and the thorough investigation of causes. And through the revision of the Commercial Code that took effect in April 2003, the Japanese government introduced US-style corporate governance that separates executive and inspective functions in corporate management – the same separation that allowed Enron and WorldCom to happen. Successive surveys (see Chapter 8) have suggested that Japan is the Asian country with furthest to go in improving standards of governance: yet the Japanese equity market remains far more attractive to outside investors than, say, Indonesia, or even China or India, which have made great strides in corporate governance. Why is this? The answer could lie either in the fact that Japan starts corporate governance reform from a much higher level, albeit something of a plateau, or simply that some Japanese firms at least consistently return high dividends to their shareholders and do not go bankrupt with the same frequency as their Indian or Chinese counterparts. Which seems the more likely explanation?

In **Korea**, SK Group, which is involved in businesses from mobile phones to engineering, had a KRW1.6 trillion ($1.4 billion) accounting scandal at its SK Global subsidiary in 2001. Chey Tae-won, the scion of the family that owns much of SK, South Korea's number three conglomerate, was convicted in June 2003 of wrongfully accruing personal wealth and damaging the group's affiliates through dubious stock trading and accounting irregularities he used to increase his stakes in the group. In October 2003, SK Group suffered the lion's share of fines dished out by South Korea's Fair Trade Commission (FTC) for making illegal transactions to support failing parts of their businesses. Prosecutors also arrested one of President Roh's closest aides, Choi Do-sool, in 2003 on charges of receiving KRW1.1 billion in bribes from SK shortly after Mr Roh's election.

SK was not the only one. In December 2003, prosecutors investigating how the country's largest conglomerate ensured the transfer of wealth and corporate control from father to son indicted a former head of Everland, a Samsung unit that runs South Korea's largest amusement park, and another Samsung executive, on charges of selling the son of Samsung Chairman Lee Kun-hee convertible bonds at prices lower than market value. The 1996 dealing allowed the 35-year-old son, Jae-yong, to make at least KRW97 billion (S$135.8 million) in illegal profits, they said. The investigation into Samsung paralleled a probe by state prosecutors into allegations that others of the nation's top businesses provided millions of dollars in bribes to politicians ahead of December 2002's presidential election.

Malaysia has scandal fatigue. In the 1990s scandal after financial scandal plagued the Mahathir administration, the largest involving spectacular unexplained losses totalling RM10 billion at Perwaja Steel, a government-backed heavy-industry project shrouded under allegations of irregularities, which appeared to encompass the transfer of RM76.4 million to a non-existent company in Hong Kong which was finally transferred to a Swiss bank account of a firm registered in the British Virgin Islands. Perception in the country is still that there is an elite above corporate governance rules, and that the elite is not above using state assets in its own interests. Actual cases, though, have become much fewer and Malaysia deserves the higher ratings universally given to it in recent years.

Even **Nepal**, it seems, is not immune. The Commission for Investigation of Abuse of Authority (CIAA) filed cases against 55 individuals including the former General Manager of Nepal Bank Limited, on charges of financial irregularities carried out while disbursing loans to different companies and business firms.

It is true that **Singapore** has largely escaped financial scandals of any magnitude. Wild accusations have been thrown around on the internet about Temasek Holdings, and the S$600 million losses incurred by the Singapore Technologies Group Micropolis, but apart from the perennial issue of alleged nepotism, not one shred of evidence has ever come to light of any wrongdoing. This is either good governance or superb information management. The worst scandal actually

65

uncovered was a relatively tame one: Singapore-listed conglomerate SembCorp Logistics, Southeast Asia's largest logistics group, uncovered in 2003 a $12 million accounting irregularity at its Indian subsidiary, SembLog India, headquartered in Chennai. Between 2000 and 2002 profits were overstated and expenses were incorrectly classified as fixed assets. The company promptly sacked six senior officials including its managing director and CFO after the irregularities were detected. The company also terminated the services of accountants PWL (India) and auditors KPMG Consulting. The company informed the Singapore Exchange that an investigation had shown that PWC India and KPMG, which used to be SembLog India's external and internal auditors respectively, did not detect the creation of fictitious revenues, expenses, documents and invoices even though these practices had been carried out over a number of years. The problem was dealt with quickly, openly and effectively.

In **Taiwan**, actual financial scandals are also hard to come by, especially accounting scandals, although 2004 was an exception to this rule. Overstretched firms were hit hard by the Asian financial crisis, but that is only arguably an issue for corporate governance. A few firms, such as Taiwan Power Company, have failed in their responsibilities, but this was a state-run utility. The Kuang San construction and food conglomerate was found guilty of economic crimes including breach of trust, document forgery and violating securities and banking laws in 2001. The main problem in Taiwan has been perceived to be 'black gold' – corruption, and in particular a link with politics. For example, a former finance minister and bank chairman was indicted for loans made to the Hotel Royal Chihpen in Taitung between 1996 and 1998 by the Farmers' Bank of China. Nevertheless, while there are numerous such scandals, Taiwan remains an awkward case for protagonists of corporate governance to explain – at least those who want to envisage a linear relationship between the quality of domestic corporate governance and a scandal-free economy.

WINNERS AND LOSERS

The key winners are the large jurisdictions where there have been significant improvements.

Perhaps most spectacular in its drive to reform has been **China**, despite its huge size and the large number of corporate scandals. Clarke argues that: 'Corporate governance (*gongsi zhili*) is a concept whose time seems definitely to have come in China.'[20] There can be little doubt that China has made more progress in improving corporate governance in the last decade than other countries have achieved in a century. Perhaps this has a lot to do with starting from a low base, but it is also explained by a strong, determined central government combined with considerable competitive pressure in the regions, and an ability and willingness to copy second to none. China's officials and academics are clearly worried that weak corporate governance is endangering the country's economic reforms. And the problem is not limited to public companies, though private companies are hidden from scrutiny because they are not obligated to publish their financial data. New laws have addressed a number of the issues of greatest concern, including information disclosure and financial fraud, but effective enforcement is by no means assured. China has learned from its own experience, and that of the United States, and is working hard to improve public trust in its companies. The 2003 CLSA report praised the progress the country has made on corporate governance. The country introduced quarterly reporting in 2002 and in June 2003 independent directors at listed companies were required to constitute a minimum of one-third of a company's board. The nation issued its first Code of Corporate Governance in 2002 and the China Securities Regulatory Commission also promulgated a series of regulations aimed at improving transparency, limiting the scope for fraud and protecting minority shareholders' rights. The CSRC has taken forceful steps to educate retail investors about the stock market as well as to deter practices such as market manipulation, fabrication of financial statements and other objectionable activities.

There is even the beginning of a backlash against corporate governance in China. Many domestic institutional and retail investors blamed 'overly aggressive enforcement' against listed companies, and other regulatory manoeuvres such as the attempted sale of state shares, for a collapse in share prices in China. A period of retrenchment (or at least a lower profile approach to enforcement) now seems likely in order to calm the markets. While it is my strong contention that China should no longer be viewed in the category of a developing economy, it remains true that in many cases, stock prices in China do not reflect corporate performance or operational cycles because institutional investors, insiders, and the listed companies themselves manipulate figures. As a result, investor psychology is not that of 'buy and hold' but rather 'buy to trade'. Chinese investors typically focused less on a company's basic performance when making investment decisions than on the names of the company's key institutional investors. Thus, managers in a Chinese listed company, unlike their Western counterparts, used to be under little pressure to improve performance and self-discipline. On the other hand, Chinese academics and senior officials have published numerous empirical studies in newspapers and academic journals on the subject of corporate governance. Some of their recommendations are clearly receiving consideration by People's Republic of China (PRC) lawmakers. Wu Jinglian, chief economist with the State Council's Development Research Center (DRC), criticized excessive intervention from the government and parent SOEs and proposed that listed companies drop their state-owned stakes. Zhang Weiying, professor at Beijing University, has recommended that the government allow company share-holders to select corporate managers and that China privatize its state banks. Dai Yuanchen, an economist at the China Academy of Social

67

Sciences (CASS), believes that more state industries should be opened to private investors. Wu and CSRC Chairman Zhou Xiaochuan have stated that a crucial obstacle to successful corporate governance of listed companies is 'insider control'.

Most of this reasoning also applies to **India,** another winner, where accounting regulations in particular, together with the rise of shareholder activism and generous quantities of FDI, are having an effect in improving standards of corporate governance to the point where Indian companies may consider listing abroad, even on the London Stock Exchange. As yet there has been little analysis of **Vietnam**, but there can be little doubt that the country has much to gain from high corporate governance standards in attracting FDI.

The losers are the previous winners, the small island economies.

Khan argues that several factors explain **Hong Kong**'s success in continuing with gradual corporate governance reforms. First and foremost is the relative strength of the financial sectors. Both the banks and the equity markets have proved to be much stronger than those in other regional economies during and after the crisis. Second, the presence of both competition and cooperation in the financial sector has made it possible to regulate effectively through the Banking Ordinance and Listing Rules and Takeover Code. A third factor is that in Hong Kong the insolvency and bankruptcy procedures are relatively straightforward. This makes exit of insolvent firms economically less costly and after such exits the system regains its vigour. Finally, although this may not be the most significant, the smallness of Hong Kong makes it easier for informal agreements to be made and kept through reputational and other relational mechanisms. Unfortunately, like Singapore, Hong Kong's relative advantage in running FBS is diminishing by comparison to its competitors. It is a loser in the corporate governance game whatever it does.

By comparison, he argues that

> the relative immunity of *Singapore*'s corporations, including family-owned and controlled corporations, from the recent financial crisis can be attributed to reasonably well-functioning financial markets, government oversight and corporation and coordination among the major domestic players in an open and competitive market structure.[21]

One up for good corporate governance, then. Singapore's problem is that whereas two decades ago it shone as a beacon of capitalist success in an Asia ravaged by war, beset by Communism and starved of capital investment, now it competes – as does Hong Kong – on a much more level playing field. Its standards of corporate governance remain the highest in Asia, at least to the extent that investors have the greatest confidence in its companies – but its comparative advantage has narrowed dramatically. As such it too is a real loser in the corporate governance game.

68

Other countries in Asia remain as neither particular winners nor losers, obliged to reform just to stand still. In this category come **Thailand**, **Malaysia** and bringing up the rear as usual, the **Philippines** and **Indonesia**, these last two countries still unable to persuade investors that they are serious about corporate governance, whatever improvements are happening in practice.

Japan remains a special case, criticized for poor corporate governance now for over a decade. Many commentators believe that Japan has lacked genuine reform, that the banking sector in particular has not increased its transparency and the bad loan problem remains. Despite recent initiatives to improve practices, corporate governance is still a weak point for most Japanese companies, according to two reports in 2003 by Standard & Poor's Governance unit. The reports ('Japan Corporate Governance in Transition: Weaknesses Remain and Challenges Continue' and 'An Overview of Corporate Governance in Japan') identified a number of weaknesses that have traditionally characterized corporate governance in Japan, i.e. 'lack of transparency and disclosure, boards consisting solely of executive directors, and cross-shareholding relationships'. It is true that Japanese firms are increasingly adopting practices long associated with US corporate governance: small boards, independent directors, and stock options, and these have attracted much publicity. For example, household products maker Kao Corp. has launched an advisory committee on executives' compensation and another to screen nominations for chairman and president; carmaker Honda Motor Co. has set up the Assets and Loan Management Committee, an advisory panel on important investment plans (see Chapter 3), and trading house Mitsubishi Corp. has established an advisory committee on corporate governance and another on global operations. But critics argue that these changes are cosmetic: 'they signify relatively little for corporate governance. Boards remain insider-dominated, and the authority of boards of directors vis-à-vis the CEO has been unchanged. Despite the spread of stock options, executive compensation is only minimally tied to the stock market, and disclosure of executive pay remains far from transparent'.[22] Things may change, however, as the weight of foreign institutional investors is increasing and exerting more pressure on companies' management. Domestic shareholders are also becoming more demanding. Some Japanese companies are responding to these growing demands by pursuing greater transparency and disclosure. Recent revisions to Japan's Commercial Code should also contribute to improve governance practices. But as the reports say, 'the pace of change remains slow', and the effort made by some cannot mask the overall weakness of regulatory structures in Japan.

Moreover, many Japanese executives have also expressed doubts about the effectiveness of any US-style governance system, inevitably citing the series of corporate scandals in the United States. Many Asian executives have doubts about the effectiveness of US-style corporate governance, according to an *Asahi Shimbun* survey of 100 major Japanese corporations. Some Asian executives, *especially in*

Japan, have been willing to stand up and be counted. For example, Fumio Sameshima, president of Japanese cement supplier Taiheiyo Cement Corp., said he did not believe that the US-style model of focusing exclusively on the interests of stockholders is the best model. Koji Suzuki, president of department store operator Takashimaya Co., said he did not think introduction of the US-style system will enhance governance. Fujio Mitarai, president of camera maker Canon Inc., said the scandal involving the New York Stock Exchange chairman who resigned amid criticism of his enormous compensation package clearly showed that the compensation committee had not worked effectively. Others complained of the difficulty of recruiting competent people from outside for committee posts.

What is it possible to conclude? In the view of the Economist Intelligence Unit (2003), Asia remains dominated by *opaque family-controlled business structures, off-balance-sheet liabilities and lack of minority shareholder rights*. As Bloomberg reported in 2002, 'Companies doctoring the books and accounting firms that falsify reports on behalf of their clients have been more the rule than the exception in Asia'. Corporate governance in Asia has as far to go as it has in some Western countries – Italy, for instance.

Chapter 3

The board of directors

- The role of the board as a whole
- Board composition
- Choosing a board
- Separation of chairman from CEO
- Access to information for directors
- Independent directors
- Directors' and officers' insurance
- Director training
- Board committees
- The nomination committee in the Asian corporation
- The remuneration committee in the Asian corporation
- Conclusion

THE ROLE OF THE BOARD AS A WHOLE

For corporate governance in Asia, the composition, function and operation of the board of directors of a public company has always possessed a peculiar fascination. In probably no other region of the world, even in the US, does the prestige of being such a director stand so high. Joining the board of directors of a company remains the career objective of many Asians, despite the objective of many governments in the region to replace this with an entrepreneurial inclination. Most respondents to surveys in Asia indicate that the board of directors constitutes the most important instrument in Asian corporate governance.

Directors are certainly faced with intractable problems in principle: resolving who is in control – management or the board, achieving critical judgement while maintaining detachment, and avoiding becoming either a model of unimaginative unanimity or a fissiparous collection of disparate individuals. There are,

71

moreover, persuasive financial and social arguments to be made for companies having a board of directors that reflects their customer base and the population at large. Studies have found that boards whose composition mirrors that of the company's customers, suppliers and employees help dispel negative stereotypes and catalyse efforts to recruit, retain and promote the best people, including women and minorities. In addition, a variety of academic research has shown a positive correlation between board diversity and relatively better share perform- ance (see Chapter 10).

But what does, or should, a board director *do*? The OECD believes that a corporate board should explicitly assume the following six specific responsibili- ties, which facilitate the discharge of the board's stewardship responsibilities:

- reviewing and adopting a strategic plan for the company;
- overseeing the conduct of the company's business to evaluate whether the business is being properly managed;
- identifying principal risks and ensure the implementation of appropriate systems to manage these risks;
- succession planning, including appointing, training, fixing the compensation of and where appropriate, replacing senior management;
- developing and implementing an investor relations programme or shareholder communications policy for the company; and
- reviewing the adequacy and the integrity of the company's internal control systems and management information systems, including systems for compliance with applicable laws, regulations, rules, directives and guidelines.

These guidelines suggest that the strategic plan is produced elsewhere – presum- ably by senior management. Directors would have to be extremely knowledgeable to be able to second-guess management, especially in relation to what is excluded from a strategic plan. What is missing in this is precise guidance as to the elements of a 'review'. Many of the other roles are also quite vague. 'Overseeing' can range from an annual site visit to intense scrutiny, to the point of actually inter- fering with management's role. 'Reviewing' can range from a line-by-line analysis to a brief skim.

Specifically in relation to the corporate governance of banks, the Bank for International Settlements, the BIS, had this to say about the role of the board of a bank:

Boards of directors add strength to the corporate governance of a bank when they:

- understand their oversight role and their 'duty of loyalty' to the bank and its shareholders;

- serve as a 'checks and balances' function vis-à-vis the day-to-day management of the bank;
- feel empowered to question management and are comfortable insisting upon straightforward explanations from management;
- recommend sound practices gleaned from other situations;
- provide dispassionate advice;
- are not overextended;
- avoid conflicts of interest in their activities with, and commitments to, other organisations;
- meet regularly with senior management and internal audit to establish and approve policies, establish communication lines and monitor progress toward corporate objectives;
- absent themselves from decisions when they are incapable of providing objective advice;
- do not participate in day-to-day management of the bank.[1]

The Singaporean regulator states that:

> Besides the objective of maximising shareholders' value, the Board also has a responsibility towards the Institution's depositors or policyholders to safeguard their interests through its oversight of the management of the Institution. The Board should establish corporate values for the Institution to ensure the professional conduct of the business.[2]

Bank directors should be able to pass 'fit and proper' tests for service. These directors should also assume responsibility for bank systems and procedures that ensure sound lending and monitoring practices, as well as the capacity to handle distressed debt.[3] 'The board also has a duty to lead and ensure that management performs in accordance with business plans and budgets.'[4] It follows that the board should meet regularly and as warranted by particular circumstances, as deemed appropriate by the board members. The board should ensure that it has due notice of issues to be discussed and all relevant information to enable it to properly consider the issues. PwC concludes that the board as a whole ideally should have:

- strategic thinking
- analytical skills, appropriate professional experience and other relevant skills
- effective communication skills
- knowledge of the organisation and industry.

The monitoring role of boards has been examined by several academic studies. For example, it is documented that board meeting frequency is related to corporate governance and ownership characteristics in a manner that is consistent with agency theory. The frequency of meeting is inversely related to firm value: boards actually *increase* their meeting in bad times. In addition, studies have found that the operating performance of firms in the sample improves following years of abnormal board activity. Studies of ownership structure and board composition using time-series analysis have suggested that firms experience substantial changes in ownership and board structure. These changes are correlated with one another: changes in ownership and board structure are strongly related to top executive turnover, prior share price performance and corporate control threats. What has always distinguished Asian companies from their Western counterparts in this regard is that the board has largely remained *isolated* from the effects of these changes. It has been rightly observed that:

> . . . common law appears to endorse the view that if a company appoints a director who is not competent, or does not possess the requisite level of knowledge or experience, the company and its shareholders should bear the consequences of their own actions. The fact that this is so despite the significant losses caused by corporate oversights at Barings in Singapore, Perwaja Steel and Renong in Malaysia, and Euro-Asia Agriculture and Peregrine Investments in Hong Kong, highlights the degree to which the law with respect to the duty of directors is out of sync with commercial realities.[5]

The company's share price may oscillate wildly, takeover threats may surround the company and the company's products and services be under public scrutiny: but it is middle management – at a pinch, senior management – which takes the brunt of these attacks. On the whole the board has ridden over it. *Until now.*

BOARD COMPOSITION

PwC argue that effective boards work *together* in the interests of the shareholders. An effective board should therefore not be not dominated by one member or factional group and it does not require members to be experts in all fields. An effective board does not just happen. It requires care, effort, thought and analysis to identify and select the right team of people to help the company with its current challenges and opportunities, to take the company forward into the future and to work in partnership with senior management, providing real oversight and value adding guidance. Different boards have different compositions of skills. The skill requirements depend on the company's size, nature, ambitions and the challenges it faces. An effective board is one that has the right mix of skills and experience and can work together as a team while encouraging diverse and healthy debate in the interests of the company and its shareholders.

There are a number of personal qualities that each director should bring to a board, regardless of their background, or the particular skills and experiences that have identified them as able to make a valuable contribution to the success of the company. Individual directors should have:

- the highest standards of personal integrity
- excellent judgment and an ability to make informed decisions within time constraints
- professional credibility
- the capacity to think strategically and to demonstrate vision
- sound communication skills
- sound inter-personal skills
- team orientation.

How do Asian companies determine the skills and professional experience they need on their board? There is no single correct answer other than to say that it is increasingly important that the directors, and particularly those serving on the audit committee, have an appropriate knowledge and understanding of financial statements and other financial reports. Beyond this, it is beholden on the incumbent directors to consider the skills of the current board and to identify any additional skills or experience that are required. Typically, a board ought to have a mix of directors with skills in:

- law
- finance, including accounting expertise
- marketing
- operations relevant to the company's activities including, where important, international experience
- key industries in which the company operates
- corporate governance
- human resources
- risk management
- mergers and acquisitions, if relevant
- specific matters, relevant to the company.

PwC say that the key is to take an informed and measured look at the skills the company needs on the board and to make an honest assessment of how the current board matches up to those skills. This does not mean, according to PwC, that individual directors who are making a valuable contribution must stand aside (No? What about board size limits?), but does require proactive steps to be taken to address any identified skill deficiencies without allowing the size of the board to expand too far. The problem with this analysis is that for the majority of companies in Asia – looking particularly at Chinese SOEs, for example, but equally so a small Singaporean IPO – the board of directors has not been hand-picked by PwC to have a suitable range of abilities, but rather, are the same individuals who have driven the company forward over decades. In the case of smaller companies, family appointments are frequent, although in Asia increasingly this is becoming much less of a problem as the second generation tend to come armed with MBAs, are sensitive to corporate governance issues and skilled in marketing and database management, and know about risk management and corporate finance issues, at least sufficiently to be able to know when to call on expert advice. For large public companies, especially those with ageing boards, perhaps there is still a problem, but looking at the PwC list, it seems very likely that a senior Asian executive would in the course of their career have picked up ample knowledge on *all* the issues raised.

This is precisely why the size of a board has become a problem in Asia. There is plenty of talent to choose from. How big should a board be? The UK average is 11 members. Lipton recommends a maximum of 10. But it is quality, not quantity, that counts and there is no single correct answer. A small board of directors of the highest calibre, with complementary skills and experience and a degree of independence, can obviously make for a more effective board than just sheer numbers of individuals. Indeed, a large board can very quickly become unwieldy and limit the opportunity for individual directors to make an effective contribution. The board size should ideally reflect the needs of your organization. Suffice to say, one size does not fit all, but smaller is preferred to larger. California Public Employees' Retirement System (Calpers) corporate governance standards for Japan, for example, promote reduction in board size, apparently for its own sake, and increase in board independence. The Corporate Governance Principles of the Corporate Governance Forum of Japan mimic these issues of board size and independence. Japanese companies, sensitive to the need for external investment, are responding to these criticisms by reducing board size, separating monitoring and operating functions, and increasing numbers of independent directors. In 1997, Sony, with great fanfare, painfully reduced its board size from 38 to 10. It renamed the directors removed from the board *shikko yakuin*, and translated this term as 'corporate executive officer'. The stated objective was to separate strategic decision-making from implementation. Under the *shikko yakuin* system, the board makes the strategic decisions, which the *shikko yakuin* then implement. Those demoted had their careers ruined, but the new corporate governance regime has never been about compassion at an individual level. The new system has spread rapidly among large Japanese companies. In a survey conducted by the Tokyo Stock Exchange in September 2000, 35.5 per cent of the respondents had already adopted the *shikko yakuin* system, an increase of 32 points from the previous survey, conducted in 1988.[6] In the case of the 2003 Sony reform, the board of directors was intended to have between 10 and

20 directors. Regulations governing the qualifications for director candidates were established in order to eliminate conflicts of interest and ensure independence. The intention was to increase the number of outside directors from the present level of three. Were these published? What is the actual number of non-executive directors? But the Honda board of directors still consists of 36 directors, including only *one* outside director, and makes decisions on important business activities and other legal matters. Is Honda performing any worse than Sony? Generalizations about board size may be inappropriate. Hoya Corp. has already instituted a board of six directors of whom three are independent directors. With half of the board comprised of independent directors, the Hoya president can be removed from office in a crisis situation on the edict of the independent members alone. In the case of Konica-Minolta, one of the aims is also to limit a characteristic practice among companies that have merged – distributing top personnel appointments evenly between each firm. To make matters more complicated, Chinese listed companies adopt a two-tier board structure, akin to German practice: a board of directors (BoD) and a supervisory board (SBR). They are also required to provide in their annual reports a supervisory board report (SBR). It appears that the usefulness of the SBR depends on the role that the supervisory board plays in corporate governance. If the supervisory board is nothing more than an 'honoured guest', a friendly adviser or even a censored watchdog, it is unlikely that the SBR will convey much useful information. By contrast, if the supervisory board acts as it should, as an independent watchdog, then the SBR would be useful. It is too early to tell whether eventually China will adopt a unitary board structure, as after all Germany has not yet done so, but the dynamic of convergence suggests that it will, as after all the two-tier structure in China does not have the deep roots that it does in Germany, especially in relation to employee participation.

There are two other issues of vital relevance to the composition of a board. First, interlocking directorates – whether it is right or necessary that directors sit on only *one* board. Interlocking directorates are not a recent phenomenon in Singapore. In any country where a substantial proportion of commercial and industrial activities are undertaken by the private sector, the importance of the role played by board interlocks should not be ignored. In Singapore and Hong Kong, the evidence is that market capitalization, board size, total assets, return on assets, return on sales, profit before tax and nature of the company (financial or non-financial) are significantly positively correlated with board interlocks. This lends support to the Bank Control Theory and Resource Dependency Theory. These findings are consistent with those of the United States and Australia, among other countries. Perhaps Singapore is an unfair example to pick, because of its small size.

Second, the issue of board diversity. The current track record of board diversity worldwide is poor. Women occupy less than a fifth of US public company boards, and racial minorities less than a tenth. Asian companies are no better, although racial issues in countries such as China, Taiwan, India and Japan are much less important than in Indonesia, Malaysia, Singapore and the Philippines, where in many cases a critical racial issue is the proportion of ethnic Chinese on boards. An easy solution, then: fill up boards with minorities. It might do something for inter-racial income distribution, but does anyone believe that the world will be a much better place if such positive discrimination is carried out in directors' appointments? The Malaysian experience with Bumiputera directorships and shareholdings suggests far from that. The role of women on Asian boards, as yet relatively insignificant, is another issue which is still for the future.

CHOOSING A BOARD

Across Asia, shareholders have the right to elect directors. Two considerations, one legal and one practical, temper this right and in some cases almost nullify it. First, in some jurisdictions, candidates for director must be nominated by the board of directors, which means that minority shareholders have no direct say in filling the slate of candidates from which directors are chosen. This practice, it has to be said, is on the retreat, as Hong Kong has shown. Second, the prevalence of controlling shareholders and the absence of mandatory cumulative voting mean that the controlling shareholders effectively select *all* of the directors, including those considered non-executive or 'independent'. OECD naturally believes that there should be a formal and transparent procedure for the appointment of new directors to the board.

As to re-election, the Malaysian system, for example, suggests that it is the board's responsibility to appoint new directors but the shareholders' responsibility to re-elect them. In this system all directors should be required to submit themselves for re-election at regular intervals and at least every three years. Re-election at regular intervals not only promotes effective boards but affords shareholders the opportunity to review the directors' performance in turn and where necessary, to replace them. This is consistent with Chapter 7 of the Kuala Lumpur Stock Exchange (KLSE) Listing Requirements which requires, among others, that a public listed company must have provisions in its articles of association for election of directors to take place every year. These Listing Requirements go on to require all directors, including the managing director, to retire from office once at least in each three years, but they shall be eligible for re-election. The problem with this approach is that so many elections can actually take shareholders' eyes off the ball, and replacement, except through natural wastage, becomes wholly exceptional. If the point is for shareholders to be able to intervene – to identify underperforming directors and to remove them where necessary – then why is a special AGM not sufficient? Is there not a risk that requiring re-election causes shareholders to become blasé about voting? This point has been picked up already: describing corporate governance as something that cannot be enforced through a set of rules, Tata Sons director, Jamshed J. Irani, disagreed with the proposed limit of three terms of three years each as recommended by the Naresh Chandra committee. He said this could be counter-productive as companies could end up losing the services of good directors, like the ones who have served on the boards of Tata companies for as long as 20 years. Tata is hardly a company which fails to deliver shareholder value, whatever its problems. Nor is there evidence yet, especially in Asia, that regular rotation of directors will actually enhance shareholder value. In Europe and the US, the successful SMEs and family-owned companies that have delivered economic growth and jobs for decades have been run by CEOs – the old expression used to be 'Managing Director' until everyone in an investment bank became one – for decades. There were rarely objections from family shareholders.

As to voting methods, the OECD encourages the use of the cumulative voting method, which is also encouraged directly in China, where the Code of Corporate Governance specifies that a company with a controlling shareholder who holds more than 30 per cent of all shares must use cumulative voting methods in elections of director. Remote voting methods such as electronic voting are also encouraged in the code, to facilitate more investors to participate in voting.

Finally, if shareholders in Asia are to exercise responsibly their power to replace directors, 'dismissal under what terms' is an issue which needs to be addressed. Remuneration committees must decide on suitable packages for departure and this must in turn be put to shareholders. Similarly with the length of notice period, how bonuses will be treated, what rules will be followed on notice, pensions and so on. There is no uniform best practice on this yet in Asia, although shareholders considering the matter ought to pay attention to the views of the major institutional investors in Asia, such as Templeton, Aberdeen and others.

SEPARATION OF CHAIRMAN FROM CEO

Many commentators have suggested further augmenting board objectivity and independence by separating the positions of chairman and CEO, following the best practice that the roles of supervisor (chairman) and supervised (CEO) ought not be combined. Separating the Chairman and CEO roles has in fact become part of the litany of the new corporate governance regime. It has gained popularity in the United Kingdom since it was recommended by the Cadbury Report in 1992. In 2003, the US Conference Board recommended that companies choose from among three alternative board structures, all of them a break from the tradition that most American corporations follow. Alternative 1: the Commission urged companies carefully to consider separating the offices of Chairman on the Board and CEO. Alternative 2: the roles of chairman and CEO should be performed by two separate individuals. If the chairman is not independent

79

according to strict stock exchange definitions, a 'Lead Independent Director' should be appointed. Non-CEO chairmen should not have any relationships with the CEO or management that compromises the non-CEO chairman's ability to act independently. Alternative 3: where the board does not choose to separate the chairman and CEO positions, or where they are in transition to such separation, a 'Presiding Director' position should be established. Under the above alternatives, the independent chairman, Lead Independent Director or Presiding Director should have ultimate approval over the information flow that goes to the board, board meeting agendas and board-meeting schedules. The aim, clearly enough, is to prevent dominance by the CEO.

In Asia the principle of separation is now accepted as best practice, as Tata Sons director Jamshed J. Irani argued in the same breath as opposing mandatory maximum terms for directors:

> The Chairman of the Board should be separate from and independent of the CEO. This would ensure an appropriate balance of power and a greater capacity of the Board for independent decision-making. This separation of roles provides the needed checks and balances to preserve the integrity in the decision-making process.[7]

In Singapore the MAS has mandated that a bank incorporated in Singapore shall appoint separate individuals to hold the appointments of the chairman of the board of directors and chief executive officer although as a transition provision:

> A bank incorporated in Singapore shall not be required to revoke any appointment of its Chairman or chief executive officer made before the coming into effect of these Regulations or any subsequent reappointment of such Chairman or chief executive officer in the same office.[8]

A fruitful area of study might be the level of 'relatedness' between chairmen and CEOs, especially in Asian companies, and whether this relatedness, however defined, makes a difference to corporate performance. A recent survey of approximately 380 listed companies show that around 60 per cent of Singapore listed companies separate the chairman and CEO roles. Of the 60 per cent that separate the two positions, however, there is a family relationship between the chairman and CEO for almost half of these companies. Further, there is a significant percentage where the chairman is actually an executive chairman. Therefore, the percentage of chairmen of Singapore listed companies who are independent directors, as defined under the Singapore Code, would be very small. Clearly even Singapore has a long way to go, especially as in Western jurisdictions this separation issue is being tightened all the time.

ACCESS TO INFORMATION FOR DIRECTORS

Every board, say the MAS, should have a procedure for directors, either individually or as a group, in the furtherance of their duties, to take independent professional advice, if necessary, at the institution's expense. Further, the management should provide all members of the board with a set of balanced and understandable management accounts of the institution's performance, position and prospects on a monthly basis to enable the board to discharge its responsibilities. The Singapore MAS believes that in order to fulfill their responsibilities, all board members should be provided with complete, adequate and timely information prior to board meetings and on an ongoing basis by the management. Board members need access to accurate, timely, comprehensive and well focused information to participate in a meaningful way as directors. Certainly, incomplete, inadequate and late information would be of little use, that much is clear, but it is always much easier to point to lateness than inadequacy. Someone has to take the editorial decision on material for the board meeting. Although directors should be diligent in keeping themselves abreast of generally available information relevant to the oversight of the institution, a major source of information about the activities of the institution must be provided by the management. The question is, though, how much information is management obliged to provide? Sony states that for all board meetings an agenda is established. For regular meetings this generally comprises reports from the CEO, finance director, business unit directors and the personnel director, major items of strategic expenditure to be approved, and other significant issues. The board is also notified of any permission given to directors and senior managers to deal in the shares of the company under the company's dealing code. Written reports are provided to the directors seven days in advance of each board meeting. In addition, the board considers at least annually the strategic plans of the group and individual businesses, and is provided with other information as requested. From time to time, and on request, directors are given the opportunity to receive presentations from management about key areas of the company's operations.

Clearly too, the board should regularly review the material it receives from management and hold management accountable for lapses in providing it with timely and accurate information. One notable empirical point is that the board should have a procedure for directors, either individually or as a group, in the furtherance of their duties, to take independent professional advice, if necessary, at the institution's expense. This much is in most codes and Singapore, Hong Kong and most other Asian companies do provide for it. But what matters more is how often the board avails itself of this procedure, and on that, companies are silent throughout Asia – although to be fair it is by no means certain that it would normally be either necessary or desirable in a typical year. MAS says that the management should provide all members of the board with a balanced and understandable management accounts of the institution's performance, position and prospects on a monthly basis to enable the board to discharge its responsibilities. So all this is undoubtedly right in general terms, but the problem surely is finding out whether in practice companies are meeting these requirements.

INDEPENDENT DIRECTORS

Nothing seems to excite protagonists of corporate governance more than the 'independence' of certain directors on the board. The rules have certainly tightened up as Asian jurisdictions follow the new global regime. New rules on independent directors were introduced throughout Asia in the aftermath of the Asian financial crisis, as shown in Table 3.1.

In 1998, listed Korean Stock Exchange firms were required to have at least one outside director, and by June 2000, large firms – those with assets of over US$1.7 billion – were required to have over half of directors independent. These independent directors required under the latest revision to company law will not be entrusted with corporate management. The requirement was introduced solely in response to the need for 'directors' who take a third-party stance in monitoring management. These board members are engaged to play the role of monitor with regard to the CEO's management decisions based on a certain degree of common sense and discernment, which does not require specialized expertise in corporate business practices. It will naturally be easier for a director from an entirely unrelated field to determine the propriety of the 'practical wisdom' in specific industries, practices which no one within the company would

Table 3.1 *Independent directors: new rules*

China	three/33% (by June 2003)
Hong Kong	two (proposal for three)
Indonesia	30% (of Komisaris)
Japan	two 'external' directors (optional)
Korea	25–50%
Malaysia	two/33%
Philippines	two/20%
Singapore	33%
Taiwan	two (plus 1 independent supervisor)
Thailand	three

Source: ACGA Ltd

Note: 19 February 2003, IQPC Conference, Sydney

82

think to challenge, practices which have become embedded within industries but which are unacceptable when viewed more widely. In fact, the ratio of outside directors in Korean-listed companies rose from 11.4 per cent in 1998 to more than 30 per cent in 2000. The Japanese system is a combination of old and new but under the optional new system, two 'external' directors are required, Malaysia requires two or 33 per cent, and the Philippines requires two or 20 per cent. In August 2001, the CSRC in China issued *Guidelines on the Establishment of a System of Independent Directors in Listed Companies* (the 'Guidelines'). By 30 June 2002, at least two members of the board of directors of all listed companies in China were required to be independent directors. And by 30 June 2003, at least one-third of the board are required to be independent directors. By June 2003, China mandated three or 33 per cent of a board to be independent. These independent directors are said to owe a duty of good faith (*chengxin*) and diligence (*qinmian*) to the company and to the entire body of shareholders. The CSRC reported that by 30 June 2002, 2,414 independent directors had been elected and appointed by shareholder meetings of the 1,187 listed companies in China. In 70 per cent of companies there is at least one accounting professional as an independent director. Half of independent directors are from academic and research institutions; another 30 per cent from intermediaries such as accounting and legal firms, and investment banks; those remaining are from other sources including the executives of other firms; professionals who are foreign nationals are allowed and encouraged to become independent directors of listed companies. Independent directors now account for about 20 per cent of all the directors in listed companies; outside directors account for about 60 per cent of all the directors of the boards of directors. The 2001 'voluntary' Singapore Code puts the threshold at one-third, following the example of the Vienot Code in France; Singapore is widely thought to be a market leader in Asian corporate governance. How does it shape up in terms of non-executives? In the draft Banking (Corporate Governance) Regulations 2003 and the draft Insurance (Corporate Governance) Regulations 2003, the MAS makes it clear that they were intended to apply to Significant Institutions (except that the provisions on Audit Committee in the Insurance (Corporate Governance) Regulations will apply to all direct insurers incorporated in Singapore), for which the board of directors shall comprise a majority of independent directors. The draft regulations themselves state that independent directors should make up at least *one-third* of the board. Thailand also mandates three. Taiwan mandates two (plus one independent supervisor), and companies have moved swiftly to adopt best practice. For example, in August 2002 Taiwan Semiconductor Manufacturing added three new directors partly to help form a special audit committee to review finances. Hong Kong currently (2004) runs on two, but it has been proposed that this ought to be raised to three.

83

However, many Asian jurisdictions are already behind the latest thinking, a function perhaps of derivative thinking. The latest US position, dating from Sarbanes-Oxley, is that a *majority* of the board of directors of listed companies must be independent. Why not? The more the better, surely, up to the optimum size of the board as a whole and provided that the independent directors meet the PwC requirements.

So much for how many of these non-executive directors are, or should be, on Asian boards. What about the qualitative aspect? Non-executive directors should be persons of calibre, credibility and have the necessary skill and experience to bring an independent judgement to bear on the issues of strategy, performance and resources including key appointments and standards of conduct. CSRC's regulations require that independent directors must spend enough time on the companies in which they hold directorship; one person cannot hold more than five directorship positions concurrently; they must actually perform the duty of due diligence and cannot just act as so-called 'flower bottles'. 'Independent directors are now quite serious', Anthony Wu, chairman of Ernst & Young's China practice, has said. 'At a few meetings I've attended they've asked (serious) questions.' Presumably that means that at many others they did not. Recent survey shows independent directors on average spend about 20 days in a company where they hold directorship. At least one of the independent directors should be an accounting professional (refers to personnel with senior professional title or certified public accountants).[9] All domestically listed companies must make necessary amendments to the articles of association to implement these requirements. And these independent directors have real powers: they must approve major related party transactions; they decide on the appointment or removal of the accounting firm; they should call an interim shareholders' meeting to appoint the outside auditing; they solicit the proxies before the convening of the shareholders' meeting; they serve as chairs of the auditing, compensation, and nomination committees. Independent directors must make up a majority of these committees. Clearly they sit at the very centre of the new corporate governance regime.

The guidelines emphasize that independent directors should fulfill their duty to uphold the interests of the company as a whole, and should pay particular attention to ensure that the interests of minority shareholders are not injured. Independent directors are also required to provide independent opinions to the board of directors or the general meeting of shareholders on important matters, specifically including, among other things, any matters which may injure the interests of 'medium and small shareholders'. Furthermore, the guidelines empower independent directors to review and approve material related transactions (over RNB 3 million or 5 per cent of the audited net assets) and retain outside advisers to provide independent financial consultant reports as a basis for their recommendations. Independent directors may also solicit proxies prior to the convening of a general meeting of the shareholders. These powers, if upheld in practice by the CSRC and relevant remedies granted by the courts, should serve to strengthen the role of independent directors as guardians of minority shareholder interests in the face of unscrupulous insiders and controlling shareholders. As with other legal protections existing in theory, the benefits to minority shareholders may be symbolic only unless listed companies can attract and retain qualified independent directors, and shareholders have recourse against directors and their insurers in the event of a breach of duty. Taiwanese directors, according to surveys, are dissatisfied with the influence of families on the corporate governance of listed companies and do not consider that outside directors on boards should be related to founding families. Boards that are packed with nominally independent directors may indeed give false comfort to retail investors, and could be positively dangerous. Strong boards are those with strong minds on board, willing to test each other and able to question and advise management, not those with all the right fixtures of independence and procedure but where everyone merrily agrees with each other almost all the time. The latter is still a common phenomenon on Asian boards. However, Asian CFOs evidently would welcome a bigger role for non-executive directors.

To be effective, corporate governance wisdom says that independent non-executive directors need to make up at least one-third of the membership of the board. The central *criticism* of the independent director system stems from uncertainty that, not having been a member of the corporate family, these board members would not be capable of properly analysing the company's business practices in order to come to an appropriate decision. If they were unable to do so, critics doubt that independent directors would prove to be useful board members. 'Non-executive directors are seen as something of a mixed blessing', notes the 2002 ACCA study.[10] 'While their role is seen as valuable, and it is generally accepted that they could contribute more to good governance and performance, there is also cultural resistance and a concern about the actual value they bring.' ACCA Malaysia noted that non-executive directors – along with audit committees – should be more involved in the appointment of auditors which would in turn protect the independent status of the audit. Increasingly, findings endorse the important role played by outside directors in the corporate governance system in Asia. However, to draw the conclusion, as some have, that because the majority of Asian executives asked considered the presence of outside directors improved corporate accountability to shareholders, this meant that the executives endorsed the agency theory perspective on corporate governance seems a step too far. The agency theory, let us remind ourselves, is about the relationship between executives and shareholders. Is it really the case that only outside directors can genuinely represent shareholder interests?

That is not all. There is widespread suspicion that in Asia (and not only in Asia) the appointment of technically independent directors is just not going to achieve the objectives its corporate governance protagonists claim for it. Jonas Astrup from the International Chamber of Commerce, for example, says that 'nothing gets past the boardroom doors here'. The example he cited was the resignation of three Global Trust Bank (GTB) directors, including the head of its audit committee. None of them, Astrup argued, felt they owed it to GTB stakeholders to explain their exit from the board. Instead, shareholders were forced to draw inferences from bits and pieces in the media and elsewhere. Apart from auditor matters (see Chapter 4), having dipped into its statutory reserves GTB also sought shareholder approval to appropriate Rs 130 crore in the share premium account to provide for bad loans. Had GTB's three directors spoken their mind in the interest of good governance, would things have been smooth sailing at the AGM? Would the regulators have been so accommodating? But investors and stake-holders knew very little about what is happening inside GTB, not even the identity of the shareholder who suddenly sold 25 lakh shares in a Rs 7 crore deal on the Bombay Stock Exchange one Thursday. That is because, in tough situations, Astrup claims that Indian independent directors only resign, citing illness or personal reasons as their excuse, but never a difference of opinion with manage-ment. Were they to ask tough questions and publicly disagree with management, critics of the lack of effective directors in India would soon find that nobody wants them as 'independent' directors anymore. It is no wonder, then, that even those who conduct corporate governance training schools advise management students that as independent directors, they should not aspire to be watchdogs and should only ask their questions very politely. This approach may not improve governance standards in India, but it will enhance their chances of becoming 'independent' directors and collect hefty sitting fees. Put bluntly, directors may start independent, but very quickly they *go native*.

But *who* is independent? The second set of OECD Roundtable recommenda-tions sought to reduce or eliminate loopholes by tightening standards for director 'independence', by making 'shadow' directors liable for their actions, by increasing sanctions for violations of duties of loyalty and care and by advocating delineation of a core set of related-party transactions (such as company loans to directors and officers) that should be prohibited outright. To qualify as inde-pendent, a director must be determined to have no 'material relationship with the listed company (either directly or as a partner, shareholder or officer of an organization that has a relationship with the company)'. This test is deliberately broad. The NYSE stated in its commentary to the proposed rule that because it is not possible to provide rules for all potential conflicts of interest, it has drafted the rule in broad terms to encourage boards to consider all relevant facts and circumstances when making the determination. However, the NYSE, which leads where others follow, has given some guidance as to how the issue should be approached. In the commentary to the proposed rule, the NYSE pointed out that the key concern is independence of the directors from management, not ownership. As such, the NYSE does not consider significant stock ownership, on its own, to preclude a finding of independence. The NYSE also suggested that the materiality of the relationship in question should be considered from the perspective of both the listed company and persons or organizations with which the director has an affiliation. To further emphasize the breadth of the analysis, the NYSE noted that material relationships extend beyond the strictly commercial and industrial realm to include, among others, banking, consulting, legal, accounting, charitable and familial relationships. A strict definition of independence is also gaining momentum in Asia: for example, in 2002 China adopted a set of rules (called a 'code', but apparently of a mandatory nature) that defines independence quite strictly, with regard to both company executives and blockholders (in the case of China, state-owned parent firms), and that provides for a fairly thorough nomination procedure.

The MAS has its own version of the NYSE 'bright line' tests for independence:

Definition of 'Independent Director'

3(1)   In these Regulations, 'independent director' means a director:
(a) who is not a substantial shareholder and is not connected to a substantial shareholder of the bank incorporated in Singapore;
(b) who is not in any of the relationships set out in paragraph (5); and
(c) who has no other relationship with the bank incorporated in Singapore or with any of its related companies or officers that could interfere, or be reasonably seen to interfere, with the exercise of the director's independent business judgment with regard to the interest of the bank incorporated in Singapore.

(2)   Notwithstanding paragraph (1)(a), a director of a bank incorporated in Singapore which is the subsidiary of another bank incorporated in Singapore (referred to in this paragraph as the 'parent bank') or of a financial holding company shall be regarded to have met the requirements of that paragraph if he is not a substantial shareholder of the subsidiary, parent bank or financial holding company, and is not connected to a substantial shareholder of the parent bank or financial holding company, as the case may be.

(3)   A person is connected to a substantial shareholder if he is –
(a) the spouse, child, step-child, brother, sister, parent or step-parent of the substantial shareholder;
(b) employed by the substantial shareholder or an affiliate of the substantial shareholder;
(c) a non-executive director of the substantial shareholder;
(d) a partner of the substantial shareholder in any firm; or

87

(e) accustomed or under an obligation, whether formal or informal, to act in accordance with the directions, instructions or wishes of the substantial shareholder.

(4) In respect of appointments of directors made on or after 17 July 2004, a person is also connected to a substantial shareholder if he is a director of an affiliate of the substantial shareholder.

(5) The relationships referred to in paragraph (1)(b) are:
(a) he is being employed by the bank incorporated in Singapore or by any of bank's related corporations, or has been so employed at any time during the preceding three financial years of the bank incorporated in Singapore; and
(b) his spouse, child, step-child, brother, sister, parent or step-parent is being employed by the bank incorporated in Singapore or by any of its related corporations as an executive officer whose compensation is determined by the Remuneration Committee of the bank incorporated in Singapore or related corporation, or if his spouse, child, step-child, brother sister, parent or step-parent has been so employed at any time during the preceding three financial years of the bank incorporated in Singapore.

(6) For the purposes of paragraph (1)(c), the relationships include :
(a) a director who is a substantial shareholder of, a partner in or an executive officer of, any corporation or firm carrying on business for purposes of profit to which the bank incorporated in Singapore has made, or from which the bank incorporated in Singapore has received, payments in the current or immediately preceding financial year exceeding S$200,000 in aggregate for that year; and (b) a director who is receiving any compensation from the bank incorporated in Singapore or from any of the bank's related corporations, other than compensation received for his service as a director, or has received such compensation at any time during the preceding financial year of the bank incorporated in Singapore.

(7) The Nominating Committee, may determine that a director who has one or more of the relationships mentioned in paragraph (1)(c), (3)(c) or (4) is nonetheless independent, if the Nominating Committee is satisfied that the director's independent business judgment and ability to act in the interest of the bank incorporated in Singapore will not be interfered with, [despite the rules above]'[11]

It all looked so good until Point 7.

The Malaysian Code of Corporate Governance is equally explicit:

IV In circumstances where a company has a significant shareholder, in addition to the requirement that one third of the board should comprise independent directors, the board should include a number of directors which fairly reflects the investment in the company by shareholders other than the significant share-holder. For this purpose, a 'significant shareholder' is defined as a shareholder with the ability to exercise a majority of votes for the election of directors.

V   In circumstances, where the shareholder holds less than the majority but is still the largest shareholder, the board will have to exercise judgment in determining what is the appropriate number of directors which fairly reflects the investment in the company by the remaining holders of the shares.

VI The board should disclose on an annual basis whether one third of the board is independent and in circumstances where the company has a signifi-cant shareholder, whether it satisfies the requirement to fairly reflect through board representation, the investment of the minority shareholders in a company. The board should disclose its analysis of the application of the best practices set out above, to the circumstances of the board.

VII Whether or not the roles of Chairman and Chief Executive are combined, the board should identify a senior independent non-executive director of a board in the annual report to whom concerns may be conveyed. Plus, he should meet with fellow non-executives.[12]

Here is the NYSE original version:

A director is presumed not to be independent if such individual or his or her immediate family member:

- receives more than $100,000 annually in direct compensation from the company (other than director and committee fees or deferred compen-sation for prior service (a pension, for example) that is not contingent on continued service);
- is an affiliate of or employed (as a professional, if a family member) by a present or former auditor of the company;
- is employed as an executive officer of another company where any execu-tives of the listed company serve on that other company's compensation committee; or
- is an executive officer or, only with respect to a director and not his or her immediate family members, if the director is an employee of another company (1) that accounts for at least 2 per cent or $1 million, whichever is greater, of the listed company's consolidated gross

revenues, or (2) for which the listed company accounts for at least 2 per cent or $1 million, whichever is greater, of the other company's consolidated gross revenues.

In each of the above circumstances, the bar on 'independence' will generally last for five years after the end of the relationship in question. To aid in the transition to this rule, however, the NYSE's amended proposal provides that for the first five years after the rule takes effect, companies need only 'look back' as far as the effective date of the rule when determining if a prohibited relationship existed. In addition to this new transition rule, the commentary indicates that this presumption can be rebutted if the board determines (and no independent director dissents) that the compensation is not material. However, that determination must be specifically explained in the company's proxy statement. (The principal changes to the bright line tests when compared to the original proposal, incidentally, were the inclusion of the $100,000 threshold in the compensation test and the inclusion of a new test based on specific consolidated gross revenue thresholds.)

In its discussion of the purpose of its own proposed rule change, the NYSE reiterated its commitment to its policy of generally deferring to home-country practices when dealing with foreign private issuers. Specifically, it stated that while foreign private issuers will be required to comply with the independence requirements of Section 301 of the Sarbanes-Oxley Act, and any rules adopted thereunder, the NYSE would not require foreign private issuers to comply with any additional rules relating to director independence. However, a foreign private issuer must disclose any significant deviation between its home country practices and the NYSE's requirements. So, Asian companies are safe for the time being, but the writing is on the wall: eventually all companies listing in the US will be expected to conform to NYSE regulations.

At least the MAS and the Malaysians are *trying*. By comparison, the Securities and Exchange Law in Korea does not yet prescribe detailed qualification requirements for non-executive directors, but prescribes only passive limitations creating criteria, which prevents certain people from becoming non-executive directors. The provisions related to the disqualifications of non-executive directors, as stipulated in the Securities and Exchange Act, are outlined in considerable detail. The Korea Listed Companies Association established 'service standards for non-executive directors' in November 2000. This standard, established on the premise that improved corporate governance strengthens corporate competitiveness and maximizes corporate value, contains comprehensive guidelines regarding the function and legal status of non-executive directors, basic authorities and duties, and remuneration. However, due to the fact that the will of the management is strongly reflected in the nomination and appointment of non-executive directors, there is a limit on the extent to which many non-executive directors are truly independent of company management.

Issued in April 2001, the Japanese *Interim Plan for the Outline of Proposed Laws for Partial Revision of the Commercial Code* included an article that made the election of at least one independent director mandatory without distinction for all large companies. Following the announcement of this plan, this particular article drew strong criticism, with those opposed frequently citing the shortage of qualified persons to serve as independent directors and the loss of corporate autonomy they felt would result. In response to this opposition, the article was excluded from the bill ultimately submitted to the Diet, and the revised law that was passed in the end does not make the election of independent directors mandatory. Although the election of independent directors was not mandated for all companies without distinction, the formation of a 'major asset committee' does require the election of at least one independent director. Moreover, at least two independent directors must be elected when a company opts to establish committees to monitor execution.

The CSRC defines 'independence' as independent from controlling shareholder-management-major business relations. The independence qualifications of the candidates for independent directors need to be checked and approved by CSRC first before they can be voted in shareholder meetings. Candidates for independent directors have to make a public declaration on their independence qualifications and their information needs to be publicized in newspapers; they cannot work for more than six years in a company.

Most listed Thai companies are controlled by majority shareholders who can appoint board members without approval of other minority shareholders through the majority vote. Critics suggest that as a result the board of directors is often neither independent from management nor accountable to small shareholders. Regulator SET therefore requires that there must be at least two independent non-executive directors on the board in order to monitor the management of the company. But the term 'independent non-executive director' excludes *only* employees of the company. In Thai family-controlling companies, the boards of directors are often composed of independent non-executive directors who are friends and family of the majority shareholders rather than qualified professionals who would monitor the management of the companies. As a consequence, the majority shareholders continue to control these companies.

The gap between this and the latest thinking in Hong Kong is now huge; www.webb-site.com believes that even legal advisers to a company should not be allowed to serve as independent directors, as they are hardly likely to oppose a transaction in the boardroom if their law firm stands to get fees out of the deal. Currently, Listing Rule 3.11(2) specifically allows a company's 'professional adviser', including lawyer, to act as an independent director. By contrast, in the mainland markets, this practice is banned (see Para IIIA5 of the CSRC Guidelines). In this respect, the mainland is already ahead of Hong Kong. This should not be thought of as a suggestion that *all* innovations in corporate governance in the West will automatically 'catch on' in Asia. Indeed, not all of them are popular in their country of origin. For example, in January 2003 a survey of 30 FTSE 100 chairmen by headhunters Russell Reynolds Association revealed strong concerns about the boardroom reforms proposed by Derek Higgs's corporate governance review. More than 80 per cent of respondents opposed bolstering the power of a senior independent director, saying this made the role 'unattractive, time-consuming and divisive' and one which few people would wish to assume. Forty per cent of chairmen opposed the suggestion that a chief executive should not become chairmen as too prescriptive.

What is the conclusion? Corporate governance has placed much stress on 'neutral' and 'unbiased' selection of independent directors for boards, and in particular for non-executive directors. But there are many problems associated with this: the traditional positive discrimination argument about selecting at best inappropriate and at worst incompetent and most likely ineffective directors instead of the 'experienced men with good contacts' (the suits) that the business really needs. Then there is unconscious bias in the selection process. Most directors will argue along the lines that an absence of relationships is not an accurate predictor of board excellence. At best, commentators have suggested, independence is a rough, observable surrogate for the hoped-for ability in auditors and directors to bring an objective judgement to bear on financial reports and management's performance and strategy.

DIRECTORS' AND OFFICERS' INSURANCE

The cost of directors' and officers' insurance policies, so-called D&O policies, sky-rocketed worldwide after Enron. Board members are 'concerned now more than at any time in history', about personal liability. Holly Gregory, partner at Weil Gotshal, claimed in 2002 that a successful search for new directors in the US was not impossible – as long as companies are willing to look beyond chief executives. Companies say they seek out chief executives because their experience gives them the required skills to help oversee a large corporation. Critics, however, question whether CEOs are really motivated to recruit like-minded executives as a way to perpetuate lavish pay packages, a sort of scratch-each-other's-back mentality.

DIRECTOR TRAINING

In addressing the role of the board in corporate governance in Asia, the first OECD Roundtable recommendation, interestingly enough, focuses on director training, voluntary codes of conduct, expectations for professional behaviour and directors' resources and authority vis-à-vis management. These recommendations aim to increase the pool of candidates who are willing and able to perform the tasks entrusted to directors and to give them the skills and authority to do their jobs. It is not clear how the two are in practice related, as, logically, if the training is to be offered to directors after they are appointed, this will do nothing to increase the pool of candidates and may even discourage individuals from putting themselves forward as independent directors, if on top of everything else they will have to spend time being trained.

Asian regulators are keen, however, that every director should receive appropriate training on how to discharge their duties on first appointment to the board. The MAS says that this should include a familiarization programme on the institution's business and risk profile, governance practices, internal controls and risk management processes. The programme should also include a briefing on the duties and responsibilities as a director. Directors should also be cognizant of relevant laws and regulations applicable to the institution.[13] In Singapore, a country where education and training are highly prized still, the MAS hardly needs to make such training compulsory, but it remains the case that proper detailed courses are quite expensive and, just as in the West, they tend to be attended by accountants and lawyers as much as, if not more than, by directors of listed companies. In China there is compulsory training for the directors of public listed companies. The objective of the training: to equip directors with a broad knowledge and understanding of rules and regulations and to keep directors informed on the latest changes in the securities industry. So far, CSRC and Tsinghua University have organized almost a dozen training programmes for independent directors and investors. A certificate of attendance is issued upon completion. There are now in China monthly training classes for independent directors, with attendees in both Shanghai and Beijing. Some 6,000 Chinese directors are being trained every year. There are now monthly training courses for directors already on board by the two stock exchanges, with the intention of training all the directors of public companies within three years. In addition, the CSRC has been instrumental in organizing investor education sessions in major cities and through the media, including the internet. In mid 2003, the Kuala Lumpur Stock Exchange (KLSE) announced a new requirement for directors of listed companies to participate in a new Continuing Education Programme (CEP), effective 1 July 2003. Issued as Practice Note 15/2003 of the KLSE listing rules, the CEP follows the Mandatory Accreditation Programme (MAP), a compulsory training initiative launched in 2001 and completed by more than 5,300 directors. The CEP aims to expand on MAP by ensuring that directors are kept up to date with relevant market issues, especially regulatory developments. Under the new scheme, directors will be able to earn points not only by attending relevant courses, but also by lecturing or writing articles (in accredited subject areas). Each director of a listed company

93

will be required to earn 48 CEP points each calendar year. These requirements apply equally to directors of Malaysian Exchange of Securities Dealing and Automated Quotation Bhd (MESDAQ)-listed companies. Under the motto 'education for life for all', the Institute of Corporate Directors (ICD) has been very active in conducting the directorship training programme, particularly in four specific corporate governance-related issues on Audit Committees, Risk Oversight Committee, Governance Committee and Financial Numeracy for Directors. In addition, the ICD has also undertaken to orient bank directors on the issues of corporate governance, a requirement of the Bangko ng Sentral Pilipinas (BSP). The Malaysian regulators fully endorse the initiative towards certification of corporate directors, particularly those who serve as independent directors, as the country's laws and regulations mandate.

There is, perhaps, a problem with training that applies in Asia still, and that is the gulf between theory and practice. Attendees at training courses want all the theory and the detail, but do not relish being tested on their practical application in difficult hypothetical case studies; they do not always recognize that their own organization is expected to follow the guidelines they are being taught, they are sometimes keen to imply the existence of conspiracy theories and underhand dealings even if none are readily to hand, and they do not always accept that failure to follow them may result in prosecution, let alone poor shareholder value. This attitude is changing though, in some cases quite rapidly, especially in countries such as Malaysia where in the past regulations have been poorly enforced. In other countries such as Singapore, a high standard of application to training is consistently observed.

BOARD COMMITTEES

How does the theory work? It is argued that in order to balance, and if necessary check, the power held by the CEO, the monitoring function of the Asian company board is strengthened through the creation of committees comprised mostly of independent directors. An important aspect of this system is the ability of the board of directors to remove the CEO from office when poor performance or rule infringement demand it. Accordingly, some have argued that the two systems under this structure – the committees comprised mostly of independent directors and the corporate executive officer system under which power and authority is centralized with the CEO – complement each other, and must therefore be introduced in tandem. It also follows that the committees comprised mostly of independent directors must function properly, and sound corporate management must be protected if a corporate executive officer system is to be introduced. In this corporate executive officer system, the CEO can single-handedly make decisions that were impossible to reach without corporate boards' resolutions in the past. The structure based on the principle of separating monitoring and execution, under which committees to monitor execution will be established, vests the audit, nominating and compensation committees, as well as the corporate executive officers, with the authority to remove the CEO.

In Asia the picture is still mixed. Hong Kong has seen a greater involvement of independent non-executive directors on boards and committees and more board committees being established.[14] The chairman retains the right to sit on committees in Malaysia. Japan, for example, amended its commercial code in May 2002, to allow companies to choose their structure of governance. The choice is among the old company law scheme of a board of directors and a separate audit board (the *kansayaku*); and a new, more US-like scheme that provides for an audit committee of the board with independent directors as a majority. The road will, of course, be long; Japanese companies have shied away from instituting a clear board committee structure that would give real responsibilities to a largely ceremonial board.

Revisions to the current Japanese Commercial Code were designed to establish a clear distinction of roles and responsibilities between oversight and operational functions within a corporation, and in particular clearly to distinguish the corporate board's oversight functions from business operation functions. Under the previous code, this distinction may not be clear because the board of directors could perform both oversight and business operation roles. In Japan companies must have at least two independent directors on their boards if they desire to adopt a structure under which committees to monitor execution would be established. Moreover, although the establishment of committees to monitor execution is possible with two independent directors, the inclusion of two independent directors on a board is not enough by itself. Having one independent director serve as a member of multiple committees is in and of itself inadvisable. The latest revision merely deems two independent directors satisfactory for the time being in deference to the practical difficulties involved in engaging a larger number of independent directors. Firms have begun to shrink their boards of directors, and many instituted the *shikko yakuin* system as noted above, to delineate the supervisory function of a board of directors from the operating responsibilities of the top management team. Many firms have announced appointments of independent directors.

With the revision of the Japan's Commercial Code effective 1 April 2003, Japanese companies are required to opt for either 'make no changes', 'establish a decision-making committee regarding major assets' or 'adopt a "Company with Committees" System'. This last alternative gives companies the option of eliminating their traditional internal auditing systems by setting up three committees, each made up of at least three board directors, the majority of whom should come from the outside. Some companies have already started to move toward the new scheme: Kikkoman, the soy sauce maker, was the first to appoint independent directors on its board; and Parco, the department store group, rapidly announced its intention to form board committees on remuneration, compensation and audit. Individual hearings with 90 presidents and chairmen of large companies who are regular members of the Japan Association of Corporate Directors (JACD) revealed that more than 10 companies plan to establish committees to monitor execution in the first fiscal year that it goes into effect (fiscal 2003), with an additional 10 or more companies planning to introduce this system in the second fiscal year.

One of the most important parts of the 'Company with Committees', the formation of a major asset committee, is considered to provide the operating committees of top management established under conventional business practices a legal status, and to clarify that the board of directors has the authority to monitor the operating committee. This revision permits the formation of a major asset committee by resolution of the board at large companies with independent directors on their boards and at least 10 board members. This committee is to be composed of at least three board members and is to be able to make decisions regarding items conventionally included under decisions to be made exclusively by the board of directors. The revised Commercial Code recognizes the body conventionally thought of as the operating committee as the highest decision-making body regarding the disposal and transfer of major assets (generally defined as the equivalent of 1 per cent or more of the company's capital), as well as large-scale debts and other management items requiring an extremely high degree of flexibility.

In April 2003, allegedly in order to ensure proactive decision-making, the Honda Board of Directors set up such an Assets and Loan Management Committee, which is responsible for deciding upon the disposal of the company's important assets and related matters. Honda has further established a Management Council, which is composed of eight representative directors and four managing directors. Along with discussing in advance items to be resolved at meetings of the board of directors, this Management Council is said to discuss important management issues as directed by the board of directors. Regional executive officers are assigned to be in charge of the business operations in each region, with the aim of heightening the autonomy of the region and ensuring speedy decision-making. In addition, regional executive councils located at each regional operation discuss important management issues in the region within the bounds of the authority conferred upon them by the Management Council. What is interesting about this description is the way in which, at last, the distinction for corporate governance purposes between the board and management is being eclipsed. Japanese companies are certainly in the forefront of making these changes.

Why have companies adopted the new system? Obviously enough, to please analysts and the government. At Toshiba Corporation, for instance, the new structure is seen as 'a means to further enhance corporate governance by reinforcing supervisory functions and management transparency, and to improve operating agility and flexibility'. The Hitachi Group has said that: 'The purposes of adopting the new structure are (1) improving the speed of management, (2) securing more transparent management practices (3) serving as part of the group companies' management strategy, and (4) improving global management.' At the Orix Corporation, a leasing company, management claimed that: 'The shift to the system ensures a more effective separation of the roles and responsibilities between the decision-making and monitoring function of the board of directors and the executive function of management.' Yasuhiko Fujiki, president of Orix Corp., said the introduction of the system in June 2003 resulted in enhanced checks on management. Supermarket operator the Aeon Company

> aims to create a system under which corporate governance with a high degree of transparency and objectivity can be realized through the clear separation of management monitoring and execution and speedy management decisions are made possible with the transfer of a large portion of authority to the corporate executive officer.

Motoya Okada, president of Aeon Co., which adopted the committee-based system in May 2003, has said the new governance structure has helped improve management transparency. Now that board committees that include outside directors have been set up, Aeon executives are being held more accountable than ever to fully explain their businesses. Finally, not to be outdone, the Sony Corporation announced in January 2003 that from June 2003 it would adopt the new optional, 'Company with Committees' system as well as new board and candidate for board rules. Sony introduced a new corporate executive officer (*Shikko-yaku*) system to complement the previous corporate executive officer (*Shikko-yakuin*) system. Corporate executive officers are in charge of management and governance for the Sony Group based on the directions of the board of directors. It is envisaged that present representative directors will be appointed as representative corporate executive officers. In order to further strengthen the distinction between oversight and business operation roles to a level beyond the requirements of the revised Commercial Code, Sony said it intended to introduce internal standards for a separation between the chairman of the board of directors and representative corporate executive officers. The board of directors will also decide the basic principles of Sony's corporate governance structure and issue 'Regulations of the Board'. The major regulations will concern upper and lower limits on the number of directors; eliminating conflicts of interest; and qualifications for director-candidates which will ensure the independence of the newly created committees. The Sony Corporation now says it will 'aim to enhance the Sony Group's corporate governance functions by further strengthening corporate governance and improving management

97

transparency of the group through boosting the role of the board as a monitoring body and clarifying executive responsibility and additional transfer of authority'. Can a system this complex, with so many layers of responsibility, ever hope to achieve this? No Japanese company has yet formed an independent board committee, observes Standard & Poor's. Disclosure is another issue of concern, with compensation of Japanese directors and senior management remaining largely opaque.

As of May 2003, 32 companies (or 14, if the 19 Hitachi Group firms are counted as one) have either shifted or said they would shift to the new system by the end of the current fiscal year. According to a January survey conducted by the Japan Association of Corporate Directors of the presidents and chairmen of 130 major member corporations, 27 of the 79 firms that responded said they had adopted or were considering adopting the new system. Not very many, is it? Extrapolating from this data, as well as from hearings conducted with top executives, more than 100 firms will have adopted the new system by the end of March 2005, and the figure is likely to grow to some 500 to 600 firms (out of some 3,500 in all) within the next four to five years. That is more impressive.

If ever a comparison were to work to one party's advantage, comparing all this diversity and complexity with the elegant simplicity of the rule MAS established for banks in Singapore would surely do so. The MAS rule simply says:

A bank incorporated in Singapore shall have:
(a) a Nominating Committee;
(b) a Remuneration Committee; and
(c) an Audit Committee.[15]

It is precisely such succinctness and all-embracing uniformity which protagonists of the new corporate governance regime are seeking in national regulations. Where Japan's regulations are numerous, replete with options and get-out clauses, in Singapore banks at least have clear instructions. What remains open to doubt, however, is whether the insistence by regulators on the creation of these committees actually brings real benefits to the shareholders of Asian corporations. While it is impossible to answer these questions completely – not least because insufficient time has passed to enable a proper judgment to be made – detailed investigation of each type of committee may shed some light on the issue.

THE NOMINATION COMMITTEE IN THE ASIAN CORPORATION

In an ideal world, nomination committees should assess the skillsets already present on the board and draw up job descriptions based on the qualities and skills required of additional members before beginning the process of finding and considering suitable candidates. It is usual practice in Asia as elsewhere that once an appointment is made the director in question should receive a letter detailing the time at work required, the responsibilities and fees for attending meetings and carrying out committee work. In addition to its recruitment function, the nomination committee is also charged with executing an annual assessment of the size, structure and skills profile of the board, with a view to making appropriate changes when the occasion arises. The nominating committee formulates the proposals regarding the election and removal of corporate directors that will be submitted to shareholders' meetings. The board of directors, however, retains the authority to appoint corporate executive officers and remove them.

The MAS says that:

> Institutions should establish a Nominating Committee to make recommendations to the Board on all Board appointments. A majority of the Nominating Committee members, including the Chairman, should be independent directors. The Nominating Committee should have written terms of reference that describe the responsibilities of its members . . . The Nominating Committee is also charged with determining annually whether or not a director is an independent director.[16]

4.2   The Nominating Committee should determine the criteria to be applied in identifying candidates and reviewing nominations. When reviewing nominations, the candidate should be a fit and proper candidate and be the best and most qualified candidate nominated for the office, taking into account the candidate's contribution and performance, including his or her track record, age, experience, capabilities and other relevant factors as determined by the Nomination Committee (e.g. attendance, preparedness, participation and candour).

4.3   The Nominating Committee is also charged with determining annually whether or not a director is an independent director.

4.4   All directors who intend to continue as a director of the Institution should be re-nominated and re-elected at regular intervals and at least once every three years.

4.5   When a director serves on multiple boards, he or she should ensure that sufficient time and attention is given to the affairs of each of the Institution he or she serves. The Nomination Committee should decide whether or not such a director is able to and has been adequately carrying out his or her duties as director of the Institution. Internal guidelines should be adopted that address the competing time commitments that are faced when directors serve on multiple boards.

99

It is always informative when examining corporate governance regulations to compare what the national regulator recommends for corporations with that advised, or insisted upon, for local banks. The MAS tells local banks:

6(1) A bank incorporated in Singapore shall have a Nominating Committee comprising five members of the Board of directors of the bank, the majority of whom, including the Chairman of the Nominating Committee, shall be independent directors.

(2) The Authority may, in any particular case approve a greater number of members not exceeding seven.

(3) Every member of the Nominating Committee shall be appointed to hold office until the next annual general meeting following that member's appointment, and shall be eligible for re-appointment.

(4) If a member of the Nominating Committee resigns, ceases to be a director or for any other reason ceases to be a member of the Nominating Committee resulting in the reduction of the number of members below five, the Board of directors shall within three months of that event appoint such number of new members as may be required to make up five members.

(5) The bank incorporated in Singapore shall obtain the prior approval of the Authority for the appointment of the Chairman and other members of the Nominating Committee.

Responsibilities of the Nominating Committee

7(1) The Nominating Committee of a bank incorporated in Singapore shall identify candidates and review all nominations for appointments of -

    (a) directors;

    (b) members of the remuneration committee;

    (c) members of the audit committee;

    (d) members of other Board committees;

    (e) the Chief Executive Officer, Deputy Chief Executive Officer, Chief Financial Officer or such other officer, by whatever name called, having the powers and duties of a Chief Executive Officer, Deputy Chief Executive Officer or Chief Financial Officer.

(2) Any bank incorporated in Singapore, which is a wholly owned subsidiary of another bank incorporated in Singapore is not required to have a Nominating Committee, if the Nominating Committee of the second-mentioned bank performs the functions referred to in paragraph (1) for the first-mentioned bank.

(3) The Nominating Committee shall determine the criteria to be applied in identifying candidates and reviewing nominations, which shall include the following:

    (a) that the requirements in regulations 4(1), 10(1) and 11(1) are complied with;

(b) that the candidate is fit and proper for the office and is the best and most qualified candidate nominated for the office, taking into account the candidate's track record, age, experience, capabilities and other relevant factors as determined by the Nominating Committee (for example attendance, preparedness, participation and candour).

Furnishing information on Nominating Committee deliberations

8(1) A bank incorporated in Singapore shall, after its Nominating Committee has concluded its deliberations –

(a) notify the Authority in writing of the particulars of the persons proposed to be appointed to the positions referred to in regulation 7(1); and

(b) furnish to the Authority such further information as the Authority may require.

(2) A bank incorporated in Singapore shall not make the appointments referred to in regulation 7(1)(a) and (e) unless it obtains the prior approval of the Authority.

The key differences lie in the exact specification of numbers and the notification procedure.

Virtually all participants and commentators on corporate governance agree that a board's process for assessing existing directors and identifying, recruiting, nominating, appointing and orienting new directors is central to enhanced governance. This function can be performed by the board as a whole, but most endorse the view that the adoption of a formal procedure for appointments to the board, with a nomination committee making recommendations to the full board, should be recognized as good practice. The board of every company should therefore appoint a committee of directors composed exclusively of non-executive directors, a majority of whom are independent, with the responsibility for proposing new nominees for the board and for assessing directors on an ongoing basis. The actual decision as to who shall be nominated should be the responsibility of the full board after considering the recommendations of such a committee.

The Malaysian Code says that the nominating committee should:

- Recommend to the board, candidates for all directorships to be filled by the shareholders or the board.
- Consider, in making its recommendations, candidates for directorships proposed by the CEO and, within the bounds of practicability, by any other senior executive or any director or shareholder.
- Recommend to the board, directors to fill the seats on board committees.

IX   The board, through the nominating committee, should annually review its required mix of skills and experience and other qualities, including core competencies which non-executive directors should bring to the board. This should be disclosed in the annual report.

X   The board should implement a process, to be carried out by the nominating committee annually for assessing the effectiveness of the board as a whole, the committees of the board and for assessing the contribution of each individual director.

Sony's nomination committee is composed of five or more directors and the majority, including the chairman, will be outside directors. However, there will be at least two internal directors.

THE REMUNERATION COMMITTEE IN THE ASIAN CORPORATION

The MAS similarly advises companies to set up a remuneration committee:

7.1   To minimize the risk of any potential conflict of interest, the Board should set up a remuneration committee comprising of a majority of independent directors.

7.2 The Remuneration Committee should be chaired by an independent director and have at least one member who is knowledgeable in the field of executive compensation, failing which the RC should have access to expert advice inside and/or outside the Institution.

7.3 The Remuneration Committee should recommend to the Board a framework of remuneration for the Board and key executives, and determine specific remuneration packages for each executive director and the CEO or PO (or executive of equivalent rank). The Remuneration Committee 's recommendations should be made in consultation with the chairman of the Board and submitted for endorsement by the entire Board. The Remuneration Committee should cover all aspects of remuneration, including but not limited to director's fees, salaries, allowances, bonuses, options, and benefits in kind. The Remuneration Committee should recommend the remuneration policies of the Institution to the Board for its approval. The Remuneration Committee should seek to ensure that the remuneration policies are in line with the Institution's strategic objectives and corporate values, and do not give rise to conflicts between the objectives of the Institution and the interests of individuals. For example, the salary scale should not be set in such a way that it encourages excessive risk taking and over-emphasises short-term performance.

Guidance Notes
8.1 In setting remuneration packages, the Remuneration Committee should be aware of pay and employment conditions within the industry and in compar-

able companies. The remuneration packages should take into account the Institution's relative performance and the performance of individual directors.

8.2 The performance-related elements of remuneration should form a significant proportion of the total remuneration package of executive directors and should be designed to align their interests with those of shareholders and link rewards to corporate and individual performance. There should be appropriate and meaningful measures for the purpose of assessing executive directors' performance.

8.3 The remuneration of non-executive directors should be appropriate to the level of contribution, taking into account factors such as effort and time spent, and responsibilities of such directors. Independent directors should not be over-compensated to the extent that their independence may be compromised. The Board may, if it considers necessary, consult experts on the remuneration of non-executive directors. The Board should recommend the remuneration of the nonexecutive directors for approval at the Annual General Meeting.

8.4 In the case of directors' service contracts, there should be a fixed appointment period for all directors, after which they are subject to re-election. In any case, service contracts should not have onerous removal clauses; neither should they be excessively long. The Remuneration Committee should consider the amount of compensation to be paid to the director in the event of early termination of the directors' contracts of service. The committee should aim to be fair and avoid rewarding poor performance.

Again, the contrast with the bank remuneration committee is not great:

Remuneration Committee

10(1) A bank incorporated in Singapore shall have an Remuneration Committee comprising at least 3 directors, the majority of whom are independent directors.

(2)　In addition to such other responsibilities determined by the Board of Directors, the Remuneration Committee shall be responsible for recommending a framework for determining the remuneration of directors and executive officers of the bank incorporated in Singapore, and for recommending the remuneration of each executive director and the chief executive officer of the bank incorporated in Singapore.

(3)　Any bank incorporated in Singapore, which is a wholly owned subsidiary of another bank incorporated in Singapore is not required to have a Remuneration Committee, if the Remuneration Committee of the second-mentioned bank is responsible for the matters referred to in paragraph (2) for the first-mentioned.

103

The Malaysian Code similarly suggests the need for remuneration commit-tees, consisting wholly or mainly of non-executive directors, to recommend to the board the remuneration of the executive directors in all its forms, drawing from outside advice as necessary. The idea is that executive directors should play no part in decisions on their own remuneration – but who is to monitor this? Membership of the remuneration committee should appear in the directors' report. Then again, the Malaysian system suggests that the determination of remuneration packages of non-executive directors, including non-executive chairmen, should be a matter for the board as a whole. The individuals concerned should abstain from discussion of their own remuneration.

The Malaysians note that:

4.9   Investor concern on remuneration practices in Malaysia is not at the level that it is in the United Kingdom, Australia and the United States. Nevertheless this disclosure requirement recognises and promotes important principles of fairness and accountability. Also, this principle implies that the report would be in the name of the board, rather than of the remuneration committee.

4.10 The company's annual report should therefore contain the details of remuneration of each director. Standards should be set which provide a rational and objective remuneration policy. For example, the objective of determining remuneration for a director might be to ensure that the company attracts and retains the directors needed to run the company successfully or linking remun-eration rewards to corporate and individual performance.

Under Japan's Commercial Code revisions of 2002, if a firm adopts the 'company with committees' structure, the amount of compensation for its direc-tors and executive officers (and how it should be awarded) is decided by a compensation committee, comprised by a majority of outside directors. On the other hand, because outside directors should not be able to set their own compen-sation, in the end the president or other directors decide on remuneration for these outside directors. If this is the case, then naturally, the independence of the outside directors would be called into question – their role is to decide compensation for those who set their own remuneration. As for Sony, the compensation committee sets the amount of compensation that each member of the board of directors and each corporate executive officer is to receive. The compensation committee's determination represents the final decision on these matters. The Sony Compensation Committee is composed of three or more directors and the majority, including the Chairman, will be outside directors. However, there will be at least one internal director. The CEO and COO do not serve on this committee.

CONCLUSION

It has always been a somewhat mysterious aspect of corporate governance that while at the level of high theory, it has always been recognized that the principle tension – indeed, almost the raison d'être of corporate governance itself – has been the potential conflict of interests between managers and shareholders, there is far more in practice about the structure and function of the board of directors than about the policing of managers. The risk with this focus surely exists within the corporation worldwide, and certainly in Asia, that while the board may be organized impeccably, senior management in the layers immediately beneath it are relatively unregulated. Divisional heads possess great authority and it must be the function of the board to rein them in where necessary and to ensure that they work in the interests of shareholders. The idea that forming a series of board committees will somehow improve the reality of honest corporate governance does seem implausible. There is a missing concept of 'influence' between the working of a committee and the board as a whole and the senior executives who lean on it. Does anyone imagine that in a typical Asian corporation a remuneration committee will decide that because the share price has slumped by a third, perhaps in line with the market, the CEO's salary should be cut by that amount? That a nomination committee will reject the nomination of a family member to a board position? Resignation will remain the only key threat for an independent director, and even that may not suffice to create the necessary total independence that the new corporate governance regime demands. Only an injection of real independence would do that – yet the role of the state within companies is universally derided by protagonists of corporate governance. It is a nice paradox.

Chapter 4

Accounting standards and procedures

- The link
- Internal audit
- The audit committee
- Potential conflict with shareholders' and board of directors' roles
- Auditor communication with audit committees
- The role of auditors
- Auditor independence
- Summary of US rules
- Summary of changes from proposals
- Audit partner rotation
- Expanded disclosure: principal accountants' fees
- Global accountancy convergence

THE LINK

For all that they are usually conjoined, as here, the question of accounting standards actually sits rather uneasily with corporate governance. Clearly a well-governed company will have impeccable accounting standards: in particular its statements of income and profits will be above reproach and its assessment of assets fair and true, insofar as both are feasible goals. But this is about what the company *does*, rather than the structure of how the company is run. Accurate accounts themselves are really a *goal* of corporate governance, not *part of it*. One way of looking at the relationship, though, is to argue that anything which allows shareholders to make informed judgements is good governance[1] and therefore to see corporate governance as providing a series of mechanisms as a result of which shareholders can be reassured that accounting malpractice has been eliminated, or at least reduced to an absolute minimum. This at least permits us free rein in talking about the issue.

The OECD takes the view that:

> While audited financial statements are often mandated by securities regula-
> tion or stock exchange requirements, what constitutes compliance with audit
> standards is rarely legislated, although the right to practise as an auditor may
> be subject to state regulation, with focus on ensuring auditor independence.
> Asian laws generally require compliance with national standards, which increas-
> ingly reflect international norms, such as IAS and ISA, as standards setters
> have recognised the practical and reputational benefits that accrue from using
> benchmarks which enjoy widespread acceptance.[2]

The current degree of convergence should not be overstated, though. The OECD
view is that

> while most Asian countries have stated that their standards broadly align with
> IAS, national variances and exceptions from 'full IAS' (a term which we are
> hearing more and more) exist in the light of differing conditions that obtain
> in individual jurisdictions. Asian Roundtable countries should work towards
> full convergence with international standards and practices for accounting,
> audit and non-financial disclosure. Where, for the time being, full conver-
> gence is not possible, divergences from international standards and practices
> (and the reasons for these divergences) should be disclosed by standards setters;
> company financial statements should repeat or reference these disclosures
> where relevant.[3]

The US implemented the Sarbanes-Oxley Act, and Asian jurisdictions have
implemented accounting reforms, mainly to render it at least very probable that
financial statements will be accurate. Likewise in Asia; echoing widely felt opinions
across the region, Professor Kazuyuki Suda of Kobe University commented that:

> According to the Korean FSS, the accounting regulatory system in Korea
> should be stiffer as moral hazards for corporate leaders and accountants has
> become 'all too common'. Two major accounting issues – underfunded and
> underexpensed pension funds, and the lack of meaningful consolidated data –
> make the valuation of some companies look even more expensive.

Such widespread convictions that accurate accounting is vital for a region's prosperity is not to say that other international organizations necessarily agree with
SOX or accept its precepts unhesitatingly or without criticism. Does the EU, for
instance, see entirely eye to eye with SEC reforms? Well, no, not exactly. UNICE,
the umbrella European Employers' Association, argues that European companies
with their main listings on European exchanges already meet tough audit
standards. In a letter to the EU Internal Market Commissioner, the UNICE

Secretary-General, Philippe de Buck, commented that the extra burdens on European companies 'go beyond what is needed to achieve the results that are sought'. The same EU Commissioner echoed these sentiments in a letter to the SEC Chairman, complaining that 'the implementation of some of the provisions of the Act might have undesirable extraterritorial consequences or they might create unnecessary difficulties for European companies'.[4] The interest for the study of Asian corporate governance is that the relationship between the EU and the SEC is not yet replicated at an Asian level. Individual Asian companies, even China, do not yet have the weight in international accountancy (or corporate finance) to determine the standards and justify exceptions. It is perfectly plausible to argue that it is precisely the lack of an institution like the EU in Asia that prevents this from happening. Asian countries acting individually inevitably end up price takers in the global accountancy standards supermarket.

Moreover, accounting itself as a discipline is still underdeveloped in countries such as Vietnam and China. The national accounting professional organization, the Chinese Institute of Certified Public Accountants, operated through the MoF, has administered and issued the professional designation 'Certified Public Accountant' (CPA) to qualified candidates only since 1988. The national examination for Chinese CPAs was introduced in 1994. The CPA firms are also licensed and required to comply with the rules and standards. The CSRC decreed that from 1 April 2002, all listed companies which plan to issue new shares must hire a foreign accounting firm to provide a supplementary audit of their accounts, before being allowed to issue any new shares. According to the head of Ernst & Young's China practice, speaking in 2002, China must therefore deal with a massive shortage of qualified accountants. He estimated that then 60–70 per cent of China's estimated 140,000 certified accountants were now aged 70 or older. And even that number is far below the 4 million the country could probably use to service its estimated 8 million operating companies. Ernst & Young and its main competitors, including the world's largest accounting firm PwC, are rapidly building up their China practices to meet the demand. But progress has been relatively slow because most new workers require extensive training, with Ernst & Young adding about 400 people a year to its China workforce, bringing its current national total to about 1,700 out of over 100,000 worldwide.

We are on firmer ground with the structure of a company which directs and supports the audit function: the audit committee and both the internal and external audit.

INTERNAL AUDIT

Supporters of corporate governance argue that the internal audit function is an integral part of an effective system of corporate governance. It is supposed to be the first line of defence for a company against accounting malpractice. So according to the OECD, a board should definitely establish an internal audit function. And where an internal audit function does not exist, the board should obviously assess whether there are other means of obtaining sufficient assurance of regular review and/or appraisal of the effectiveness of the system of internal controls within the company. The board needs to explain, in summary, the means that exist for obtaining such assurance of regular review and/or appraisal, so the internal audit function should be construed as including outsourcing. There are a number of other things the internal audit function, contracted out or not, needs to do right. The board or the audit committee should determine the remit of the internal audit function, which should encompass the evaluation of risk and monitoring of the effectiveness of the system of internal control. An independent and adequately resourced internal audit function must be able to provide assurance to the board in respect of systems of internal control, while the board or the audit committee should determine the general direction or remit of the internal audit function within the standards developed by the internal audit profession and with the understanding that the internal audit function should be independent of the activities it audits and the audits should be performed with impartiality, proficiency and due professional care. What Asian board these days does not do all these things?

Regional regulators echo the OECD view. For example, the MAS takes the view that:

> The Board should ensure that an internal audit function that is independent of the activities audited is established. The primary role of the internal auditor is to objectively review and evaluate the Institution's activities to maintain or improve the efficiency and effectiveness of its risk management, internal controls, and corporate governance. Internal auditors must understand the Institution's strategic direction, objectives, products, services and processes. They should communicate their findings to the Board or its Audit Committee and management.

Guidance Notes

11.1 The Internal Auditor's primary line of reporting should be to the chairman of the Audit Committee. The Internal Auditor should have unfettered access to the Board or its Audit Committee.

11.2 The scope of the Internal Auditor's remit should be clear and appropriate for the risks of the Institution, including those risks arising from proposed new lines of business or products.

11.3 There should be a process for discussion of internal audit reports with the business or support areas under review. Issues raised in internal audit reports should be clear and prioritised for action. Reports should be timely and distributed to the appropriate management personnel.

11.4 There should be processes for ensuring recommendations raised in internal audit reports are dealt with in a timely manner. Outstanding exceptions or recommendations should be closely monitored.

11.5 The Audit Committee should at least annually, review the adequacy of the internal audit function. The Internal Auditor's responsibilities include, but are not limited to, the following duties: (a) Evaluate the reliability, adequacy, and effectiveness of the Institution's internal controls and risk management processes. (b) Ensure that the Institution's internal controls result in prompt and accurate recording of transactions and proper safeguarding of assets. (c) Determine whether the Institution complies with laws and regulations and adheres to established policies, and whether management is taking the appropriate steps to address control deficiencies.

11.6 The Audit Committee should ensure that the internal audit function has adequate resources and has appropriate standing within the Institution.

11.7 The Audit Committee should approve the appointment, resignation or dismissal of the head of internal audit.

11.8 The Internal Auditor should at least meet the standards set by nationally or internationally recognised professional bodies including the Standards for the Professional Practice of Internal Auditing set by The Institute of Internal Auditors.[5]

Faced by this exemplary set of standards, a sceptic can surely only argue that the problem is that such guidance still needs to be issued: most of it ought to be self-evident.

To take a practical example of an Asian corporation, Honda's position is that its board of corporate auditors is composed of four corporate auditors, including two outside corporate auditors. In accordance with the rules of auditing policy and the apportionment of responsibilities as determined by the board of corporate auditors, each corporate auditor audits the execution by directors of their duties through various means, including attendance at meetings of the board of directors and inspections. Two outside corporate auditors were elected at the company's ordinary general meeting of shareholders held on 24 June 2003 and they comprise half the number of corporate auditors so as to strengthen their independence. In connection with this, a Corporate Auditors' Office was newly established in April 2003 to provide direct support to the board of corporate auditors. In order to ensure a proper auditing of the company's accounts, the board of corporate auditors and the board of directors receive auditing reports based on the Commercial Code's Audit Special Exceptions Law, the Securities and Exchange Law, and the Securities Exchange Acts of the USA. In addition, they supervise the election of independent auditors, their remuneration and non-audit services.

The problems with internal audit in Asia are not to do with the composition of the division, the professionalism of the people working for it or the immediate standards that they follow, although to some extent even the most assiduous of internal audits can be deceived from time to time by a particularly evasive manager. The problems relate much more to the fact that the head of internal audit within a company is still an employee of the company itself. If, for example, as happened at Parmalat as well as many other companies in Asia as elsewhere, the survival of the company itself depends on hiding black holes in accounts, then an internal auditor, or any other whistleblower for that matter, will undoubtedly be self-destructing. Knowing how difficult it can be even for well-qualified candidates to gain re-employment at short notice, how much more difficult is it – especially in Asia – for candidates from failed firms to get re-employed, especially if they themselves have been instrumental in organizing its downfall, whether or not that downfall was inevitable at some point in the future. That is the problem: *an inbuilt structural tendency for internal audit to self-censor.*

THE AUDIT COMMITTEE

This inbuilt tendency is very obvious when looking at the relationship between the internal audit function and the audit committee to which it should report.[6] The audit committee has especial importance in the new global corporate governance regime, but it rests critically on the notion that it possesses genuine independence because of the independent directors sitting on it. Taking Singapore as an example of current best practice in Asia, the MAS says that the board should establish an audit committee with a set of written terms of reference that clearly sets out its authority and duties. The audit committee plays an important role in establishing, maintaining and developing the control systems and compliance culture within the institution. It provides independent oversight of the institution's financial reporting and internal controls. It should work closely with the internal and external auditors to provide a system of checks and balances within the institution. As the audit committee oversees the internal audit function and evaluates the external audit function, it is therefore imperative that it should also be independent. The audit committee should be comprised of only non-executive directors. The majority of the audit committee, including the chairman, should be comprised of independent directors. Most Asian codes suggest that there 'should' be an audit committee, and the usual number of proposed directors to serve on it is three. Either all of them or a majority are expected to pass the national tests for independence – the Smith report in the UK advocated that they should be entirely composed of independent directors – and the chairman is almost invariably expected to be independent.

To avoid conflict of interests, members of the Audit Committee should not be part of the executive committee or any management committee that takes part in the management of the institution. The board should ensure that the members of the audit committee are appropriately qualified to discharge their responsibilities. At least two members should have accounting or related financial management expertise or experience. The audit committee should have express authority to investigate any matter within its terms of reference, full access to and the cooperation of management, full discretion to invite any director or executive officer to attend its meetings and reasonable resources to enable it to discharge its functions properly. The duties of the audit committee should include keeping under review the scope and results of the audit, its cost effectiveness and the independence and objectivity of the external auditors. The audit committee is supposed to review the independence of the external auditors annually. Where the auditors also provide a substantial volume of non-audit services to the institution – and this is on the decline, in Asia as much as elsewhere – the audit committee should keep the nature and extent of such services under review, seeking to balance the maintenance of objectivity and value for money. The audit committee is expected meet with the external auditors, internal auditors and appointed actuary, where applicable, without the presence of the institution's management, at least annually.[7] Is this really likely to be sufficient when it matters, i.e. when there are severe problems with the accounts which may be being hidden from the audit committee or of which they have only superficial knowledge?

The SEC has required national securities exchanges and national securities associations (self-regulatory organizations) to prohibit the listing of securities of issuers not in compliance with the audit committee requirements of the Sarbanes-Oxley Act of 2002. The new Rule 10A-3 under the Securities Exchange Act of 1934 requires issuers listed or quoted on an self-regulatory organization (SRO) to comply with the following standards:

> Each member of the audit committee of the issuer must be independent according to the specified criteria. To be considered independent, a member of an audit committee may not, other than in his or her capacity as a board or committee member, either (a) accept any consulting, advisory or other compensatory fee from the issuer or its affiliates, or (b) be an affiliated person of the issuer or any subsidiary of the company.

The SEC relied upon existing SRO standards; the independence criteria do not, for example, preclude independence on the basis of other commercial relationships, such as the sale or purchase of goods. These additional relationships would be covered by the independence requirements adopted by the SROs. Under the 'no compensation' prohibition, disallowed payments include payments made directly or indirectly (e.g. those made to a spouse or other relative, or to an entity that provides accounting, consulting, legal, investment banking or financial advisory services to the issuer, but not, for instance nonadvisory financial services such as lending relationships, maintaining customer accounts or brokerage services). The SEC also clarified that prohibited compensatory fees would not include the payment of fixed compensation amounts to an audit committee member under a retirement plan that is not contingent on continued service. With regard to the 'affiliated person' prohibition, the SEC adopted, as proposed, a safe harbour that a person will not be deemed to control the issuer (and will, therefore, not be an affiliate) if the person is not an executive officer or beneficial owner of more than 10 per cent of any class of voting equity securities of the issue, with no presumption that a greater than 10 per cent shareholder would automatically be deemed an affiliate, independence of a shareholder owning more than 10 per cent of the securities of the issuer depending on a 'facts and circumstances analysis' of control. The executive officer of an affiliate, a director who also is an employee of an affiliate, and a general partner or managing member of an affiliate are also deemed to be 'affiliated persons'.

The rule provided two exemptions from the independence requirements that are available for both domestic and foreign listed issuers:

- *IPO issuers* The rule requires new issuers to have at least one independent audit committee member at the time of listing, a majority of independent members within 90 days and a fully independent audit committee within one year of listing.
- *Overlapping board relationships* An audit committee member who sits on the board of directors of an issuer and an affiliate of the issuer is exempt from the 'affiliated person' prohibition if, except for being a director on each board, the member otherwise meets the independence requirements with respect to both entities.

An employee of a foreign private issuer who is not an executive officer is exempt from the independence requirements if the employee is elected to the board or audit committee pursuant to the issuer's governing law or documents, an employee collective bargaining or similar agreement or other home country legal or listing requirements. This exemption is intended to accommodate issuers from countries such as Germany that require employee representatives to serve on the board.

Recognizing that controlling shareholders are more common among foreign issuers than among domestic issuers, the rule provides that an audit committee member is exempt from the 'affiliated person' prohibition if the member is an affiliate of the issuer or a representative of the affiliate the member has only observer status on, and is not the chair of, the audit committee, and neither the member nor the affiliate is an executive officer of the issuer. Where the audit committee member is a representative of the shareholder, the shareholder (as well as the audit committee member) may not be an executive officer. An audit committee member is exempt from the 'affiliated person' prohibition if the member is a representative of a foreign government or foreign governmental entity that is an affiliate of the issuer, and is not an executive officer of the issuer. The SEC made clear in the adopting release that this exemption is not limited to just one foreign government representative and that more than one member of the committee can qualify under this exemption.

With respect to the latter two exemptions, the audit committee member would still need to satisfy the 'no compensation' prohibition of the independence requirements.

To accommodate companies that issue multiple classes of securities on various markets, the SEC adopted, as proposed, an exemption from the audit committee requirements for additional listings of securities by an issuer at any time the issuer is subject to the requirements as a result of the listing of a class of its common equity or similar securities on an SRO. The SEC also adopted an exemption for listings of non-equity securities of a consolidated or majority-owned subsidiary of a parent issuer, if the parent issuer is subject to the audit committee requirements as a result of the listing of its equity securities. Certain countries, such as Brazil and Japan, require or provide for auditor oversight through a board of auditors or similar body, or statutory auditors. In the final rule, the SEC made several modifications to the proposed exemption. The rule provides that a foreign private issuer will generally not be subject to the audit committee requirements of Rule 10A-3 if the issuer has a board of auditors or similar body, or has statutory auditors (collectively, a 'Board of Auditors'), established and selected pursuant to home country legal or listing provisions expressly requiring or permitting such a board or similar body:

- The Board of Auditors is required to be either separate from the board of directors, or composed of one or more members of the board of directors and one or more members that are not also members of the board of directors.
- The Board of Auditors is not elected by management of the issuer and no executive officer of the issuer is a member of the Board of Auditors.
- Home country legal or listing provisions set out standards for the independence of the Board of Auditors from the issuer or its management.
- The Board of Auditors, in accordance with applicable home country legal or listing requirements or the issuer's governing documents, is responsible, to the extent permitted by law, for the appointment, retention and oversight of the work of the issuer's outside auditors.

The remaining requirements of Rule 10A-3, such as the complaints procedures requirement, the authority to engage advisers requirement and the funding requirement, apply to the Board of Auditors to the extent permitted by law. For foreign issuers relying on this exemption, the term 'audit committee' in Rule 10A-3 refers to the issuer's Board of Auditors. In the final rule, the SEC made clear that the Board of Auditors would be subject to the 'audit committee financial expert' disclosure requirements:

- The audit committee must be directly responsible for the appointment, compensation, retention and oversight of the work of the issuer's outside auditors.
- The audit committee must establish procedures for the receipt, retention and treatment of complaints regarding accounting, internal accounting controls or auditing matters, including procedures for the confidential, anonymous submission by employees of concerns regarding questionable accounting or auditing matters.
- The audit committee must have the authority to engage independent counsel and other advisors, as it determines necessary to carry out its duties.
- The issuer must provide appropriate funding for the audit committee.

The SEC also attempted to address commentators' concerns regarding specific areas in which foreign corporate governance arrangements differ significantly from US practices. To that end, the SEC made several refinements in the final rule to the following exemptions for foreign private issuers: listed domestic issuers had to comply with the new requirements by the date of their first annual shareholders' meeting after 15 January 2004, but no later than 31 October 2004; foreign private issuers and small business issuers had to comply by 31 July 2005. No ifs, no buts: issuers must comply.

Asian companies looked at the extensive fundraising possibilities as well as the trailblazing path of the SEC and, for the majority, decided: we too had better have audit committees. In Hong Kong as recently as 1997, only 12 companies among the 553 listed companies had audit committees' disclosures in their annual reports. By 2003 this proportion had practically reversed. The clear trend in Asia is to follow best practice as laid down by SOX above. Did this of itself improve their audit function? Doubtful.

Moreover, the US rule applies only to listed companies. A domestic reporting company that is not listed is only required to disclose in its proxy statement whether it has an audit committee established in accordance with the rule and, if so, whether the members of the committee are independent. The non-listed company must choose one of the approved SRO definitions of audit committee independence, and must state which definition it has used. A foreign private issuer that is not listed on an SRO and that has an audit committee financial expert on its board must choose one of the approved SRO definitions of audit committee independence, and determine whether its financial expert is independent according to that definition. But of course a large Asian family company does not have to have an audit committee; and what would it mean if it did? US regulations do *not* prohibit domestic venture capital firms from investing in Asian companies that do not have audit committees, although it is worth saying that few now would.

What should the audit committee do? Recognizing 'the critical role played by audit committees in the financial reporting process and the unique position of audit committees in assuring auditor independence', the SEC rules, consistent with Section 202 of SOX, require that the audit committee pre-approve all audit, review and attest services, as well as all engagements for permissible non-audit services, unless it is entered into pursuant to pre-approval policies and procedures established by the audit committee. If the latter, which the SEC states is equally valid, such policies and procedures must be detailed as to the particular service, may not include delegation of the audit committee's responsibilities to management and must be disclosed as discussed below. The SEC noted in its adopting release that it expects that pre-approval policies and procedures would be 'prudent and responsible' and, further, that audit committees would establish policies for the maximum period in advance of the service that the approval may be granted. In addition, the SEC noted that Section 202 of the Act allows the audit committee to delegate to one or more of its members the authority to grant pre-approval of non-audit services, including tax services, and all audit, review and attest services so long as the pre-approval policies are detailed as to the particular service approved, the audit committee is informed of each service and the pre-approval policies do not delegate the audit committee's responsibilities to management. A small cop-out permits this to be waived for non-audit services that (i) were not recognized to be on-audit services at the time of engagement, (ii) constitute less than 5 per cent of the total revenues paid to the auditors during the same fiscal year, and (iii) are promptly brought to the attention of the audit committee and approved prior to completion of the audit. As the SEC noted, this *de minimis* exception is intended to mitigate the costs of inadvertent violations of the Act and the rules. Thus, it is not intended as a safe harbour on which to rely prospectively, and Asian companies are certainly aware of this need to separate out audit from non-audit service provision by accountants (see 119–21).

Most Asian codes expect the audit committee to appoint and deal with the auditor, as well as reviewing the internal audit function and the financial statements of the company and comparing them with the results of the auditors. The duties entrusted to an audit committee involve monitoring whether management is managing the company in a fair and proper manner that complies with the basic management policy and mid to long-term management plans adopted by

116

the board of directors. The committee should review the level of progress made on mid- to long-term plan targets and to ensure audit management efficiency. As such, it is vested with broader powers than conventional corporate auditors used to have in the past. For instance, audit committees are the bodies that carry out the board of directors' monitoring function set forth in Article 260, Paragraph 1 of the Commercial Code now in force in Japan. Japanese regulators admit that the audit committee system there was modelled after the US audit committee. But as with most Asian adoptions of the US system, there are small, but sometimes significant, differences: in this case, while the US-style committee used only to conduct the audits required by law that focus mainly on accounting data, Japanese audit committees undertake certain auditing functions required by law that used to be carried out by conventional corporate auditors, in addition to their role of evaluating the extent to which the objectives set by the board of directors have been achieved. As Derek Higgs said,

> The tasks that are being heaped on it [the audit committee] and the skills that are being required of it are pretty large. If you develop a range of significant and important roles for the audit committee, you might come close to the end of the unitary board system because the audit committee becomes the supervisory board within the board.

The MAS has laid down quite precise guidelines for how the audit committee of a bank, for instance, ought to operate:

> (1) A bank incorporated in Singapore shall have an AC comprising at least 3 directors, all non-executive, the majority of whom, including the chairman, shall be independent directors.
> (2) The AC shall, in addition to such other responsibilities determined by the Board of directors or provided under written law, be responsible for reviewing the scope and results of audits carried out in respect of the operations of the bank incorporated in Singapore, the cost effectiveness of the audits, the independence and objectivity of external auditors, and the adequacy of the internal audit function of the bank incorporated in Singapore.
> (3) Any bank incorporated in Singapore, which is a wholly owned subsidiary of another bank incorporated in Singapore is not required to have an Audit Committee, if the Audit Committee of the second-mentioned bank is responsible for the matters referred to in paragraph (2) for the first-mentioned bank.

By comparison the MAS Guidelines for insurers – listed companies in Singapore have been mandated to establish audit committees for over a decade – are similar:

117

(1) A direct insurer shall have an Audit Committee comprising at least 3 directors, all non-executive, the majority of whom, including the chairman, shall be independent.

(2) The AC shall, in addition to such other responsibilities determined by the board of directors or provided under written law, be responsible for reviewing the scope and results of audits carried out in respect of the operations of the direct insurer incorporated in Singapore, the cost effectiveness of the audits, the independence and objectivity of external auditors, and the adequacy of the internal audit function of the direct insurer incorporated in Singapore.

It is fascinating to compare the two guidelines, and both with SOX. You cannot put a piece of paper between the two Singapore guidelines, except for the obvious enough point about subsidiaries. Noticeably missing is any suggestion that the audit committee can delegate any of its work to one of its members, but other than that, the provisions of SOX are little advance on the Singapore Code. What really matters is how the individual audit committees of different institutions actually work, and whether their operation is sufficient to ensure the highest quality of accounting reporting. To argue that Singapore has almost completely escaped accounting-related scandals because of the audit committee is to confuse correlation with cause; after all, Singapore was also pretty much accounting scandal-free in the years before the introduction of compulsory audit committees for listed companies in 1991.

POTENTIAL CONFLICT WITH SHAREHOLDERS' AND BOARD OF DIRECTORS' ROLES

SOX clarifies that the audit committee requirements are not intended to override any requirement under an issuer's constituent documents or home country legal or listing provisions for shareholders to ultimately vote on, approve or ratify such requirements. The SEC also recognized that some foreign jurisdictions prohibit the full board of directors from delegating certain responsibilities to a committee, such as the ability of directors to submit nominations or recommendations to shareholders on the appointment in the final rule clarifies that none of the audit committee requirements conflicts with any legal or listing provisions in an issuer's home jurisdiction that require such responsibilities to be vested with shareholders or the full board of directors. What the SEC had in mind in this case is that the audit committee requirements relate instead to the assignment of responsibility between the audit committee and management. However, even where there is a specified role for shareholders or the board of directors, if the issuer provides a recommendation or nomination regarding such responsibilities to shareholders, the SEC takes the view that the audit committee or the body performing similar functions must be responsible for making the recommendation or nomination, to the extent permitted by national law throughout Asia.

AUDITOR COMMUNICATION WITH AUDIT COMMITTEES

The SEC's rules require each accounting firm registered with the Oversight Board that audits a company's financial statements to report (orally or in writing) to the audit committee prior to filing the related audit report with the SEC:

- all critical accounting policies and practices used by the company, including critical accounting estimates, the selection of initial accounting policies, reasons why certain policies are or are not considered critical, and how current and future events affect that determination;
- all material alternative accounting treatments that have been discussed with management, including the ramifications of their use and the auditors' preferred treatment; and
- other material written communications between management and the auditors that would facilitate auditor and management oversight by the audit committee (e.g. management representation letters, internal controls reports, schedules of material adjustments and proposed reclassifications, listings of adjustments and reclassifications not recorded, engagement letters and independence letters).

At the time SOX was drafted, there was some confusion about the level of detail that management should provide to audit committee members: the final rules were clarified to make clear that the rules only required communication of 'material' alternate accounting treatments and were not meant to require reporting on the application of accounting principles to relatively small transactions or events. Common sense, in other words, was meant to apply. This has always been applied in Asia where there have been, as yet, no major conflicts between audit committees and auditors.

THE ROLE OF AUDITORS

As the OECD has said, laws across Asia require listed companies to have their financial statements audited by an independent auditor. There is a great range across Asian jurisdictions, however, in the capabilities, experience, standards and practices of external auditors. In some instances, the quality and independence of audits have fallen short. In Thailand, for instance, measures are being taken to cut the number of listed companies an accounting firm can audit from 300 to 50, on the twin bases that no one firm ought to have so much influence over the market and that so many companies can hardly be an incentive to accurate

119

accounting. With degrees of frequency that vary by jurisdiction, Asian auditors have certainly approved financial statements that vary greatly from existing accounting standards, even after allowing for wide discretion in characterizing specific events and treatments. As in other regions, shortcomings arise from a combination of factors, which may include bias, inexperience, ignorance and negligence. The proper function of auditors, says the Malaysian Code, is to report to the company's stakeholders on the accuracy of the company's accounts. Shareholders appoint them at the AGM, or EGM. In practice, external auditors worldwide have been appointed by finance directors and confirmed by share-holders. The audit committee should select external auditors on the basis of their qualifications, expertise and resources, effectiveness and independence (how else?). The external auditors should independently report to shareholders in accordance with statutory and professional requirements, and independently assure the board on the discharge of their responsibilities under D.I and D.II under Part 1 of this Code in accordance with professional guidance. This points up the dual responsibility of the auditors – the public report to shareholders on the statutory financial statements and on other matters as required by the listing requirements; and additional private reporting to directors on operational and other matters.

AUDITOR INDEPENDENCE

The SEC has progressively tightened regulations related to the non-audit services that, if provided to an audit client, would impair an accounting firm's inde-pendence. There are two main parts of this independence. First, because of the importance in the process of the audit committee itself, the requirements are essentially that the audit engagement team may not audit services to the issuer for more than five or seven consecutive years, depending on the partner's involve-ment in the audit, except that certain small accounting firms may be exempted from this requirement. No accounting firm may audit an issuer's financial state-ments if certain members of management of that issuer had been members of the accounting firm's audit engagement team within the one-year period preceding the commencement of audit procedures. The auditor of an issuer's financial state-ments must report certain matters to the issuer's audit committee, including 'critical' accounting policies used by the issuer; and require disclosures to investors of information related to audit and non-audit services provided by, and fees paid to, the auditor of the issuer's financial statements. Second, under the final rules, an accountant would not be independent from an audit client if an audit partner received compensation based on selling engagements to that client for services other than audit, review and attest services.

SOX says that to be considered independent, a registered public accounting firm that audits a public company's financial statements would not be permitted to provide, contemporaneously with the audit, any of the non-audit services listed in Section 201 or any other service the Oversight Board determines by regulation to be impermissible. These prohibited services include:

- bookkeeping or other services related to the accounting records or financial statements of the audit client;
- financial information systems design and implementation;
- appraisal or valuation services, fairness opinions, or contribution-in-kind reports;
- actuarial services;
- internal audit outsourcing services;
- management functions or human resources;
- broker or dealer, investment adviser, or investment banking services; and
- legal services and expert services unrelated to the audit.

In general, a registered independent public accountant can provide non-audit services that are not otherwise prohibited, including tax services, to a public company audit client only if the activity is approved in advance by the company's audit committee. Similarly, the audit committee of a public company generally must pre-approve all audit and permissible non-audit services to be provided by the company's external auditor.

While rules such as these are common in Asia, for instance in the Singapore and Malaysian Codes of Corporate Governance, the OECD is right to suggest that they are not yet universal. For example in China, although the listing rules require the external auditors of listed companies to have CPA licences, most of these appointments are awarded without a public tendering process. Information on how and why a CPA firm is selected remains confidential within the 'insider' circle of the top management. Furthermore, and completely against best practice, there is no requirement for disclosure of auditor fees versus non-audit fees in the annual reports. Not yet, anyway. The Chinese regulators are currently in the process of setting rules on auditor rotations. Once implemented, it will be a positive step in enhancing auditor independence and another example of how a key Asian jurisdiction is closing the gap between Western and Asian practice.

SUMMARY OF US RULES

The rules are intended to, among other things:

- strengthen the existing auditor independence rules, in some respects going beyond the requirements of the Act;

121

- clarify the scope of non-audit services prohibited to be performed by a company's outside auditor;
- specify the audit committee pre-approval requirements in respect of audit and non-audit services;
- require that critical accounting policies and other material written communications between management and registered audit firms be reported to the audit committee;
- require mandatory rotation of certain audit partners, as well as a 'time-out' period after that, with the timing for each depending on the partner's involvement in the audit;
- address auditor conflicts of interest arising from audit partner compensation and employment by issuer clients;
- require disclosures of information related to audit and non-audit services provided by, and fees paid to, a company's outside auditor.

SUMMARY OF CHANGES FROM PROPOSALS

The final rules were adopted substantially as proposed, although some important changes were made. Below is a summary of some of the most significant changes from the original proposals:

- The SEC clarified the scope of certain prohibited non-audit services.
- The audit partner rotation rules were changed from the proposals to provide a five-year rotation period and a five-year 'time-out' period for lead and concurring partners and a seven year mandatory rotation period with a two year 'time-out' period for certain other audit partners depending on the partner's involvement in the audit, and to exempt all other audit partners.
- The SEC added an exemption to the rules related to avoiding conflicts arising from employment with an audit client to exclude from such rule members of an audit engagement team that provide less than ten hours of services during an annual audit period, and also provided additional exemptions for conflicts created through mergers or acquisitions and for emergency or unusual circumstances.
- The SEC also clarified the determination of the time period during which members of an audit engagement team may not take a position and serve in a financial reporting oversight role at an issuer client by providing a uniform date for all members of the engagement team.
- The SEC narrowed the rules related to compensation of partners for non-audit services to apply only to audit partners, not every member of an audit engagement team, and specified that the compensation must be based on an audit partner's procuring engagements to provide non-audit services.

122

These rules have had an impact on foreign accounting firms that conduct audits of foreign subsidiaries and affiliates of US issuers, as well as of foreign private issuers.

In accordance with Section 201(a) of the Act, the SEC rules prohibit auditors registered with the Public Company Accounting Oversight Board, certified public accountants and public accountants in connection with an engagement for which independence is required from performing the following non-audit services for an audit client during the audit and professional engagement period:

- bookkeeping or other services related to the audit client's accounting records or financial statements;
- financial information systems design and implementation;
- appraisal or valuation services, fairness opinions, or contribution-in-kind reports;
- actuarial services;
- internal audit outsourcing;
- management functions or human resources;
- broker-dealer, investment adviser or investment banking services;
- legal services; and
- expert services unrelated to the audit.

The rules provide a transition period for the provision of prohibited non-audit services. The safest rule to follow is that an accountant is not deemed to be independent if at any time during the audit and professional engagement period any person who is a part of the audit engagement team earns or receives compensation based on performing or procuring an engagement to provide a service other than an audit, review or attestation. With respect to the prohibitions on bookkeeping, financial information systems design and implementation, appraisal, valuation, fairness opinions or contribution-in-kind reports, actuarial services, and internal outsourcing services, the final rules clarify that the provision of such services will cause the auditor to lack independence unless it is reasonable to conclude that the results of these services will not be subject to audit procedures during an audit of the audit client's financial statements. In its adopting release, the SEC noted that the change from 'reasonably likely' in the proposals to 'unless it is reasonable to conclude' in the final rules was intended to emphasize the responsibility the audit firm has in making the determination that the provision of these services will not be subject to audit procedures.

In its final rules, the SEC took the position that expert services, which the Act includes in the list of prohibited services but which the SEC had expressly decided not to prohibit at the time it adopted its existing rules, may impair an accountant's independence as to an audit client. The rules prohibit the provision of expert services on the grounds that it violates the basic principle that an auditor should not act as an advocate for its audit client. Specifically, auditors would be prohibited from providing expert witness or other services, including accounting advice, opinions or forensic accounting services, in connection with the client's participation in a legal, administrative or regulatory proceeding, including providing forensic accounting services to the audit client's counsel in connection with an SEC enforcement investigation or serving as an expert witness in a utility rate setting proceeding in support of an audit client's request for an increase in fees.

The SEC's rules, however, would not prohibit an auditor from assisting the audit committee in its own investigation of a potential accounting impropriety or complying with the auditor's obligations under Section 10A of the Exchange Act to search for fraud material to an issuer's financial statements and keep the audit committee informed of its findings, so long as the auditor did not take on the role of an advocate. For example, an auditor may render forensic services to the audit committee and share its work product with the audit committee's counsel. Similarly, an auditor would be permitted to testify as a fact witness to its audit work for a particular audit client. Moreover, an accounting firm that, after receiving appropriate authorization from an audit client's audit committee, had prepared an audit client's tax returns could appear as a fact witness in tax court to explain how the returns were prepared. The SEC noted that should a litigation arise or an investigation be commenced at the time the auditors were conducting their investigation, the completion of their procedures would not be deemed prohibited expert services so long as the auditors remain in control of their work and do not become subject to the direction or control of counsel to the issuer.

The rules permit tax services such as tax compliance, tax planning and tax advice to continue to be provided to an audit client if they have been pre-approved by the client's audit committee and are not, in effect, prohibited legal or expert services. Tax services that might be regarded as prohibited legal or expert services include representing an audit client before a tax court, which would involve an accountant's serving as an advocate for his or her client, and formulating tax shelters, which may require the accountant to audit his or her own work, assume a management function or become an advocate for a client in seeking to minimize tax obligations or defend novel tax issues. In Hong Kong, shareholder activist David Webb has been assiduous in tracking the other work done by auditors for every public company of which he is a shareholder. In the case of the Hong Kong Exchange, for instance,

> On the reappointment of auditors, you will be happy to learn that the only non-audit work performed by PricewaterhouseCoopers was tax compliance work, for a fee of $564,000. We always ask this question at every listed company whose AGM we attend, because there is increasing concern about conflicts of interest. We were satisfied that in this case, there were none.

In India, an example of the type of problem which can emerge was GTB's heavily qualified audit report for 2002. Auditors PwC pointed to the accounts being prepared on a going-concern basis, despite a substantial erosion of net worth, based on the bank's future capital infusion plans. The auditor said that 'utilisation of statutory reserves below the line after the net loss for the year' to provide for non-performing assets was not in conformity with generally accepted accounting principles, although GTB had the permission of the Reserve Bank of India (RBI) to do so. Similarly, PwC said GTB had not provided for over Rs 311 crore of advances that had been restructured after the year-end, saying that the restructured loans were substantially secured and interest had been serviced until the end of March 2003. Also, it made no provision for Rs 181 crore of assets acquired against certain debts. Yet, GTB was not annoyed; its annual report said it will apply to the RBI for reappointing PwC as auditor. But as the AGM approached, newspaper reports said that M. Bhaskara Rao & Co. might replace PwC as statutory auditor. The RBI was believed to have cleared the new auditor even ahead of the AGM. This is very poor governance indeed. In Japan, Standard & Poor's has described the *kansayaku* (corporate auditor) system as problematic, on the basis that many corporate auditors are former company employees and cannot be considered completely independent.

AUDIT PARTNER ROTATION

It is interesting that on auditor rotation Asia might finally with some justice take credit for being first in the field. South Korea's Financial Supervisory Service (FSS) ordered listed companies to rotate 67 per cent of their auditors every three years in 2001, the US and Japan imitated the reform bill in 2002 and 2003 respectively. The China Securities Regulatory Commission (CSRC) and the Ministry of Finance have issued a joint document requiring companies to rotate their auditors every five years in a step towards tightening corporate accounting standards. In 2003 Korea decided to rotate all company auditors, or the accounting firm itself, every six years, and the US began to carry out research into the reform bill, according to FSS accounting supervision director Jung Yong. Most local accounting firms resist the rotation of accounting firms. Shin Chan-soo, head of the Korean Institute of Certified Public Accountants (KICPA), strongly opposed the reform bill. In the US, accountants were overridden: Section 203 of SOX requires the lead audit partner and the reviewing partners directly involved in an audit, review or attest engagement to rotate off the engagement after five consecutive fiscal years. The SEC's rules implement this provision by requiring that the lead and concurring partners rotate after five consecutive fiscal years as the lead or concurring partner on an engagement and require a five-year 'time-out' period after that. Unlike the original proposals, which also proposed to

125

extend the rotation requirements to all other partners on the audit engagement, the final rules only extend rotation and time-out period requirements to certain other partners performing audit services. In addition to the lead and concurring partners, the rotation rules also apply to a set of partners defined as 'audit partners'. The rules require that 'audit partners', other than the lead and concurring partners, must rotate off the engagement after seven consecutive years and then are subject to a two-year 'time-out' period. As defined by the rules, 'audit partners' are those partners who have responsibility for decision-making affecting the audit or who maintain regular contact with management and the audit committee. In addition to the lead and concurring partners, 'audit partners' include all partners who serve the client at the parent or issuer level, other than 'specialty' partners. Further, the lead partner on significant subsidiaries (those constituting 20 per cent or more of consolidated revenues or assets of the client) is included within the definition of 'audit partners'. Other partners that do not fall within the term 'audit partners' are not subject to the rotation requirements. A partner could, in compliance with the rotation requirements, serve either as a lead partner on a significant subsidiary or as an 'audit partner' at the parent or issuer level for two years prior to becoming the lead or concurring partner on the engagement and still be able to serve in that capacity for five years. The rotation and time-out requirements would apply to 'tax' partners who perform significant tax services related to the audit and necessary to its completion, but not to partners providing tax compliance or tax planning services pursuant to audit committee pre-approval. 'National office' partners who serve as technical resources for the audit team and may be consulted on issues related to a specific client on a regular basis would not be considered members of the audit engagement team and, thus, would not be subject to the rotation requirement. In order to allow firms to establish an orderly transition of their audit engagement teams, the SEC adopted transition rules for the partner rotation requirements.

A registered public accounting firm would not be considered independent of a public company audit client if the lead audit partner having primary responsibility for the audit, or the audit partner responsible for reviewing the audit, had signed for five consecutive years. The SEC's final rule on auditor independence requires the lead and concurring partners to rotate after five years and, upon rotation, to be subject to a five-year 'time out' period. In addition, the SEC's final rule imposed a seven-year rotation requirement on certain other audit partners on the audit client's engagement team followed by a two-year 'time out' period. These partner rotation rules are intended to strike a balance between the need to bring a fresh look to the audit engagement and the need to maintain continuity and audit quality. The SEC's final rules also contain an exemption from the rotation requirements for small accounting firms, i.e. firms with fewer than five public company audit clients and fewer than ten audit partners, provided an audit quality review condition is met. Similar rules on rotation have now been followed by Asian jurisdictions such as Singapore, Pakistan and South Korea, and others may follow.

EXPANDED DISCLOSURE: PRINCIPAL ACCOUNTANTS' FEES

To enable investors to better evaluate the reliability of financial statements and the independence of the auditors that prepare them, the SEC's rules expand disclosure of fees paid for audit and non-audit services to include, in addition to audit fees and 'all other fees' (disclosure as to which is currently required for US issuers), audit-related fees and tax fees. Non-US issuers will now be required to provide disclosure for all four categories of fees. The final rules clarified that audit fees are expected to include all fees for services to comply with Generally Accepted Auditing Standards (GAAS). The disclosure is required to be included in a company's proxy or information statement and incorporated by reference into its annual report. Companies that do not file proxy statements, including non-US issuers, are required to include the disclosure in their annual reports on Form 10-K, 20-F or 40-F. (Asset backed issuers are exempt.) Audit fees include fees for services that generally only the independent auditor can provide, such as comfort letters, statutory audits, attest services, consents and assistance with and review of SEC filings. Audit-related fees include fees for employee benefit plan audits, Merger's and Acquisitions (M&A) due diligence, accounting assistance and audits in connection with proposed or consummated acquisitions, internal control reviews, and consultations concerning financial accounting and reporting standards.

Tax fees include: (i) tax compliance, including the preparation of tax returns, refund claims and tax payment planning services, and (ii) tax consultation and planning, including assistance and representation in connection with tax audits and appeals, M&A and employee benefit plan tax advice, and requests for rulings or tax advice from taxing authorities. Disclosure is required for the two most recent fiscal years rather than only for the most recent fiscal year, as is currently required. Other than for the audit fees category, the rules also require a description, in qualitative terms, of the types of services provided under the remaining three categories.

GLOBAL ACCOUNTANCY CONVERGENCE

A global corporate governance regime requires, of course, global accountancy standards. Is it so obvious? The OECD view is that:

> As a result [of the argument in favour of convergence], even if a proposed national standard is 'better' than its international counterpart, the value of

comparability may militate in favour of adopting the international standard. This situation may be particularly true for smaller jurisdictions, where cross-jurisdictional comparability may yield greater relative benefits. Adoption of established and tested international standards also permits greater devotion of local resources to implementation and enforcement and helps to insulate standards setters from external pressures.

Singapore, Hong Kong and other countries that have completely adopted, or almost completely adopted, international accountancy rules are apt to take a public position in favour of international harmonization which plainly would prejudice their position of comparative advantage. There was a time, for instance, when the only straight stockbroking play in Asian markets in which fund managers could invest was in Singapore – which led to the firm Vickers Ballas (now taken over) being valued at an astronomic Price/Earnings Ratio (P/E Ratio). As China and India become alternative – and much larger – destinations for funds, this can hardly be attractive news for the smaller Asian countries.

IAS are increasingly becoming the benchmarks for accounting and have been endorsed for multinational securities offerings and cross-border listings by the International Organization of Securities Commissions (IOSCO) and the Bank for International Settlements. IAS and International Standards of Audit (ISA) were also identified as the key standards to follow by the Task Force on the Implementation of Standards of the Financial Stability Forum (FSF). The world's largest accounting firms and the International Federation of Accountants (IFAC), which represents the accounting and audit profession on the international level, support the use of both IAS and ISA. The FSF also identified the IOSCO Objectives and Principles of Securities Regulation as a key standard to follow and the IOSCO International Disclosure Standards for Cross-Border Offerings and Initial Listings by Foreign Issuers provide specific guidance on the content of non-financial disclosure. The most difficult challenge is the International Financial Reporting Standards (IFRS)/US GAAP (Generally Accepted Accounting Principles) convergence. It is natural for the biggest capital market with the most well-developed standards to expect other countries to converge with its standards. Thus, companies that want access to America's capital markets are required to adopt US GAAP or, at least, to provide a US GAAP reconciliation. The Singapore-incorporated companies that have had an eye on a US listing can attest to the time, effort and costs expended in understanding the differences between Singapore and US GAAP.

The Sarbanes-Oxley Act directed the SEC to carry out a study on the adoption of a principles-based accounting system. The study report, published recently, recommended principles-based or objectives-oriented standards, which avoid the use of percentage tests that allow financial engineers to achieve technical compliance while evading the intent of the standard. In the wake of the corporate accounting scandals that led to the watershed Sarbanes-Oxley legislation, there were suggestions that US GAAP had become too rules-based. The SEC study recognized that certain standards are rules-based (for instance, accounting for leases and consolidation of special purpose entities) and noted that 'continuing to move towards objectives-oriented standard setting in the US would increase the speed and likelihood of convergence'.

A fresh start began with the Norwalk Agreement, a memorandum of understanding signed between the International Accounting Standards Board (IASB) and the Financial Accounting Standards Board (FASB) in September 2002. The IASB and FASB each acknowledged their commitment to the development of high-quality, compatible accounting standards that could be used for both domestic and cross-border financial reporting. They would use their best efforts to make their existing financial reporting standards fully compatible as soon as practicable. They would also coordinate their future work programmes to ensure that, once achieved, compatibility is maintained. A short-term project was launched to remove a number of differences identified for resolution in 2003. The US Securities and Exchange Commission (SEC) welcomed the Norwalk Agreement and senior officials had indicated that if sufficient progress was made in converging and also in creating an effective infrastructure for interpretation and enforcement, the SEC would consider allowing non-domestic companies to file in the US using IFRS without reconciling to US GAAP.

A secondary, though extremely important, issue is the global convergence of financial statement reporting. At a broader level, undisclosed off-balance-sheet financing also increases systemic risk to the economy where such financing is widespread. Following the restructuring of the international accounting standard-setting body in 2001, now called the International Accounting Standard Board (IASB), the new international accounting standards developed and published by IASB are known as International Financial Reporting Standards (IFRS). Nevertheless, IAS (approved and issued under the previous constitution) continue to be applicable and of equal standing with IFRS unless and until they are amended or withdrawn. Like the International Accounting Standards (IAS) set up by the Financial Accounting Standards Board, there are around 34 codified International Financial Reporting Standards in existence. Adoption of a common standard for preparing financial statements would ensure that interpretations made from reading a statement by a person is no different from that made by any other person in a different part of the world. The adoption of IFRS would also make consolidation of financial statements of foreign subsidiaries of a holding company much easier. Currently, companies are required to follow the accounting and reporting standards prescribed by the host country when preparing their accounts. Frequently these standards are at variance with those followed by the parent company, making consolidation very difficult. Hence, parent companies are required to reconcile the difference to ensure uniform treatment for every

129

item before the consolidated statements are prepared. The EU has now endorsed IFRS: a critical step towards achieving a global financial reporting framework. For Asian companies, adoption of the IFRS along with IAS would translate into less paperwork in the form of restatement of accounts when they plan to approach investors overseas. After harmonization of accounting standards across the globe, accounting bodies are now proposing a common financial statements reporting standard for preparation of annual accounts. According to the OECD:

> At present, jurisdictions in Asia diverge widely in the degree to which they have adopted international standards and practices such as IAS. For some jurisdictions, full convergence represents a relatively short and easy step. For others, full convergence can involve a long and difficult journey.

The Confederation of Asian Pacific Accountants (CAPA), an association of national accountancy organizations, has commissioned a study to take stock of the progress by member countries. CAPA President, Robin Hamilton Harding, has said the countries would need to work towards convergence of international standards with their own standards to ensure that inference drawn from financial statements by anyone is the same.

The OECD has pointed out that, as regional regulators and practitioners know, international standards can be complex and hard to introduce; a move to full compliance with IAS can also impose substantial costs, requiring additional training and financial and human resource commitments at the company, professional firm and standards-setter levels. Moreover, under certain market conditions, a shift in accounting standards can sharply cut property values and reported earnings, potentially destabilizing markets and financial systems. For these and similar reasons, local conditions from country to country may require adoption of standards, such as IAS, individually (rather than all at once) and/or at differing speeds. But, such local conditions should be used neither to politicize the standards-setting process nor to encourage the adoption of standards that diverge from internationally-recognized benchmarks. During the transition to full convergence, standards setters should disclose where local standards and practices diverge from IAS (and the reasons for these divergences); company financial statements should reference specific disclosures where they apply to specific items and yield materially different results.

In Hong Kong, the Society of Accountants' president Roger Best pressed ahead with accounting reform by rolling out some 15–18 new standards, for example on the measurement and disclosure of financial instruments, which industry players say may result in significant increases in earnings volatility for some Hong Kong companies. The standards, IAS 32 and 39, were revised and issued by the IASB. They require investments to be measured at market value and companies no longer being given the option to measure some of these investments at cost. No such requirement yet existed in Hong Kong, but as usual, Asia catches up fast these days: the Korean Standards Association (KSA) was planning to issue the standard on financial instruments soon so that it would become effective on 1 January 2005 at the earliest, but no later than 2006. Best said:

> There is a concern that a number of companies that might be affected by the standards will have to change some of their internal accounting systems in order to capture all the information necessary. We might need to give those entities time to make those changes.

Hong Kong, Taiwan, Singapore (and the EU countries) are in the category of countries that have regulatory requirements to converge with IFRS. Accounting standards in Singapore are now set by the CCDG: Singapore standards were closely modelled on IFRS originally and the country will adopt IFRS, except where there were particular reasons for deviation. The government says that there will continue to be instances where Singapore practice needs to be different from the IFRS, but these would probably be rare and related to matters of interpretation or detail, rather than principles. One example of a local accommodation that the CCDG considered necessary is the treatment of long leasehold land in the standard on leases. According to the IFRS, land has an indefinite life and cannot be treated as a fixed asset (finance lease) if title to the land is not expected to pass at the end of the lease term. Thus, the cost of acquiring leasehold land would be treated as pre-paid lease payments. The CCDG modified the standard so that long leasehold property may be classified either as a fixed asset or as an operating lease based on the principle in the IFRS (i.e. whether the lease transfers to the lessee all the risks and rewards incident to ownership of the facility that is on the land). As Singapore standards have been closely modelled on the standards of the IASB and its predecessor since 1977, Singapore has similar reasons to converge with IFRS as the EU, or any other country for that matter – the removal of barriers to cross-border listings and becoming a competitive and dynamic knowledge-based economy with economic growth, better jobs and social cohesion. The benefits of convergence will accrue to Singapore companies, its financial and capital markets and, ultimately, the Singapore economy. Although there may not be many companies that at present stand to benefit from cross-border listings, the soft infrastructure needs to be in place for future developments.

Other countries that have a formal convergence plan include Malaysia and Hong Kong.

In Indonesia, the Financial Accounting Standards Board (DSAK) of the Indonesian Institute of Accountants is continuing its policy of harmonizing Indonesian Financial Accounting Standards (PSAK) with IFRS.

131

Exposure drafts issued and outstanding are as follows:

- Revision to PSAK 8, Events after the Balance Sheet Date. Issued in July 2002. This standard would replace that portion of PSAK 8, Contingencies and Events after the Balance Sheet Date, that addresses events after the balance sheet date. The portion of PSAK 8 that addresses contingencies is replaced by PSAK 57, Estimated Liabilities, Contingent Liabilities and Contingent Assets. In preparing this exposure draft, DSAK referred to IAS 10 (Revised 1999), Events after Balance Sheet Date.
- Limited Revision to PSAK 58, Discontinuing Operations. Issued in August 2002. The revision to PSAK 58 is limited to paragraph 40 on presentation of disclosures.
- Revision to PSAK 16, Fixed Assets. Issued in August 2002. This exposure draft would replace PSAK 16, Fixed Assets and Other Assets, particularly regarding accounting treatment for revaluation of fixed assets. In this exposure draft, the accounting treatment for fixed assets is harmonized with other PSAKs such as:

  - PSAK 22, Accounting for Business Combinations
  - PSAK 26 (Revised 1997), Borrowing Costs
  - PSAK 46, Accounting for Income Tax
  - PSAK 48, Impairment of Assets
  - PSAK 57, Estimated Liabilities, Contingent Liabilities, and Contingent Assets.

  In preparing this exposure draft, DSAK referred to IAS 16 (Revised 1998), Property, Plant and Equipment, and local regulations on related matters.

In addition, another board – known as The Central and Regional Governmental Accounting Standards Committee (KSAP) – was established under a decree of the Minister of Finance to develop governmental accounting standards. KSAP issued the following exposure drafts in October 2002:

- Conceptual Framework for Governmental Accounting
- Governmental Accounting Standards (PSAP) 1, Presentation of Financial Statements
- PSAP 2, Budget Realization Statements
- PSAP 3, Cash Flow Statements.

In preparing the above exposure drafts, KSAP referred to sound international practices, considered the specific situation in Indonesia, including regulations, accounting practices, and human resources, and a transition period to tolerate the preparedness of reporting entities. Specifically, KSAP referred to:

- International Public Sector Accounting Standards (IPSAS) of IFAC
- PSAK
- Governmental Accounting Standards developed by the US Governmental Accounting Standards Board
- Financial Accounting Standards developed by the US Financial Accounting Standards Board.

July 2002 update

Consistent with the objective of harmonizing between Indonesian Pernyataan Standar Akuntansi Keuangan (PSAK/Statements on Financial Accounting Standards) and the International Accounting Standards, at present the Board of Financial Accounting Standards of Indonesia is discussing the following:

- Revision to PSAK 24, Accounting Retirement Benefit Cost
- Revision to PSAK 16, Fixed Assets and Other Assets
- Revision to PSAK 30, Accounting for Leases
- A new accounting standard on agriculture.

Also, the Board has published accounting standards for Syariah banking as follows:

- Framework for the Preparation and Presentation of Financial Statements of Syariah Banking
- PSAK 59, Accounting for Syariah Banking.

October 2001 update

The Financial Accounting Standards Board (Dewan Standar Akuntansi Keuangan, or DSAK) of the Indonesian Institute of Accountants is continuing its policy of harmonizing Indonesian Financial Accounting Standards (PSAK) with IAS. The following standards are effective for periods beginning on or after 1 January 2001 (their equivalent IAS is indicated for reference):

- PSAK 19 (Revised 2000), Intangible Assets (IAS 38)
- PSAK 31 (Revised 2000), Accounting for Banking (including disclosure requirements in IAS 30)
- PSAK 46, Accounting for Income Tax (IAS 12). This standard is effective for periods beginning on or after 1 January 1999 for companies issuing publicly traded securities, while for other companies, this standard is effective for periods beginning on or after 1 January 2001

133

- PSAK 55 (Revised 1999), Accounting for Derivatives and Hedging Activities
- PSAK 57, Estimated Liabilities, Contingent Liabilities, and Contingent Assets (IAS 37).

The following standards will be effective for periods beginning on or after 1 January 2002 (their equivalent IAS is indicated for reference):

- PSAK 5 (Revised 2000), Segment Reporting (IAS 14)
- PSAK 58, Discontinuing Operations (IAS 35).

Exposure drafts of PSAK issued and outstanding are as follows:

- Conceptual Framework for the Preparation and Presentation of the Financial Statements of Shariah-based Banks. This standard is largely based on the conceptual framework of IAS, but adjusted to reflect Islamic laws and philosophies.
- Accounting for Shariah-based Banks. This standard is largely based on the Accounting, Auditing, and Governance Standards for Islamic Financial Institutions promulgated by the Accounting and Auditing Organization for Islamic Financial Institutions (based in Bahrain).

January 2001 update

The Financial Accounting Standards Board (Dewan Standar Akuntansi Keuangan) of the Indonesian Institute of Accountants (IAI) is continuing its policy of harmonizing Indonesian Financial Accounting Standards (PSAK) with IAS.

The following standards are effective for periods beginning on or after 1 January 2000 (their equivalent IAS is indicated for reference):

- PSAK 45, Financial Reporting for Non-profit Organizations
- PSAK 48, Impairment of Assets (IAS 36)
- PSAK 52, Reporting Currencies.

The following standard is effective for periods ending on or after 31 December 2000 (the equivalent IAS is indicated for reference):

- PSAK 56, Earnings per Share (1AS 33).

The following standards will be effective for periods beginning on or after 1 January 2001 (their equivalent IAS is indicated for reference):

- PSAK 19 (Revised 2000), Intangible Assets (IAS 38)
- PSAK 31 (Revised 2000), Accounting for Banking (including disclosure requirements in IAS 30)
- PSAK 46, Income Tax Accounting (IAS 12)
- PSAK 55 (Revised 1999), Accounting for Derivatives and Hedging Activities.

The following Standards will be effective for periods beginning on or after 1 January 2002 (their equivalent IAS is indicated for reference):

- PSAK 5 (Revised 2000), Segment Reporting (IAS 14)
- PSAK 58, Discontinuing Operations (IAS 35).

The Board has issued an exposure draft on Provisions, Contingent Liabilities and Contingent Assets (IAS 37) that is currently being considered for issue as Standard PSAK 57.

Another project on which the Board is expected to issue an Exposure Draft in the next twelve months is Accounting for Shariah Banking.

According to the GAAP 2001 survey by the 'Big 7' accounting firms, reviewing progress toward convergence in over 60 countries, approximately 20 countries are responding to the challenge of convergence with an active agenda and proposed changes to national requirements. Matters had improved *dramatically* by the following year. According to the GAAP Convergence 2002 survey of 59 countries, only Iceland, Saudi Arabia and Japan did not intend to converge with IFRS 2001. This survey infuriated the Japanese. Authorities there pointed to the fact that the Accounting Standards Board of Japan (of the Financial Accounting Standards Foundation) was established as an accounting standards setter of Japan. They also remarked:

[the report] does not exactly describe our stance on convergence. We regret that this report blows up relatively tiny difference between other countries and us, due to inadequate categorisation. In the recent developments of accounting standards in Japan, harmonisation with international standards has always been primary concern. For instance, we have already introduced the accounting standard for financial instruments, similar to IAS 32 and 39, the standard for pensions, similar to IAS 19, and many standards similar to international standards, for example the Business Accounting Council published the Opinion concerning Revisions of the Auditing Standards, the Opinion concerning Revisions of the Interim Auditing Standards, and the Opinion concerning Establishment of the Accounting Standard for the Impairment of Fixed Assets. Accompanied by the amendment of the Commercial Code, the

Ministerial Decree concerning Financial Statements of Joint-Stock Companies (Kabushiki-Kaisha) and some other Ministerial Decrees were integrated into the Enforcement Regulations of the Commercial Code. Auditing Standards were drastically revised: The Auditor's Consideration concerning the Going Concern Assumption was issued.

Critics of the progress of Japanese accounting standards complain that *still* on consolidation (the point at which many differences with international accounting standards are said to occur), an offshore subsidiary of a Japanese company does not need to apply consistent accounting rules or disclose information about 'immaterial' subsidiaries, which may conceal large offshore liabilities. For example, an entity's consolidated financial report may represent an arithmetical addition of its Mexican, Japanese, British and US subsidiaries' business activities that have been prepared in compliance with their respective accounting standards, resulting in meaningless consolidated numbers.

Among other Asian countries, Indonesia, Thailand and China are in the category of countries that either have a convergence policy announced, or a plan that is under development but not finalized. As to India, the President of the Institute of Chartered Accountants says that it has done some work on prescribing financial reporting standards, but that it would be a long haul before India and most of the world adopted a common financial reporting standard: 'It would be difficult to achieve uniformity in its entirety.' China is also in the process of bringing its accounting system closer to IAS, especially in the areas of business combinations and segment reporting. For example, the Supreme Court has issued an Ordinance on the procedures for shareholders suing directors and management in case of losses due to false disclosure by the company.

As noted in GAAP 2001 – A Survey of National Accounting Rules Section 3 – Country Summaries, by Andersen, BDO, Deloitte Touche Tohmatsu, Ernst & Young, Grant Thornton, KPMG and PricewaterhouseCoopers, Chinese accounting may differ from that required by IAS because of the absence of specific Chinese rules on recognition and measurement in the following areas:

- uniting of interests (IAS 22.8);
- provisions in the context of acquisitions (IAS22.31);
- employee benefit obligations (IAS 19);
- discounting of liabilities (IAS 37.45);
- the treatment of an issuer's financial instruments (IAS 32.18/23);
- the derecognition of financial assets (IAS 39.69);
- hedge accounting for derivatives (IAS39.142); and
- the treatment of the cumulative amount of deferred exchange difference on disposal of a foreign entity (IAS21.37).

136

There are no specific rules requiring disclosures of:

- a primary statement of changes in equity, exceptions for joint stock limited enterprises (IAS 1.7);
- the fair value of financial instruments (except for listed investments) (IAS 32.77);
- the fair value of investment properties (IAS 40.69);
- discontinuing operations (IAS 35);
- diluted earnings per share (IAS 33.47); and
- the current or FIFO cost of inventory when LIFO is used (IAS2.36).

There are also inconsistencies between the PRC standards and IAS. Under the PRC standards:

- certain subsidiaries with dissimilar activities can be excluded from consolidation (IAS 27.14);
- subsidiaries are excluded from consolidation if intended for sale, even if previously consolidated (IAS 27.13);
- for most business combinations accounted for using purchase accounting, the identifiable assets and liabilities of subsidiaries acquired are consolidated based on their book values (IAS 22.40);
- either provisions for major overhaul costs or deferral of incurred major overhaul costs are allowed (SIC 23);
- trading and derivative financial assets and liabilities are generally not held at fair value (IAS 39.69/93);
- proposed dividends are accrued (IAS10.11);
- deferred tax accounting is uncommon and, when done, is calculated on the basis of timing differences, with the deferral method or the liability method allowed (IAS12);
- definition of extraordinary items is wider (IAS 8.6/12);
- certain disclosures relating to primary segments (for example, acquisitions and depreciation of assets) are not required (IAS 14.57/58); and
- there are no rules addressing the consolidation of special-purpose entities (SIC 12).

In certain enterprises, other issues could lead to differences from IAS: under some circumstances, finance leases can be recognized at the undiscounted amount of minimum lease payments (IAS 17.12); and there is no specific requirement for segment reporting to be prepared (IAS 14.44).

Differences between the existing PRC standards and IAS have narrowed considerably. However, there are still some major differences in key areas such as consolidation basis, provisions and off-balance sheet treatment. On the other

137

hand, since the new national accounting standards became effective over the past two years, key areas where PRC standards and IAS have started to converge include business combinations, lease accounting, impairment of assets, pre-operating expenses, foreign currency translation, the calculation of earning per share, and segment reporting. China has accelerated improvements to its accounting standards in 2004: according to the head of the accounting department at the Ministry of Finance, the government body planned to promulgate more than 20 new accounting standards in the near future. These will cover areas such as:

- government grants and assistance
- presentation of financial statements
- earnings per share
- discontinued operations
- segment reporting
- foreign currency translation
- business combinations.

The official also claimed that with two laws and two regulations governing accounting practices now on the books, a framework aligning China's accounting and reporting practices with global standards has been established. To demonstrate China's commitment to applying the new system, the central government ordered that all 189 state-owned enterprises (SOEs) directly under the central government adopt the new accounting system by 2005, following joint stock and foreign-invested enterprises. It is expected that the new system will be applied by more than 100 such SOEs next year.

In India, the last few years have seen the Institute of Chartered Accountants of India introduce new accounting standards that have radically changed the face of corporate accounts. In 2002, for example, new accounting standards were introduced, covering areas such as impairment of assets, financial reporting of interests in joint ventures, the treatment of intangible assets, interim financial reporting, discontinuing operations, consolidated financial statements, deferred taxation and related party disclosures. Reforms have covered *inter alia* these areas:

- *Segment reporting (AS17)*: This accounting standard mandates disclosure of the revenues and profits of the different product segments of a company or the performance of the different geographical segments in which it operates. For example, a company may have two or more lines of business, and an investor would want to know how each of these businesses is performing so that he or she can judge whether the company is extracting full value from each business or whether it would be better off selling some of the businesses. Since this type of analysis is not possible from the aggregated data, segment-wise reporting is absolutely essential for the analyst. Now that segment reporting has been extended to quarterly data, investors know exactly how each business segment is performing.

■ *Accounting for deferred taxes (AS22)*: Taxes on income should ideally accrue in the same period as the revenue and expenses to which they relate. Indian analysts recognize, though, that in many cases taxable income may be significantly different from the accounting income. The main reason is that there are differences between items of revenue and expenses as appearing in the statement of profit and loss and the items which are considered as revenue, expenses or deductions for tax purposes. It is also because there are differences between the amount in respect of a particular item of revenue or expense as recognized in the statement of profit and loss and the corresponding amount which is recognized for the computation of taxable income. The net result of many allowances that companies availed of was to defer the payment of tax. AS 22 now mandates that accounts have to be adjusted for such deferral, and this has already had a significant impact on many reported profits.

■ *Consolidated financial statements (AS21)*: These statements are intended to present financial information about a parent and its subsidiaries as a single economic entity. They incorporate the financial statements of all the subsidiaries of a company to present a consolidated accounting statement, enabling an analyst or an investor to get a snapshot of the position of the entire group. In an environment where inter-group transactions are common and siphoning off of resources to group companies has been widespread, consolidation of accounts is of immense help to investors. A related standard is AS 23, 'Accounting for Investments in Associates in Consolidated Financial Statements' which sets out principles and procedures for recognizing the effects of the investments in associates on the financial position and operating results of a group.

■ *Impairment of assets (AS28)*: This comes into effect from 2004–5, and will ensure that a company's assets are carried in its books at no more than their recoverable amount. An asset is carried at more than its recoverable amount if its carrying amount exceeds the amount to be recovered through use or sale of the asset. If this is the case, the asset is described as impaired and this statement requires the enterprise to recognise an impairment loss.

■ *Intangible assets (AS26)*: This prescribes the accounting treatment for intangible assets that are not dealt with specifically in another accounting standard. This statement requires an enterprise to recognize an intangible asset if, and only if, certain criteria are met. It also specifies how to measure the carrying amount of intangible assets and requires certain disclosures about intangible assets. Besides the accounting standards, the ICAI also has guidance notes, and recent topics include how to account for stock options.

139

Indian journalists ask, will accounting standards and guidance notes prevent companies from fudging their accounts? Perhaps not, but the ICAI's Statement on Standard Auditing Practices (SAP) tries to establish standards on the auditor's responsibility to consider fraud and error in an audit of financial statements: when planning and performing audit procedures and evaluating and reporting results, auditors must consider the risk of material mis-statements in the financial statements resulting from fraud or error. Add to all this the Securities and Exchange Board of India's (SEBI) insistence on quarterly disclosures, and the substantial changes in disclosure norms made by the RBI for financial companies and banks, and it is clear that financial reporting in India Inc. has come a long way in the past decade. The SEBI committee on accounting standards has also recommended a number of new measures to improve corporate disclosures and make it difficult for companies to commit irregularities. The committee headed by Y. H. Malegam suggested among other things:

1 Companies to disclose annually the loans and advances given to the subsidiary and associate companies.
2 A limited audit of the quarterly results of companies from the first quarter of FY 2003–4 and full audit of the half-yearly results from fiscal 2003–4.
3 A risk report which should form a part of the annual report.

The committee has invited suggestions from the public on these measures.

There is still a long way to go, but with rapid harmonization of Chinese, Indian and even Indonesian accounting standards, as demonstrated, this area is not likely to remain for much longer a zone of comparative advantage for Singapore and Hong Kong in Asia as it so demonstrably has been for the past two decades or more. Moreover, the accounting gap in terms of principles is closing every year between Asia and the West. The best-governed companies in Asia now report income which is qualitatively equal, if not superior – especially in terms of long-term reliability – to that of US or European companies.

Chapter 5

Corporate governance and corporate strategy

- The link between governance and strategy
- Managing risk
- A spanner in the works
- Rewarding performance: the board
- Rewarding performance: the shareholders
- Related party transactions
- Corporations and politics
- Corporate governance and corporate social responsibility
- Conclusion

THE LINK BETWEEN GOVERNANCE AND STRATEGY

This is the most difficult part of an analysis of corporate governance, and the least discussed. What does it make companies do differently? So difficult is this relationship to disentangle, indeed, that:

> Enterprise Governance is an emerging term that CIMA and others use to describe a framework that covers both the corporate governance and the business management aspects of the organisation. Achieving a panacea of good corporate governance that is linked strategically with performance metrics should enable companies to focus all their energies on the key drivers that move their business forward. . . . Enterprise governance considers the whole picture to ensure that strategic goals are aligned and good management is achieved.'[1]

This concept of enterprise governance, however much one might suspect that the concept has been developed for the sake of it, perhaps has something to recommend it. After all, the conformance dimension of enterprise governance has had significant coverage in recent years and, in particular, in the last few years following the various corporate scandals. In contrast, the performance dimension does not lend itself as easily to a regime of standards and audit. Instead, it is desirable to develop a range of best practice tools and techniques that need to be applied intelligently to different types of organization. These tools and techniques are very much the domain of the professional accountant in business. The focus here is on helping the board to make strategic decisions and understanding its appetite for risk and its key drivers of performance. Implementation of strategy and its ongoing relevance and success must then be assessed on a regular basis.

> Management cannot run the company without any reference to corporate strategy. The CEO and the senior management team must take the initiative to formulate corporate strategy and orient the corporation towards a strategic direction. They ensure that such a strategy is realistic and solidly based on the operating realities they face on a day-to-day basis. They also try to invest on such a strategy all their prudence, imagination, and foresight to a point where they have a deep sense of ownership over it. They should in fact be fully committed to it. When it is presented to the Board of Directors, they should be forthcoming with all the information, analysis, and thinking that went into its preparation. These they share with the corporate directors liberally. They should be open to the corporate directors' advice and counsel. They may be asked questions, consider options, weigh certain perspectives they may never have thought of. In the final analysis, with the Board's guidance, a decision is reached and a resolution is adopted. This decision rests within the competence and responsibility of the Board.[2]

There are a range of tools and techniques, e.g. scorecards, continuous improvement, strategic enterprise systems, which can help boards to focus on strategic direction and its implications for all areas of the business, but these are not often dealt with as a coherent whole by the board. One of the proposals of the enterprise governance project is to address this 'oversight gap' by developing a 'strategic scorecard' for the board to ensure that good governance applies equally to the performance aspects of the business. This should be forward looking and reflect the issues that are truly critical to company success. The scorecard should embrace the strategic objectives of the enterprise, the value drivers, the milestones, the timing of intended achievements and the risks that need to be managed. Following recent scandals, e.g. Enron, Worldcom, etc., the emphasis has been on 'traditional' corporate governance issues – what we have termed the conformance dimension. However, it is also important to reject a one-sided emphasis on the structures of corporate governance, taking an integrated approach and not over-emphasising control – recent UK corporate problems such as those at Marconi have typically been strategic failures.

As Marakon Associates analysts have argued, 'overlooking management improprieties is not the only way boards have let down shareholders in recent years'.[3] They cite a number of examples, e.g. Ford, Kmart, Vivendi and Nortel, where boards have failed to steer management away from decisions that damaged long-term shareholder value. However, there are some fundamental problems with using shareholder value as the measure of board performance, which corporate governance has not yet properly addressed. The link between governance and corporate strategy, especially in Asia, remains extremely fragile. It is surprising how little public discussion of the balance between effective corporate strategy on the one hand, and investor protection on the other, actually occurs. Part of the problem with the development of corporate governance in Asia, however, is that investors are well aware of this disparity. Put bluntly, does an investor care if management is raking large sums out of the company in excess of stated remuneration, if the CEO rides roughshod over the board of directors, if the company's accounts lack precision, and if the independent directors of the company are actually mere figureheads, if the company consistently delivers good shareholder value? Putting together an argument on this score involves two strands of reasoning. The first is a free rider argument: any individual group of shareholders may not care, but shareholders as a collective group must, because unscrupulous new companies (or companies currently in trouble) may use the lack of honesty to mislead some fresh group of shareholders. Second, however, there is the distinction that must be made between the short and long term. Aman Mehta, Worldwide CEO of HSBC, argued that corporate governance is increasingly recognized as vital in securing investment flows, but he bravely and unfashionably recognized that in itself corporate governance as it current exists will not suffice:

> We need also to go to the heart of how companies set and implement their strategy . . . [in the 1990s] we saw industry sector after sector go for rapid growth. Not just the internet, not just the TMT sector, but right across the board. Maximising shareholder value was name of the game.

His first target is mergers and acquisitions:

> These high expectations of growth both encouraged and were encouraged by companies expanding through acquisition and/or moving into new business areas . . . despite the growing body of academic research that shows that at least half of all mergers actually destroy shareholder value, often catastrophically.

Yet corporate governance has absolutely nothing to say about management that takes on mergers and acquisitions activity, provided the proper procedures of

143

consultation and advice have been taken. The second issue that the HSBC chief raised was new markets. In the 1990s, he observes, foreign direct investment leapt upwards, but he cautions that:

> Building a business is a long-term process, and it is the financing partnership that is important, not any one deal. The major responsibility here lies with management. . . . Well thought through and well-executed corporate strategy should be the driver. Then the capital markets will work perfectly effectively in support.

The Marakon analysts distinguish between the internal and external aspects of corporate governance where the external dimension focuses on the board while the internal dimension focuses on the role of the CEO and executive management team and their relationship with the rest of the organization in driving value growth This view is consistent with the framework of enterprise governance. According to this line of reasoning, companies need to be successful in creating value, which is not just about ensuring that the board works well, but that the company's strategy is the right one and is implemented well. Superior performance will not arise from making the right decisions about the wrong issues, or from diligent pursuit of unprofitable aims. This is why the famous Ernst & Young study, *Measures That Matter*, dating from 1998 – admittedly pre-Enron, but not before human nature – identified corporate strategy and its execution as the number one non-financial factor determining corporate value.

Japanese firms, interestingly, are most open about the way in which corporate governance reform must be envisaged in the context of overall group strategy, and this may influence international fund managers in retaining an investment in the Japanese market. For example:

> Yamaha Motor aims to maximize the group's management performance and to enhance the Company's auditing capability to better monitor and supervise management. To this end, we have established a corporate governance system designed to promote greater transparency, soundness and objectivity in management, and are committed to taking all necessary measures to realize these governance objectives under the system. In consolidating our management structure, we have adopted a highly autonomous in-house company system and a regional headquarters system, and are honing the group's competitive edge by capitalizing on the systems' twin synergy. We intend to evolve this consolidated management structure into a still more autonomous system.[4]

Part of the problem, however, is that profit maximization is far from being a relatively straightforward index against which to measure the performance of managers. Added to this, many firms are subject to direct or indirect pressure from the state to achieve non-economic goals, such as the preservation of an industry for national security purposes or the generation of employment in key rural areas, and these may be even more difficult to detect, measure and compare to corporate governance levels. Lest it be thought that China is the only country where commentators have observed companies not pursuing value maximizing strategies, in Japan:

> We cannot ignore the fact that while there are some excellent Japanese companies such as Toyota Motor Corp. and Kao Corp., there are also numerous firms that were unable to swiftly decide to abandon unprofitable businesses. So, what sort of corporate governance is effective in ensuring that shareholders can recover their investments? The keystone of corporate governance is how management commits itself to guaranteeing to the market that investors can recover their investments. Judging from this, it can be said that providing management with incentives in the form of performance-linked compensation is the most important key to corporate governance.

MANAGING RISK

The relationship between risk management and corporate governance has not yet been explored in sufficient depth. In the US, since the case of *Ward* v. *Hunt*, a failure to carry out adequate risk management can be construed as a failing by directors warranting legal action by shareholders. In Asia this is most certainly not yet so.

A SPANNER IN THE WORKS

What about companies that have a deep-seated problem with commercial strategy in the first place? In the past three decades, China has made persistent efforts to improve the efficiency of its SOEs, including delegating SOEs more management decision-making power, contracting with managers to improve their performance, and establishing a modern enterprise system to make SOEs properly independent players in the market. A typical academic protagonist of good corporate governance like Donald Clarke argues that:

> A fundamental dilemma of Chinese [corporate governance] stems from the state policy of maintaining a full or controlling ownership interest in enterprises in several sectors. The state wants the enterprises it owns to be run efficiently, but not solely for the purpose of wealth maximization. A necessary element of state control of an enterprise is the use of that control for purposes such as the maintenance of urban employment levels, direct control over sensitive industries, or politically motivated job placement.[5]

145

This in turn, he argues, creates several problems. The first one is that many of these goals are not easily measured and there is no obvious way of balancing them one against the other. The presumption here is that a difficulty of balancing goals is an intrinsic problem, but even if it is, Western corporations also have a balancing act to follow: in countries such as Germany, for instance, shareholder value maximization is still not accepted as the sole purpose for a corporation. That there are monitoring problems arising from multiple goals, however, no one would deny. Clarke's second objection is that the policy of continued state involvement sets up a conflict of interest between the state as controlling shareholder and other shareholders. Clarke is able to cite the fact that Chinese firms without dominant state ownership have been shown in several studies to outperform firms with dominant state control – but this of course reflects the type of firms which have been released from state control. Strategic heavy industry, Stern Stewart & Co. has demonstrated, is not good at returning high shareholder value – maybe as the company suggests because it is so intensive in its use of capital.

Because the Chinese government clearly does not have a singleminded policy of value maximisation, it follows that a necessary element of state control of an enterprise must be the use of that control for purposes other than the maximization of its wealth as a shareholder – purposes such as the maintenance of urban employment levels, direct control over sensitive industries or politically motivated job placement. This in turn undoubtedly creates several problems to which it is fair for Clarke to point. First, many of these goals are not easily measured and there is no obvious way of balancing them one against the other. This creates monitoring difficulties. Second, the policy of continued state involvement sets up a conflict of interest between the state as controlling shareholder and other shareholders. In using its control for purposes other than value maximization, the state exploits minority shareholders who have no other way to benefit from their investment. (It is interesting that such criticisms were not made against, for instance, British Airways in its very profitable post-privatization monopoly years. Only when an enterprise underperforms, apparently, is a state stake criticized.) The state wants to make SOEs operate more efficiently by subjecting them to a new and different set of rules – the rules of organization under the 'modern enterprise system'.

Current policy regarding SOEs is essentially to abolish the form by corporatizing them, i.e. converting them into some form of company governed by the Company Law: (a) a CLS, the approximate equivalent of the large stock corporation in Western countries, (b) a limited liability company (LLC), intended for a much smaller and more closely knit group of investors or (c) a wholly stateowned limited liability company (WSOLLC), a special type of LLC that may be wholly owned by a state agency. This process, which does not necessarily involve privatization – it all depends, after all, on who owns the shares in the converted company – is already well underway. The corporatization policy has many purposes. They include the raising of equity capital for SOEs following conversion to the corporate form, the expansion of state control in some sectors through leverage, and the improvement of the management of state assets through the implementation of a new organizational form. A secondary consideration in passing the Company Law was also the promotion of growth in the non-state sector via the provision of a new organizational form. Some of these purposes are discussed below in more detail. A final point to note about corporate governance laws and institutions (CGLI) reforms is that despite talk of the state withdrawing from the economy, it is firmly committed to retaining control over enterprises in several sectors: national security-related industries, natural monopolies, sectors providing important goods and services to the public, and important enterprises in pillar industries and the high-technology sector. Indeed, part of enterprise reform involves a magnification of the scope of direct state control through leverage. In the traditional economic system, the state (through one or more of its agencies) was the sole owner of a SOE and exercised full control over it. Corporatization, through the institution of divisible equity shares, allows non-state investors to contribute to the enterprise, while they remain in a minority. As a former senior policymaker observed, with an equity stake of a mere 6 per cent, the state controls the 94 per cent of 'social capital' in the Guangzhou Light Industrial Group, and the enterprise is classified as 'state-controlled'. The state maintains the same level of control it had before, but now over a larger pool of assets, and in a fashion rather reminiscent of an Italian family.

It is still widely believed in China that the corporate form, through its separation of ownership (in the hands of shareholders) from control (in the hands of management), will be a cure for the ills of the SOE, which are diagnosed as stemming from the unity of ownership and control (in the hands of the state). Commentators envisage managers trying to run a business subject to constant bureaucratic interference from the government agency in charge of the enterprise and told to meet various and conflicting goals. Corporatization therefore is supposed to separate state ownership from state control, and thereby free managers from such interference so that they can pursue efficient and profitable operations. But, in the view of the corporate governance protagonists, both the diagnosis and the solution are fundamentally flawed. The solution is flawed because it assumes that the goal of the state owner in the new system is profits. The policy of corporatization does not involve a renunciation by the state of its ambition to remain the direct owner of enterprises in a number of sectors, and this ambition makes no sense if profits are the only objective. But state-owned enterprises were thus always controlled, both at the enterprise level and at the level of the administrative body in charge of them, by human beings who did not own the enterprise. Devolving more power to enterprise managers or corporatizing SOEs does little to address this problem. Moreover, policy-makers also found that they had to alter rules to take account of continuing state ownership. Additionally, the need to provide for the special circumstances of state sector enterprises ended up 'hijacking the entire Company Law', so that instead of state sector enterprises being made more efficient by being forced to follow the rules for private-sector enterprises, potential private sector enterprises had to follow rules that make sense only in a heavily state-invested economy. 'Told you so' is largely the response of supporters of corporate governance.

Since the unity of ownership and control was never really the problem in the first place, it follows that the separation of ownership from control cannot be the solution. Yet to the evident surprise of the Western commentators, much Chinese commentary continues to view the separation of ownership from control not as a regrettable concomitant of the division of labour between suppliers and managers of capital but as a positive good to be pursued for its own sake because it appears to be a necessary feature of the 'modern enterprise system'. Far from fearing the Berle and Means model of the corporation, in which shareholders are widely dispersed and unable to exercise any meaningful control, reform-minded commentators have seemed to welcome it, if not worship it. Indeed, concentrated shareholding is viewed by many as almost a perversion of the ideal of widely dispersed shareholding. Yet calls for government-owned enterprises to be independent of government 'interference' are calls for nothing short of utter non-accountability for management. Given that the assets were contributed to the enterprise by a government agency – certainly not by the managers – it seems reasonable for the agency to have some say in how the assets are used. The issue, of course, is what kind of targets the agency sets for the manager, and how it evaluates his or her performance. But that is a reason to propose changes in how the state manages its agents, not to cease managing them entirely. This is a line of reasoning which appeals to quite different state involvement in assets – in Singapore, for instance, where corporate governance is never construed as targeting the dominant or minority shareholdings in firms such as Singtel and Singapore Technologies by government fund managers such as Temasek or the Government Investment Corporation of Singapore (GIC). The Singapore government wants to have its cake and eat it when it comes to state involvement in firms, and the Chinese are only easier targets because their SOEs are visibly less efficient.

The problem of multiple objectives is certainly a real one throughout Asian corporations, not just SOEs. As a complex organization of human beings arranged into various subgroups, all with their own objectives, the state does not, and in the view of the political right cannot, produce a single, consistent set of targets for its agents to maximize. This debate is so evidently a political one that it is impossible to ignore. Moreover, control over SOEs in the traditional system was often divided among multiple agencies – one or more for labour, management, production targets, inputs, etc. – none of which had to internalize the costs of the decisions of the other. Thus, it was difficult for anyone, had they been so inclined, to make and enforce a trade-off among competing objectives. Even where there is a single monitoring body, like the CSRC or the MAS, that body may itself have several objectives: for example MAS is both the central bank and the economic and financial regulator. The regulator may not even know itself how the costs and benefits of achieving different state objectives should be measured and traded off against each other, and thus can hardly be an effective monitor of managers charged with achieving those objectives.

The policy of 'corporatization' is explicitly intended to solve the problem of multiple controllers with multiple objectives. First, the interests of the various state agencies involved in the enterprises are reduced to a common denominator – equity – and quantified. Second, the new shareholders have only a single way in which to voice their interests – shareholder voting – in which the majority rules, thus eliminating conflicting goals. Third, despite their conflicting interests, the new shareholders now also have a common interest: distributable profits. Thus, diversification of the shareholder base, even where share ownership is not private, is intended to result in a stronger focus on the single target of profitability. The theory has much to commend it. In practice, however, a large number of corporatized Chinese SOEs remain dominated by a single state shareholder that exercises its control either through formal channels, such as shareholder voting, or through traditional channels, such as the acknowledged authority of the Communist Party's organizational department over personnel appointments in key state-owned and state-controlled enterprises, whether or not corporatized and listed on the stock market. Singapore is a lot more subtle, but the same structural relationships are taken for granted at the national level. Not only that, but they meet with political approval at the grassroots,[6] just as they do in Continental Europe, however uncomfortable this might be to US academics.

Many Western analysts of the monitoring problem in the state sector point to the absence of an ultimate principal as a key problem. According to this analysis, an agent of the state monitors the enterprise managers, and another agent must monitor the monitor, but no matter how far up the chain of monitors we go, we never run into an ultimate principal – or to be more accurate, the ultimate theoretical principal in the case of state ownership, the citizenry of China, is far too dispersed and powerless to play any real role. As a result, effective monitoring cannot take place because there is nobody in the chain of monitors with the appropriate incentives; nobody who is entitled to the increase in asset value that effective monitoring would bring about. Corporatization is intended to replace a pliant and negligent state owner with profit-seeking shareholders that will monitor management more effectively. But was state ownership per se ever the problem? Certainly, the current structure can be blamed for many problems. Even if the state as principal had mutually consistent and easily measurable goals, its agents – the monitors of the enterprise managers – might not monitor well for those goals. Actual supervision and monitoring is carried out by local

149

officials who are appointed and salaried by local government. Even if those officials perfectly represented the interests of their principal, local government's interests can often conflict with those of the centre. And in practice, of course, the effectiveness of local officials' monitoring is compromised both by their incentives to shirk and in many cases by their simple lack of skills to understand which actions would increase or decrease enterprise value.

Yet while the lack of an ultimate human owner can be a source of considerable agency costs, these costs need not be crippling. There are many successfully functioning institutions such as charities and parastatals that do not rely on having individual or group owners watching for free cash flow, and even among those who do, many are so remote – governments and pension funds, for example – that they function successfully with an ultimate human 'owner' so distant as to be absent for all practical purposes. Thus, although the absence of an ultimate owner – i.e. a human being with both control over the agent below him or her and a right to the residual – is an obstacle to efficient monitoring, it is not an insuperable one or even perhaps the greatest one. It is hard, therefore, to see why state employees should be inherently incapable of monitoring effectively, given the right targets, skills and incentives. The problem with state monitoring is far more likely to be found in the lack of these elements, not in the lack of an ultimate human principal. But the truth of Clarke's point that 'Whatever the importance of a human monitor at the top of the chain, corporatization as currently practiced will not bring it about' must be admitted. When SOEs are corporatized and share interests allocated or sold, the new shareholders are, for the most part, either state agencies or other entities that are owned, directly or indirectly, by the state. This is true whether or not such companies are listed on China's stock markets. Such entities may well be structured with the intention that they be profit-seeking, but if they are in fact able to pursue profits effectively, that would only show that private ownership was not necessary in the first place. No amount of restructuring can eliminate the cost of the absent principal if state ownership is retained, since the latter necessarily entails the former. Despite the reformist ambition animating the corporatization project, state sector considerations remain strong. As the owner of state sector firms, the state may reasonably stipulate how they should be run. But it is not necessary to stipulate at the same time the fine details of how non-state parties should associate.

REWARDING PERFORMANCE: THE BOARD

SEC Chairman William Donaldson once called on corporate boards to rein in pay and perks for CEOs, saying that 'In some cases, the CEO has become more of a monarch than a manager' – which of course meant that to remove him usually meant a coup d'état rather than a sacking. Donaldson once told a group of business leaders that investor anger has been made worse 'by the perception and, in many cases, unfortunately, the reality that those at the top have not shared their loss – that those at the top have continued to enjoy massive salaries, bonuses and perks unrelated to performance'. Donaldson did not propose any specific reforms. Instead, he told companies and directors that there was no one-size fits all reform.[7]

A rash of corporate accounting abuses that began with the Enron collapse has generated multiple efforts to improve corporate governance, financial disclosure, executive compensation practices (especially the granting, valuation, and expensing of stock options), and shareholder rights. Aligning pay with performance has become a mantra of corporate governance. These 'abuses' of executive pay were brought to light partly by the slowing global economy and partly by the way that 'excessive' executive compensation was tied to company stock prices in the form of stock options. Calpers now aims to use the pension systems of companies in which it invests to spur broad-based compensation plans that go way beyond top executive officers. 'Broad-based equity compensation plans create enduring value for the corporations that adopt them', Calpers investment chief Angelides has said. He has a plan under which Calpers and Calstrs would only invest in companies that grant less than 5 per cent of their total equity compensation to the top five executives and give less than 25 per cent of shares awarded as pay to executives and directors of the company. The guidelines would also call on companies to provide a vesting schedule for stock options of at least four years. Certainly, as Ernst & Young identified as early as 1998 in the *Measures That Matter* paper, dizzyingly narrow Gini coefficients of pay make for unhealthy companies with envious employees and an impoverished corporate culture. In that sense, the Calpers strategy makes sense for purely selfish investment reasons. Abuses in stock option granting practices, coupled with the likelihood that the Financial Accounting Standards Board will require companies to expense their stock options, have subsequently led to a decline in the use of stock options and renewed interest in and granting of restricted stock. Once stock options lose their preferred status as a low-cost incentive (when the bargain element in the stock option exercise becomes a charge to earnings), performance-based long-term incentives will garner renewed interest and use. According to Aon Consulting in the US,[8] the use of stock options actually decreased in 2003, reversing a long-standing trend.

Heightened awareness of executive compensation will lead boards of directors and, in particular, their compensation committees, to more carefully scrutinize the intended effects and actual results of their company executive compensation. MAS believes that:

> there should be a formal assessment of the effectiveness of the Board as a whole and the contribution by each director to the effectiveness of the Board. The performance of the Board would be measured by the extent to which the

Institution's objectives have been met. An assessment of the Board's performance should include both the performance of the entire Board and also the role and involvement of individual Board members. Remuneration practices should provide incentives that will act in the best long-term interests of the Institution, and aid in managing risk prudently as well as achieving other business objectives, without compromising the ongoing viability, solvency and reputation of the Institution.

Guidance Notes

5.1   The Board should develop objective performance criteria. Such performance criteria should address how the Board has enhanced the value of the Institution, taking into account depositors' or policyholders' interests. The performance criteria should also include the use of other qualitative measures such as the setting of strategic directions and achievement of strategic objectives, quality of risk management and adequacy of internal controls. These performance criteria should not be changed from year to year, and where circumstances deem it necessary for any of the criteria to be changed, the onus should be on the Board to justify this decision.

5.2   The Board should implement a process for assessing regularly, the effectiveness of the Board as a whole and for assessing the contribution by each individual director to the effectiveness of the Board. There should be in place an enforceable mechanism to replace ineffective directors.

Asian codes of corporate governance are agreed in recognizing that the level and composition of remuneration should be appropriate to attract, retain and motivate the directors to run the company successfully. The component parts of remuneration should be structured so as to link rewards to corporate and individual performance, in the case of executive directors. In the case of non-executive directors, the level of remuneration should reflect the experience and level of responsibilities undertaken by the particular non-executive concerned. In Western countries, attitudes to remuneration for board members are changing to bring them in line much more with shareholder value and other goal-based criteria. For example, UK plastics and flooring manufacturer Low & Bonar has attempted to tackle the problem of 'golden farewells' for departing executives by adopting a new remuneration package that will reduce the notice period of executives who consistently fail to meet performance targets. The Association of British Insurers, who favour a non-statutory approach to curbing excessive executive payouts, said: 'It shows that companies can use their imagination to produce innovative solutions to this problem.' The Honda company says that:

> With regard to the directors, the term of their office is limited to one year and the amount of remuneration payable to them is determined according to

a standard that reflects their contributions to the Company. The goal is to heighten maneuverability so as to cope with any changes in the management environment.

How ought such long-term compensation to work? A proper corporate governance perspective requires examination of total compensation level and the mix of compensation, compared to industry peers, before any conclusions are made about the appropriateness of the compensation of a particular executive. One other thing that fund managers like to see in companies introducing performance share plans is that they do not just tag these performance shares onto the existing compensation packages. Rather, the potential value of the shares that the CEO may get should be explicitly taken into account in calculating total compensation. For example, if a CEO received $1 million last year in total compensation, inclusive of incentive pay, the performance shares he is entitled to this year should not be treated just as incremental compensation to this $1 million. His other components of compensation may have to be adjusted downwards to reflect this new compensation component, although it may not be an exact adjustment if he is giving up fairly certain compensation in exchange for risky performance-based compensation.

When evaluating the adoption of performance share plans by companies, therefore, supporters of corporate governance argue that investors should expect to see these kinds of features:

- Benchmarks that articulate well with shareholder value creation. Performance share plans should include some form of shareholder return target.
- Performance targets that are sufficiently challenging, requiring a minimum level of performance and providing for increasing awards for increasing levels of performance.
- Performance share awards that provide long-term incentives, rather than reward primarily short-term performance.

Mak Yuen Teen of the National University of Singapore argues that:

Just as many Singapore companies jumped onto the stock option bandwagon when stock options were in vogue, without thinking carefully through its design and implementation, there is a risk that the same thing will happen for performance shares. Investors should look carefully at what is meant by 'performance', when companies introduce performance share plans. Performance share schemes, if not properly designed and implemented, may not achieve their objectives and may result in the over-compensation of senior

153

executives (like some stock option plans have done). That would not be good for corporate governance in Singapore.[9]

The problem, as Professor Mak rightly says, is what is actually meant by performance. There is no one single measure. There are serious inherent dangers in using almost any kind of shareholder value criterion: no one is prepared to argue seriously for the one that would really be in shareholders' interests, something like a discounted cash flow based long-term shareholder value remuneration system with each board director effectively holding payments as loans until a final reckoning at some distant point in the future, with full recovery in the hands of the company in the event of premature death or retirement. That would *really* focus directors on the long-term interests of the company, and if it were generous enough and sufficiently widely adopted, it would not act as a disincentive. In the absence of any proper alignment, Mak calls for something which will be stringent enough to convince shareholders that the recipients deserve the rewards. Performance shares are the preferred method of the moment, replacing share options now these must be expensed. Relative performance evaluation, as Mak argues, has the advantage of filtering out industry effects and helps to isolate the extent to which good or poor performance is attributable to the company, rather than the industry, but shareholders need to be extremely careful in determining the plausibility of the index to which the individual company is being compared.

REWARDING PERFORMANCE: THE SHAREHOLDERS

Common shares of the same class carry a right to pro rata portion of dividends. Asian jurisdictions differ as to whether dividends may only be paid out of net profits of the company. They also differ on whether there are regulations governing the timely payment of dividends. Singapore, Taiwan and Vietnam do not have regulations on this score, although the former two countries most definitely do not need them as investors would vote with their feet if they felt slighted in respect of dividends, to which the local investment communities have always been very sensitive. In other jurisdictions, investors are entitled to appropriate dividends, however defined, within a month or so of the declaration of financial results by the company. This is another example where China is in advance of Hong Kong so far as governance is concerned – or at least arguably. Hong Kong follows the traditional model and leaves it up to the company; China mandates a two month maximum period.

RELATED PARTY TRANSACTIONS

This topic falls in the borderline between conventional corporate governance issues and enterprise governance. It may be tempting to take commercial advantage of the opportunity presented by a related party transaction, but according to the strict standards of corporate governance this opportunity should always be rejected by a listed company. For a private company, however, the matter remains murky. Although legal regimes in Asia typically provide rules for the approval of extraordinary transactions, in some cases, insider shareholders (and those allied to them) are not disqualified from voting to approve transactions where they have an interest on both sides. For example, as David Webb points out, the Hong Kong Listing Rules include trustees of trusts in the definition of connected persons, but they do not explicitly include any company controlled by the trustee. Webb cites the example that a director of the Hong Kong Exchange is a beneficiary of a trust which has majority control of a property company which has granted a lease to a subsidiary of the Exchange. Although the trustee is an 'associate' of the director and hence a connected person, the company the trustee controls is not a connected person. So the property company is free to deal with the Exchange and the transactions are not deemed to be connected transactions. To close the Listing Rule loophole, the definition of 'associate' should be changed to include companies controlled (30 per cent or more) by the trustees of any trust of which the director, substantial shareholder or his family is a beneficiary. A further detail that in his view needs amending is that, since beneficiaries of trusts can also be non-individuals, the rule should apply to all substantial shareholders (including companies and other entities), not just those who are human beings.

CORPORATIONS AND POLITICS

BP, the UK's biggest company, has ceased making political donations worldwide as criticism mounts about corporate influence on government policy. The world's third-largest private sector oil group donated $840,000 (£600,000) in the US in 2002, and its close relations with the British government – with key executives moving between the two – have left it dubbed 'Blair Petroleum', although it has made no political donations in Britain for a decade. Lord Browne, BP's Chief Executive, told a meeting of the Royal Institute of International Affairs at Chatham House in London that large multinationals must tread warily from now on.

> We must be particularly careful about the political process because the legitimacy of that process is crucial both for society and for us, a company working in that society. That is why we've decided, as a global policy, that from now on we will make no political contributions from corporate funds anywhere in the world. We'll engage in the policy debate, stating our views and encouraging the development of ideas, but we won't fund any political activity or any political party.

155

We hear very little about political donations from companies in Asia: as yet, the matter is hardly relevant in China; in other jurisdictions there is already state funding of political parties. In Korea, however, the matter has already become a live one, but the boot is on the other foot: 'in February 2002 . . . the Federation of Korean Industry (FKI) announced that its members would no longer comply with 'unjustified demands' for political funds.'

CORPORATE GOVERNANCE AND CORPORATE SOCIAL RESPONSIBILITY

Criticism of shareholder value leads naturally to a discussion of corporate social responsibility (CSR) and its relationship with corporate governance in Asia. According to Corporate Social Responsibility consultants MHCi[10] in 2001

> there is increasing advocacy of a broader and more inclusive concept of corporate governance that extends to corporate responsibility and has a wider concept of 'stakeholder' than that used by the OECD. These ideas are reflected in the King Report for South Africa, the Commonwealth principles of business practice, the UK's Tomorrow's Company etc.

If high corporate governance standards are necessary to penetrate global, especially Western, markets there must be a strong argument to the effect that they will not work alone. Coca-Cola, for example, may not have considered the international media attention when its bottling plant in Kerala, India, was alleged to have caused drought for local farmers by siphoning off important sources of groundwater. Examples like this show that virtually every decision to create value for shareholders has positive or negative consequences for other stakeholders like employees, communities, customers, people on a mission and the public at large. Closing a large manufacturing plant in a small community might improve manufacturing efficiency and create shareholder value, but it would also create a lot of pain for the people who lose their jobs and for the communities in which they live. A major investment in new manufacturing capacity, however, might add value for shareholders, create new jobs and bring additional revenue into the community's economy. It is virtually impossible today to create shareholder value without creating consequences, good or bad, for other stakeholders. So managers today must increasingly address other stakeholders' concerns, through both their actions and the information they provide on the consequences of those actions.

In Asia, studies have shown that both consumers and companies value price, quality and brand name as the top factors for purchasing decisions. But companies still fail to perceive social issues as an important factor that is valued at the top by a significant portion of the consumers (55.7 per cent consumers ranked social issues in top three). This fact suggests that companies need to improve their

156

understanding of the consumer's expectations to gain the competitive advantages. This fact is also felt in the marketing companies too:

> Marketers may not feel motivated to change until more Asians demand greenness with their purchasing power. For a decade or more Asian marketing experts have pointed out that those who wish to capture some of the North American, European or Austrian markets need to be better prepared to make their products meet the standards now being demanded by consumers there.[11]

Another study using the Hong Kong retail industry obtained similar results.

Many private investors are now seeking guidance through organizations such as the Association for Sustainable and Responsible Investment in Asia (ASrIA), and its international counterparts, in order to make informed decisions about socially responsible investment (SRI) (Loh, 2001). Within the SRI framework, companies are measured according to their adherence to the triple bottom line principle, i.e. taking into account social and environmental considerations in addition to the standard financial criteria:

> Business leaders don't have to wait, indeed increasingly they can't afford to wait, for governments to pass and enforce legislation before they pursue good practices in support of international human rights, labour and environmental standards within their own operations and in the societies of which they are part. The public increasingly expects corporations to act in a socially responsible way. . . . With globalisation has come the growing sense that we're all responsible in some way for helping promote and protect the rights of our neighbours, whether they live on the next street or on the next continent.

> (Mary Robinson, former Irish President
> and UN Human Rights Commissioner, May 2002)

So what about specific corporate practices? Take predatory lending, for instance. Predatory lending is the widespread, booming practice of targeting poor communities for loans that are designed to strip their wealth and home equity. It frequently victimizes the elderly and minorities, and is affiliated with many major banks' holdings. Ban it? Regulate it?

The benefits that the corporation receives from society imply certain responsibilities, including key elements of corporate governance, such as transparency, the sanctity of contracts and respect for the institutions of the society as a whole. Good corporate citizens recognize that fundamental workers' rights are human rights and must be respected, and are values which should be shared by employers and employees alike. These rights include freedom of association, the right to bargain collectively, prohibition of forced and child labour and discrimination, provision of a safe and healthy workplace, the payment of a living wage and job security. Consequently, companies should extend their responsibility beyond their shareholders and be liable to civil society as a whole. The broadening of the perception of social needs by companies, in terms of extending their liabilities beyond the needs of stakeholders, can become an important asset for the company. It can build new unique competencies distinctive from its competitors' and can yield good reputation and credibility. There is much evidence of this from Western markets, e.g. from the high correlations between the Dow Jones Sustainability Index and the Dow Jones market index. A criticism, to be fair, of the 'evidence' provided by this correlation is that the missing 'X' factor, 'the well-governed company' factor, causes both the good shareholder value performance and the high scores on sustainability, corporate governance and corporate social responsibility. Both CLSA and the ACGA agree that nothing can compare with the highest standards of transparency and accountability. Quality of management and boards is the key that ties in companies with good corporate governance together with higher financial ratios and relatively better shareholder value performance than low CSR companies. *Good companies in the West tend to be good all-round, and Asia is already going the same way.*

Critics suggest that in fact the greatest obstacle to good corporate citizenship is the behaviour of the retailers and merchandisers of Europe and North America, aided and abetted by suppliers and subsidiaries in Asia and elsewhere in the world. But, the excesses of exploitation have forced many to accept the idea that enterprises have obligations to workers who are not their direct employees. The often blatant disregard of these rights has been tragic for workers, we should not forget. In Pakistan it is estimated that 20 million children work. Half of those in bonded labour die by the age of 12. In the Dominican Republic and in Central America workers are beaten up and suffer death threats for trying to organize trade unions to defend their rights.

Evidence of the emergence of shared workplace values is fortunately also appearing in the corporate codes of conduct arena where multi-stakeholder efforts such as the Ethical Trading Initiative and SA8000 are gathering ground. Unilaterally producing and trumpeting a code of conduct was the first corporate response to consumer concerns at abuses, including child labour. Most such codes were totally inadequate in content, were rarely implemented and in any case had little or no follow-up procedures. In reality they were mere public relations exercises and some have rightly described them as 'fig leaves for exploitation', which raises interesting questions about how the corporate governance of these companies works and how audit trails for the approval of such abuses can be detected, right up to board level. Continuing trade union and NGO pressure forced some companies to rethink their approach to workplace values; so were born multi-stakeholder codes of conduct. A good example is SA8000 managed by Social Accountability International. Global corporations, trade unions, NGOs, academics and inter-governmental representatives together produced a standard firmly anchored in the International Labour Organization (ILO) Conventions. They developed a set of procedures to make these values come alive with detailed management systems for their implementation and monitoring. Today, companies adopt SA8000 and make it a contractual obligation that their suppliers comply with the code. They put in place detailed management systems for implementing and monitoring the operation of SA8000. An independent verification results in full workplace audits every three years with surveillance audits at six-monthly intervals. The aim is to secure a continuous improvement in workplace conditions. Significant workplace changes are beginning to result from the implementation of SA8000. One plant recently certified in India after vigorous efforts to meet the standard has seen major improvements in wages and working conditions. The company recognizes that the cost of compliance is high but feels that it will be repaid in improved productivity and quality of production. The real contributions of codes such as SA8000 is their vindication of what trade unions have been saying all along – not only about the importance of labour law and employment relationships but about the need for international treaties to force multinational companies to have and apply labour policies on an international basis. We know that corporations will only adopt standards if it is in their commercial interest to do so, or if they are regulated to make it compulsory.

Greenpeace is promoting the Bhopal Principles to address concerns about corporate accountability across a wide range of issues:

1 *Implement Rio Principle 13.* States must as a matter of priority enter into negotiations for a legal international instrument, and adopt national laws to operationalize and implement Principle 13 of the Rio Declaration, to address liability and compensation for the victims of pollution and other environmental damage.

2 *Extend Corporate Liability.* Corporations must be held strictly liable without requirement of fault for any and all damage arising from any of their activities that cause environmental or property damage or personal injury, including site remediation. Parent companies as well as subsidiaries and affiliated local corporations must be held liable for compensation and restitution. Corporations must bear cradle-to-grave responsibility for manufactured products. States must implement individual liability for directors and officers for actions or omissions of the corporation, including for those of subsidiaries.

3 *Ensure Corporate Liability for Damage beyond National Jurisdictions.* States must ensure that corporations are liable for injury to persons and damage to property, biological diversity and the environment beyond the limits of national jurisdiction, and to the global commons such as atmosphere and oceans. Liability must include responsibility for environmental cleanup and restoration.

159

4 Protect Human Rights. Economic activity must not infringe upon basic human and social rights. States have the responsibility to safeguard the basic human and social rights of citizens, in particular the right to life; the right to safe and healthy working conditions; the right to a safe and healthy environment; the right to medical treatment and to compensation for injury and damage; the right to information and the right of access to justice by individuals and by groups promoting these rights. Corporations must respect and uphold these rights. States must ensure effective compliance by all corporations of these rights and provide for legal implementation and enforcement.

5 Provide for Public Participation and the Right to Know. States must require companies routinely to disclose to the public all information concerning releases to the environment from their respective facilities as well as product composition. Commercial confidentiality must not outweigh the interest of the public to know the dangers and liabilities associated with corporate outputs, whether in the form of pollution by-products or the product itself. Once a product enters the public domain there should be no restrictions on public access to information relevant to the environment and health on the basis of commercial secrecy. Corporate responsibility and accountability must be promoted through environmental management accounting and environmental reporting which gives a clear, comprehensive and public report of environmental and social impacts of corporate activities.

6 Adhere to the Highest Standards. States must ensure that corporations adhere to the highest standards for protecting basic human and social rights including health and the environment. Consistent with Rio Declaration Principle 14, States must not permit multinational corporations to deliberately apply lower standards of operation and safety in places where health and environmental protection regimes, or their implementation, are weaker.

7 Avoid Excessive Corporate Influence over Governance. States must cooperate to combat bribery in all its forms, promote transparent political financing mechanisms and eliminate corporate influence on public policy through election campaign contributions, and/or non-transparent corporate-led lobby practices.

8 Protect Food Sovereignty over Corporations. States must ensure that individual States and their people maintain sovereignty over their own food supply, including through laws and measures to prevent genetic pollution of agricultural biological diversity by genetically engineered organisms and to prevent the patenting of genetic resources by corporations.

9 Implement the Precautionary Principle and Require Environmental Impact Assessments. States must fully implement the Precautionary Principle in national and international law. Accordingly, States must require corporations to take preventative action before environmental damage or heath effects are incurred, when there is a threat of serious or irreversible harm to the environment or health from an activity, a practice or a product. The existence of scientific debate or uncertainty must not deter the adoption of safer alternatives where they are known to be available. Governments must require companies to undertake environmental impact assessments with public participation for activities that may cause significant adverse environmental impacts.

10 Promote Clean and Sustainable Development. States must promote clean and sustainable development, and must establish national legislation to phase out the use, discharge and emission of hazardous substances and greenhouse gases, and other sources of pollution, to use their resources in a sustainable manner, and to conserve their biological diversity.

There are still exceptions, even in the West, but they are becoming fewer and more far between. By contrast, Professor Michael Hopkins of Middlesex University believes that Asia still has a long way to go in implementing CSR:

> The term corporate social responsibility has swept Europe like a storm in the past few years. Links with corporate governance are also just beginning to appear. In Asia, I have seen that corporate social responsibility has appeared in most countries of the region but few companies, if any, have gone much further than reviewing their philanthropic responsibilities. The reputation of Asian companies for good levels of corporate governance is, again, confined to only a few companies and countries. For instance, only a few firms in Hong Kong, Singapore, India, the Philippines, Malaysia appear to take CSR and corporate governance seriously. Others, particularly in poorer countries such as Pakistan, Sri Lanka, Iran are still in the grip of robber-barons. While in the giant, China, CSR has only just appeared on the radar screen and then mainly from western prompting.

Aman Mehta, CEO of HSBC, agrees:

> In Asia, for example, balancing the need for development with the need for protecting the region's environment will be challenging, but worthwhile. And trying to rapidly match Western ideals of being environmentally correct will be impossible and, most likely, fruitless.[12]

CONCLUSION

As has been pointed out, in Asia we still do not know 'how ownership structures influence not only firm performance and valuation, but also other corporate

161

policies such as investment patterns and financing structures'.[13] Reading only corporate governance and CSR literature one would be surprised to discover that Japan's GDP per capita was so high or that China attracted such an enormous proportion of world FDI in recent years. Corporate governance research has wandered a long way from an integrated approach to delivering long-term shareholder value and making a contribution to the national and global economy and welfare.

Economic Performance
Corporate Governance and Finance

After reporting corporate deficits in FY'01 for the first time since our foundation, we at Matsushita have made drastic reforms in our management structure, with a firm determination to attain a V-shaped performance recovery. In January 2003, the motto "Today we re-declare our founding" was announced at the Annual Management Policy Meeting. Our management structure is undergoing a significant transformation from a "heavy and slow" company to a "lean and agile" Matsushita.

Management System

In FY'03, with the view of establishing autonomous management at each business domain of Matsushita, a reform took place expediting optimum management operation under the Group-wide management system.

■ Framework of Management Reform
1. Matsushita has implemented an "Executive Officer System" tailored to the domain-based management in order to integrate the comprehensive strength of all Group companies. Moreover, a "Group Managing Directors & Officers Meeting" has been introduced as an organization for consulting on corporate strategy issues.
2. With the aim of establishing corporate governance best suited to the diversified scope of its business fields, Matsushita will further strengthen its corporate auditor system by having management personnel, who are well-versed in day-to-day operations at operational fronts, participate in decision-

making on corporate strategies and mutual supervisory functions.
3. The remuneration system for Members of the Board of Directors and Executive Officers has been revised. The new system based on the same criteria, specifically CCM and cash flows, is intended to accomplish the goal of increasing corporate value in the interest of shareholders.

● Reform of the Board of Directors
By delegating authority to Executive Officers, the Board of Directors will concentrate its functions on corporate strategies and supervision, thereby clarifying the supervisory functions of the Board of Directors and the business executive functions of the Executive Officers. As participation of those at the operational fronts in the Board of Directors is necessary, supervisory functions and executive functions will not be completely isolated. Also, the Board of Directors itself will be reduced in number to promote swift decision-making.

● Executive Officer System
The Board of Directors will elect and appoint Executive Officers who are to assume responsibility for the execution of business throughout the entire Matsushita Electric Group. Members of the Board of Directors and Executive Officers are equal, in terms of rank and status, and their business results are evaluated based on the same criteria and are accordingly reflected in their compensation.

● Advisory Board
Since FY'98, an Advisory Board consisting of three selectees from outside the company and Matsushita's top management has been established for achieving management that is open to society.

■ Overview of the Advisory Board
Members: Three advisors from outside the company, Members of the Board of Matsushita
Meetings: Three times a year
Themes in the Past:
  "Issues for Matsushita as Viewed from Outside the Company"
  "New Business Strategies in a Network Society"
  "Efforts toward the Sustainable Society"

Mid-Term Management Plan "Value Creation 21"

In FY'01, with "deconstruction" and "creation" as keywords, Matsushita launched its "Value Creation 21" plan. This plan entails transformation of the company's business and profit structures from a 20th century-type business model characterized by mass production and mass sales of standard products into a "Super Manufacturing Company" for the 21st century. The plan also aims at constructing new business models that bring about synergy effects among devices, sets, and service businesses.
In FY'02, the management focus shifted to "creation." The management system reform took place to restructure businesses and organizations, and to enhance its effectiveness. By realigning Group companies into 14 business domains, overlapping of businesses was eliminated and the concentration of development resources became possible. In addition, at each domain company, autonomous management has been promoted with emphasis on consolidated cash flows on a global basis. Evaluation of each domain company was narrowed down to two standards, capital cost management (CCM) and cash flows (CF), to create a system that enables the Head Office to carry out fair and sound evaluation and follow-up. Through a system of complete empowerment and capital governance, we are aiming at accomplishment of the "Value Creation 21" plan in FY'03.

Corporate Outline and Financial Information
matsushita.co.jp/ir/en/

■ Matsushita Electric Group Management System

Financial Information

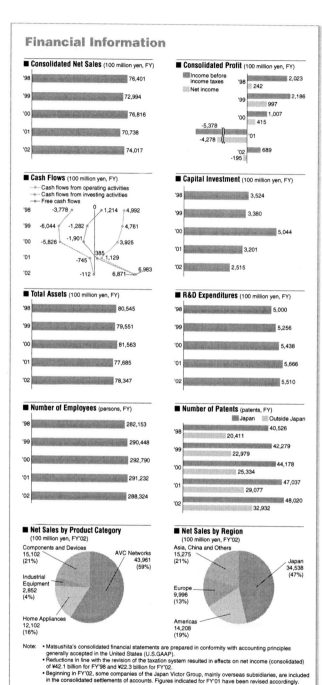

■ Consolidated Net Sales (100 million yen, FY)

'98	76,401
'99	72,994
'00	76,816
'01	70,738
'02	74,017

■ Cash Flows (100 million yen, FY)

--○-- Cash flows from operating activities
--●-- Cash flows from investing activities
--●-- Free cash flows

'98	-3,778	0	1,214	4,992
'99	-6,044	-1,282		4,761
'00	-5,826	-1,901		3,925
'01	-745	385	1,129	
'02	-112		6,871	6,983

■ Total Assets (100 million yen, FY)

'98	80,545
'99	79,551
'00	81,563
'01	77,685
'02	78,347

■ Number of Employees (persons, FY)

'98	282,153
'99	290,448
'00	292,790
'01	291,232
'02	288,324

■ Net Sales by Product Category
(100 million yen, FY'02)

Components and Devices 15,102 (21%)
AVC Networks 43,961 (59%)
Industrial Equipment 2,852 (4%)
Home Appliances 12,102 (16%)

■ Consolidated Profit (100 million yen, FY)

■ Income before income taxes
▨ Net income

'98	2,023 / 242
'99	2,186 / 997
'00	1,007 / 415
'01	-5,378 / -4,278
'02	689 / -195

■ Capital Investment (100 million yen, FY)

'98	3,524
'99	3,380
'00	5,044
'01	3,201
'02	2,515

■ R&D Expenditures (100 million yen, FY)

'98	5,000
'99	5,256
'00	5,438
'01	5,666
'02	5,510

■ Number of Patents (patents, FY)

▨ Japan ▢ Outside Japan

'98	40,526 / 20,411
'99	42,279 / 22,979
'00	44,178 / 25,334
'01	47,037 / 29,077
'02	48,020 / 32,932

■ Net Sales by Region
(100 million yen, FY'02)

Asia, China and Others 15,275 (21%)
Japan 34,538 (47%)
Europe 9,996 (13%)
Americas 14,208 (19%)

Note: • Matsushita's consolidated financial statements are prepared in conformity with accounting principles generally accepted in the United States (U.S.GAAP).
• Reductions in line with the revision of the taxation system resulted in effects on net income (consolidated) of ¥42.1 billion for FY'98 and ¥22.3 billion for FY'02.
• Beginning in FY'02, some companies of the Japan Victor Group, mainly overseas subsidiaries, are included in the consolidated settlements of accounts. Figures indicated for FY'01 have been revised accordingly.

Global Risk Management

Along with business globalization, the importance of risk management is increasing throughout the world. In November 2002, the Overseas Risk Management System was established to respond 24 hours full time globally. With "Human Safety" and "Company's Credibility" built on the fundamental principles of our Management Philosophy of "Customer-Comes-First," we are committed to responding promptly as expected by the society and customers. In concrete terms, "Risk Management" is incorporated into business plans and undertaken by top executives in the daily business activities.

TOPICS

Socially Responsible Investment (SRI)

In recent years, the concept of Socially Responsible Investment (i.e. investment taking into consideration social aspects such as environmental issues and human rights, in addition to corporate financial aspects) is rapidly spreading mainly in Europe and the U.S. For two consecutive years in FY'01 and FY'02, Matsushita was selected for inclusion in FTSE4Good, the socially responsible investment index created by the British FTSE Group. Also in Japan, we were ranked the top name (as of October 2002) in the "SRI Social Contribution Fund – Wing for Tomorrow" of the Asahi Life Asset Management Co., Ltd.

Chapter 6

Corporate transparency

- Why disclose?
- But disclose *what*?
- Conclusion

WHY DISCLOSE?

The pressure to improve transparency is spearheaded by the Singapore government. It reckons that transparency – in how the stock market works and in the way listed companies communicate with their investors – is a vital ingredient for an active and successful stock market, and especially one that hopes to assume the mantle of being a regional exchange.

Disclose, disclose, disclose. That was the resounding message for Asian business by Linda Tsao Yang, Acting Chairman, Asian Corporate Governance Association, Hong Kong SAR. Companies that adopt honest disclosure 'will gain the confidence of investors and get access to capital without paying high-risk premiums', she said. Pronouncements like this could be cited ad infinitum.

BUT DISCLOSE *WHAT*?

It is surely a fundamental point about commercial advantage that companies need to retain commercial confidentiality and secrecy about areas such as the following:

- research and development under way, including successes and failures;
- planned product introduction;
- dates, type of media, geographic location and expenditure on marketing initiatives;
- format and content of advertising material;
- hiring policies;

- planning for M&A;
- intentions to raise capital through equity or bond markets or through private equity.

Every jurisdiction permits companies commercial confidentiality over these areas.

It is not, however, so clear what aspects of corporate strategy good corporate governance mandates ought to be disclosed. Best corporate governance practice, however, would suggest disclosure of some or all of the following:

Accounting policies. In September 2002, the CSRC issued a regulation regarding the acquisition of a significant holding in a listed company. Annual reports of the majority of Asian listed companies now specify their accounting policies and in particular all divergences from 'full IAS'.

By contrast, the SEC requires disclosure in proxy statements and annual reports of the use of any exemption to Rule 10A-3 (an issuer availing itself of an exemption must disclose its reliance on such exemption and its assessment of whether, and if so how, such reliance will materially adversely affect the ability of the audit committee to act independently and to satisfy the other requirements of the rule), and the identification of the audit committee in proxy statements and annual reports; for issuers that have not separately designated an audit committee, the rule requires the issuer to disclose that its entire board of directors is acting as the audit committee. The SEC also requires corresponding updates to the audit committee independence disclosure in proxy statements. Related to the recent adoption of disclosure requirements for 'audit committee financial experts' of foreign private issuers, the SEC is requiring that a foreign private issuer disclose whether its audit committee financial expert (if it has one) is independent, as that term is defined in the SRO listing standards applicable to the issuer. For foreign issuers with a board of auditors, the SEC clarified that the term 'audit committee' for these purposes refers to the board of auditors.

For instance, despite objections from foreign companies listed on US stock exchanges to the personal certification requirement, no exemptions will be brooked. The SEC accepted that overseas companies were subject to different legal regimes, and that different bodies bore responsibility for the accuracy of disclosure documents. Alan Beller, head of the SEC's corporate finance division, said that the Sarbanes-Oxley Act had necessitated fresh action: foreign companies had lived with US legal requirements for decades, and that the new rules were quite general in nature. Foreign companies have been exempted from the requirement that large companies file their financial reports more quickly than in the past (the annual report deadline will be shortened from 90 to 60 days).

China already had in place a fairly complete regulatory structure of disclosure requirements. The PRC Securities Law includes various general requirements for information disclosure. Well before its passage in late 1998, interim regulations specifying disclosure obligations were already in place, in particular the 1993 Provisional Regulations for Administration of the Issuance and Trading of Shares, the Implementation Rules for Information Disclosure of Companies Publicly Issuing Shares (Trial Implementation) and the Provisional Measures on Prohibition of Securities Fraud. These served to establish basic mandatory public disclosure requirements by means of such documents as a company's prospectus, listing particulars, annual report, interim reports and reports on material and extra-ordinary events. Since 1994, the CSRC has released dozens of detailed rules governing the form and content of disclosure documents, in the form of a series of Detailed Rules for Content and Format of Information Disclosure and Rules for Compilation and Reporting of Information Disclosure, among various other circulars and regulations. The recent Regulations for Corporate Governance of Listed Companies, discussed below, also provide further articulation of disclosure requirements with specific reference to shareholder rights. In January 2003 the CSRC issued revised guidelines for corporate annual reports and accounts, requiring among other things that managers and financial executives guarantee in writing that the reports and accounts contain no major errors or misleading information. The revised rules also standardize the format of the annual report summary by including a reporting format in an appendix.

Potential defendants.   Who has a duty of disclosure? Beller said of the SEC action: 'Part of the current exercise is to simply cut through all of that and say that if you are a CFO or CEO you have a personal responsibility for disclosure', which is now the SEC rule. By comparison, subject to CSRC findings on liability, the Circular exposes a broad range of potential defendants to civil liability. It is not only listed companies that may be liable to pay compensation. Their directors, supervisors and managers, and those of their underwriters, may together have joint and several liability for misleading disclosures or material omissions in dis-closure documents causing investors to suffer losses in securities transactions. Any 'specialized firms' and individuals providing 'relevant' documents to an issuer are also obligated to strictly carry out their professional duties and guarantee the authenticity, accuracy and completeness of the documents they issue, thereby extending the range of potential plaintiffs to include lawyers, accountants, asset appraisers and other professional advisers. Holders of at least 5 per cent of outstanding shares also have disclosure duties. Various CSRC Disclosure Rules also address specific requirements applicable to professional advisers. This is now typical of Asian practice, which comes close to the SEC principle without imposing in all cases the same personal responsibility on CEOs and CFOs.

Quarterly reporting.   Here's an idea that is going nowhere fast: it is a good example of one of the problems of copying. Asian jurisdictions jumped onto the quarterly reporting bandwagon – to be fair, there was a considerable debate about its

167

wisdom and advisability in Singapore and Hong Kong – but what did it achieve? Are not short-termism and concomitant dangers reinforced by such reporting? At least, it is possible that this may occur without responsible investment by long-term investors – including precisely those major institutional investors who form the backbone of determined corporate governance in Western jurisdictions, but who in many cases remain absent from Asian stock exchanges.

In China, the CSRC has proposed to revise its guidelines on quarterly reporting. They clarify that quarterly results need not be audited if there are no specific requirements from the CSRC or the stock exchanges. Quarterly reports should include information about significant accounting policy changes, error corrections, and explanations for any changes in the scope of consolidation. Disclosure is also required about changes to any senior executive management positions or controlling shareholders, serious court cases and final rulings, and the total amount of guarantees and cash assets entrusted to other institutions. The Kuala Lumpur Stock Exchange (KLSE) requires all enterprises whose debt or equity securities are publicly traded to publish interim financial reports every three months. In Singapore, recommendations in favour of quarterly reporting were made by corporate governance advisory committees (although to be fair there was also disquiet publicly voiced from respected circles), and it is already required of listed companies with market capitalisation of S$75 million or more. Smaller companies have been exempted until 2005 when a review will be conducted.

For the record, Table 6.1 shows the position with respect to quarterly reporting as it stood in 2003.

Table 6.1 *Comparison of quarterly earnings disclosure requirements*

Country	Regulation
China	All listed companies since 1999
Taiwan	All listed companies except shipping firms
Japan	TSE requires quarterly disclosure of sales from FY 2003 and everything from FY 2004
Korea	Banks since September 1999
	Other listed and registered companies since 2000
Singapore	All listed companies since January 2003
Hong Kong	All companies listed on GEM already disclose
	Quarterly reporting for all listed companies proposed January 2002
US	All listed companies
Germany	All companies listed on MDAX – top 100 companies

Source: Goldman Sachs

Those in favour argue that timely and reliable quarterly financial reporting improves the ability of investors, creditors and other interested parties to understand and be able, to a certain extent, to assess an organization's capacity to generate earnings and cash flows, and its financial condition and liquidity situation. Those against, such as Tata Sons director Jamshed J. Irani, say that while they of course endorse good governance practices, overlegislation will defeat the purpose. 'For example, quarterly financial disclosures often make managers take decisions to boost the quarterly performance which may not be good in the long term.' This was precisely the point made by senior corporate figures in Singapore, even though in neither case were they listened to, such is the force of the new corporate governance regime.

In September 2002, the CSRC issued a regulation regarding the acquisition of a significant holding in a listed company.

Acquisitions. In November 2002, in support of earlier regulations, the CSRC issued the following new disclosure rules relating to acquisition of listed companies that are effective from 1 December 2002. These rules were added to the CSRC's Standard for the Form and Content of Information for Disclosure by Companies with Securities Issued to the Public:

- No. 15, Report of Changes in Shareholdings in Listed Companies
- No. 16, Report for the Acquisition of Listed Companies (30 per cent or less interest)
- No. 17, Offering Report for Acquisitions (greater than 30 per cent interest)
- No. 18, Directors report of acquiree companies
- No. 19, Offering Report Exemption Application.

Auditors. The OECD has called for the disclosure of all ownership financial relationships between auditors and the company, and this is clearly best practice already.

Core business. In Malaysia, it has already been established that a definition and scope of the company's core business is another area for disclosure.

> Core business is concerned about the core competency of the company and the tacit acknowledgement that management should not go into new business helter-skelter without a careful evaluation of its abilities and resources. The road to PN4 status should be avoided.

Dividend policy. Dividend policy must be articulated and is important in the long term for shareholders. A stated dividend policy must be present first before arguments regarding its contents and appropriateness can be forwarded. Common shares of the same class carry a right to pro rata portion of dividends. As a legal matter, Asian countries differ as to whether dividends may only be paid out of net profits of the company (OECD, 2003).

Income.   According to the first companies scored under the revised *Business Times* Corporate Transparency Index (CTI), listed firms are disclosing more in their cashflow statements but could improve by providing a better breakdown of expenses and liabilities.

Ownership and changes in ownership.   A number of Asian corporate governance frameworks require disclosure by shareholders whose ownership exceeds certain thresholds, typically 5 per cent. The OECD reports that less widespread, however, is the application of attribution rules to take into account ultimate or beneficial ownership or to require disclosure of voting agreements that have the effect of raising voting control above the disclosure threshold provided for by law, regulation or listing requirement.

Personnel policies.   This has been the Cinderella of corporate governance. 'Having the right people' has been recognized worldwide as being a major contribution to long-term shareholder value, but the disclosure of criteria for executive selection, the involvement of recruitment consultancies, personnel issues within the firm, retention rates and other personnel issues are not customarily disclosed by Asian corporations to their shareholders.

Related party transactions.   These come under the category of items which ought not to exist at all within the well-governed company, but if they ever do occur, whether inadvertently, dredged up from the past, or as a result of a breach of company regulations, they should be disclosed as soon as possible.

Self-dealing/related-party transactions should be subject to both banking and corporate-governance restrictions. All Asian governments should introduce measures, or enhance existing measures, to provide non-controlling shareholders with adequate protection from exploitation by controlling shareholders. These measures should include, among other things: (i) strengthening disclosure requirements (particularly of self-dealing/related party transactions and insider trading); (ii) ensuring that regulators have the capacity to monitor companies for compliance with these requirements and to impose substantial sanctions for wrongdoing; (iii) clarifying and strengthening the fiduciary duty of directors to act in the interest of the company and all of its shareholders; (iv) prohibiting indemnification of directors by companies for breaches of fiduciary duty; and (v) providing shareholders who suffer financial losses with private and collective rights of action against controlling shareholders and directors.

The OECD notes that real problems remain in disclosing the terms of the transactions and insider-shareholders' interest in them; www.webb-site.com, which is an excellent source of practical examples of corporate governance failings, notes that in Hong Kong the Listing Rules (HK) for Chapter 21 companies require disclosure of individual investments in the annual report, including any investment that represents 5 per cent or more of net assets and at least the 10 largest investments. Regulatory note: this listing rule is grossly inadequate, because shareholders only find out once a year, up to 4 months after the year end, what investments their company owns. In the case of Hong Kong company CTGCI, it was not until the results were published on 15 April 2003, 14 months after the IPO, that shareholders found out where their money had been invested. In India now in annual reports, companies now provide related party transactions that highlight whether there are material transactions with either promoters or their group companies.

'Relevant facts'. Disclosure requirements potentially applicable to foreign investors in China have been evolving quickly. For example, an April 2002 CSRC release requires, among other things, that an FICLS intending to list its shares make detailed prospectus disclosures of risk factors relating to such items as: overseas suppliers, customers and technical services; risks relating to possible changes to PRC tax laws, regulations and policies favouring FIEs; possible changes to laws, regulations and policies impacting technology transfers from the country in which its foreign parent is incorporated to China. In India, 2003 saw a key development in that companies had to make available consolidated accounts for all companies. In essence, this did away with the opacity that existed in the form of a web of subsidiaries and joint ventures, with little information on the impact of these on the health of the parent company. Unravelling inter-company transactions and the true picture of profitability is now possible, an invaluable tool for any shareholder.

Retrospective performance. Results three months after the event are just not good enough. Time is clearly of the essence for financial reporting. In Singapore, one of the most transparent of jurisdictions in Asia, the Statement of Accounting Standard (SAS) 1 on Presentation of Financial Statements states that the objective of financial statements 'is to provide information about the financial position, performance and cash flows of an enterprise that is useful to a wide range of users in making investment decisions', but that 'the usefulness of financial statements is impaired if they are not made available to users within a reasonable period after the balance sheet date'. In other words, the longer it takes a company to release its results, the less useful the information becomes, which is quite right. One of the salient, and damning, findings of the Singapore Corporate Transparency Index exercise – which sought to measure the degree of openness of listed Singaporean companies and how fast they disseminate information by studying not only the content of their interim report but also the way in which they went about communicating this content – was that the majority of companies took far too long to release their results. Frequently, investors had to wait almost three months to get a terse lowdown on what happened in the first half of the financial year, being the six months to 30 June. All companies listed on the Singapore Exchange (SGX) with a calendar financial year (ending 31 December) are in fact required, as a condition of listing, to release their interim results within three months of the half-year ending, that is by the end of September for interims for period to 30 June. Of the 275 companies that reported interims for the first half of a year, 28 (10.2 per cent) reported in July, 100 (36.5 per cent) reported in August, and a whopping 147 (53.3 per cent) in September. Furthermore, the most popular week for the release of results was the last week of September, when 62 reported. SingTel, reporting quarterly data for three months to 30 June, managed to release their results on 28 July. And the big four banks all released within five weeks of their half-year end.

A research report from JP Morgan highlighted just how varied Asian markets in fact are in the timeliness of their financial reporting. Published in August, the report analysed 172 large and liquid Asian companies in order to calculate the average number of days taken between close of books and reporting a variety of data, including quarterly, semi-annual and consolidated annual results. Hong Kong companies fared worse than their Asian counterparts in the reporting of interim results: they took an average of 66 days between books close and reporting. For consolidated annual reports, Hong Kong companies were fourth slowest with an average of 97 days (only Indonesian, Korean and Taiwanese firms performed more poorly). While Hong Kong did score well in quarterly reporting, the sample size was extremely small – only three companies – because quarterly reporting is not mandatory. Some Asian companies compared well against international blue-chips (as reflected in the reporting practices of eight multinational firms: GE, Nokia, GM, Glaxo SK, Royal Dutch Shell, Vodafone, Intel and Phillip Morris). Indian companies in particular stood out for being much faster at quarterly reporting, while those in Taiwan and Thailand also did well, according to JP Morgan. But when it came to consolidated annual reports, only one country – Australia – was close to the international average of 59 days. Thai companies led the Asian pack at just 71 days, while Singaporean and Indian firms reported after an average of 83 and 84 days respectively. Indonesian companies gave investors the longest wait – an average of 132 days (though some were much faster). JP Morgan singled out certain Asian companies for exceeding required regulatory standards and taking governance seriously, including Infosys Technologies and Hughes Software from India, TSMC from Taiwan, and ST Engineering from Singapore.

Remuneration policies and practice.   All companies above a certain size – no one is really clear what that is – ought to disclose their remuneration policies. MAS says:

Principle 7: There should be a formal and transparent procedure for fixing the remuneration packages of individual directors. No director should be involved in deciding his own remuneration. The Board should establish a broad framework for directors' remuneration.

The Malaysian Code suggests that the company's annual report should contain details of the remuneration of each director. Linked to this is an expectation that remuneration structures and their link to performance ought to be disclosed. Listed companies generally have no difficulties with this, especially as they usually have in place some form of performance pay related to the share price. Ask the directors of a mid-sized private company to do the same, however, and whether you ask in Singapore or London you will almost certainly get the same answer: there is no policy, it just depends on what we believe the company can afford to pay in dividends at the end of the financial year. Best corporate governance practice here for a listed company is to state publicly absolutely every last cent paid to directors and senior managers. Loans are out, following Sarbanes-Oxley, and there is no detail too small, especially for a listed company, for release to potential investors.

Risk management methodologies. In practice, this increasingly means ticking a box marked 'mark to market' and it does not yet, it seems, involve disclosing the detail of exact positions in the market which is deemed to fall under commercial confidentiality, the traditional foe of disclosure in corporate governance.

CONCLUSION

The quality of information disclosure depends on the standards under which it is prepared and presented. The OECD Principles identify three types of standard that underpin a strong disclosure regime: accounting, audit and non-financial disclosure. Good disclosure requires the provision of material information. Material information is information the omission or misstatement of which could influence the economic decisions made by the users of information. In this area, companies often express concern about the costs of complying with disclosure requirements while regulators wish to ensure that the information demanded genuinely furthers regulatory objectives. Applying the concept of materiality in developing disclosure requirements helps companies and regulators to decide what information is truly relevant. The general definition of materiality, however, may lend itself to differing interpretations. In Asia, where interpretation in practice has been rather liberal, a number of companies have fallen significantly short of national and international standards. Failures have included:

173

- hiding of large enterprise debts through related-party transactions and off-balance sheet financing, such as cross-guarantees within corporate groups;
- insufficient reporting of contingent liabilities, particularly loan guarantees granted to related and unrelated parties;
- insufficient segment information that would have revealed the risks related to specific sectors such as real estate; and
- failure to use mark-to-market accounting where appropriate.

Gradually, all Asian jurisdictions are seeing standards of disclosure improve, with the result that a surfeit of information now faces investors, just as it does in Europe and the US.

Corporate Governance and Other Information

Corporate Governance

The Company

In the interests of its shareholders, the Company is committed to high standards of corporate governance and devotes considerable effort to identifying and formalising best practices.

The Company is listed on the stock exchanges of Hong Kong and New York, and its shares are majority held by a private company, Bowenvale Limited ("Bowenvale"), incorporated in British Virgin Islands, with a 68.9% holding. Bowenvale is, in turn, held by China International Trust and Investment Corporation ("CITIC") and SES GLOBAL S.A. ("SES GLOBAL"). CITIC controls 50.5% of the economic interest and 50% of voting rights of Bowenvale whilst SES GLOBAL controls 49.5% and 50%, respectively. Under the shareholders agreement of Bowenvale, CITIC and SES GLOBAL are each entitled to appoint, and remove, up to four directors to the Board of the Company.

The Board

The Board is composed of 13 members, eight of whom are appointed by the shareholders of Bowenvale, CITIC and SES GLOBAL, three independent non-executive directors and two executive directors, who are also the Chief Executive Officer and the Deputy Chief Executive Officer of the Company.

The Chairman and the Deputy Chairman of the Board are appointed by CITIC and SES GLOBAL from one of their nominated directors, and the posts are rotated biennially between CITIC and SES GLOBAL.

The Board is scheduled to meet on a quarterly basis and additional Board meetings are held if and when required. The Board also holds private sessions at least once a year without the presence of management.

The Board deals with strategic and policy issues and approves corporate plans, budgets, and monitors the performance of the management. The day to day operation of the Company is delegated to the management. The Board has established a framework of corporate governance and is supported by three committees, the Audit Committee, the Business Development Committee and the Renumeration Committee, each of which has defined terms of reference covering its authorities and duties. The chairman of these committees reports regularly to the Board on the matters discussed.

Audit Committee

The Audit Committee, chaired by an independent non-executive director, is composed of five members, two non-executive directors and three independent non-executive directors. The Chairman and some of its members have extensive knowledge and experience in financial matters. The Chief Executive Officer, the General Manager Finance and other management staff attend meetings by invitation, as do the external auditors. The Committee examines any matters relating to accounting principles and practices adopted by the Company, and discusses auditing, internal control and financial reporting matters.

Audit Committee (continued)

In recognition of the fact that the independent auditors are ultimately accountable to the Audit Committee, the Audit Committee shall have the sole authority and responsibility to select, evaluate and, where appropriate, replace the independent auditors (or to nominate the independent auditors for shareholders approval), and shall approve all audit engagement fees and terms and all non-audit engagements with the independent auditors. The Audit Committee shall consult with management, including the principal financial officer, but shall not delegate these responsibilities.

The Audit Committee is scheduled to meet at least two times a year to review the audit reports, status of the Company's audits, internal controls, and the interim and final results of the Company prior to recommending them to the Board for approval.

The Audit Committee also holds private sessions with the external auditors without the presence of management.

Business Development Committee

The Business Development Committee is composed of three non-executive directors. The Committee meets quarterly before each Board meeting. The Chief Executive Officer and other management staff also attend the quarterly meetings. The Committee is tasked to review all corporate plans, budgets and any new and ongoing projects or ventures and make recommendations to the Board for consideration and approval.

Remuneration Committee

The Remuneration Committee is composed of three members, of whom one is an independent non-executive director and the other two, non-executive directors. The Committee is chaired by the independent non-executive director. The Committee is scheduled to meet at least once a year. The Committee also holds private sessions without the presence of management.

The Committee formulates the remuneration guidelines and policies for the Board's approval. The Committee ensures that the remuneration offered is appropriate for the duties, and in line with market practice. The Committee may engage external professional advisors to assist and/or advise the Committee, if and when necessary.

Disclosure Committee

To conform to recommendations arising from the Sarbanes-Oxley Act, a Disclosure Committee has been formed. The Committee is composed of seven management staff and chaired by the Deputy Chief Executive Officer.

The Committee's prime function is to ensure that the Chief Executive Officer and the Chief Financial Officer are informed of any material facts concerning the Company that should be publicly disclosed.

Disclosure Committee (continued)

The Committee is responsible for considering the materiality of the information and determining disclosure obligations on a timely basis. The Committee will have overall coordinating responsibility for the Company's public disclosure, including announcements, statements and circulars to the public or stockholders, and reports to the regulatory bodies. The Committee will organise and supervise the disclosure process.

The Committee is also responsible for regularly reviewing the structure of the operations and principal reporting lines and confirming that the disclosure procedures take account of any changes in the structure and principal reporting lines.

Shareholder Relations

The Board recognises its accountability to shareholders for the performance and activities of the Company and attaches considerable importance to the effectiveness of its communications with shareholders. To this end, an Investor Relations Sector has been established as part of the Company's website, www.asiasat.com, to provide information to shareholders about the Company. This is in addition to other corporate communications with shareholders, such as circulars, notices, announcements, interim reports and annual reports, copies of which can also be found on the website.

The interim report and annual report contain a full financial review and an operational review.

Guidelines on Conduct

The Company periodically issues notices to its Directors and employees reminding them that there is a general prohibition on dealing in the Company's listed securities during the blackout periods before the announcement of the interim and annual results.

OTHER INFORMATION

Directors' Interests

As at 30th June, 2003, as recorded in the register required to be maintained under Section 352 of the Securities and Future Ordinance ("SFO") or otherwise notified to the Company pursuant to the Model Code for Securities Transactions by Directors of Listed Companies under the Rules Governing the Listing of Securities on The Stock Exchange of Hong Kong Limited, the following directors have the following interests in the shares in the Company:

(i) Ordinary shares

Peter Jackson and William Wade had a personal beneficial interest in 163,500 and 5,000 ordinary shares respectively in the Company.

Directors' Interests (continued)

(ii) Options to subscribe for ordinary shares in the Company under the Share Option Scheme.

The following table discloses movements in the Company's share options for the six months ended 30th June, 2003:

	Option type	Outstanding at beginning of the period	Granted during the period	Cancelled/ lapsed during the period	Outstanding at end of the period
Directors					
Mi Zengxin	C	100,000	—	—	100,000
Romain Bausch	C	100,000	—	—	100,000
Edward Chen	C	50,000	—	—	50,000
Ding Yu Cheng	C	50,000	—	—	50,000
R. Donald Fullerton	C	75,000	—	—	75,000
Ju Weimin	C	50,000	—	—	50,000
Li Tong Zhou	C	50,000	—	—	50,000
Jürgen Schulte	C	50,000	—	—	50,000
Robert Sze	C	75,000	—	—	75,000
Peter Jackson	A	335,000	—	—	335,000
	B	150,000	—	—	150,000
	C	430,000	—	—	430,000
William Wade	A	316,000	—	—	316,000
	B	114,000	—	—	114,000
	C	330,000	—	—	330,000
Total Directors		2,275,000	—	—	2,275,000
Employees	A	1,067,500	—	—	1,067,500
	B	1,574,000	—	—	1,574,000
	C	2,233,000	—	—	2,233,000
Total Employees		4,874,500	—	—	4,874,500
Grand Total		7,149,500	—	—	7,149,500

Details of specific categories of options are as follows:

Option type	Date of grant	Vesting period	Exercise period	Exercise price HK$
A	4th February, 2002	Fully vested	4th February, 2002 - 25th November, 2006	17.48
B	4th February, 2002	Fully vested	1st October, 2002 - 30th September, 2009	17.48
C	4th February, 2002	4th February, 2002 - 3rd February, 2004	4th February, 2004 - 3rd February, 2012	14.35

Directors' Interests (continued)

The closing price of the Company's shares immediately before the date of grant on 4th February, 2002 was HK$14.85.

The fair values of the options granted as at 30th June, 2003 measured as at the date of grant on 4th February, 2002 for option types A, B & C as defined below were HK$6.00, HK$6.90 and HK$8.16 per option respectively. The following significant assumptions were used to derive the fair value using the Black-Scholes option pricing model:

Option type	A	B	C
Expected life of options	$4\frac{5}{6}$ years	$7\frac{2}{3}$ years	10 years
Expected volatility based on historical volatility of share prices	56%	51%	51%
Hong Kong Exchange Fund Notes rate	5.08%	5.47%	5.99%
Expected annual dividend yield	1.62%	1.62%	1.62%

For the purpose of the calculation of fair value, no adjustment has been made in respect of options expected to be forfeited, due to lack of historical data.

The Black-Scholes option pricing model requires the input of highly subjective assumptions, including the volatility of share price. Because changes in subjective input assumptions can materially affect the fair value estimate, in the directors' opinion, the existing model does not necessarily provide a reliable single measure of the fair value of the share options.

SUBSTANTIAL SHAREHOLDERS

As at 30th June, 2003, according to the register required to be kept under Section 336 of the SFO and information otherwise reported to the Company, the following persons held an interest of 5% or more in the shares in the Company:

Name	No. of shares	%
Bowenvale Limited	268,905,000	68.9
Able Star Associates Limited	268,905,000[1]	68.9
China International Trust and Investment Corporation	268,905,000[1]	68.9
SES Finance S.A.	268,905,000[2]	68.9
SES GLOBAL S.A.	268,905,000[2]	68.9
Commonwealth Bank of Australia	20,665,600[3]	5.3

Notes:

(1) Able Star Associates Limited ("Able Star") controls 50% of the voting rights of Bowenvale Limited ("Bowenvale"). Able Star is wholly-owned by CITIC Asia Limited ("CITIC Asia") which in turn is wholly-owned by CITIC International Holdings Limited ("CITIC International") which is a wholly-owned subsidiary of China International Trust and Investment Corporation ("CITIC"). Accordingly, Able Star, CITIC Asia, CITIC International and CITIC are deemed to be interested in the 268,905,000 shares in the Company held by Bowenvale.

(2) SES Finance S.A. ("SES Finance") controls 50% of the voting rights of Bowenvale, SES Finance is a wholly-owned subsidiary of SES GLOBAL S.A. ("SES GLOBAL"). Accordingly, SES Finance and SES GLOBAL are deemed to be interested in the 268,905,000 shares in the Company held by Bowenvale.

(3) Commonwealth Bank of Australia ("CBA") is interested in 20,665,600 shares in the Company by virtue of its corporate interest in the following companies which are interested in shares in the Company.

Companies controlled by CBA	No. of shares held
(i) First State Investments International Limited, an indirect wholly-owned subsidiary of CBA held under First State Investment Management (UK) Ltd, SI Holdings Ltd, First State Investments (UK Holdings) Ltd, Colonial First State Group Ltd, The Colonial Mutual Life Assurance Society Ltd, Colonial Holding Co (No. 2) Pty Ltd, Colonial Holding Co Pty Ltd and Colonial Ltd	7,695,200
(ii) First State Investment Management (UK) Limited, an indirect wholly-owned subsidiary of CBA held under SI Holdings Ltd, First State Investments (UK Holdings) Ltd, Colonial First State Group Ltd, The Colonial Mutual Life Assurance Society Ltd, Colonial Holding Co (No. 2) Pty Ltd, Colonial Holding Co Pty Ltd and Colonial Ltd	12,022,900
(iii) First State Investments (Hong Kong) Limited, an indirect wholly-owned subsidiary of CBA held under First State (Hong Kong) LLC, First State Investments (Bermuda) Ltd, First State Investment Managers (Asia) Ltd, Colonial First State Group Ltd, The Colonial Mutual Life Assurance Society Ltd, Colonial Holding Co (No. 2) Pty Ltd, Colonial Holding Co Pty Ltd and Colonial Ltd	947,500
(iv) First State Investments (Singapore), an indirect wholly-owned subsidiary of CBA held under First State Investments Holdings (Singapore) Ltd, First State Investments (Bermuda) Ltd, First State Investment Managers (Asia) Ltd, Colonial First State Group Ltd, The Colonial Mutual Life Assurance Society Ltd, Colonial Holding Co (No. 2) Pty Ltd, Colonial Holding Co Pty Ltd and Colonial Ltd	907,500

Note: First State Investments (Singapore) holds the 907,500 shares for First State Investments (Hong Kong) Limited. Accordingly, the interest of First State Investments (Singapore) duplicates the interest of First State Investments (Hong Kong) Limited.

Purchase, Sale or Redemption of Own Securities

During the six months ended 30th June, 2003, neither the Company nor any of its subsidiaries purchased, sold or redeemed any of the Company's securities.

Arrangement to Purchase Shares or Debenture

Save as disclosed above, at no time during the period was the Company, or any of its subsidiaries, a party to any arrangements to enable the directors of the Company to acquire benefits by means of the acquisition of shares in, or debentures of, the Company or any other body corporate.

Code of Best Practice

None of the directors of the Company are aware of any information that would reasonably indicate that the Company is not, or was not for any part of the six months ended 30th June, 2003, in compliance with the Code of Best Practice as set out in Appendix 14 of the Rules Governing the Listing of Securities on The Stock Exchange of Hong Kong Limited.

Practice Note 19 of the Listing Rules

Pursuant to paragraph 3.7.1 of Practice Note 19 of the Rules Governing the Listing of Securities of The Stock Exchange of Hong Kong Limited, the Company discloses that the covenants relating to the loan facility of HK$1,950 million (US$250 million) for a term of five years require (a) CITIC and SES GLOBAL between them to maintain beneficial ownership of more than 75% of the ordinary issued share capital of Bowenvale Limited, which is a substantial shareholder of the Company; and (b) Bowenvale Limited to maintain beneficial ownership of at least 51% of the issued share capital of the Company.

Closure of Register of Members

The Register of shareholders of the Company will be closed from 9th to 16th October, 2003 (both days inclusive). In order to qualify for the interim dividend, all transfers, accompanied by the relevant share certificates, must be lodged with the Company's Hong Kong Branch Share Registrars, Computershare Hong Kong Investor Services Limited at Rooms 1712-1716, 17th Floor, Hopewell Centre, 183 Queen's Road East, Hong Kong for registration not later than 4:00 p.m. on 8th October, 2003. The interim dividend will be paid on or about 18th November, 2003.

HITS AND MISSES *Producing an impressive annual report is a game of hit and miss. Below are our favorites.*

HITS	
China Mobile	Well-reported governance issues, including directors' interests.
Bharat Petroleum	Financial history spans 25 years, with sources and proceeds of funds.
Infosys	Outstanding three-year ratio analysis. "Intangible Assets Scoresheet" a rare plus.
Bank Mandiri	An enhanced MD&A, and signed financial reporting responsibility.
Ajinomoto	Total capital breakdown and interest coverage ratio shown; global network mapped.
CLP Holdings	"Financial Results and Position at a Glance" is a benchmark.
IOI Corp	Outstanding financial overview and highlights, with a rarely-encountered quarterly progress report.
Wipro	US GAAP statements and reconciliation as a separate section.
MISSES	
CJ Corp	Short on business review, shallow on financials, and vague on segments.
Mitsubishi Corp	For a company with 182 business units, the financial analysis lacks substance.
CNOOC	Very poor share information. Not a single share item is highlighted.
Daiwa House	What's the use of a three-page financial review?
Petrochina	A Chinese giant deserves more than two pages of business operating review.
Ranbaxy Labs	A hollow, one-page "MD&A Report" filed as an appendix.
ORIX	A lack of visuals. Must annual reports look boring?
Honda Motor	Has yet to pick up on discussion of corporate governance and risk analysis.

THE BEST OF THE LOT *Winners by Category*

Category	Winner	Comments
Business Overview	Sony	The company "At a Glance" is a model to follow - compact and intelligible, with key three-year charts and outlook for the coming year.
Executive Statement	Sony	A 15-page "Message from Top Management" is strategy-oriented, substantial and to-the-point.
Share/Investor Information	Aditya Birla Group of Companies	Features monthly stock prices over 12 months compared against the index, distribution of shareholdings, and categories of shareholders.
Financial Highlights	IOI Corp	Offers "Performance Indicators", "Financial Indicators" and - in a rare move - very detailed "Quarterly Results".
	IOI Properties	Investor-oriented financial condition indicators, with worthwhile ratios, backed by charts.
Financial Review	DBS Group	A 20-page MD&A, with a business overview and selected financial data over three years (including a dozen meaningful ratios). Useful description of bad loans and interest rate risk.
Financial History	Matsushita Electric	A 24-page "Fact Book" with numbers spanning six years, including sales and income over 18 quarters, segment data, recent alliances, and number of patents.
Financial Objectives and Outlook	Chugoku Electric Power	Features previous and new targets over 1-3 years, with equity ratio, ROE, ROA, income and free cash flow. Lays out "The Future Shape of Chugoku Electric" over four years.
Board, Management, Governance	ECGO	Matter-of-fact biographies of directors, disclosing their involvement in committees. Thorough description of management remuneration, including warrants.
Risk Factors and Management	United Overseas Bank	A 20-page section, separate from financial review, on the five types of risks. Bad loans (secured and unsecured) and provisions filed by country and industry.
Social and Environmental Responsibility	BHP Billiton	A separate report features a target scoreboard of legal compliance and environmental incidents, from waste minimization to land management, with lively case studies.
Use and Value of Charts	Singapore Airlines	The charts pace the financial review and back historical data, placed strategically to complement each other.
Use of Covers	RoadShow Holdings	A flashy screen that changes images by angle fits well with the personality of this media advertising company.
Design and Visuals	ST Engineering	Boldly went from book format to a newspaper format with two sections, one of which highlights financials. Original, highly readable, informative.
Report Theme	EGCO	The theme, "The World is Our Home" is smart, solid and sustained, backed by a green visual route and a symbolic illustration.

THE BEST AND THE REST:
CFO ASIA'S ANNUAL REPORTS SURVEY

	Company	Country	Score		Company	Country	Score
1	Sony	Japan	●●●●	54	Grasim Industries	India	●●
2	CLP Holdings	Hong Kong	●●●▸	55	Ayala Corp	Philippines	●●
3	United Overseas Bank	Singapore	●●●▸	56	Tanjong	Malaysia	●●
4	DBS Group	Singapore	●●●▸	57	United Broadcasting	Thailand	●●
5	IOI Corp	Malaysia	●●●▸	58	Next Media	Hong Kong	●●
6	Foster's Group	Australia	●●●▸	59	Bridgestone	Japan	●●
7	Singapore Technologies Engineering	Singapore	●●●▸	60	BAT Malaysia	Malaysia	●●
8	Teijin	Japan	●●●▸	61	Samsung Electronics	South Korea	●●
9	Singapore Airlines	Singapore	●●●	62	TelecomAsia	Thailand	●●
10	Yamaha Motor	Japan	●●●	63	Toray Industries	Japan	●●
11	Honda Motor	Japan	●●●	64	China Mobile (Hong Kong)	Hong Kong	●●
12	Daiwa House	Japan	●●●	65	Dr. Reddy's Laboratories	India	●●
13	Esprit Holdings	Hong Kong	●●●	66	Tokyo Gas	Japan	●●
14	China Petroleum & Chemical Corp (Sinopec)	China	●●●	67	Johnson Electric	Hong Kong	●●
15	MTR Corp	Hong Kong	●●●	68	Bharat Petroleum	India	●●
16	Electricity Generating Public Company (EGCO)	Thailand	●●●	69	Bank Mandiri	Indonesia	●●
17	Mitsubishi Corp	Japan	●●●	70	Telekom Malaysia	Malaysia	●●
18	Maybank	Malaysia	●●●	71	Wharf Holdings	Hong Kong	●●
19	BHP Billiton	Australia	●●●	72	Fraser & Neave	Singapore	●●
20	Itochu	Japan	●●▸	73	Hysan Development	Hong Kong	●●
21	All Nippon Airways	Japan	●●▸	74	Chugoku Electric Power	Japan	●●
22	Matsushita Electric	Japan	●●▸	75	Cathay Pacific Airways	Hong Kong	●●
23	Reliance Industries	India	●●▸	76	Omron	Japan	●●
24	Kao Corp	Japan	●●▸	77	Tokyo Electron	Japan	●●
25	Rolta India	India	●●▸	78	Wipro	India	●●
26	AMMB Holdings	Malaysia	●●▸	79	CNOOC	Hong Kong	●●
27	CapitaLand	Singapore	●●▸	80	Daiwa Securities	Japan	●●
28	Coles Myer	Australia	●●▸	81	Nissin Food Products	Japan	●●
29	IOI Properties	Malaysia	●●▸	82	Swire Pacific	Hong Kong	●●
30	Singapore Exchange	Singapore	●●▸	83	Beijing Datang Power Generation	China	●●
31	Del Monte Pacific	Singapore	●●▸	84	Total Access Communication	Thailand	●●
32	Singapore Press Holdings	Singapore	●●▸	85	Hongkong & Shangai Banking (HSBC)	Hong Kong	●▸
33	Keppel Corp	Singapore	●●▸	86	Hero Honda	India	●▸
34	Sun Hung Kai Properties	Hong Kong	●●▸	87	Evergreen Marine	Taiwan	●▸
35	Hindalco Industries	India	●●▸	88	NEC	Japan	●▸
36	Infosys Technologies	India	●●▸	89	Yamaha Corp	Japan	●▸
37	Indian Rayon	India	●●▸	90	SSI	India	●▸
38	Indo Gulf	India	●●▸	91	United Microelectronics (UMC)	Taiwan	●▸
39	Tom.com	Hong Kong	●●▸	92	Crosswave Communications	Japan	●▸
40	Hutchison Whampoa	Hong Kong	●●▸	93	Legend Holdings	Hong Kong	●▸
41	RoadShow Holdings	Hong Kong	●●	94	Ayala Land	Philippines	●▸
42	SembCorp Industries	Singapore	●●	95	Cheung Kong Infrastructure	Hong Kong	●▸
43	ORIX	Japan	●●	96	San Miguel	Philippines	●▸
44	Ajinomoto	Japan	●●	97	Ranbaxy Laboratories	India	●▸
45	Canon	Japan	●●	98	Internet Initiative Japan	Japan	●▸
46	Sumitomo Mitsui Banking	Japan	●●	99	Sapporo Breweries	Japan	●▸
47	NTT	Japan	●●	100	Larsen & Toubro	India	●▸
48	Asahi Breweries	Japan	●●	101	SingTel	Singapore	●▸
49	First Pacific	Hong Kong	●●	102	Wah Sang Gas Holdings	Hong Kong	●▸
50	Hang Seng Bank	Hong Kong	●●	103	Sumitomo Electric	Japan	●▸
51	PCCW	Hong Kong	●●	104	CJ Corp	South Korea	●▸
52	News Corp	Australia	●●	105	Shin Satellite	Thailand	●▸
53	Indian Aluminium	India	●●				

CORPORATE GOVERNANCE REPORT

1. CORPORATE GOVERNANCE PHILOSOPHY:

Monsanto India Limited is a subsidiary of Monsanto Company, USA and is committed to adapting the best global practices of Corporate Governance. Corporate Governance envisages commitment of the company towards the attainment of high levels of transparency, accountability and business propriety with the ultimate objective of increasing long term shareholders' value, keeping in view the needs and interests of all other stakeholders.

2. BOARD OF DIRECTORS:

The Board comprises of Executive and Non-Executive Directors. The present strength of the Board is seven Directors comprising of one Executive Director, three Independent Non-Executive Directors and three Non-Executive Directors, including the Chairman of the Company. The Executive and Non-Executive Directors are accomplished professionals and experts in their respective corporate fields.

Monsanto Company, USA has certain rights enshrined in the Articles of Association pertaining to the appointment of Directors.

The Board has a formal schedule of matters reserved for its consideration and decision, which includes reviewing Company performance, internal control system and issues coming out of internal/statutory audits.

Mr.Brett D. Begemann was appointed as a Chairman in place of Mr.B.K. Chiu w.e.f. 16th January, 2002.

The details of the Directors on the Board of your Company are given below:

None of the Directors is a member of more than 10 committees or acts as a Chairman of 5 committees across all companies in which he is a Director.

Seven Board Meetings were held during the year on following dates:

1. 22nd May, 2001
2. 25th July, 2001
3. 20th September, 2001
4. 27th October, 2001
5. 28th January, 2002
6. 8th March, 2002
7. 27th March, 2002

The time gap between any two consecutive meetings is not more than four months.

3. SHAREHOLDERS' / INVESTORS' GRIEVANCES COMMITTEE:

In compliance of the requirement of Corporate Governance under the Listing Agreement with the Stock Exchanges, the Company has constituted a Shareholders'/Investors' Grievances Committee on 20th January, 2001 to look into issues relating to shareholders, including share transfers. The committee constitutes of:

Mr. R.C. Khanna   - Chairman
Mr. Sekhar Natarajan - Managing Director
Dr. S.P. Adarkar   - Non-Executive Director
Mr. H.C. Asher   - Non-Executive Director
Mr. Ajai Jain   - Counsel (Legal & Taxation) &
                        Company Secretary is the
                        Compliance Officer of the Company.

The company received 183 correspondences/complaints during the year, which have all been resolved.

Shares Transfer System: The Company's shares are in compulsory Dematerialisation Segment.

Name of Director	Category	No. of Board meetings attended	No. of other directorships held	Attendance at the last AGM
Mr. Brett D. Begemann	Chairman & Non-Executive Director	Nil	1	N.A.
Mr. Sekhar Natarajan	Managing Director	7	5	Yes
Dr. S.P. Adarkar	Independent Non-Executive Director	7	13	Yes
Mr. R.C. Khanna	Independent Non-Executive Director	7	6	Yes
Mr. H.C. Asher	Independent Non-Executive Director	7	22*	Yes
Mr. Wan Wah Chung	Non-Executive Director	Nil	1	No
Mr. C.Y. Wong	Non-Executive Director	Nil	-	No

*Includes directorship in private companies/alternate directorship

Share Transfer in physical forms are presently registered and option letter for simultaneous dematerialisation of shares are being sent within a period of 20 days from the date of receipt, provided the documents are complete and the shares under transfer are not in dispute. The share certificates duly endorsed are being immediately dispatched after expiry of 30 days from the date of option letter to those who have not opted for simultaneous transfer cum dematerialisation. The total number of equity shares in physical form transferred during the year was 710643.

4. AUDIT COMMITTEE:

This Committee has been constituted on 20th September, 2001 and its members are:

Mr. R.C. Khanna	- Independent & Non-Executive Director-Chairman of the Committee
Dr. S.P. Adarkar	- Independent & Non-Executive Director
Mr. H.C. Asher	- Independent & Non-Executive Director
Mr. Ajai Jain	- Secretary of the Committee
Mr. Sekhar Natarajan	- Managing Director-Permanent Invitee

The Chief Financial Officer, Internal Auditor and a representative of the statutory auditor will be the invitees at the Audit Committee meeting as and when required.

One Audit Committee meeting was held on 27th October, 2001 and attended by all the members of the Committee and also by Chief Financial Officer and statutory auditors of the Company.

5. PECUNIARY RELATIONSHIP OR TRANSACTION WITH THE COMPANY OF NON-EXECUTIVE DIRECTORS:

The Non-Executive Directors have no material pecuniary relationship or transaction with the Company in their personal capacity.

REMUNERATION OF DIRECTORS:

The details of remuneration paid to the Executive Director in the financial year are given in Note 5 of Notes to Accounts.

Independent Non-Executive Directors viz. Dr. S.P. Adarkar, Mr. R.C. Khanna and Mr. H.C. Asher were paid commission of Rs.1,40,000/- each (for the year ended 31st March, 2001) after adoption of the accounts at the Annual General Meeting held on 25th July, 2001 and also sitting fees for attending various meetings.

The Company does not have any Stock Option Scheme. However, the Managing Director and every employee of the Company participate in the Global Stock Option Plan/ Stock Appreciation Rights Plan of Monsanto Company, USA.

6. GENERAL BODY MEETINGS:

Particulars of Annual General Meetings (AGM) held during last three years:

	Date	Venue	Time
49th AGM	22nd July, 1999	M.C.Ghia Hall, Bhogilal Hargovindas Bldg, 2nd Floor, 18/20, Kaikhushru Dubash Marg, Mumbai-400 001.	10.30 a.m.
50th AGM	14th July, 2000	M.C.Ghia Hall, Bhogilal Hargovindas Bldg, 2nd Floor, 18/20, Kaikhushru Dubash Marg, Mumbai-400 001.	10.30 a.m.
51st AGM	25th July, 2001	M.C.Ghia Hall, Bhogilal Hargovindas Bldg, 2nd Floor, 18/20, Kaikhushru Dubash Marg, Mumbai-400 001.	3.00 p.m.

No postal ballots were used/invited for voting at these meetings.

7. DISCLOSURES:

The details of transaction with the Company, which are either under direct or indirect control of holding company i.e. Monsanto Company, USA are given in Note 19 of the Notes to Accounts. Besides these, the Company has no material transaction with its promoters, directors or the management, their subsidiaries or relatives, etc. that may have a potential conflict with the interest of the Company.

The Company has complied with all regulatory requirements on capital market and has not been imposed any penalty/ strictures by the Stock Exchanges or SEBI or any other statutory authority.

8. MEANS OF COMMUNICATION:

Half-yearly report sent to each household of Shareholders	No, as the result of the Company is published in the newspapers
Quarterly results - Newspapers in which results are normally published	1) The Economic Times, Mumbai 2) Navakal/Maharashtra Times, Mumbai
Any Website, where displayed	Yes, at the site www.monsantoindia.com
Whether it also displays official news releases and the presentation made to Institutional Investors or to the analysts	Yes

9. GENERAL SHAREHOLDER INFORMATION:

1. Annual General Meeting:
   - Date and Time   : 23rd July, 2002 at 10.30 a.m.
   - Venue   : M.C.Ghia Hall, Bhogilal Hargovindas Bldg, 2nd Floor, 18/20, Kaikhushru Dubash Marg, Mumbai - 400 001.

2. Financial Calendar   : 1st April to 31st March

3. Date of Book Closure   : 9th July, 2002 to 16th July, 2002

4. Dividend Payment Date   : 23rd July, 2002

5. Listing on Stock Exchanges   : The Stock Exchange, Phiroze Jeejeebhoy Towers, Dalal Street, Mumbai – 400 023.
   - : National Stock Exchange of India Ltd., Exchange Plaza, 5th Floor, Plot No.C/1, G-Block, Bandra-Kurla Complex, Bandra (West), Mumbai – 400 051.
   - : Delhi Stock Exchange Association Ltd., DSE House, 3/1, Asaf Ali Road, New Delhi –110 002.

6. Listing Fees   : Listing fees of all the Stock Exchanges for the year 2002-03 has already been paid.

7. Registrar and Share Transfer Agents   : Intime Spectrum Registry Limited, 260, Shanti Industrial Estate, Sarojini Naidu Road, Mulund (West), Mumbai – 400 080.

8. Monthly Highs & Lows of market price on Bombay Stock Exchange (BSE) & stock performance during the year 2001-02:

Period (Year 2001-02)	High (Rs.)	Low (Rs.)	Sensex
April'01	792	680	3676
May'01	1045	755	3759
June'01	994	901	3651
July'01	970	860	3513
August'01	959	430	3359
September'01	430	325	3267
October'01	370	326	3083
November'01	399	315	3377
December'01	391	258	3500
January'02	427	320	3466
February'02	550	416	3758
March'02	635	475	3758

MARKET PRICES OF THE COMPANY'S SHARES DURING THE YEAR 2001-02 ON BSE

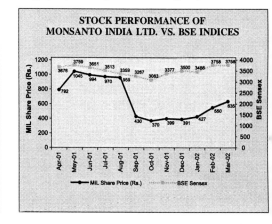

STOCK PERFORMANCE OF MONSANTO INDIA LTD. VS. BSE INDICES

9. Distribution Schedule & Shareholding Pattern as on 31st March, 2002:

DISTRIBUTION SCHEDULE		
Category	No. of Shareholders	No. of Shares
Upto 5000	7176	907835
5001 - 10000	205	151949
10001 - 20000	74	110480
20001 - 30000	22	53125
30001 - 40000	14	48921
40001 - 50000	9	41757
50001 - 100000	12	86563
100001 and above	14	7230544
TOTAL	7526	8631174

SHAREHOLDING PATTERN		
Category	No. of Shares	%
Promoters	6227022	72.15
Mutual Funds	2037	0.02
Nationalised Banks	820	0.00
Bodies Corporate	216570	2.51
Public	2007569	23.26
NRI/FIIs	177156	2.06
TOTAL	8631174	100.00

10. Stock Code
   - The Stock Exchange, Mumbai : 524084
   - National Stock Exchange of India Ltd. : MONSANTO (Symbol)
   - Delhi Stock Exchange Association Ltd. : 5874
   - International Securities
     Identification Number (ISIN) : INE274B01011

11. Dematerialisation of shares and liquidity : 15.40% of the paid-up capital of the Company has been dematerialised as on 31st March, 2002.

12. Outstanding GDRs/ADRs/Warrants or any Convertible instruments : N.A.

13. Plant Locations :
   a) 1, 4 & 5, Madhuban Industrial Estate, Madhuban Dam Road, Rakholi, Silvassa-396 240, Union Territory of Dadra & Nagar Haveli.
   b) Moka Road, Srivara Village, Bellary-583 103, Karnataka.
   c) Bapirajagudem Village, Pedavegi Mandal, Vijaya Rai Post, West Godavari Dist.- 534 475, Andhra Pradesh.

14. Address for correspondence:
   i) Intime Spectrum Registry Limited, 260, Shanti Industrial Estate, Sarojini Naidu Road, Mulund (W), Mumbai-400 080.
   ii) Monsanto India Limited, Ahura Centre, 5th Floor, 96, Mahakali Caves Road, Andheri(E), Mumbai-400 093.

10. BRIEF RESUME & OTHER INFORMATION IN RESPECT OF MR. SEKHAR NATARAJAN - MANAGING DIRECTOR, MR. R.C. KHANNA - DIRECTOR AND MR. C.Y. WONG - DIRECTOR, SEEKING RE-APPOINTMENT AT THE ENSUING ANNUAL GENERAL MEETING:

(i) Mr.Sekhar Natarajan, aged 48, joined the organisation in 1980 and has vast experience in finance, marketing and business operations in India. Currently, he is the Lead for South Asia and is responsible for managing/monitoring the business in all of South Asia. Mr.Natarajan is a qualified Chartered Accountant and Cost Accountant.

His other Directorships include: Mahyco Monsanto Biotech (India) Ltd., Parry Monsanto Seeds Ltd., Monsanto (Bangladesh) Limited, Mahyco Vegetable Seeds Limited, Maharashtra Hybrid Seeds Company Limited and Energen International Limited. He is also a member of the Shareholders'/Investors' Grievances Committee of the Company.

(ii) Mr. R.C. Khanna is 76 years old, and his qualifications are B.Com. (Lond.) F.C.A. (Eng. & Wales), A.C.M.A., F.C.A., A.I.C.W.A. He joined the Board of Directors of the Company in 1975. He is a Chartered Accountant and has vast experience in matters relating to corporate finance and taxation.

His other Directorships include: Ador Technopak Limited, Cooperheat India Pvt. Ltd., Kotak Mahindra Asset Management Co. Ltd., Tata Chemicals Limited, Schrader Duncan Limited and Shriram Investments Limited. He is also Chairman of the following Committees viz. Kotak Mahindra Asset Management Co. Ltd. – Audit Committee, Tata Chemicals Limited – Audit Committee and Monsanto India Limited – Audit Committee & Shareholders'/Investors' Grievances Committee.

(iii) Mr. C.Y. Wong is 49 years old. Mr. Wong is currently the manufacturing manager for South-East Asia and South Asia, i.e. Malaysia, India, Pakistan, Thailand and has the responsibility for long-term strategic planning and direction of the manufacturing operation in the regions. His total experience is of about 23 years and his association with Monsanto is of about 19 years. He has vast experience in Engineering, Operations and setting up of new manufacturing sites.

Mr. Wong is a qualified engineer with B.Sc. in Mechanical Engineering, Master of Engineering from University of Liverpool, certificate in Managerial Accounting from University of Pertanian Malaysia and certificate in Marketing Management from Malaysian Institute of Management. He is not a Director/Member of any other Company/Committee.

The Board of Directors
Monsanto India Limited

Re: Auditors' Certificate on Corporate Governance

We have examined the compliance of conditions of corporate governance by Monsanto India Limited for the year ended on 31st March, 2002 as stipulated in Clause 49 of the Listing Agreement of the said Company with the Stock Exchanges.

The compliance of conditions of corporate governance is the responsibility of the Management. Our examination was limited to procedures and implementation thereof, adopted by the company for ensuring compliance of the conditions of corporate governance. It is neither an audit nor an expression of opinion on the financial statements of the Company.

In our opinion, and to the best of our information and according to the explanations given to us, we certify that the company has complied in all material respects with the conditions of corporate governance as stipulated in the above mentioned Listing Agreement. Attention is however invited to Paragraph 4 of the Corporate Governance Report of the Board of Directors regarding the number of audit committee meetings held during the year.

As required by the Guidance Note issued by the Institute of Chartered Accountants of India, we have to state that according to the information and explanations given to us, no investor grievance is pending for a period exceeding one month against the Company as per the records maintained by the Shareholders' and Investors' Grievances Committee.

We further state that such compliance is neither an assurance as to the future viability of the Company nor the efficiency or effectiveness with which the Management has conducted the affairs of the Company.

For **Deloitte Haskins & Sells**
Chartered Accountants

P. B. Pardiwalla
Mumbai: May 22, 2002   *Partner*

MANAGEMENT DISCUSSION AND ANALYSIS REPORT

Industry Structure & Development: With over 400 Million acres under cultivation and over 60% of our population dependant on agriculture, the well being of our people and economy depends to a great extent on the performance of the agriculture sector. Both the Crop Protection (CP) industry and Seeds industry play a crucial role in the agriculture sector. The CP industry helps in protecting crops from damage by weeds, pests, insects and fungus, both pre and post harvest. The seeds industry provides high quality varietal and hybrid seeds for farmers which help him to improve yields of his crops.

The CP industry is commonly referred to as the pesticides industry and is regulated under a separate statute, the "Insecticides Act, 1968". The seed industry is again regulated by an independent statute called the "Seeds Act, 1966" which specifies very stringent conditions and norms for the commercialisation of seeds.

The two main activities in the CP industry are manufacturing of technical grade pesticides and formulations from these technical grade pesticides. Technical grade pesticides are manufactured indigenously as well as imported. The Indian CP industry is highly fragmented with the presence of large manufacturers operating on a national level and several small and regional players.

The Indian seed industry can be broadly divided in two categories- field crop seeds (FCS) and vegetable seeds. This industry too has a few large producers operating at the national level and a number of small and regional producers and marketers.

In an extremely competitive industry, continued growth depends on bringing new products and technologies through a strong Research & Development platform and the ability to invest and develop new markets through in-field farmer level work.

Opportunities & Threats: The fortunes of our Ag industry is influenced and closely linked to the growth and development of the overall agricultural sector. With the steady increase in the population, land available for cultivation is shrinking. This means we need higher yields to feed a growing population. High yields generally can be assured by saving loss of crop from the losses caused by weeds, pests and insects. Higher yields can also be driven by better quality of seeds.

This is a positive side for the long-term prospects of the CP and Seeds industry. In addition, current government policies encourage the growth of the food processing industry and exports of agro-based products.

The use of hybrid seeds is still very low in India and farmers still prefer to save and use their residual crop as seed for next season. But awareness about, the high yield and good quality of produce from hybrid seeds, attracting them to switch over to new varieties of hybrid seeds, is growing.

The farmers' acceptance of modern technologies of farming and availability of hybrid seeds in several regions is also a positive indication for the growth of the seeds industry.

Reform of the agriculture sector has not yet been touched upon and farm sizes and poor farm economies of scale still compel most farmers to still use old technologies/practices. This affects volume growth in the use of pesticides and new varieties of hybrid seeds.

The dependence on the monsoon is again a major threat to an agriculture-based industry. The growing campaign by environmentalists against the use of pesticides, and the increasing stress on huge investments on effluent treatment, and excessive excise duty on pesticides (this, when fertilisers are exempt from such duties) are other areas of concern.

Productwise Performance: Thanks to timely monsoons, the agriculture sector is poised for a 5.7% growth in 2001-02, against a negative growth of 0.2% in the last year. Both our agrochemical as well as seed businesses have performed well. Our agrochemicals business grew by 20% with growth coming in from our *Machete*, *Roundup* and *Leader* herbicides. With the weakening Sri Lankan and Bangladeshi currencies, we managed to hold on to our export business.

Our seeds business has grown by 33% backed by our good corn and sunflower hybrids and a growing export business.

Financial Performance: Although the overall margins have improved, our agrochemical margin continues to be under pressure because of lower realisation and competing molecules. Our seed margins have been slightly improved due to superior germplasm and better adoption.

Our cost management efforts have yielded good results during the year. Good cash collections have also helped us reduce our working capital costs during the year.

Outlook : Several factors have a major bearing on our performance and results: the state of economy, market conditions and monsoon trends, to name a few. The Indian Meteorological Department has predicted one more year of good monsoon for this year, which augurs well for our industry and our Company.

MANAGEMENT DISCUSSION AND ANALYSIS REPORT

We hope to continue with our focus on the growth of our business which will depend on our ability to penetrate untapped markets as well as capturing a greater share of the existing market.

The Company will also continue to focus on better cost management to maintain its competitiveness in the market place.

Risks & Concerns: The Company depends on imports for most of its technical material and hence the business is susceptible to the volatility of the exchange rates and import duties. The overall economic slowdown has also affected most segments of the economy including the agriculture markets. Competition in the market place continues to have an impact on our realisations and also exerts pressure on our margins.

A good, evenly distributed monsoon, is always a crucial player in the growth of the agriculture sector and related industries.

Internal Control System: Your Company's management continuously reviews the internal control system and procedures to ensure orderly and efficient conduct of business. Your Company adheres to its written corporate policies with respect to all transactions, financial reporting and budgeting.

The Company regularly conducts internal audits either through external or internal resources to monitor the effectiveness of internal control in the organisation.

The Constitution of an Audit Committee during the year has further strengthened the overall control on the business.

Human Resources: The Company has 384 employees as on 31st March, 2002. Our Development, Performance and Rewards system is linked to our global HR systems and helps us to build an organisation that will help us be successful in India. Training needs are regularly identified and internal and external trainers were hired regularly to impart training.

We have built a team-driven organisation where all employees work together to create our future.

Cautionary Statement : The statement made in this report describing the Company's projections, expectations and estimations may be a forward looking statement within the meaning of applicable securities laws and regulations. Actual results may differ from those expressed or implied in this report due to the influence of external and internal factors which are beyond the control of the Company.

For and on behalf of the Board of Directors

R C Khanna   **Sekhar Natarajan**
Director   *Managing Director*

Date: May 22, 2002

Chapter 7

Codes of corporate governance

- Introduction
- Coded objectives
- Now we are six
- All singing from the same hymn sheet
- Case study 1: Singapore
  - Key principles
  - Board structure
- Case study 2: China
- Work without end

INTRODUCTION

One of the key ingredients to the corporate governance recipe as practised worldwide has been the development of codes of corporate governance. Looking at the way such codes have been introduced, changed and amended over the years is a good way of examining the legalistic progress of corporate governance.

A word of caution, first, about codes. They lack three essential elements that characterize legal norms:

1 that the procedure for their drafting and of sanctions is established in the Constitution or the organic law of the State and that it is presumed that they express the wish of the citizens ('Laws do not oblige because they are accepted by the wish of the people . . . the people will dictate its wish through suffrage' (Digesto romano, Lib. 1 tit. III, 32, paragraph I));

2 that they are mandatory for all and evenly applied 'without fear or favour'; and

3 that their violation or unfulfilment leads to a sanction which emanates from a legal or administrative source and which is sufficiently strong to deter repeated breaches of the code.

They therefore occupy a legal limbo, and their strength depends on enforcement. The power of a code in Singapore is very different, as a result, from a code in the Philippines or Indonesia. They may say the same thing, but that is only the beginning of it.

Moreover, as Professor Annie Koh, a forceful and dynamic Finance Professor at Singapore Management University, has noted, although in the last few years, Singapore, Malaysia and Thailand have all introduced codes of corporate governance, these tend to focus on *listed* companies. 'Private companies should behave like good public companies from day one', she has said. Her silent admonition that one day they may need to tap the share markets and so should prepare themselves is certainly a fair point, but it is also worth noting that even private companies may need injections of capital – private equity is the biggest and most spectacular example, of course – but equally, private companies may accept finance from business angels, relatives and friends. Professor Koh didn't say this, but Chinese New Year will always tend to pass more peacefully if everyone is convinced that even if adverse business conditions cannot be helped, at least no one has fraudulently absconded with anyone else's money.

The codes themselves, though, are of course impressive documents.

CODED OBJECTIVES

Why have a code? Why did Malaysia, for instance, find it necessary or desirable to introduce a Code of Corporate Governance? The Malaysian code, as with others in Asia, ostensibly aims to set out principles and best practices on structures and processes that companies may use in their operations towards achieving the optimal governance framework. These structures and processes exist at a micro-level which include issues such as the composition of the board, procedures for recruiting new directors, remuneration of directors, the use of board committees, their mandates and their activities. 'The need for a code was inspired in part by a desire for the private sector to initiate and lead a review and to establish reforms of standards of corporate governance at a micro level. This is based on the belief that in some aspects, self-regulation is preferable and the standards developed by those involved may be more acceptable and thus more enduring.' If one believed that the private sector in Malaysia really did spontaneously get together and agree on the desirability of the code, then who could argue with the sentiment expressed?

The extent to which it was a copy even in concept was explicitly acknowledged by the Malaysian authorities. 'The level of awareness and attention generated by the Cadbury Report has been phenomenal. The report has struck a chord internationally, and it has provided a yardstick against which standards of corporate governance are being measured:

> The role of the code is to guide boards by clarifying their responsibilities, and providing prescriptions strengthening the control exercised by boards over their companies. . . . In developing the code we have been mindful of developments in other jurisdictions. We have endeavoured to keep the discussion at an international level. Standards developed for Malaysia must measure up to international thinking on this subject.

The problem with this kind of copying is, as mentioned in Chapter 2, its potential two-dimensionality. Confronted with a code embedding an alien spirit to business, but which has the apparent support of the government, the natural response of the Asian business – or indeed the Mediterranean one – is to go along with the fad of the moment, and conform to what is being asked of it. But the danger of a conformity without intent is its narrow boundaries: the codes must continually be rewritten precisely because there is no internal business impulse to better governance. Perhaps not even in the Anglo-American model is this impulse fully internalized.

NOW WE ARE SIX

Most Asian countries now have codes of corporate governance – indeed, have had them for some time.

- In January 2002, the CSRC released its Code of Corporate Governance for Listed Companies in **China**. The code emphasizes the importance of credibility and integrity and identifies the relationships between shareholders and directors, executives and management, and trustors and the trustees. The code requires that all annual general meeting details comply with PRC Company Law. Requirements for directors and supervisors as well as stakeholders' rights and related items are articulated. The code also sets additional disclosure requirements of corporate governance for listed companies.
- The Institute of Chartered Accountants of **Sri Lanka** delivered its *Report of the Committee to Make Recommendations on Matters Relating to Financial Aspects of Corporate Governance* as early as December 1997.
- The **Malaysian** Code on Corporate Governance was developed by the Working Group on Best Practices in Corporate Governance (JPK1) and subsequently approved by the High Level Finance Committee on

193

Corporate Governance. JPK1 was chaired by the Chairman of the Federation of Public Listed Companies. The members of the JPK1 comprised a mix of private and public sector participation. The code was claimed to be principally an initiative of the private sector as indicated by the membership of JPK1. The high-level Finance Committee on Corporate Governance then formulated the Malaysian Code on Corporate Governance in March 2000. As of 1 June 2001, revised KLSE Listing Requirements spelt out that listed companies must disclose the extent of their compliance with the best practices encapsulated in the code.

- The Institute of Chartered Accountants of **Pakistan** delivered its recommendations on, and the Securities and Exchange Commission of Pakistan issued immediately afterwards, the Code of Corporate Governance for Pakistan in March 2002.
- The codemakers have not been idle in **Hong Kong**, either. The Stock Exchange issued a Code of Best Practice as early as December 1989, and revised it in June 1996, February 1999 and August 2000, when it produced the SEHK, Model Code for Securities Transactions by Directors of Listed Companies. HKSA, New Corporate Governance Guide on Formation of Audit Committees (January 1998).
- In **Thailand**, the Stock Exchange of Thailand (SET) first published a 'Code of Best Practice for Directors of Listed Companies' in December 1997.

It is perhaps tempting to separate out those countries which took action before the Enron and Chinese scandals broke, such as Singapore and Malaysia, and those which only took action afterwards, like Pakistan.

ALL SINGING FROM THE SAME HYMN SHEET

'Code convergence' is a reality. In other words, since the Asian financial crisis there has been a marked convergence towards 'global best practice' in new corporate governance codes of virtually all major economies. US scandals have had a paradoxical effect: slowed the pace of change and undermined credibility of US standards, while also making governance reform more important. Sarbanes-Oxley is partially restoring US reputation. Code convergence continues.

CASE STUDY 1: SINGAPORE

The Singapore government responded to the Asian financial crisis by taking a number of initiatives to strengthen its financial sector and improve the competitiveness of its economy. Following the recommendations of the Corporate Finance Committee in 1998, Singapore has been steadily moving from a merit-based regime, under which the securities regulator judges the quality of the companies to be listed, to a disclosure-based regime, where the market evaluates the companies based on more complete information. This move not only changes the role of regulators; it also requires fundamental changes to the legal and regulatory framework, accounting and auditing standards, codes of best practice and the role of third-party watchdogs such as the news media and investors' associations. With this in mind, the Ministry of Finance, together with MAS and the Attorney General's Chambers, spearheaded a comprehensive review of corporate regulation and governance. As part of this exercise in December 1999 it formed three private sector led committees to review and recommend regulations and corporate practices *modelled after international best practices*, with the predictable aim of increasing Singapore's competitiveness in the global economy. One of these committees, the Corporate Governance Committee (CGC), conducted a detailed study to: review, develop and promote best practices in corporate governance among the publicly listed companies in Singapore; examine international best practices and benchmarks in order to formulate corporate governance principles and recommend corporate governance practices suitably modified to the local environment; and recommend a framework to enhance and promote higher standards in corporate governance.

The CGC completed its review and submitted its final report and an accompanying Code of Corporate Governance in March 2001. In their deliberations, the Corporate Governance Committee opted for a balanced approach, very similar to the approaches adopted in the UK and Canada. In general, the intent of the code is not to prescribe corporate behaviour in detail but to essentially secure sufficient disclosure so that investors and others can assess a company's performance and governance practices and respond in an informed way. The government announced its acceptance of all the CGC's recommendations on 4 April 2001.

The guidelines are built upon the Code of Corporate Governance issued in 2001 by the CGC, set up by the Ministry of Finance, the Authority and Attorney-General's Chambers. The Singapore Code of Corporate Governance came into effect from 1 January 2003, for all listed companies which hold their annual general meetings from this date. While the code itself does not require compliance, its adoption as a part of the Singapore Exchange's Listing Manual does state that listed companies make certain related disclosures in their annual reports. The CGC proposed that all companies listed on the Singapore Stock Exchange be required, as a requirement in the Listing Manual, to give a complete description of their corporate governance practices with specific references to each of the guidelines set out in the code, and where they deviate from these best practices, they should disclose these non-compliance with appropriate explanations in their annual reports for Annual General Meetings (AGMs) held from 1 January 2003 onwards. In line with these recommendations, the relevant sections of the Listing Manual have been revised by the Singapore Exchange. Listed companies are now indirectly required to adopt the best practices set out in this code, for they will be required to disclose the extent of their compliance and any deviations in those annual reports presented at AGMs held after 1 January 2003.

The Singapore government describes its Code of Corporate Governance as 'a critical milestone in strengthening our disclosure-based regime'. What is so special about the code? It sets out principles and best practices in four main areas of governance, namely, board matters, remuneration, accountability and audit, and communications with shareholders. Listed companies are now required to describe their corporate governance practices in their annual reports, as well as disclose and explain areas of deviation from the code.

Key principles

Board matters

- An effective board is essential to lead and control the company.
- There should be a strong and independent element on the board, with independent directors making up at least one-third of the board.
- Separation in the roles of chairman of the board and CEO of the company is necessary to ensure an appropriate balance of power.
- A formal and transparent process is required for the appointment and re-election of directors.
- Complete, adequate and timely information should be provided to the board by the management.

Remuneration matters

- The level and mix of remuneration should be appropriate to attract, retain and motivate the directors.
- There should be clear disclosure of the company's remuneration policy, level and mix of remuneration, and the procedure for setting remuneration.

Accountability and audit

- The board is accountable to the shareholders.
- An Audit Committee with written terms of reference should be established.
- The board should meet with internal and external auditors without the presence of company's management.
- It must be ensured that the management maintains a sound system of internal controls.

■ An internal audit function should be established.

Communication with shareholders

■ Adequate disclosure of corporate governance structure and practices are a crucial part of communications.
■ It is essential to engage in regular, effective and fair communication with shareholders.
■ Greater shareholder participation at Annual General Meetings should be encouraged.
■ Key personnel, including the auditors, should attend AGMs to answer shareholders' queries.

Board structure

In addition to the establishment of an audit committee (AC) which is a current requirement under the Companies Act, the Singapore Code recommends the establishment of two other board committees: the remuneration committee (RC) and nomination committee (NC).

The requirements for membership on these board committees are summarized in Table 7.1.

Before implementing the recommendations of the CGC, the board of directors of listed companies need to examine their existing corporate governance frameworks and policies, so as to properly align and improve its practices, at a reasonable cost and effort. Potential questions that all listed companies will need

Table 7.1 *Requirements for membership on board committees: three committees*

	Audit committee	Nomination committee	Remuneration committee
Size	At least three members	At least three members	–
Chairman	Independent	Independent	Independent
Composition	All non-executive, majority independent	Majority independent	Majority independent
Critical skills/ knowledge	At least two having accounting or financial management expertise or experience	–	At least one with knowledge of executive compensation or access to expert advice

to ask, before steps are taken to forge ahead with their corporate governance initiatives, are:

- What is our current status and extent of compliance with the Singapore Code?
- Does the board have the right mix of competencies? Has the board's written terms of reference been drawn up/updated?
- Is the board and are the individual directors subject to any formal assessment of effectiveness?
- Nomination and remuneration committees – have these been appropriately established and constituted with a set of relevant terms of reference?
- Does the audit committee need to be restructured such that it comprises only of non-executive and a majority of independent directors? Does its terms of reference need to be revised?
- Is there adequate disclosure regarding directors' and the top five key executives' remuneration packages?

Although the provisions of the code are not mandatory, the Singapore government reports enthusiastically that an August 2003 Ernst & Young survey of the annual reports of 30 large locally listed companies found that all had generally complied with the principles set out in the Code of Corporate Governance. For instance, all 30 companies surveyed have a nominating committee and had appointed an independent director to be the chairman of the audit committee as recommended by the code. This compared very favourably to observations taken two months before the code was introduced, which showed that the average total score was only 21 per cent. ACCA discovered that two months before the code became effective only 54 per cent of Chief Financial Officers in Singapore had reviewed their corporate governance practices (ACCA, 2002).

In 2003, the Financial Reporting Council (FRC) of the UK published the new Combined Code. This was based on the proposed revision of the Combined Code (1998) in the report by Derek Higgs on the role and effectiveness of non-executive directors, which incorporated the recommendations on audit committees by Robert Smith. Perhaps the most significant changes in the code are the expanded definition of director independence, an increase in the recommended proportion of independent directors from one-third to a majority of the board for larger listed companies, and separate Chairman and CEO with the Chairman being an independent director. There is also a clearer specification of non-executive directors' duties, an increased role and more stringent guidelines on membership of the audit committee, as well as an increased emphasis on the need for internal audit and control functions. Further, the new code allows for some differences in corporate governance arrangements for larger and smaller

companies, particularly pertaining to the number and proportion of independent directors on the board and the number of members on certain board
committees.

At a stroke, the Singapore Code was rendered obsolete. As Professor Mak of
NUS observed, while the Singapore Code specifies that there should be a 'strong
and independent' non-executive element on the Board, it makes no specific
mention of the role that non-executive directors (NEDs) have to play on the
board to ensure good corporate governance, for example in direct contact with
shareholders. To some extent the differences can be explained by the fact that
unlike in the UK major shareholders in Singapore tend to be families or government, and non-executive directors are often related to them or are their nominees.
In fact, as Professor Mak rightly argues, the concern in Singapore is likely to be
quite the opposite – major shareholders having too much direct communication
with and influence over non-executive directors. His choice of language on the
next point is revealing: whereas the Singapore Code recommends that the nominating committee decide whether or not a director – including an NED – is able
to adequately carry out his duties, the UK Code (2003) goes further and places
the responsibility on the NEDs to also 'undertake that they will have sufficient
time to meet what is expected of them'. The UK Code (2003) also includes a
schedule which provides guidance on the liability of NEDs and how NEDs should
exercise care, skill and diligence in discharging their responsibilities. As noted
above (Chapter 3) the latest practice is for a majority of the board to be made
up of non-executive directors, whereas the Singapore Code calls for only one-
third to be so. Another fresh development in the Combined Code is that
independence for directors is now expected to include independence from major
shareholders as well as from management. This expanded definition of independence is also adopted by the corporate governance codes in countries such as
Canada and Malaysia, although the US continues to define independence primarily
as independence from management. Honours are pretty much even with respect
to board committees, with in some instances the Singapore Code beating the
Combined Code in its insistence on disclosure and its specification for the composition of certain committees. For example, the Singapore Code recommends
that the board reports to shareholders annually the remuneration of not just the
directors, but also the top five key non-director executives of the company.
Likewise audit committees remain a best practice recommendation in the UK,
while in Singapore, it has been legally required for listed companies since 1991.

CASE STUDY 2: CHINA

The corporate scandals and capital flight cases that emerged in mid-2001 prompted
officials at CSRC and other state regulatory bodies to put corporate governance
at the top of their list of priorities for 2002. Reflecting this commitment, in

January 2001 CSRC issued the Code of Corporate Governance of Listed Companies in China.

The two key documents are: the *Code of Corporate Governance for Listed Companies in China* (China Securities Regulatory Commission – CSRC, State Economic and Trade Commission, 7 January 2001) and the *Guidelines for Introducing Independent Directors to the Board of Directors of Listed Companies* (China Securities Regulatory Commission – CSRC, State Economic and Trade Commission, 16 August 2001).

The code is a set of comprehensive rules covering basic principles for corporate governance of listed companies, the means for the protection of investors' interests, and the ethical requirements for directors, supervisors, managers and other senior management members. In particular, the code emphasizes that listed companies must be operated in an independent manner and sets out the minimum disclosure regarding corporate governance such as: (1) the composition of the board of directors and the supervisory board; (2) the performance and evaluation of the board of directors, the supervisory board and the independent directors; (3) the composition and work of the specialized committees of the board of directors; and (4) specific plans and measures to improve corporate governance. The code aimed to introduce solid corporate governance in listed companies by elevating requirements on accounting procedures and information disclosure, introducing independent directors' systems, and tightening the supervision of corporate management. CSRC officials who drafted the code, and other similar legislation in the past, used the US legal and regulatory systems as models. Though the code directly addresses many of the existing problems in China's financial sector, it will only prove effective if company managers honestly implement – and CSRC strictly enforces – its provisions. Yet these provisions are promising. For example, the code expands the rights of shareholders. Article 2 states that minority shareholders should have equal status with other shareholders and Article 4 gives shareholders the right to protect their interests through civil litigation and other legal approaches. Article 8 requires that listed companies make a genuine effort to use modern telecommunications technologies in shareholders' general meetings to improve shareholder participation. And Article 11 gives institutional investors more weight in the decision-making process, including in the nomination of directors. The code attempts to strengthen the roles of the boards of directors and supervisors. According to Articles 29 and 31, a listed company must establish transparent procedures to select the board of directors, and a listed company in which the controlling shareholder owns a stake in excess of 30 per cent should adopt a cumulative voting mechanism to ensure the voting interests of minority shareholders. Article 49 requires listed companies to introduce independent directors who do not hold any other positions within the company. Articles 60 and 61 state that members of the board of supervisors must be permitted access to information related to operational status and be allowed

200

to hire independent intermediary agencies for professional consultation, without interference from other company employees. Finally, the code includes specific provisions on information disclosure. Articles 88 and 89 require the listed company to disclose promptly any information that may have a substantial impact on the decision-making of shareholders or associated parties. Articles 13 and 14 require the listed company to fully disclose prices of related party transactions and prohibit it from providing financial collateral to related entities. Article 92 requires the listed company to promptly release detailed information on controlling shareholders. And Articles 25 and 27 require controlling shareholders to honour the independence of the listed company and to avoid interfering or directly competing with the listed entity.

WORK WITHOUT END

Asian codemakers are, of course, shooting at a moving target. Just as Asia has caught up with the concept and implementation of codes of corporate governance, Europe is making matters more complicated. The latest Combined Code in the UK contains 39 'principles', 14 main and 25 supporting, and 'provisions' – detailed points of best practice and annual reports must specify whether or not these are being applied. Professor Mak says that he believes that:

the U.K. Code (2003), together with developments elsewhere in countries such as the U.S. and Australia, means that the 'goalposts have moved'. While the Singapore Code recommends that at least one-third of the Board should be independent of management, the U.K., U.S. and Australia are now advocating that a majority of the Board should be independent. Further, in these countries, the concept of independence has been considerably tightened, especially in terms of relationship between directors and major shareholders, and business or other relationships that directors may have with the companies whose boards they sit on and with the management of these companies. The calls to have two separate individuals holding the Chairman and CEO positions have grown louder. Even in the U.S., where the combined CEO-Chairman model is heavily entrenched, the recent NYSE/Richard Grasso episode has given considerable ammunition to proponents of a separation there. . . . Other aspects where changes should be considered in the light of changing global practices include wholly independent board committees (especially the audit and remuneration committees), more transparency in pay practices for directors and senior executives, 'whistleblowing' provisions to provide employees with avenues to bring to the Board's attention serious improprieties by management and to protect these employees, and greater responsibility on institutional investors to play a pro-active role in corporate governance of companies.

He is absolutely right about the goalposts; Asian countries are continuing to revise their codes in response to the challenge. For example, in Hong Kong,

> It had planned to release the revised Code in December 2003. This will now be delayed until Q1 2004. At the same time the significant Listing Rules changes relating to corporate governance will be submitted for approval by the SFC.

In 2004 the Singapore government, unsurprisingly, responded to the Combined Code by announcing commensurate improvements to the Singapore Code. And by the time that Singapore, Hong Kong and other Asian jurisdictions adopt the provisions embedded in the Combined Code, the US and UK will be ready with new ones, which Asian regulators have not thought of because they have been so busy implementing the last lot. The goalposts are being moved deliberately. This is *regulatory colonialism*.

Chapter 8

The role of active shareholding in Asia

- The role of active shareholding in corporate governance
- The basis of action
  - Introduction
  - Summary of proxy voting guidelines
- The legal background in Asia
- Asia just doesn't have much yet
- Conclusion

THE ROLE OF ACTIVE SHAREHOLDING IN CORPORATE GOVERNANCE

Throughout Asia, it is now recognized that shareholders delegate the detailed and 'day-to-day' decision-making of the corporation to the board of directors, but that they can, if they see the need, participate in significant corporate decision-making processess through various legal measures. They can attend shareholders' meetings, make shareholder proposals, solicit proxies and convene extraordinary shareholders' meetings. Shareholders can also resort to seeking criminal or administrative investigations to seek the accountability of management. Civil lawsuits can be time consuming and it is difficult to obtain enough evidence to prevail in litigation. In recent years, corporate governance advocates – particularly public employee pension fund investors like Calpers and Hermes in the West – have tended to focus on issues such as greater independence for the board of poorly performing companies, and the quicker and less troublesome removal of underperforming CEOs. Pressure applied by corporate governance advocates and large institutional investors has certainly resulted in changes of leadership at several major Western companies, as reported by Booz Allen Hamilton in 2002, but this has yet to happen in Asia.[1] In the Asia-Pacific region, the same study reported that the number of transitions was essentially constant from 1995 through 2000, and there remains a conviction that orderly transition is almost certainly better for the stock markets, just as it is for the electorate. The OECD Principles provide that 'institutional investors and nominee shareholders should consider the costs and benefits of exercising their voting rights' but currently, institutional investors in Asia still prefer to vote with their feet. With thousands of companies to choose from, who can be surprised?

THE BASIS OF ACTION

This is how one major international investor, Fidelity, views its responsibilities as an investor and how it believes they should be exercised.

Introduction

Fidelity's mutual funds are managed with one overriding goal: to provide the greatest possible return to shareholders consistent with governing laws and the investment policies of each fund. In pursuit of this goal, the Fidelity funds take two basic types of action: (1) buy and hold securities they believe will appreciate in value, and sell securities they believe are less likely to appreciate in value; and (2) exercise their rights as shareholders to support sound corporate governance within companies in which the funds invest.

At Fidelity, the first type of action – buying and selling securities – is based on searching the globe for investment opportunities company by company, issue by issue. In that spirit, Fidelity portfolio managers make their investment decisions – to buy, hold or sell – based on this research.

The exercise of shareholder rights is generally done by casting votes by proxy at shareholder meetings on matters submitted to shareholders for approval. For example, the election of directors or the approval of a company's stock option plans for officers or employees. At Fidelity, formal written guidelines followed by all of the Fidelity Funds have been established for proxy voting by the Board of Trustees of the Fidelity Funds. The purpose of these guidelines (summarized below), is simple: to promote accountability of a company's management and board of directors to its shareholders; to align the interests of management with those of shareholders; and to increase disclosure of a company's business and operations.

Fidelity believes sound corporate governance should achieve three key objectives:

1 *Accountability*. There must be effective means in place to hold those entrusted with running a company's business accountable for their actions. Management of a company must be accountable to its board of directors; the board, in turn, must be accountable to shareholders, who are the company's owners. Promoting

accountability can take many forms. These include enforcing rules and laws imposing duties on officers and directors; protecting shareholder voting rights; ensuring rigorous scrutiny of a company's financial statements by independent, outside auditors; and maintaining free and open markets to allow for the re-allocation of capital and transfers of corporate control.

2 *Alignment of management and shareholder interests.* The interests of a company's management and board of directors should be aligned with the interests of the company's shareholders. This means, for example, that salary and equity-based forms of compensation paid to management should be designed to reward management for doing a good job of creating value for the shareholders of the company.

3 *Effective disclosure.* The third objective is to promote timely disclosure of important information about a company's business operations and financial performance. This is intended to enable investors, individual and institutional alike, to make informed decisions on when to buy, sell or hold a company's securities.

To promote these objectives, specific proxy guidelines – *Fidelity Funds' Proxy Voting Guidelines* – were established by the Board of Trustees of the Funds, after consultation with Fidelity. (The Proxy Voting Guidelines are reviewed periodically by Fidelity and by the Independent Trustees of the Fidelity Funds, and, accordingly, are subject to change.)

The guidelines recognize that a company's management is entrusted with the day-to-day operations of the company, as well as longer term strategic planning subject to the oversight of the company's board of directors. The guidelines also recognize that the company's shareholders – the owners of the company – must have final say over how management and directors are performing, and how shareholders' rights and ownership interests are handled.

Fidelity's proxy voting guidelines generally address three types of proposal submitted to shareholders: (1) proposals seeking approval of *equity-based compensation*, including stock option plans; (2) proposals relating to changes in corporate control; and (3) proposals that affect *shareholder rights, including voting rights.*

Summary of proxy voting guidelines

Equity-based compensation plans

APPROVAL OF PLANS OR PLAN AMENDMENTS

Fidelity encourages the use of reasonably designed stock-related compensation plans that align the interests of corporate management with those of shareholders by providing officers and employees with an incentive to increase shareholder value. While we evaluate plans on a case-by-case basis, the guidelines generally call for withholding our vote for plans or plan amendments that do not meet the following conditions:

- The dilution effect of new shares authorized, plus the shares reserved for issuance in connection with all other stock related plans, should not exceed 10 per cent. However, for companies with a smaller market capitalization, the dilution effect should not exceed 15 per cent. If the plan does not meet this test, the dilution effect is also evaluated in the light of any unusual factor involving the company.
- The minimum exercise price of stock options should be no less than 100 per cent of fair market value on the date of grant.
- Neither the board of directors nor its compensation committee should be authorized to materially amend a plan without shareholder approval.
- The granting of awards to non-employee directors should not be subject to management discretion, but rather should be pursuant to non-discretionary grants specified by the plan's terms.
- The plan should not authorize the re-pricing of stock options (including the cancellation and exchange of options) without shareholder approval.
- The restriction period for restricted stock awards (RSAs) normally should be at least three years. RSAs with a restriction period of less than three years, but at least one year, might be acceptable if the RSA is performance based.
- Stock awards other than stock options and RSAs should be identified as being granted to officers/directors in lieu of salary or cash bonus, and the number of shares awarded should be reasonable.

RE-PRICING OF OUTSTANDING OPTIONS

Fidelity generally will withhold its authority on the election of directors if, within the most recent year and without shareholder approval, a company's board of directors or its compensation committee has re-priced certain outstanding options held by officers or directors exceeding certain percentages depending on the size of the company.

MEASURES DEALING WITH TAKEOVERS

The Fidelity guidelines generally oppose measures that are designed to prevent or obstruct corporate takeovers. Such measures tend to entrench current management. In our free capital markets system, the active trading of a company's securities and the potential transfer of corporate control through takeover – hostile or otherwise – must be permitted to occur.

206

SHAREHOLDER RIGHTS PLANS

The guidelines recognize that there are arguments both in favour of and against shareholder rights plans, also known as poison pills because they can prevent someone from buying more than a certain percentage of a company's stock without management approval. We believe the best approach is for the company to put its case to shareholders by letting them vote on a plan. We generally respond to the adoption or extension of a shareholder rights plan in accordance with the following guidelines:

- If, without shareholder approval, a company's board of directors has instituted a new poison pill plan, extended an existing plan or adopted a new plan upon the expiration of an existing plan during the last year, we generally withhold votes on the election of directors at the Annual Meeting following such action.
- Fidelity may vote in favour of a rights plan with 'sunset' provisions: if the plan is linked to a business strategy that will – in our view – likely result in greater value for shareholders, if the term is less than five years, and if shareholder approval is required to reinstate the expired plan or adopt a new plan at the end of this term.
- We generally support shareholder resolutions requesting that shareholders be given the opportunity to vote on the adoption of rights plans.

GOLDEN PARACHUTES

The guidelines oppose the use of accelerated employment contracts that will result in cash grants of greater than three times annual compensation (salary and bonus) in the event of termination of employment following a change in control of a company. In general, the guidelines call for voting against such 'golden parachute' plans because they impede potential takeovers that shareholders should be free to consider. Adoption of such golden parachutes generally will result in withholding of the Fidelity Funds' votes for directors who approve such contracts and stand for re-election at the next shareholders' meeting.

INCREASES IN AUTHORIZED COMMON STOCK

The guidelines generally call for approval of increases in authorized shares, provided that the increase is not greater than three times the number of shares outstanding and reserved for issuance. In calculating shares outstanding and those reserved for future issuance, the guidelines take into account shares reserved for stock-related plans and securities convertible into common stock, but not shares reserved for any poison pill plan.

'BLANK CHECK' PREFERRED STOCK

The guidelines generally call for voting against proposals to authorize preferred stock whose voting, conversion, dividend and other rights are determined at the discretion of the board of directors when the stock is issued. Although so-called 'blank check' preferred stock typically is used for legitimate financing needs, it also can be issued in an anti-takeover situation. To protect Fidelity Fund shareholders, while still providing financing flexibility to management, Fidelity generally votes in favour of the authorization of preferred stock if the company's board of directors specifically agrees to the following provisions:

- The voting rights of a series of preferred stock are limited to one vote per share.
- The preferred stock will not be issued in an anti-takeover situation unless shareholders have approved the issuance in advance.

CLASSIFIED BOARDS

The guidelines view the election of a company's board of directors as one of the most fundamental rights held by shareholders of the company. Because a classified board structure prevents shareholders from electing a full slate of directors at Annual Meetings, the guidelines generally call for voting against classified boards. Fidelity generally will vote in favour of shareholder proposals to declassify a board of directors unless a company's charter or governing corporate law allows shareholders, by written consent, to remove a majority of directors at any time, with or without cause.

SHAREHOLDER RIGHTS

Fidelity's guidelines view the exercise of shareholders' rights – including the rights to act by written consent, to call special meetings and to remove directors – to be fundamental to corporate governance.

Corporate governance is argued to relate to international fund management in the following way. There is a close relation between corporate governance and the portfolios held by investors. Most firms in countries with poor investor protection are controlled by large shareholders, so that only a fraction of the shares issued by firms in these countries can be freely traded and held by portfolio investors. The prevalence of closely-held firms in most countries helps explain why these countries exhibit a home bias in share holdings and why US investors underweight foreign countries in their portfolios. A hypothetical estimate of the world portfolio of shares available to investors who are not controlling shareholders (the world float portfolio) differs sharply from the world market portfolio. In regressions explaining the portfolio weights of US investors, the world float portfolio has a positive significant coefficient but the world market portfolio has no additional explanatory power. Not all agree. It has also been suggested that foreign direct investment in Asia may not have positive effects on corporate governance at all.

Foreign firms that enter Asian markets will have little effect if they only seek to take advantage of any lower standards of transparency and governance, rather than to implement higher standards, and foreign capital and globalisation has done little to improve anything much.[2]

was the comment of one academic writing as recently as 2003.

The ACCA stands firmly behind the belief that shareholder activism is a fine route to good corporate governance. It has declared:

Investor mindsets have to undergo a paradigm shift from passivity to activism if shareholders want to stand up for their rights. Improving regulations in each country are giving investors the tools and legal recourse to confront companies on poor practice.

THE LEGAL BACKGROUND IN ASIA

Legally, according to the OECD, Asian legal regimes tend to demand shareholder approval of the following:

- Amending the company's founding documents (e.g. statutes, articles of incorporation, etc.).
- Changing the terms, conditions or relative rights of the company's shares.
- Electing directors.
- Major transactions, such as merger, sale of substantially all of the company's assets outside of the ordinary course of business, or an acquisition of assets outside of the ordinary course of business that represents a significant increase in the company's overall assets.

Some jurisdictions also require shareholder approval of dividends. Typically, the majority required for approval of fundamental changes ranges from two-thirds (in Vietnam and Taiwan) to three-fourths (in Bangladesh, Malaysia, Pakistan and Singapore). There is considerable range in the minimum prior notice required for shareholder meetings. Such notice varies from 7 days in Vietnam to 30 days in China and Chinese Taipei.[3]

Asia is teeming with legislation to enhance shareholder rights and make shareholder activism easier, too. In China the January 2002 release of the *Regulations for Corporate Governance of Listed Companies* (the 'Regulations') marked according to some commentators a substantial movement toward meaningful investor protection in China. In addition to providing a general mandate for protection of shareholder rights, the Regulations also require that corporate governance structures ensure that all shareholders, especially minority shareholders, enjoy equality. Clarke adds that although they may for the time being establish

209

theoretical rights without access to legal remedies in court, other provisions of the Regulations are also aimed specifically at protecting shareholders' (especially minority shareholders') rights:

- The right to bring court or other proceedings to enjoin illegal actions of meetings of the shareholders and the board, as well as to require the company to sue directors, supervisors, managers whose violating conduct has injured the company.
- Listed companies take active steps to maximize shareholder participation at general meetings.
- Disclosure and 'arm's length' requirements in connection with related party transactions, and taking effective steps to ensure that related parties do not harm the company by monopolizing procurement and sales channels, etc.
- Implementation of effective measures to prevent embezzlement of company assets and funds by shareholders and related parties, and a ban on granting security interests in favour of shareholders and related parties.
- Imposition of a general duty of good faith and other special duties on controlling shareholders.
- Qualifications of candidates for seats on the board are to be disclosed well in advance of elections.
- Requirement of cumulative voting for directors when the controlling shareholder holds over 30 per cent of voting control, for the express purpose of protecting medium and small shareholders.
- Directors are bound to duties of loyalty, good faith and diligence, are to act in the best interests of all shareholders and treat all shareholders fairly.
- Independent directors have a specific duty to protect the interests of 'small and medium' shareholders.

Considering that China's contemporary capital markets are still a relatively new phenomenon, China's legislators and the CSRC have done an admirable job of establishing a framework for disclosure and shareholder protection. Key among the systemic problems within China's listed companies has always been concentrated share ownership – the largest shareholder stake in listed companies averaged 44.9 per cent, according to a July 2001 issue of *China Securities*, while the second-largest shareholder typically owned a mere 8.2 per cent. With such a disparity, majority shareholders can easily ignore minority investors and use information asymmetries – whereby board directors and senior managers have access to key information regarding a stock price before individual investors – to falsify the books and defraud new investors.

More than 60 per cent of listed companies' shares (both A and B shares) in China were not in circulation, according to CSRC at one time. The considerable amount of non-tradable shares in the market makes management indifferent to the fluctuations in stock prices and the rights of minority shareholders. Meanwhile, external supervision by government industry regulators, and the media, remains limited. Since most listed firms emerged out of state-owned entities, the government in many cases owns more than half, and in some cases up to 80 per cent, of a company's shares. Typically, however, the state does not exercise its rights as a shareholder to influence management effectively. In fact, majority government control of listed companies can make it difficult for systems managers to build healthy corporate governance systems and enhance profitability. Because of the expense and difficulties facing a small shareholder attempting to assert its rights against a listed company, the requirement that the CSRC establish a violation before damage claims proceed to court could serve in practice to reduce barriers to individual shareholders seeking compensation. At the same time, this requirement tends to deprive the courts of an important function and opportunity for their development along US lines. From a more cynical standpoint, this also underscores the Chinese government's underlying ambivalence toward meaningful empowerment of the courts to the exclusion of central administrative and regulatory processes. The inescapable question remains in the minds of pro-corporate governance commentators: will China's capital markets ever realize their full potential contribution to the Chinese economy until the rule of law and a truly independent judiciary are established? With all this the authors of the OECD White Paper would reluctantly agree. The political issue is fundamental: the link between a Western model of almost everything, and especially corporate law and administration, and wealth creation.

Then the OECD report takes a tilt at Asian jurisdictions themselves. By their nature, the OECD argues, the standards underpinning the equitable treatment of shareholders also require greater resources to investigate and wider discretion to enforce than the bright line rules by which shareholders' rights are implemented. In Asia, difficulties for regulators and courts can be magnified by the use of complex, interlocking ownership structures that often cut across national boundaries, as well as by the prevalence of informal agreements and relationships that leave no paper trail for investigators or litigants to follow. There are specific charges, too. Certain jurisdictions, such as India, Korea, Philippines and Thailand, are singled out for prohibiting voting *in absentia* – such an outrage, apparently, to insist that shareholders actually attend AGMs; but then how can huge international pension funds actually attend the AGM of each of the companies they invest in? – while Singapore limits the number of proxy cards provided to nominees to two per nominee. Some jurisdictions also prohibit split or partial voting by nominees, thereby making it impossible for nominees to cast votes in accordance with the instructions of their principals. It is not uncommon for jurisdictions to permit only shareholders of the company to serve as proxies for other shareholders. Moreover, some jurisdictions permit the chairman of the meeting,

211

who is usually closely aligned with management or insider shareholders, to determine the outcome of a vote by asking for a show of hands. Of course, secret voting is the only acceptably format, so far as the OECD is concerned. Parliamentary democracy has always been thus, at least since 1832, and naturally, what is right for the UK Parliament must be right for the Asian company as well. The OECD further suggests that laws and listing requirements also frequently fail to require companies to provide verifiable confirmation that votes were properly tabulated and recorded. Not content with attacking the legislation, the OECD also lists a number of practices across Asia which, it believes, prevent or impede effective shareholder participation in shareholder meetings. These practices include:

- Numerous companies scheduling shareholder meetings on the same day.
- Meetings being held in inadequate or inconveniently located facilities.
- Untimely or ineffective notice of meetings.[4]
- Inadequate information concerning agenda items.
- Fixing a record date that precedes the date the meeting is announced.
- Unreasonable restrictions on persons who may serve as proxies.
- Prohibitions on voting *in absentia*.
- Unreasonable restrictions on the ability of shareholders to place issues or initiatives on the agenda and to ask questions of the board.
- Vote by voice or show of hands.
- Failure to record the conducting and outcome of meetings in ways that are verifiable.

It is no surprise to see that these most specific of allegations are not backed up with the identification of the culprits, which is lamentable given the rest of the report's insistence on the importance of enforcement. An exception was a report in the Singapore *Business Times* that:

a local bank recently met a UK-based fund which is also its shareholder to enlighten the fund on its preference share issue. But no such meeting was held for analysts, despite requests. The reason cited was the bank was in a 'close season' as its fiscal 2002 results are scheduled for release soon. Wasn't the meeting with the UK fund, therefore, a selective disclosure violation? This is not an isolated case. There are many such confidential meetings that take place with fund managers, and neither the investing public nor SGX is privy to them.

What seems clear, moreover, is that the OECD is rather dredging the bottom of the barrel in terms of legislation. Apart from these relatively few limitations, there are splendid opportunities for shareholder activism established in Asian legal jurisdictions. The problem is not the legal framework. The OECD cannot help much any more, at least not until it starts naming and shaming.

ASIA JUST DOESN'T HAVE MUCH YET

Divorce statistics in Asia are still lower than in the West, albeit they are rising. And the relationship between a company, especially its CEO, and its shareholders is widely envisaged in Asia as similar to that of a family's relationship with its head. The parallel extends to the earning capacity – the company earns and the shareholders receive. Western critics should think hard about this point.

China would like more shareholder activism, but it remains exceptionally unusual in the Chinese market. The market still has a relatively short history and is dominated by individual, rather than institutional, investors. As of end-March 2003, a mere 10 per cent of the Shanghai and Shenzhen A-share companies were also listed on markets open for foreign investors, and less than 1 per cent of the A-share companies had cross-border capital programmes. Major international investors such as Calpers have still to decide to invest in the Chinese market. Campaigns for CSR issues have had some success, but detailed shareholder-motivated changes in individual company actions have yet to blossom.

In **Hong Kong**, David Webb has almost single-handedly, it seems, put share-holder activism on the map. For example, his Project Vampire (Vote Against Mandate for Placings, Issues by Rights Excepted) seeks to amend the Listing Rules, which allow directors to choose who owns the company by granting them a mandate to issue new shares up to 20 per cent of existing shares, to whomever they choose at any discount they choose. Webb urges shareholders to vote against the general share issue mandate unless it complies with his recommendations, based on international best practice, which are:

1 The mandate to issue shares for cash, other than by a rights issue, shall be in respect of not more than 5 per cent of the issued shares a the time of the mandate.
2 The discount for shares issued other than by a rights issue shall not exceed 5 per cent.
3 The mandate to issue shares for other purposes, including acquisitions, shall be for not more than 20 per cent of the issued shares.

The Hong Kong Exchange has continued to seek the maximum authority to issue new shares under its own listing rules. So Webb opposed that, and although he did not win the vote in 2003, there is increasing opposition to this management proposal by listed companies. Noting, however, fewer votes on technical proposals, Webb wondered 'whether those investors really understood

213

the other proposals, which are more technical in nature, or simply chose to abstain on them'. What Webb did succeed in doing was getting himself elected to the Board of the Hong Kong Exchange, against the recommendations of the existing directors, although whether this was on the principle of 'better the barbarian within the walls than the barbarian without' we shall perhaps never know. He himself said that:

> It goes against the grain for institutional investors to oppose management, and they only do so if they feel very strongly, so this sends a clear message that shareholders have had enough of the way HKEx has been run by vested interests, including the brokers who have held all the elected seats since the company was listed, at which time they owned 100 per cent of it. Many have since sold their shares, and yesterday's election marks at least the beginning of the end of broker dominance which has impeded market development.

In **India**, one company director said that 'a very tiny majority of the over 25 million shareholders in the country are conscious of their rights and even fewer know how to exercise their rights'.[5] Those that do, such as Greenpeace, are often seen as representative of Western interests. It is true that protagonists of ethical investment have seen India as a suitable location to influence company policy. Greenpeace activists stormed Hindustan Lever's 2003 AGM using proxies gained from friendly shareholders. They first 'prepared' those present on the possible fallout on their holdings if the former employees of the now-closed unit at Kodaikanal (in Tamil Nadu) sued the company for allegedly exposing them to mercury contamination. They then grilled the HLL management on the company's plan to remedy the damage done to the environment, the health of the former workers and the community at large. The management presented its own defence, which Greenpeace found inadequate. Indian commentators criticized 'vigilante shareholder activism' based on

> outsider interference in what is essentially a business relationship between the company and those who own it. Vigilante activists groups have gone on to dictate the manner in which business is done across the globe and India, often to the detriment of both individual choices and the larger good.[6]

Other targets have included companies using child labour.

In **Japan**, recent steps taken by investors show that at least some of them will no longer go along quietly with the status quo: money-management firms are now being required by public pension fund sponsors to vote their shares according to a predetermined set of voting guidelines, and to report back on how they voted. For example, the Public Pension Fund Association, which handles pensions for workers who have pulled out of their employers' pension funds, as well as assets from dissolved pension funds, is pressing its asset-management firms to exercise their voting rights. It voted against 15 out of 150 management proposals at shareholders' meetings last year and aims over the next couple of years to build a structure enabling it to screen out troubled firms with two yardsticks: earnings and corporate governance standards. It may also use the shareholder activism tactics of Calpers (the California Public Employees' Retirement System) as a model for its own activities. Calpers itself has teamed up with Sparx Asset Management in Japan and Relational Investors LLC in California to set up a pilot Japan Corporate Governance Fund. Worth $200 million, the fund is established to make significant investments in a small number of Japanese companies and 'collaborate with management to increase the value of the companies for the benefit of shareowners, employees and other stakeholders'. The Pension Fund Association has expressed an interest in teaming up with Calpers. Such an alliance could have a dramatic impact on how Japanese companies view corporate governance. M&A Consulting, headed by former bureaucrat Yoshiaki Murakami, has been making hostile bids for Japanese companies since 1999. Corporate governance protagonist Murakami sees shareholder value becoming the new Japanese standard, given new accounting regulations and enhanced visibility, the unwinding of cross-shareholdings, growing foreign ownership and an ageing society combined with massive under-funding in the pension system. He pushes companies to focus on cash flow and profit, core businesses, capital efficiency, board monitoring, executive compensation aligned with the interests of shareholders, higher dividend payouts and share buybacks. Individual shareholders with high net worth are also becoming more activist-oriented. Chozo Nakagawa, who invested in 3,000 shares of financial services company Nippon Shimpan, has initiated a JP¥46 billion class-action suit against its directors. Nakagawa quit his job last July to prepare for the lawsuit. He studied commercial law on his own and plans to act without hiring a lawyer. Kanehide Yoneyama is a major shareholder in Sekiwa Real Estate, Yuraku Real Estate and the retailer Konaka. Yoneyama started investing in stocks seriously in 1998, using funds he earned while running his own business. As a major shareholder of auto-parts maker Kiriu, Yoneyama pressured management to raise production efficiency and ultimately encouraged the eventual sale of Kiriu to Unison Capital. Yoneyama is now tilting at Konaka, where he has become the fifth largest shareholder, with 1.02 million shares.

Korea is getting more than its fair share of shareholder activism in Asia, and the corporate sector is widely thought by outside commentators to be much the better for it. Shareholder activism was pretty much nonexistent until it was initiated in 1997 by the People's Solidarity for Participatory Democracy (PSPD), led by Dr Hasung Jang, a charismatic Korea University finance professor. PSPD's minority shareholder campaign's first target was Korea First Bank and it has since then expanded its activities to easy targets such as Samsung Electronics,

SK Telecom and Hyundai Heavy Industries. PSPD methods also include shareholder proposals, proxy solicitations, convening extraordinary shareholders' meetings and policy recommendations. Certain recommendations such as the dismissal of directors or auditors cannot be subject to shareholder proposals, however, as limited by law. The only way that shareholders may propose such changes remains through extraordinary shareholders' meetings. For example, in April 2003 a Monaco-based private equity fund called Sovereign Asset Management announced that it had quietly bought up the single largest stake – 14.99 per cent – in SK Corp., Korea's top oil refiner and a flagship of SK Group, the country's third-largest conglomerate. The ultimate aim of the move was transparent: Sovereign hoped eventually to cash in on what it saw as a company worth much more than its low stock valuation. But Sovereign's media-shy New Zealand-born principals justified the investment in terms that resonated throughout South Korea: in a press release, the fund stated its goal was to turn SK Corp. into 'a role model for corporate governance and shareholder value for Korean business'. Watch this space, then.

In **Malaysia**, shareholder activism was supposedly stimulated by the formation of the Minority Shareholders Watchdog Group, which was founded by five of the country's leading institutional investors (but at the behest of the government): the Employees' Provident Fund, Permodalan Nasional Berhad, Armed Forces Fund Board, Pilgrims Fund Board (Tabung Haji) and the Social Security Organisation. However, this organization received more publicity when it was set up than for anything it did afterwards. To be fair, Professor Chee Keong Low does not agree with this pessimistic analysis:

> The MSWG scored its first widely publicized victory as a shareholders' group by mustering investor support to thwart the proposal by Maruichi Steel Tube Limited ('Maruichi') to acquire a 32.5 per cent interest in Malaysian Merchant Marine Limited ('MMM'). The transaction would not have been controversial but for two factors namely, the vendor was the managing director of MMM and the cash consideration represented a premium of some 310 per cent over the last traded price when the proposed acquisition was announced. Maruichi had in fact disbursed funds to the amount of RM99.9 million, being the full amount payable for the transaction, when the vendor unexpectedly requested for a rescission of the same. By consenting to the rescission, Maruichi incurred no financial loss and recovered all the amounts that it had paid. The success achieved by MWSG in this case attests to the importance of shareholder activism and provides a concrete illustration of how this can contribute towards enhancing corporate governance practices across East Asia.[7]

In **Singapore**, the whole question of shareholder activism is moot. Certainly, shareholders have demonstrated a new-found willingness to press company directors for answers, most notably in the case of the domestic banks, which have pursued questionable strategies in respect of acquisitions, for instance. Bank AGMs in Singapore are no longer always the placid affairs they used to be. However, the majority shareholder in many successful Singapore businesses remains the state, often mediated through state-owned companies such as Temasek Holdings or through the Government Investment Corporation (GIC). Smooth relations between shareholder and management usually ensue, and when there are management problems, such as occurred in 2003 at Singapore Airlines, the government does not hesitate still to wade in with solutions. If the government is the indirect majority shareholder of Singapore Airlines, is such interference an example of good *corporate* governance, calling management to account, or poor *national* governance, because of the blurred dividing lines between the state and the private sector? Or both? It is no surprise that the rules of the corporate governance game sometimes still appear very strange in Asia, not least to the electorate, who were keen to see the problems of Singapore Airlines sorted out quickly and fairly.

CONCLUSION

Currently, a number of Western international funds are either only interested in Asia from the standpoint of distressed debt or liquidation purchases, such as the Carlyle Group which does have representation in Asia, or are standing out of investment altogether in jurisdictions such as China, as does Calpers. These are precisely the institutional investors with the will, the know-how and the resources to make shareholder activism work. When foreign investors do participate in companies, as evidence from Asia shows, they are more stringent in their demands for the accurate employment of capital. The process is changing as domestic activists push national fund managers to more determined preservation of their shareholder value, but it is globalization which is really driving shareholder activism in Asia, together with the awkward mix of shareholder value and CSR which accompanies such activism.

Chapter 9

Measuring corporate governance

- Introduction
- PERC evaluation of countries
  - The Corporate Library and GovernanceMetrics International
- CLSA and ACGA combine forces
- Ranking companies
- Academic corroboration
- The stance of the ratings agencies
- Flaws of the measurement process
- Measuring transparency
- From measurement to consultancy

INTRODUCTION

The first thing to recognize is that there is a problem – or a challenge. Some concepts, like road safety, are readily amenable to statistical analysis, if not to complete unanimity over results. Others, such as beauty, are evidently in the eye of the beholder. Our subject matter falls somewhat in between: like style, *corporate governance is hard to define but easy to recognize*. Demand for corporate governance ratings has certainly increased in the new millennium, so for example credit rating agencies such as Moody's and Standard & Poor's moved into rating corporate governance alongside agencies such as the ACGA and firms such as KPMG. This clearly underscores the growing importance of corporate governance in global investment decision-making, but precisely because of the proliferation of methodologies and suppliers there is no universal acceptance of the way to measure it. KPMG China observed in 2003 that good governance is still hard to gauge, stressing that complying with all the rules does not necessarily mean a firm is being well run. KMPG argue that it follows that organizations that rate governance need to develop more meaningful and measurable yardsticks and firms need to communicate their governance processes even more effectively. Managers themselves are finding it hard to gauge exactly what the reforms mean precisely for their companies. Asked whether companies are better governed now than they were before Enron became a household name, the largest group of respondents – 45 per cent of the executives – said that there was no way of telling. Mostly this seems reasonable, except that the proliferation of different measurements of corporate governance – including, be it said, KPMG – has made it more difficult for this to be achieved. It is very likely that different firms, and indeed countries, will score differently depending on the type of measurement used and the weighting within it of different aspects of corporate governance. Clearly there are conceptual problems with measurement: for example, should an otherwise exemplary Indian company be penalized for not presenting its accounts in IAS format, when it is specifically required to do otherwise under Indian accounting regulations? These issues are producing factional adherence to different methodologies, although there has not yet been sufficient track record for these methodologies to be able to study how this factional adherence is working in practice. But what is important to recognize is that corporate governance evaluation, measurement and scoring has now become itself a competitive marketplace.

PERC EVALUATION OF COUNTRIES

A 2003 survey of expatriates' perception of corporate governance in Asia by the Political and Economic Risk Consultancy (PERC) group revealed a slight improvement in expatriates' overall perceptions from the year before: 'To give Asia its due, the one country where perceptions have deteriorated the most in the past year is the USA.' The survey results ranked Singapore as having the highest corporate governance level in Asia: 'Singapore has done an excellent job of promoting itself as a place striving for better corporate governance.' Japan and Hong Kong ranked second and third respectively, reflecting an understanding by Western expatriates of the differences between local corporate standards and their own. South Korea and Malaysia shared fourth place and the Philippines came in fifth. At the other end of the scale, Thailand, Indonesia, where 'the legal system is viewed more as a threat than an institution that offers protection', and India were scored barely better than Vietnam, and China, which was rated 'anything but transparent'.

The Corporate Library and GovernanceMetrics International

These companies also released a metric in 2002. According to Nell Minow, Editor of the Corporate Library, 'In light of the new standards that have been issued

219

Box 9.1 RUSSIAN INSTITUTE OF DIRECTORS CORPORATE GOVERNANCE RATING METHODOLOGY

We divide the various real and perceived corporate governance risks into 8 categories and 20 subcategories, each with a clearly defined risk weighting and guidelines for their allocation. While no assessment of the risks involved could be 100 per cent scientific, we believe this methodology allows us to be reasonably objective in comparing companies on the basis of their corporate governance profile.

We assign penalty points, thus the higher a company's rating, the higher the risks we associate with it. We find that our model produces results largely consistent with market perceptions of the corporate governance risks – we believe companies that receive more than 35 penalty points are extremely risky, while we view those with a rating below 17 as relatively safe.

Main categories for calculating corporate governance risks

Transparency: Max = 14

We subdivided transparency into four subcategories – the availability of Western, audited accounts, the existence of an ADR program, the timeliness of AGM/EGM notifications and a company's overall reputation for openness.

US GAAP/IAS accounts: Max = 6

Ranges from 6 for companies that are 'allergic' to international accounting standards (usually with good reason), to 0 for those with several years of US GAAP or IAS accounts.

Reputation for openness: Max = 4

Estimated by the relevant analyst, taking into account the presence and quality of a company's investor relations department, the openness of management, and the availability of the operating data necessary to construct accurate earnings models.

ADR program: Max = 2

Two penalty points for no intention to issue ADRs, 0 for an existing Level 2 or 3 program.

AGM/EGM notifications: Max = 2

Companies unable to deliver AGM agendas to shareholders receive 2, those with irregular or delayed notifications get 1.5.

Assignment of penalty points by category

Low transparency		14
US GAAP/IAS accounts	6	
Reputation for openness	4	
ADR program	2	
AGM/EGM notifications	2	
Dilution		13
Authorized but unissued shares	7	
Portfolio investors hold blocking stake	3	
Charter protection	3	
Asset transfers/transfer pricing		10
Controlling shareholders	5	
Transfer pricing	5	
Mergers/restructuring		10
Mergers	5	
Restructuring	5	
Bankruptcy		12
Overdue accounts payable or tax arrears problems	5	
Indebtedness	5	
Financial management	2	
Ownership restrictions		3
Restrictions on foreign ownership or voting	3	
Corporate governance initiatives		9
Board composition	3	
Corporate governance charter	2	
Foreign strategic partnership	1	
Dividend policy	3	
Registrar quality		1
Total		**72**

Dilution: Max = 13

The threat of possible unfair or economically unjustified dilution is perceived as one of the largest risks for shareholders. The presence of a large number of authorized shares – which could be issued at the board's discretion – often indicates a higher probability that a dilutive issue may be upcoming. Reasonable and abusive share issues can be distinguished by whether a placement has clearly stated goals, whether a company's Charter contains protection against dilution, and whether minority investors can block board decisions over new issues.

Authorized but unissued shares: Max = 7

The number of penalty points depends on the amount of shares authorized relative to those outstanding and the level of certainty investors have regarding the purposes of a planned issue.

Portfolio investors hold 25 per cent blocking stake: Max = 3

We award 3 penalty points if outside shareholders are unable to block any unfavorable issue.

Charter protection: Max = 3

The absence of Charter provisions granting preemptive rights or other measures protecting against dilution result in 3 penalty points.

Asset transfers / transfer pricing: Max = 10

Manipulation of assets and dubious pricing techniques are often hard to prove, but are sometimes possible to identify from close examination of financial statements and the trading techniques used by a company. Evidence shows that these practices, while sometimes invisible to investors, create the most serious drain on shareholder value.

Controlling shareholders: Max = 5

We give companies 5 penalty points for having a controlling shareholder with a poor track record on corporate governance. If this shareholder happens to be the Russian government, meaning the company may operate for the benefit of the state rather than other shareholders, it receives 3 points.

Transfer pricing: Max = 5

An unclear trading environment or extensive use of offshore and/or affiliated trading companies leads to an increased risk of transfer pricing, and is penalized by 1–5 points.

Mergers/restructuring: Max = 10

If a company is on the verge of merger or serious restructuring this creates the risk that assets may be lost or merger terms unfair, increasing short-term uncertainty.

Mergers: Max = 5

Companies with no upcoming merger are given 0, those with announced merger terms 2, while those with uncertain terms, where the mergers are perceived to have a likely negative effect on investors, get the maximum 5 penalty points.

Restructuring: Max = 5

This is measured based on the public availability and feasibility of a planned restructuring program and the actual steps management has already taken towards implementation.

Bankruptcy: Max = 12

Any approach to measuring bankruptcy risk is unlikely to be straightforward. Many Russian companies have overdue payables or have defaulted on their debt obligations, but this does not automatically drag them into bankruptcy proceedings. At the other extreme, if a politically powerful structure expresses a strong interest in a company's assets, it could successfully initiate bankruptcy at a relatively stable enterprise. We have tried to use a flexible approach towards measuring bankruptcy risk, which is essentially arbitrary and expresses our understanding of the situation.

Overdue accounts payable or problems with tax arrears: Max = 5

Attempts to initiate bankruptcy, third parties actively buying a company's debt on the market, and large tax or payable arrears contribute to this risk measure.

Indebtedness: Max = 5

Penalty points are assigned on the basis of a company's perceived ability to service its financial debt. The maximum 5 points are allocated to companies that have defaulted on their debt obligations.

Financial management: Max = 2

The quality of a company's financial management significantly contributes to its ability to extricate itself from complex debt situations and bankruptcy threats.

Ownership and voting restrictions: Max = 3

Occasionally, companies have introduced restrictions on minority or foreign ownership or AGM/EGM voting. We believe it is appropriate to penalize such companies in our rating system, as being unable to influence a company's decisions increases the threat that minority investors' rights could be violated.

Corporate governance initiatives: Max = 9

This is a broadly defined measure of management's willingness to share profits with outside shareholders and treat them fairly, as well as investors' ability to channel their concerns to the board. We would also note that this measures only the formal steps taken by management to improve its relationship with minority investors, and is not an attempt to guess management's intentions.

Board composition: Max = 3

Representatives of minority shareholders or well-known independent industry experts serving on the board usually help to instill confidence that minority shareholders will at least be informed of the board's activities and have their concerns heard.

Corporate governance charter: Max = 2

If company takes the initiative and introduces a corporate governance charter explicitly stating its policy towards outside shareholders, this is generally received positively by the market and reflected by 0 penalty points.

Foreign strategic partnership: Max = 1

The presence of a foreign strategic investor working closely with management increases the chances of more civilized policies.

Dividend policy: Max = 3

This indicator assesses not only the existence of a clearly stated dividend policy, but also the adequacy of the dividends paid and timeliness of these payments.

Registrar quality: Max = 1

This factor was more significant in the past, and registrar quality is becoming less relevant. Nevertheless, we believe that companies should be penalized for using captive registrars instead of the services of larger, professional companies.

Source: Russian Institute of Directors

by the New York Stock Exchange, these metrics will really help shareholders distinguish between companies that are paying attention and those that aren't'.

CLSA AND ACGA COMBINE FORCES

So much for perceptions: what about ratings of the reality? ACGA has been monitoring corporate governance developments in 11 Asian markets since the publication of its first regional report in 2000, while the CLSA has produced governance scores for Asia since 1999. The CLSA global survey initially looked at the corporate governance standards of 115 companies in 25 developing countries. Now the Asia survey alone looks at 380 companies in 10 Asian economies (Table 9.1). The survey divides the corporate governance into 7 categories which are discipline, transparency, independence, accountability, responsibility, fairness and social awareness.

In 2003, ACGA joined CLSA[1] in the production of its 'CG Watch 2003' report.[2] The 2003 report showed a vast disparity in quality. Helped by its new Code of Corporate Governance, Singapore took the top spot with a rating of 7.7, up from 7.5 in 2000. It is fascinating to see the reciprocity of the corporate governance game here: how can it be that a code *itself*, irrespective of whether

Table 9.1 CLSA governance scores, February 2002

Country	Country score (%)	CG rules (%)	Enforcement (%)	Company scores (%)
Singapore	74	80	70	32–81
Hong Kong	72	80	60	41–89
India	59	80	50	45–91
Taiwan	58	70	50	42–90
Korea	47	60	30	45–78
Malaysia	47	90	25	27–87
China	44	45	30	30–69
Thailand	38	75	20	35–77
Philippines	36	60	20	34–75
Indonesia	29	40	10	17–59

Source: ACGA Ltd

it is actually followed, can contribute to a higher national corporate governance score? True, Singapore companies tend to adhere to it, but that is what matters, not the existence of the code itself. Second again was Hong Kong with a score of 7.3, which was basically unchanged from the year before. In this case the report accurately pinpointed specific problems such as the failure of the Hong Kong Association of Minority Shareholders (HAMS) to get off the ground, business pressure to water down some of Hong Kong Exchanges and Clearing Ltd's corporate governance amendments to its Listing Rules (including the withdrawal of a proposal to require quarterly reporting for Main Board companies) and a controversial transaction involving the disposal of Boto Holdings's core plastic Christmas tree and garden accessories business as among the reasons for Hong Kong's second place showing. Other scores were India, 6.6; Taiwan, 5.8; South Korea and Malaysia, both 5.5. A satisfactory but could-do-better report card was returned by companies in Taiwan, Korea and Malaysia. Singled out for showing the greatest improvement since CLSA began producing the reports in 2001 were South Korea and Malaysia.

In need of significant improvement are firms in Thailand, 4.6; China, 4.3; the Philippines, 3.7; and 'the perennial laggard', Indonesia, 2.2. CLSA say that in these countries in particular, corporate governance is more a matter of form over substance, backing up the Political and Economic Risk Consultancy (PERC) perceptions with the conclusion that enforcement of legislation still raises doubts as to how serious these governments really are about raising governance standards. According to CLSA, too, Japan remains the with the most to do to improve governance. KPMG agree; they argue that whereas the wounds inflicted on the reputation of US business have started to heal, their evidence as of 2003 'clearly pegs Japan as the country with furthest to go in improving standards of governance; our research into corporate transparency reinforces the point, with Japanese firms making only marginal improvements since last year'.

Two pieces of evidence which are worth mentioning were derived from the 2001 report. First, a strong correlation appeared in the study between high corporate raters and countries with strong macro corporate governance environments. Companies from South Africa (5.5 weighted average), Hong Kong (6.8), Singapore (7.4), Mexico (6.1) and Brazil (4.7) were represented in the top quartile. By contrast, the study noted that half the companies from Poland (3.3), Russia (2.1), Pakistan (3.1), Indonesia (3.2), Turkey (4.4), the Philippines (3.3) and Korea (3.8) fell in the bottom quartile. The correlation between corporate governance and financial ratios was strong for most Latin American and Asian markets. Second, the study's executive summary concluded that across global emerging market sectors, transport, manufacturing, metals/mining and consumer (goods) had the highest average corporate governance scores; petrochemicals, pharmaceuticals and infrastructure scored the lowest. Correlations to financials were stronger for sectors that were less strong on corporate governance, e.g. infrastructure, property and conglomerates.

CLSA themselves do not want to put too much emphasis on the exact numbers, although it is worth saying that governments in the region appear to be paying more attention to their position on the CLSA scoring system than perhaps any other aspect of corporate governance. They say that their most recent surveys show general improvement in the regulatory environment and greater efforts being made towards better enforcement in Asia, but they urge that investors still need to take action and be wary of corporate shenanigans. Recent reports confirm that corporate governance remains a key to investment decisions and valuation metrics at both the macro and micro levels. But there is little room for complacency: while there have been improvements, some markets have regressed or remain unchanged. CLSA stated:

> We noted regulatory improvement and some tightening of enforcement. But avenues for redress by minorities remain lacking; and unless controlling shareholders are 'disincentivised' from taking advantage of their listed entities, Asia risks being seen as merely cosmetic in its CG reforms.

Of the 380 companies surveyed, the average corporate governance score was 62 per cent, 4.1 points higher than the 2002 average of 57.9 per cent, which was up on the previous year's 55.9 per cent. Among large regional capitalized stocks, HSBC Holdings, Infosys Technologies, TSMC, KT Corp., BAT Malaysia, Public Bank, Singapore Press Holdings, ST Engineering and Standard Chartered all scored high corporate governance scores. *CG Watch*'s 2003 star performers in Hong Kong included banks HSBC and Standard Chartered Bank, global trading firm Li & Fung, retailer Esprit, consumer technology company V-Tech, property developer Kerry Properties and newspaper publisher SCMP Group Ltd. The top ten high-CG/strong performing firms in the 2001 study were HSBC (Hong Kong), Infosys (India), Singapore Airlines, HDFC Bank (India), Li & Fung (Hong Kong), Neptune Orient Lines (Singapore), Richemont (South Africa), CLP (Hong Kong), SA Breweries plc (South Africa) and Singapore Press Holdings. The bottom ten low-CG/poor performing firms, on the other hand, were Indocement (Indonesia), Lukoil (Russia), Indah Kiat (Indonesia), Pakistan Telecom, Fauji Fertilizer (Pakistan), UEM (Malaysia), Indofood (Indonesia), Dewan Salman (Pakistan), Hub Power (Pakistan) and Metro Pacific (Philippines).

Many companies that have been the subject of corporate governance scrutiny are reluctant to publicize their scores, particularly if they have not done well. *CG Watch* now only publishes the top half of the companies it surveys. 'Companies have been touchy about reports if their corporate governance is not quite up to the mark. We tried [publishing them] in early reports and it caused too much aggravation.'[3] Disclosure, it seems, does not extend to corporate governance measurement – a nice contradiction.

The biggest jump in scores came from the discipline category where the average score rose by 8.6 percentage points. 'This is one of the easiest areas for companies to increase their scores by a greater stated commitment to corporate governance tenets – e.g. discussion in annual reports, become transparent on financial targets etc.', *CG Watch* said. The report also cautioned that averages usually hide wide extremes of scoring. 'Against our 62 per cent average corporate governance score is a 75 percentage point range – the lowest score in our sample is 17.4 per cent while the highest is 92.9 per cent', the report declared, adding that companies with weaker corporate governance scores generally scored lower on independence and responsibility. For example, the lowest 10 companies in the sample scored 9 per cent for independence, 18 per cent for responsibility and 24 per cent for fairness. The average corporate governance score for this group was just 29 per cent, or 60 percentage points lower than the top 10 companies. 'Key in having good overall corporate governance is transparency and fairness,' said *CG Watch*.

RANKING COMPANIES

The EIU criteria for assessing a firm's corporate governance are shown in Box 9.2.

> ## Box 9.2 EIU CRITERIA FOR ASSESSING CORPORATE GOVERNANCE
>
> 1   Thorough oversight of company finances by qualified independent directors free of pressure from management and with funds to hire their own expert consultants.
> 2   Absence of any conflicts of interest on the part of outside directors – relationships with their own businesses, consulting contracts, and so forth.
> 3   A well-balanced board by skill and age, selected by a nominating committee independent of the CEO.
> 4   Top executive compensation that is convincingly tied to longer-term performance on a variety of criteria. Linking incentive pay more closely to relative performance against competitors, both financially and in the market, is sensible.
> 5   Tightening up of holding requirements that limit the ability of executives and directors to unload shares at a peak.
> 6   Regular meetings of outside board members away from the CEO.
> 7   Comprehensive and regular briefing of the board on strategic questions, followed by open debate.
> 8   A board that knows how to stay out of operational questions and focuses on the big picture.
> 9   Accessible financial accounts that clearly set out the principles behind, and consequences of, significant accounting policies and decisions.
> 10 Transparent information on, and explanation of, corporate decisions on matters of both strategy and governance.

ACADEMIC CORROBORATION

In conjunction with the preceding corporate governance structure, insider trading rules are weakly enforced in Southeast Asia. For example, the first legal case brought against insider trading occurred in 1996 in Indonesia, and in over six decades of stock trading in Manila, no individual has ever been prosecuted, convicted or jailed for insider trading or price manipulation. Given the corporate governance structure and the still lax enforcement environment just described, it is widely suspected that insiders of the richest-family-controlled conglomerates frequently trade on their private information, often through affiliated brokerages. In interviews with more than a dozen brokers and analysts in the Philippines and Indonesia, academics found that relative to other companies, the stock price for the companies controlled by the richest families reflects the information in earnings at an earlier time. This finding is consistent with the

Table 9.2 *Corporate governance: business under scrutiny*

Transparency research methodology and results

The top 10 companies (in terms of market value) in the USA, Japan, UK, France and Germany were assessed in terms of the degree of openness they displayed in publicly available information (notably the investor relations section of their web sites and the annual reports) on various corporate governance issues. The companies scrutinized are shown below:

USA	UK	Japan	France	Germany
General Electric	BP	NTT DoCoMo Inc	Total Fina Elf	Deutsche Telecom
Microsoft	GlaxoSmith Kline plc	Toyota Motor	Aventis	Allianz
Exxon Mobil	Vodafone Group	NTT	L'Oreal	Siemens
Wal-Mart Stores	HSBC Holdings	Sony Corp	Sanofi Synthelabo	SAP
Citigroup	AstraZeneca	HondaMotor Co	BNP Paribas	Daimler Chrysler
Pfzer	Royal Bank of Scotland	Takeda Chemical	Vivendi Universal	Munich Re
Intel	Lloyds TSB	Mitsubishi Tokyo Financial Group	Axa	Deutsche Bank
Johnson & Johnson	Barclays	Nissan Motor	France Telecom	EON
AIG	Diageo	Canon Inc	Carrefour	BMW
IBM	HBOS PLC	Seven-Eleven	Orange	Bayer

Each company was assessed on 29 different issues ranging from disclosure on executive pay, information on non-executive directors, retention of auditors and ease of voting at the AGM over a three-week period in July 2002. A single researcher undertook all the research to assure consistency of perspective.

Each company was scored on the following basis:

    0 – information was not available
    1 – the information was there, but hidden
    2 – easily found, but hard to understand/ or incomplete
    3 – easily found, understandable and complete enough to answer the question

Source: EIU

229

notion that insiders of the companies controlled by the richest families are particularly aggressive in trading on their proprietary knowledge of the information in earnings before these earnings are reported to outsiders. They reported that at least half of the interviewees volunteered that a major portion of their analysis involved trying to identify trades by insiders to help their clients to mimic these trades. For example, in a recent insider trading scandal in the Philippines, a major owner of BW Resources used 32 trading accounts (11 of which were in code numbers), numerous personal associates, and 8 member brokers to carry out his stock price manipulation scheme.

Hong Kong is one of the most effectively regulated markets in Asia. As a result, relative to insiders of Southeast Asian companies, insiders of Hong Kong companies are likely to have fewer opportunities to trade on their private information. Therefore, if particularly aggressive insider trading for Southeast Asian companies controlled by the richest families explains the pattern of information flow into stock price, it would be expected that this telltale pattern will be weak or nonexistent for Hong Kong companies. Academic studies support this – they found further support for the insider trading interpretation based on tests that assume the presence of a strong incentive for insider trading: (i) when there is a large change in earnings, and (ii) before the first legal case in a country is brought against insider trading. Moreover, they claim that test results were robust to controls for company-specific size, growth and risk, as well as to alternative measures of the flow of information into stock price. They found that value-relevant information flows into stock price earlier for companies in which insiders have relatively more opportunities and incentives to trade on their private information, suggesting that stock price is more informative for such companies. Related to this observation, these results support the conjecture in Ball, Kothari and Robin (2000, p. 48) that 'poor public disclosure does not necessarily impede the flow of information into stock prices, since the information flow can occur instead via the trading of informed insiders', and because stock markets and financial service industries are more developed in Hong Kong than in Southeast Asia, they argued that there is more information spillover across companies controlled by the same richest family in Hong Kong. Their test results provide evidence that directly counters this expectation. They provide evidence that for companies in Indonesia, Malaysia, the Philippines and Thailand, the flow of the value-relevant information contained in annual earnings into stock price occurs earlier for the companies controlled by the richest families. This pattern of information flow is especially pronounced when there is a strong incentive, as proxied by a large change in earnings or by no insider trading cases having yet been prosecuted in a country, to trade on inside information. They did not find similar evidence in the relatively well-regulated market of Hong Kong. These results are consistent with the contention that insiders of the richest-family-controlled companies in Southeast Asia are particularly aggressive in trading on

230

their proprietary knowledge of the value-relevant information in earnings before these earnings are reported to the public.

Based on tests using 1989 to 1996 data for companies in Indonesia, Malaysia, the Philippines and Thailand, academics found that relative to other companies, the flow of the value-relevant information contained in annual earnings into stock price occurs earlier for the companies controlled by the richest families. This pattern of information flow is especially pronounced when there is a strong incentive, as proxied by a large change in earnings or by no insider trading cases having yet been prosecuted in a country, to trade on inside information. These results are robust to controls for company-specific size, growth, and risk, as well as to alternative measures of the flow of information into stock price. They did not find similar evidence in the relatively well regulated market of Hong Kong or for family-controlled companies overall. Their results were consistent with the contention that insiders of Southeast Asian companies controlled by the richest families are particularly aggressive in trading on their proprietary knowledge concerning the information in annual earnings before these earnings are reported to outsiders. Overall, these findings confirm the usual understanding of how corporate governance structure affects the flow of information into stock price, suggesting that a company's share price is more informative for companies in which insiders have relatively more opportunities and incentives to trade on their proprietary information. Considered in conjunction with the results reported earlier, these results suggest that it is richest family control, rather than family control per se, that is associated with particularly aggressive insider trading in Southeast Asian markets. An important implication here is that in future studies that attempt to document the economic consequences of the corporate governance structure in Southeast Asia, an especially effective approach might be to separately examine the companies controlled by the richest families.

THE STANCE OF THE RATINGS AGENCIES

Standard & Poor's (S&P) has created a program that examines individual companies' governance practices and produces a score that can be used by outside investors to compare them to their competitors. Companies can use the service to garner an evaluation of how their governance and financial practices are perceived by the public. Standard & Poor's took four years to develop its Corporate Governance Score (CGS) system. It began as an emerging market service to help gauge governance in some lesser developed capital markets, but Enron prompted S&P to roll out the service to US and European companies. S&P scores companies in four different categories: ownership structure, financial stakeholder relations, financial transparency/information disclosure, and board and management structure. Under these general categories, the rating agency considers numerous sub-categories – things such as concentration and influence of ownership, voting and shareholder meeting procedures, independence of the company's auditor, anti-takeover provisions, and the like. Although Standard & Poor's publishes country governance analyses from time to time, it is important to note that it does not currently score individual countries. However, consideration of a country's legal, regulatory and market environment is an important element in the overall analysis of the risks associated with the governance practices of an individual company. For example, two companies with the same company scores, but domiciled in countries with contrasting legal, regulatory and market standards, present different risk profiles should their governance practices deteriorate, i.e. in the event of deterioration in a specific company's governance standards, investors and stakeholders are likely to receive better protection in a country with stronger and better enforced laws and regulations. However, in Standard & Poor's opinion, companies with high corporate governance scores have less governance-related risk than companies with low scores, irrespective of the country of domicile.

CGS reflects Standard & Poor's assessment of a company's corporate governance practices and policies and the extent to which these serve the interests of the company's financial stakeholders, with an emphasis on shareholders' interests. These governance practices and policies are measured against Standard & Poor's corporate governance scoring methodology, which is based on a synthesis of international codes, governance best practices and guidelines of good governance practice. Companies with the same score have, in the opinion of Standard & Poor's, similar company specific governance processes and practices overall, irrespective of the country of domicile. The scores do not address specific legal, regulatory and market environments, and the extent to which these support or hinder governance at the company level, a factor which may affect the overall assessment of the governance risks associated with an individual company.

From the investor's point of view, say S&P, the CGS can provide a trusted and independent assessment, based on global best practice and therefore comparable internationally. It is also an opinion on the reality of good corporate governance within a company, as well as its commitment to the form of good corporate governance. In doing so, they argue that it helps create a more appropriate view of the risks involved in their existing or potential investments. At a seminar in 2003 in Indonesia the telling point was made that:

> In the case of S&P, their rating credibility is maintained because investors could compare companies in different countries with same ratings . . . A company with a B+ rating will of course be compared with a company with a similar rating in Singapore, Malaysia, the United States or in Europe.

Box 9.3 S&P SCORING METHODOLOGY

A CGS is articulated on a scale of CGS 1 (lowest) to CGS 10 (highest).

CGS 10 and CGS 9 – a company that, in Standard & Poor's opinion, has **very strong** corporate governance processes and practices overall. A company in these scoring categories has, in Standard & Poor's opinion, few weaknesses in any of the major areas of governance analysis.

CGS 8 and CGS 7 – a company that, in Standard & Poor's opinion, has **strong** corporate governance processes and practices overall. A company in these scoring categories has, in Standard & Poor's opinion, some weaknesses in certain of the major areas of governance analysis.

CGS 6 and CGS 5 – a company that, in Standard & Poor's opinion, has **moderate** corporate governance processes and practices overall. A company in these scoring categories has, in Standard & Poor's opinion, weaknesses in several of the major areas of governance analysis.

CGS 4 and CGS 3 – a company that, in Standard & Poor's opinion, has **weak** corporate governance processes and practices overall. A company in these scoring categories has, in Standard & Poor's opinion, significant weaknesses in a number of the major areas of governance analysis.

CGS 2 and CGS 1 – a company that, in Standard & Poor's opinion, has **very weak** corporate governance processes and practices overall. A company in these scoring categories has, in Standard & Poor's opinion, significant weaknesses in most of the major areas of analysis.

Important note

A CGS is based on current information provided to Standard & Poor's by the company, its officers and any other sources Standard & Poor's considers reliable. A CGS is neither an audit nor a forensic investigation of governance practices. Standard & Poor's may rely on audited information and other information provided by the company for the purpose of the governance analysis. A CGS is neither a credit rating nor a recommendation to purchase, sell or hold any interest in a company, as it does not comment on market price or suitability for a particular investor. Scores may also be changed, suspended or withdrawn as a result of changes in, or unavailability of, such information.

Source: S&P

From the company's point of view the CGS can provide a way of demonstrating its commitment to the substance as well as the form of good corporate governance; it also enables non-textbook corporate governance structures to be independently assessed from inside the company. In doing so the company could over time capture the corporate governance premiums that are available in the global financial market. Companies were not slow to jump on the S&P bandwagon. The Hong Kong Stock Exchange & Clearing Ltd (the holding company of the Stock Exchange of Hong Kong) showed its own commitment to good corporate governance practice – or its awareness of a good PR coup at least – by being the first Asian company to publish its Corporate Governance Score from Standard & Poor's: a very good CGS-8.3. It has recommended that its member companies also go through this process.

Like CLSA, Standard & Poor's has found clients equally reticent to go public with its corporate governance ratings, a service it launched in 2001 which is separate from the agency's credit ratings reports. 'Most of the companies we've done have chosen not to go public', admitted Calvin Wong, managing director for governance services, Asia-Pacific. The service was conceived in 1998 after the Asian financial crisis. 'Seven to eight is strong and nine to ten is very strong,' Mr Wong explained. The scores of companies which do not wish to be publicized are kept confidential. 'The companies take our scoring and use it for internal purposes. They get a clear roadmap if they want to improve. In most cases, the companies know they have issues. If they improve, they might go public later', he said. Interest in S&P's corporate governance rating service has come from a variety of companies, although Mr Wong singled out China's state owned enterprises (SOEs) – those that are either about to privatize or have already done so – as the most enthusiastic. 'It makes sense because governments tend to lead the movement for better corporate governance', he said, referring to the SOEs.

> On the other hand, governments are partially an obstacle to better corporate governance because they like to be in control. But their control may not be in the best interests of other shareholders. Management is aware of that tension and would like to be more independent of government practices. Having the analysis that highlights that tension can be helpful.

Another point he made was that many companies would like to see their competitors obtain corporate governance ratings before they go through the process themselves so they have a better idea of what they might be up against. 'An oil company wants to see how other oil companies have done before it goes ahead,' he said. S&P is prepared for the business to grow slowly.

> It's still early days and I think the market has yet to get comfortable with the quantification of corporate governance. We have a vested interest in seeing it

grow but I'm not surprised that as with any new product, it takes a while for the market to get accustomed to it and see the value proposition.

By contrast to the massive S&P endeavour, Moody's announced in June 2002 that it would henceforth incorporate corporate governance variables into its credit rating methodology, which some analysts felt was even more important to the high profile of corporate governance than hiving it off into a separate index.

Euromoney has been ranking companies for corporate governance since the mid-1990s. *Euromoney* asks market analysts at major banks and research institutes in Asia to nominate the top three firms in each of the countries or sectors they covered. The analysts were asked to bear in mind 'market strength, profitability, growth potential and quality of management and earnings'. *Euromoney* magazine received nominations for 699 firms for all categories from 136 replies. It favours SingTel and Keppel Corp in Singapore. It subdivides its categories into Most Transparent Companies, Most Accessible Management and Treatment of Minority Shareholders. In Singapore Fraser & Neave found a mention for its exemplary treatment of minority shareholders, Shipping group Neptune Orient Lines (NOL) won a mention under the Most Improved Company award. Venture Corp. was included in the Most Convincing Strategy category, and Hyflux was the only local firm on the Best Small Company list, ending joint ninth. On the negative side, SembCorp Industries was listed under the Least Impressive Management category. DBS Group Holdings was featured in the Least Impressive Investor Relations table, a seeming contradiction, given its listing under the Most Accessible Management category.

If the *Euromoney* rankings provide an indication as to which companies were then deemed to have had good corporate governance, it will be interesting to see if they are exempt from financial scandals in the coming years, as surely good corporate governance is persistent, if not contagious.

The international agencies are not the only players in the ratings game, however. Singapore itself, for example, is developing a new Corporate Governance Index for domestic listed companies, to measure the quality of their corporate governance practices. The Singapore Institute of Directors, which is spearheading the project, gave DBS its inaugural Best Managed Boards Award. The award recognizes the bank's efforts to build a diverse and independent board. The judges singled out the boards of DBS along with runners-up Keppel Corp., SIA Engineering and ST Engineering for their good governance practices. Two relatively new listings, massage chair maker OSIM International and ornamental fish breeder Qian Hu, were also commended for their willingness improve their corporate governance.

By comparison to the clarity of corporate governance ratings in Singapore, the measurement of corporate governance in India is caught in a unique domestic quagmire. Commentators rightly suggested that any rating (governance ratings

Table 9.3 Euromoney *ratings: Singapore (2002)*

Position	Company	Votes
1	DBS	54
2	SIA	49
3	Singapore Telecom	31
4	ST Engineering	29
5	Noble Group	27
6	Keppel Corporation	15
7	CapitaLand	12
8	Creative Technologies	10
9	OCBC	10
10	Venture Corporation	7

Table 9.4 Euromoney *ratings: Korea (2002)*

Position	Company	Votes
1	Samsung Electronics	57
2	Kookmin Bank	51
3	LG Electronics	24
4	Korea Telecom	20
5	Hana Bank	15
6	Samsung Fire & Marine	13
7	Posco	12
8	Kepco	10

more so) is more of an opinion and may come with a number of caveats. The objectives of the whole exercise should be very clear, methodology should be standardized and validated and communications transparent, lest it results in extra burden for the regulators to prove their pro-activeness in overseeing the rating agencies. It must be feared that in India precisely the reverse appears to be happening and that obfuscation, circumlocution and obscurantism threaten to blight the entire process of corporate governance measurement. Observers have pointed to three major challenges facing corporate governance ratings in India. First, regulators do not seem to have set clear objectives in relation to the capital

Table 9.5 Euromoney *ratings: Indonesia (2002)*

Position	Company	Votes
1	Astra International	49
2	Unilever Indonesia	39
3	Telkom Indonesia	26
4	HM Sampoerna	17
5	Caltex Pacific Indonesia	14
6	Ramayana Lestari Sentosa	12
7	Bank Central Asia	10
8	Bank Mandiri	8

Table 9.6 Euromoney *ratings: Taiwan (2002)*

Position	Company	Votes
1	TSMC	112
2	UMC	21
3	Acer	14
4	Chinatrust	12
5	Asustek Computer	11
6	AU Optronics	10
7	Hon Hai Precision	9
8	Fubon Financial	8
9	Compal	8
10	China Steel	8

markets. Second, there is insufficient accumulated knowledge on corporate governance and a great amount of fluidity in the theory at present. Bizarrely, for example, the Securities and Exchange Board of India (SEBI) says that it would like to ensure that the rating assigned to a bond issue by a company converges with its corporate governance (CG) rating over the long term. Why bother with both, then? In the short run, there could still be a difference between the two ratings, said Mr Pratip Kar, Executive Director, SEBI, adding that companies that had scored well in terms of good governance should ultimately see their initiatives reflected in their bond ratings as well. The third challenge is to assign

Table 9.7 Euromoney *ratings: Thailand (2002)*

Position	Company	Votes
1	Siam Cement	59
2	Thai Farmers Bank	35
3	AIS	21
4	Thai Union Frozen	20
5	Shin Corp	16
6	PTTEP	16
7	Banpu	13
8	DTAC	12
9	Siam City Cement	12
10	Bangkok Bank	9

Table 9.8 Euromoney *ratings: China (2002)*

Position	Company	Votes
1	Legend	41
2	China Mobile	37
3	TCL	31
4	CNOOC	24
5	Petrochina	17
6	China Resources	16
7	Sinopec	13
8	Cosco Pacific	10
9	Asiainfo	9
10	Denway Motors	9

adequately explained ratings to the companies in the context of global markets. Additionally, although there are two corporate governance rating agencies – CRISIL (following Standard & Poors) and ICRA (like Moody's) have started giving Corporate Governance Ratings – they have promptly been caught in a controversy regarding whether the former is laxer in assigning ratings than the latter. CRISIL gave the highest ratings to HDFC, HDFC Bank and Hero Honda and second level to Dabur. ICRA gave a second level to ITC and Godrej and a level 4 to Easab India. No one quite knows why.

Table 9.9 Euromoney *ratings: Malaysia (2002)*

Position	Company	Votes
1	BAT	58
2	Public Bank	40
3	YTL	28
4	Maybank	26
5	Tanjong	25
6	Genting	25
7	Maxis	19
8	Petronas	13
9	Sime Darby	12
10	IOI Corp	9

Table 9.10 Euromoney *ratings: Philippines (2002)*

Position	Company	Votes
1	Ayala Corporation	77
2	Globe Telecom	31
3	Bank of the Philippine Islands	24
4	San Miguel	22
5	SM Prime	19
6	Jollibee	15
7	PLDT	12
8	Ayala Land	7
9	Petron Corp	5
10	Metrobank	4

FLAWS OF THE MEASUREMENT PROCESS

There are two types of flaw with the measurement process. The first type we may call *internal*, where the measurement process fails *by its own lights*. A company with a high score ends up proven guilty of accountancy fraud, for instance. The most celebrated internal failure of the corporate governance measurement process comes from Europe, where the Corporate Governance Authority, a private CG rating company which relied on self-assessment, produced a high rating for

Ahold, the Danish company which was demonstrated spectacularly to have falsified its accounts. It would not be surprising for a similar event to transpire in Asia because corporate governance measurement is in its infancy and is dependent to a large extent on the information provided by companies themselves. True, absolutely thorough accountancy research could have identified Enron's problems in advance, but there is no guarantee that similar problems with fraud and inequitable treatment of minority shareholders by Asian companies will easily come to light.

Second, however, there are the *external* problems with corporate governance measurement, which are that many CSR activists and others concerned with social justice believe that insufficient, if any, weight is given in corporate governance analysis to measuring the impact of companies on the health and safety of their employees, on the environment and on wider stakeholders. For example, Asian construction companies may have excellent corporate governance, but the death rate among workers on Asian construction sites is still greater than in Western countries. *No* work-related death among a workforce ought to be acceptable, but accident rates do matter, and they do not feature in corporate governance analysis. Critics believe that the constituent elements of corporate governance measurement are too narrow to merit such widespread attention and priority by companies: that they can even distract companies from their social role.

MEASURING TRANSPARENCY

This is likewise a matter of surveys, although it is important to note that transparency almost inevitably forms part of wider corporate governance surveys and ratings. In 2003, for the second year running, the Economist Intelligence Unit assessed the transparency of the top ten firms by market capitalization in France, Germany, Japan, the UK and the US. Each company was scored for the provision and accessibility of information (notably in the investor relations section of their websites, annual reports and SEC filings) on 29 governance issues ranging from disclosure on executive pay and information on nonexecutive directors to retention of auditors and ease of voting at the annual general meeting. A total of 310 senior executives participated in the EIU online survey on corporate governance. The survey was conducted in June and July 2003. The good news: information is getting easier to find. In August 2002, 32 per cent of the companies EIU looked at did not have a separate section on corporate governance either on their website or in their annual report. In August 2003 this proportion had fallen to 24 per cent (and Japan alone accounted for three-quarters of the laggards). With the exception of Japan, most companies now provide clear information on the various committees and supervisory boards responsible for auditing and executive compensation.

240

The BT Corporate Transparency Index (CTI) was launched in July 2000 to assess the level of disclosure in financial results released by Singapore-listed companies. Based on the scores, the level of corporate transparency has actually dropped for 2001 from 2000. This round, only 51 companies chalked up more than the 50-point 'pass mark'. That's just 18.3 per cent of the total number of 278 companies with a financial year ending 31 December. In the previous year, 68 out of the 268 (that's 25 per cent) scored more than the 'pass mark'. Perhaps the deep recession has diverted the attention of some companies from the demands of transparency to what they perceived as more crucial 'bread and butter' issues. The CTI was revised in 2003 to put greater emphasis on the quality of disclosure. Like the previous CTI, it scores financial results based on two broad segments: content, which covers the balance sheet and profit and loss data, together with other items such as the narrative commentary; and context, which covers other factors such as timeliness and the means of dissemination. The main change is that the revised CTI gives a 60 per cent weighting to content and 40 per cent to context – unlike the old CTI which gave equal weighting to content and context – to underscore the importance of the quality of financial statements. Other changes were also made, to take into account changes in reporting requirements. Scoring is conducted by an in-house team which appraises not only the quality of the information disclosed (BT call that 'content') but also how effectively that content is communicated to the investors (labelled 'context').

Overall, BT now reported that the quality of disclosure was encouraging, as indicated by the distribution of scores. Of the 23 companies that reported their 2002 full-year results in January: one scored more than 90 points on the CTI out of a possible 100; 22 per cent scored between 80 and 90 points; 35 per cent scored between 70 and 79 points and 17 per cent scored between 50 and 69 points. At the lower end of the scale, 22 per cent scored fewer than 50 points. The revisions to the CTI mean a direct comparison with previous scores cannot be made. However, one general observation is that some companies that did well before did not score as highly under the revised CTI with its emphasis on content. Fish breeder Qian Hu Corp, which scored 90 points for its 2001 financial statements, scored only 78 for its 2002 results. Chartered Semiconductor Manufacturing also saw its score fall, from 86 for 2001 to 76 for 2002, with one factor being its poor disclosure of borrowings. But other companies improved their scores. Healthcare group Osim International topped the list with 91 points for its 2002 results, a big jump from 74 for 2001, mainly because its latest financial statement was almost as detailed as an annual report. Publisher SNP Corp also registered a big improvement with 66 points for 2002 (2001: 44 points) as a result of improving its balance sheet and cashflow statements. Other companies that improved their scores include Singapore Food Industries, Keppel Corp., Keppel Land and Raffles Holdings. BT scored companies that reported their 2002 results in February, followed by those reporting in March, before

241

tallying the final rankings for all companies reporting 2002 results. Companies reporting for financial years ending in March, June or September 2003, as well as other months, will be scored after their results are released. Firms commented:

> SingTel is committed to best practice in corporate governance and has progressively improved its level of corporate transparency over the years. Good corporate governance protects the interests of all shareholders, while greater transparency benefits investors as they understand the company and its operations better, and can therefore make informed decisions.

SingTel started quarterly reporting of its financial results in June 2000, three years before it became mandatory. The company also has regular communications with investors and the media, providing access to senior management at briefings and news conferences. For fair and timely disclosure to all investors, there is also effective use of various communications channels for dissemination of corporate news and developments, as well as financial and other relevant disclosures.

In the 2003 Securities Investors Association of Singapore's Most Transparent Company Awards, Keppel Land beat off tough competition from Singapore Airlines (SIA), which took second place overall to win the Best Annual Reports Award. In third place overall, and the Best Annual Report Award runner-up, was last year's winner, ST Engineering. The award for the best annual report went to Keppel Land, which can lay claim to be one of Singapore's most investor-friendly and most transparent companies. In the Sesdaq category of the ARA, Gul Technologies took the Grand Award while top place in the Statutory Board category went to the Housing and Development Board.

FROM MEASUREMENT TO CONSULTANCY

In 2003 the ACGA launched a corporate governance assessment service for Asian companies, insurers and investment managers. The service is called the 'ACGA Quick Assessment'. According to Francois Roy, Chief Analyst, ACGA, the decision to provide the market with a 'quick' assessment was deliberate on ACGA's part.

> There is of course a place and a need for in-depth assessments of companies in Asia. But few Asian companies feel comfortable with outsiders coming in and asking questions about their directors and managers, and how they perform. Even progressive companies want to know more about what corporate governance reform involves before committing to a process of reform.

According to the ACGA, their Quick Assessment service seeks to complement existing corporate governance surveys in Asia. Its main focus is an assessment

242

of the quality – or substance – of the transparency and accountability within a company, which is followed by recommendations on how a company could improve, and prioritizes these suggestions into a practical governance plan. ACGA says that it has designed its Quick Assessment to be easily understood and to save companies time and money, and claims that it is a response to what many Asian companies, investors and insurers say they need: a good-value and concise report on how to improve corporate governance and manage related risks.

Clearly also, firms such as KPMG are seeking to use their Corporate Governance measurement scorecards as a route into corporate governance consulting, in Asia as elsewhere in the world. And why not?

Chapter 10

Corporate governance and company performance

- Behold the good news
- Why is it so?
- Mine is better than yours
- Wait a minute . . .

BEHOLD THE GOOD NEWS

Protagonists of good corporate governance have never been slow in coming forward with the argument that what's good for corporate governance is good for the share price. According to S&P Managing Director Andrea Esposito, 'those companies with strong corporate governance cultures have more stable earnings per share'. With regard to the recent spate of corporate calamities, the President of the Institute of Chartered Accountants in England and Wales, Peter Wyman, remarked in 2002 that 'behind every headline case is a failure of corporate governance'. James McRitchie, the Editor of CorpGov.net, is equally forthright:

> There is no question that globalization of capital is on the rise. Countries and companies that seek to attract investors will need high scores on governance rating systems if they are to obtain low cost financing. Long term investors will seek markets where their legal rights are known and protected and where those using their money can be held accountable.

Policy-makers have reinforced this conclusion that a good corporate governance regime is central to the efficient allocation of international capital.[1]

The effect of corporate governance on share price performance used to be something of a contentious issue. For years, the review of literature and field studies very surprisingly failed to find a strong correlation between corporate performance and good governance. The common wisdom was that well-governed corporations should be well-managed corporations and, by extension, deliver high shareholder value, and had been for centuries, but it consistently failed to be proven. Then came a spate of papers and reports which apparently proved it. The evidence – and there is a great deal of it – now all points one way on this. Good corporate governance for a firm is positively correlated with shareholder value. 'If the market can wield sticks to deter bad practice, it can also dangle carrots to encourage higher standards of corporate behaviour.'

Among many such studies, academics from Harvard and Wharton found that a sample of US firms with stronger shareholder rights enjoyed higher firm value, higher profits, higher sales growth and lower capital expenditures during the 1990s. Several research papers presented evidence suggesting the following: company performance increases with effective governance and board independence;[2] greater incidence of financial fraud occurs when the proportion of outside directors on boards is low;[3] board independence and separation of CEO and board chair reduces the extent of earnings manipulation;[4] fees paid to the external auditor are higher resulting from higher quality audit work, for companies with more independent boards, boards that meet more often, and boards with a greater number of directors who serve on other publicly traded boards;[5] audit committee characteristics: a good audit committee is one that has independent members, has members with financial expertise, and meets regularly. Companies committing accounting fraud are less likely to have audit committees;[6] greater incidence of accounting fraud occurs when audit committee independence declines and when financial and accounting expertise of the committee is low;[7] the quality of earnings is positively related to the accounting and finance expertise of audit committees;[8] companies in financial distress are more likely to receive going concern audit qualifications when audit committee independence is greater;[9] audit committees with high financial competence have a more active and effective interface with internal audit, e.g. review internal audit programmes, hold longer meetings with chief internal auditor and review management's interaction with internal auditing.[10]

In Asia there has been a flurry of similar papers, all drawing the same unremarkable conclusions. Academics[11] constructed a corporate governance index (CGI) for almost all listed Korean public companies and reported strong evidence that higher CGI is correlated with higher firm market values. Moderate improvements in corporate governance result in an increase of market capitalization by 16 per cent of the company's book asset value or 35 per cent of the company's book value of common equity. This study suggested that an increase of one standard deviation in the index increases the level of buy-and-hold return of that firm's share by about 5 per cent for the holding period of the year 2001. Also, evidence shows that a qualitative increase in corporate governance (they in fact quantified it), increases the level of buy-and-hold return by 4–6 per cent over a year period. Conclusions from another paper[12] show that firms with profitable

245

investment opportunities, more reliance on external financing and more concentrated ownership have higher-quality governance and disclose more. Firms
with higher governance and transparency ratings are valued higher and invest
more. Moreover, these relations are stronger in countries that are less investor-
friendly, demonstrating that individual firms do adapt to poor legal environments
to achieve efficient governance practices. The importance of corporate governance was illustrated in a paper presented by Kim *et al.*, showing that corporate
governance is an important factor explaining firm value and firm return in the
Korean market.

Yet another paper[13] found that whereas debt constrains the expropriation
of dispersed shareholders by the professional managers of autonomous US corporations, in European and Asian corporate groups, debt can facilitate the
expropriation of minority shareholders by the controlling shareholder. Evidence
is presented that effective European capital market institutions let informed
outside suppliers of capital control the leverage of group affiliates; the lower
leverage of those more vulnerable to expropriation indicates that outsiders
perceive debt to facilitate expropriation. Ineffective Asian capital market institutions let controlling shareholders determine the leverage of group affiliates; the
higher leverage of those more vulnerable to expropriation indicates that debt
facilitates expropriation. On the other hand, academics in Hong Kong[14] found
that both disclosure and non-disclosure corporate governance mechanisms have
a significantly negative effect on the cost of equity capital. In addition, the effect
of non-disclosure governance mechanisms is more profound than that of disclosure on the cost of equity capital. Specifically, after controlling for beta and
size, when a firm improves its aggregate non-disclosure corporate governance
ranking from the 25th percentile to the 75th percentile, they found that its cost
of equity capital was reduced by roughly 1.26 percentage points, while the corresponding reduction in the cost of equity capital for the same improvement in
disclosure is 0.47. Finally, they found that country-level investor protection and
firm-level corporate governance are both important in reducing the cost of equity
capital. Their findings suggested that, in emerging markets where infrastructural
factors such as the legal protection of investors and the overall level of corporate
governance are not well established, reducing the expropriation risk by strengthening overall corporate governance appears to be more important in reducing
the cost of equity capital than adopting a more forthright disclosure policy. Does
Asia, however, count any more as a series of emerging markets?

Mention should also be made of a series of papers cited as forthcoming in one
paper[15] examining performance issues in relation to ownership. Lins examined
ownership and valuation of 1,433 firms in 18 emerging markets, half of which
are in Asia, finding that firm value is lower when controlling management group's
control rights exceed cash flow rights, and that large non-management control
rights blockholdings are positively related to firm value – both effects more so

in countries with low shareholder protection. Claessens suggests that a cause for this is that, in emerging markets, large non-management blockholders can act as a partial substitute for missing institutional governance mechanisms. Country-specific studies on the relations between ownership and performance generally find consistent evidence. Joh examined ownership structures and accounting performance for almost 6,000 publicly traded and private firms in Korea prior to the financial crisis, concluding that accounting performance was positively related to ownership concentration while negatively related to the wedge between control and ownership. Interestingly, the negative relationships between owner-ship wedge and profits were stronger in bad years measured by low GNP growth rates, perhaps indicating as Claessens suggests that agency problems are more severe when economic conditions are weak, or at least disguised when the economy improves. Moreover, profits were negatively related to investment in affiliated companies (more so for listed companies) but positively related to investment in unaffiliated companies. Another study by Chang also reported a negative relation between ownership wedge and performance for about 400 Korean chaebol (group)-affiliated firms. He argues that controlling owners use inside information to acquire equity stakes in more profitable or higher growth affiliated firms and transfer profits to other affiliates through internal transactions. Other studies cited reports that family-controlled firms with high levels of control have lower financial performance than family-controlled firms with low levels of control and firms that are widely held, and that firm value is higher when control-ling owners hold less than a majority of a firm's board seats. One conclusion (admittedly not from Asia, but perhaps all the more remarkable for that) was: 'strong-owner-controlled firms behave much more like their manager-controlled counterparts than weak-owner-controlled firms. This finding suggests that powerful shareholders who are mainly insiders are not necessarily perfect monitors of top managers' behavior'.[16]

It seems as if the unsurprising conclusion is that tight family control may be inferior to a Western model, but it beats confusion and lack of definite control hands down.

Perhaps the argument in Asia can be pushed further, with awkward conse-quences for the protagonists of the new corporate governance regime. Wiwattanakantang[17] reports for Thai firms that the presence of controlling share-holders is positively correlated with higher accounting performance. Moreover, family controlled firms display higher performance, concluding that the benefits of family ownership are in part due to low agency problems of Thai firms, because they typically do not adopt pyramidal ownership structures, although perform-ance was lower when controlling owners were also in top management. Such a relationship is strongest when controlling owners do not possess a majority owner-ship stake of their firms. Another Thai study concluded that the accounting performance of Thai firms declined after their IPO, and that the extent of the decrease in performance is much greater in Thailand than in the United States. They document an interesting curvilinear relationship between managerial owner- ship (excluding indirect shareholdings) and post-IPO change in performance that is consistent with the entrenchment and the alignment effects, and which will be of use to fund managers.

Professional firms agree. In an attempt to shed light on how shareholders perceive and value corporate governance, McKinsey & Co. conducted three separate surveys involving more than 200 institutional investors between 1999 and 2000. The three regions covered were Asia, the US and Europe, and Latin America. Three-quarters of the respondents reported that board practices were 'at least as important as financial performance when they evaluate companies for investment'. Over 80 per cent said they would 'pay more for the shares of a well-governed company than for those of a poorly governed one with a compar- able financial performance'.

> Although the McKinsey survey said measuring the actual market price impact of the premiums would prove difficult, 'the amounts [investors] are prepared to pay leave little doubt that good governance does feed through. The fact that most of the investors say that they already take corporate governance into account when making investment decisions is a powerful argument for corporate governance reform. We consider Investors were willing to pay 18 per cent more for the shares of a well-governed company.'

In a survey by McKinseys in 2002, a significant majority of responding investors indicated that they would be willing to pay as much as 30 per cent more for shares in companies that demonstrate good corporate governance practices. A subsequent study, also by McKinsey[18] reiterated this finding. It revealed that companies with better corporate governance had higher price-to-book ratios, an indication that investors do reward good governance by paying a premium for the shares of those companies that are well governed. According to this survey, companies can expect a 10–12 per cent boost to their market valuation by going from worst to best on any single element of governance. Good corporate governance helps to maintain overall market confidence, renew the countries' industrial bases, attract long-term investment capital, sustain economic growth and ultimately enhance nations' overall wealth and welfare. In fact, there is a widely held perception that good corporate governance leads to good corporate results.

The findings of a similar study of emerging markets conducted by CLSA in 2001 are probably best known. CLSA found strong correlations, especially among large-capitalized companies, between corporate governance and stock price performance, and valuations and financial performance ratios (see Figures 10.1, 10.2, 10.3). For instance, while the average return on capital employed (ROCE)

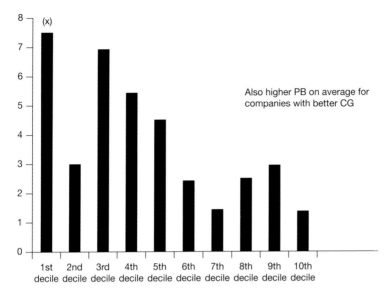

Also higher PB on average for companies with better CG

Figure 10.1 *PB of 100 largest gem stocks by CG decile (2000)*

Source: CLSA emerging markets

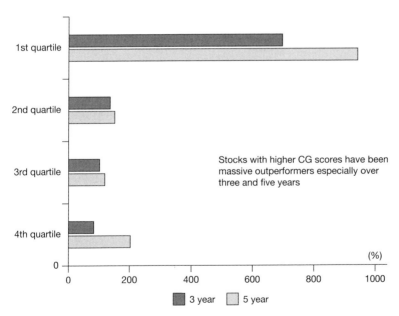

Stocks with higher CG scores have been massive outperformers especially over three and five years

■ 3 year ☐ 5 year

Figure 10.2 *Three- and five-year share price performance of 100 largest gem stocks by CG quartile*

Source: CLSA emerging markets

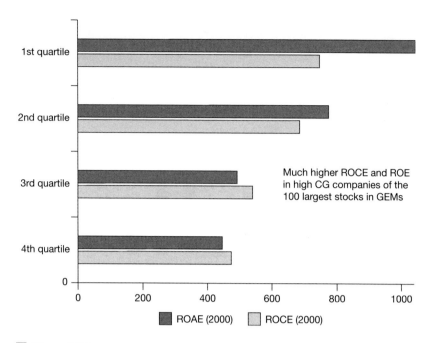

Figure 10.3 *Returns to corporate governance – global emerging markets 100 largest stocks*

Source: CLSA emerging markets

for the largest 100 firms was 23.5 per cent for fiscal year 2000, companies that were ranked in the top quarter of corporate governance yielded an average ROCE of 33.8 per cent as compared to an average ROCE of 16 per cent for those in the bottom half of the corporate governance rankings.[19]

The 2003 CLSA report concludes noticeably more modestly that investing in companies with good corporate governance definitely gives investors some protection from the worst blowups. But all of these studies indicate that good corporate governance pays dividends and, by implication, that poor corporate governance could lead to company failure. Indeed, the consensus view is that a breakdown in corporate governance was largely to blame for the corporate collapses during the Asian Economic Crisis, Enron, WorldCom and indeed almost everything, including national performance.

As in the corporate ratings, markets with low macro CG scores have seen 'substantial de-ratings and risk being marginalized by investors. In the lower half of our macro CG ranking, Korea, Thailand, Malaysia, China, Philippines, Indonesia, Pakistan and Russia have seen greater-than-50% declines (US$ terms) in their market indices over the past three and five years.[20]

250

A recent report covering the Malaysian market also seems to confirm investor predilections. The bulk of institutional players have indicated their willingness to pay a premium of 10–50 per cent for companies with excellent corporate governance practices, according to a joint KLSE–Pricewaterhouse Coopers Corporate Governance Survey in 2002. The survey found that 15 per cent of the respondents would pay more than 50 per cent premium for excellent corporate governance practices. Notably, 44 per cent are willing to pay 10–20 per cent extra, while 40 per cent would pay 21–50 per cent premium. Only 1 per cent would be happy with 1–9 per cent premium. The institutional groups include unit trust fund and asset managers, large private investment funds including insurers and government funds, and their influencers such as heads of research and heads of institutional sales. 'Institutional groups unanimously indicated that they would pay at least a 10 per cent premium to companies with excellent corporate governance practices', said PwC executive chairman Datuk Raja Arshad Uda. The other respondents to the survey were listed companies and independent non-executive directors. Of the total, there were 91 institutions, 201 companies, and 329 directors. Speaking at the release of the survey on 25 April, he said the corporate governance gap between Malaysia and other Asia-Pacific jurisdictions like Singapore, Hong Kong and Australia had narrowed since the last survey in 1998. 'All three target groups, the institutional groups, the independent non-executive directors and the public-listed companies confirm that the corporate governance regime in Malaysia has improved', he said. According to the survey, 96 per cent of directors, 93 per cent of the institutions and 84 per cent of the companies specified that corporate Malaysia has improved on corporate governance. In addition, Raja Arshad said a significant proportion of companies indicated they have exceeded the minimum reporting requirements for annual reports due to greater regulatory focus on corporate reporting. About 61 per cent of the companies stated that they have 'exceeded' the minimum level of disclosure in their respective annual reports as opposed to 52 per cent in the 1998 survey.

WHY IS IT SO?

Why does CLSA feel share prices and corporate governance are linked? They believe that a key reason is that corporate governance is a reflection of the quality of management. Higher calibre management clearly realize that high corporate governance standards are not just what investors are seeking, but also what is required to keep checks and balances in their company for long-term sustained high operating performance, while preventing corporate abuse and mismanagement. Another reason for the correlation, CLSA claimed, is that since investors have their pick of markets around the world, they can use corporate governance benchmarks as an investment yardstick. The huge menu of possible stock investments open to the global fund manager means the investor will be much more careful about investing in companies with poor corporate governance standards.

MINE IS BETTER THAN YOURS

If the arguments above are correct, then not only can companies steal a competitive march through the implementation of good corporate governance, but countries can, too. If Jackson Tai, Vice Chairman, DBS, believes what he says, he buys this argument wholesale:

> In Asia, we have to demonstrate to the outside world that we have centres of excellence here, that we can be transparent, that we are leading the industries that we serve in. It's important that the world sees that. And good governance differentiates Singapore and can differentiate our companies here.

McKinsey certainly agrees with this sentiment. Given the results of their surveys, McKinsey urged companies and policy-makers to take note. 'If companies could capture but a small part of the governance premium that is apparently available, they would create much greater shareholder value', McKinsey said as early as 1999. 'Moreover, companies that fail to reform their governance will find themselves at a competitive disadvantage when they try to obtain capital for growth. High governance standards will prove essential to attracting and retaining investors in globalised capital markets; failure to reform will probably hinder companies with global ambitions.'

However, this argument is double-edged. CLSA found that this performance relationship is clearest in markets where corporate governance is of biggest concern. The premium that investors would be willing to pay for such companies varied country by country. Investors were willing to pay 18 per cent more for the shares of a well-governed company from the US or Britain than for those of a company with similar financial performance but poorer governance practices. By the same token, they would be willing to pay 22 per cent more for a well-governed Italian company and 27 per cent more for the same in Indonesia. It follows inexorably from this argument that an Indonesian company has more to gain in percentage terms by following scrupulous corporate governance practices than a similar company in Singapore or Hong Kong.

WAIT A MINUTE . . .

Are there any caveats or downsides to this line of reasoning? Yes – this is where the analysis is really interesting. The first and obvious caveat is about the direction of causality. Does corporate governance contribute to a high share price, or does having a high and rising share price allow companies the luxury of undertaking corporate governance measures second to none? The CLSA reports, for example, call the connection a 'correlation' and carefully qualifies that by saying a correlation does not in itself prove causation. Clearly, though, they do not believe the causation works the other way round.

Second, the studies might not have got it all right anyway. For example, with regard to the effects on performance, some studies indicate that executive boards of directors controlled by outside directors tend to have fewer research and development expenses. Some have also argued that these boards tend to not follow through on consistent innovation strategies aimed at the creation of new areas of business and venturing. On the other hand, incentive contracts are not immune to criticisms regarding their capacity to align the interests of managers and shareholders, inasmuch as managers carry out their options shortly before the bad news and postpone this exercise after the good news, securing in this way their interests from the impact fluctuations of their management decisions.

Moreover, it seems that a longer time horizon is essential when it comes to demonstrating the impact of strong corporate governance on shareholder value. The report said that companies with high corporate governance scores 'tend to have high return on equity and economic value added ratios'. As a rule, companies with higher and/or improving scores had share prices that outperformed the average of companies surveyed in each market, while those with poorer scores underperformed, particularly over a time frame spanning three to five years. According to the CLSA, over short periods the outperformance of high-scoring stocks is tenuous. Over three years, the top quartile companies outperformed the average by just five percentage points. But over the past five years, stocks in the top 25 per cent of the CG survey outperformed their markets by an average of 35.2 percentage points while those in the bottom 25 per cent underperformed by 25 percentage points. Correlations are tricky things; there is quite a lot of white noise in even the best statistics, and a performance superiority of just 5 per cent is not enough to raise itself out of the white noise. There might be other reasons, too, why the particular five year period analysed demonstrated the performance data shown.

Third, is corporate governance the real determinant? In December 2001, academics[21] analysed the impact of corporate governance institutions, ownership structures and external capital market constraints on company returns on investment by using a sample of more than 19,000 companies from 61 countries across the world. This kind of multivariate data analysis is extremely difficult to do, and its conclusions are notoriously debatable, but this study, at least, showed that first of these three sets of institutions, the origin of a country's legal system proves to be the most important. Companies in countries with English-origin legal systems earn returns on investment that are at least as large as the cost of capital. Second, differences in investment performance related to a country's

253

legal system dominate differences related to ownership structure. If this argument is taken to its logical conclusion, then corporate governance reform in countries that are not blessed with English-origin legal systems like Singapore and Hong Kong (which do, it has to be admitted, still top the Asian corporate governance league tables, albeit by a diminishing margin) might as well forget it. Even if this is not so, it suggests that they may be labouring under a permanent disadvantage. But according to World Bank research in 2002,[22] although firms in countries with weak overall legal structures have on average lower governance rankings, firm-level governance is correlated with variables related to the extent of the asymmetric information and contracting imperfections that firms face, sales growth (proxy for the growth opportunities) and intangibility of assets; firms that trade shares in the US have higher governance rankings, especially so in countries with weak legal systems; good governance is positively correlated with market valuation and operating performance and this relationship is *stronger* in countries with weaker legal systems. So perhaps companies in Indonesia and the Philippines should not give up after all. Third, strong external capital markets improve the investment performance of companies. These conclusions do not threaten the supportive studies, not exactly, but they do tend to suggest that corporate governance itself may be secondary to the country's legal system *as a whole*. Bankruptcy legislation is often cited as an example of a parallel and related area which 'needs to be right' before corporate governance can really work. Intellectual property rights are another – both areas in which China has recently carried out legislative reform.

Fourth, as Claessens admits, the costs of inferior corporate governance may not be born entirely by the shareholders:

> It is important to note that the identified governance problems of Asian corporations do not necessarily imply that investors are worse off. The reviewed evidence indicates that shareholders discount stocks according to perceived corporate governance issues. This means that stock markets are increasing the cost of capital for firms with greater corporate governance problems and controlling owners/managers ultimately bear some of the agency costs.[23]

Then there is the argument about shareholder value in general. Foreign shareholders in Asia tend to attach great importance to short-term corporate performance rather than long-term continuance of the firm. In a 2003 survey of the Indian IT industry, no fewer than 88.5 per cent of respondents agreed that Corporate Governance is a must in gaining a competitive advantage. But it is interesting to note that none of the five companies ranked profitability as the top benefit gained by employing corporate governance. Two companies ranked FDI at the top, two companies ranked improved stakeholder relations at the top, and one company ranked enhanced image and brand at the top. Corporate governance enhances business competitiveness by integrating corporate social responsibility into every aspect of corporate management. Since corporate reputation serves as a useful and powerful asset/resource for companies to develop its competencies, and outperform competitors, companies that accommodate the needs of a wider range of stakeholders are more likely to yield good reputation and credibility than those which do not. The study concludes that corporate governance is not yet a necessity for successful competition in the Indian IT sector but if local and regional companies wish to enter the global market, they will need to employ good corporate governance strategies.

It is perfectly possible to conclude that the importance of corporate governance for the firms in which Asian shareholders invest lies *not* in the security of investment that they will receive, as this depends much more in practice on good management and corporate strategy, but in the strategic benefits to precisely that strategy of being able to penetrate Western markets. In that sense, good corporate governance scores are a 'language' which Western investors speak, and to attract Western capital, it is simply necessary to speak that language.

Chapter 11

Policing corporate governance: compliance and enforcement

- The perennial problem
- Who is responsible?
- Identifying culprits
- Mechanisms of enforcement
- Sanctions
- Conclusion

THE PERENNIAL PROBLEM

Let me start by making a prediction. In years to come, when convergence has been largely achieved in international accounting standards, when codes of corporate governance are indistinguishable the one from the other except for nuances of locality and language, and when the optimum structure for a board, the role of independent directors, the nature of remuneration for directors and executives, and all the other structural paraphernalia of corporate governance are distinguished largely by sector and company size rather than jurisdiction – a triumph of globalization – there will still be articles written and studies commissioned on compliance and enforcement. This will never go away. Asia will be no exception to this.

This line of reasoning suggests that 'much of corporate governance reform is actually an attempt to reduce the personalistic nature of business transactions' (Kang forthcoming). In this view, the elimination of cronyism – always the main criticism made of the corporate scene in the Philippines and Indonesia, and in the past, Malaysia and China too – is more or less synonymous with good corporate governance. It can be achieved by increasing property rights, reducing uncertainty, cutting the transaction costs of making and keeping agreements and securing property rights in the absence of neutral enforcement agencies. 'The point is that if the laws and other political institutions are unreliable, businessmen and politicians will find other ways to conduct their business' (Kang forthcoming). Implicit in this reasoning is that if these deficits can be addressed, improved corporate governance will in turn lead to greater economic welfare. The Italian experience alone should be sufficient to refute this argument: Italy, as the collapse of the Parmalat conglomerate amply demonstrated, has all these weaknesses and more, but is a highly affluent Western society. In Italy, as in the Philippines, status is still measured by exemption from the normal process of law. A society dominated by corruption cannot hope to achieve high standards of corporate governance.

Without regular inspections, ad hoc inspections, fraud task forces, independent scrutiny, active international investment with vigorous shareholders, a lively investigative media unhampered by state control and censorship, and guarantees of severe punishment for offences coupled with a high clear-up rate, the chances for successful compliance are not great. And even with them all, as in the US or the EU, flagrant abuses and corruption continue regularly. What chance is there for such a huge jurisdiction as China or Indonesia, without the resources to police consistently and with every incentive for individual firms to free-ride? For a long time, the CSRC in China was understaffed and had no real enforcement powers. As a result, only since 2002 have executives begun receiving prison sentences and personal fines, rather than the company being fined. The CSRC is seeking to make regular checks on listed companies on the issues of accounting, disclosure, related party transactions, use of funds, etc. In 2001, about 300 companies went through regular checks, while special checks were made on about 80 firms, and 32 firms were under legal investigation. These numbers are being increased each year. All firms have already completed self-assessment (but so what?). CSRC has also instituted delisting procedures as mandated by Chinese Company Law – at least 10 companies have been delisted from the main board and moved to an over-the-counter share transfer system commonly known as the Third Board. So the CSRC is at least trying. It is also important to remember that this is against a background of some 2000 listed firms, but the CSRC and other regulatory agencies in China, as in other countries in Asia, only have limited resources. There is no point in anyone clamouring for better corporate governance standards without costing their implementation – and, one might argue, weighing this against expenditure on other much needed investment such as infrastructure or health care. As the OECD itself has said, implementation and enforcement require increased commitment of human and monetary resources. In this regard, Asian policy-makers also need to balance the sophistication of rules and procedures with their ease and cost of implementation.

At present, we have not even reached a point in Asian corporate governance beyond compliance with rules, rather than the spirit of the rules. Recently, the Association of Chartered Certified Accountants (ACCA) commissioned a study, polling 200 Asian Chief Financial Officers (CFOs) from the top 300 companies in China, Malaysia and Singapore for their opinions on corporate governance.

257

The picture that emerged from the findings indicates that Asian corporate governance still focuses more on disclosure and compliance, rather than enhancing transparency. In 1999 the OECD said: 'Asia doesn't need better laws [let alone more codes or refinements of codes]; Asia needs better enforcement and better court systems.' Not that this sentiment, as we have seen, stopped them from encouraging just that. The OECD has now recognized, in 2003, after several years, that getting Asia to pass state of the art corporate governance legislation is one thing, whereas matching advances in rules with advances in implementation and enforcement is quite another matter. 'Passing new laws regarding outside directors is of little value if there are not truly "independent" directors to be found, and if the laws are not enforced.' It was still the same old story five years later: '. . . even more basic to progress, is leadership from the uppermost reaches of government that exemplifies and demands integrity, professionalism and even-handedness in public service.' However, there is growing pressure to put more enforcement mechanisms into those guidelines. The challenge which the OECD recognizes is to do this in a way consistent with market-oriented procedures by creating self-enforcing procedures that do not impose large new costs on firms. Of course, the OECD is not responsible for enforcement, but it is responsible for introducing new codes and rules. It cannot be blamed for enforcement failures.

So it suggests that all Asian countries should continue to strengthen regulatory institutions that: (i) establish high standards for disclosure and transparency; (ii) have the capacity, authority and integrity to enforce these standards actively and even-handedly; and (iii) oversee the effectiveness of self-regulatory organizations.

To be effective, the OECD admits, regulators must have a sufficient number of highly-trained personnel to monitor company compliance and to ensure that accounting and auditing self-regulatory organizations carry out their responsibilities. In addition, regulators and shareholders must also have at their disposal a range of options for sanctioning wrongdoing by accountants, auditors, company officers, directors and insiders and/or for seeking redress. Finally, underlying these requirements, must be leadership from the upper reaches of government that establishes a mandate for active and evenhanded enforcement and that sets an example of integrity and professionalism. Having this last, however, does not necessarily guarantee all the others, as China in particular has discovered.

So the OECD readily admits that the credibility – and utility – of a corporate governance framework rest on its enforceability. But its pious wish-list must be infuriating to the overworked regulators of Asian countries. Securities commissions, stock exchanges and self-regulatory organizations with oversight responsibilities should therefore continue to devote their energies to implementation and enforcement of laws and regulations. Court systems should further strengthen their expertise and capacity to adjudicate corporate governance

258

disputes efficiently and impartially, including through establishment of specialized commercial courts and promotion of alternative dispute resolution. Both agencies and courts ought to develop procedures that are objective, understandable, open and fair. In addition to enforcing the law, public decision-making should inform the future behaviour of market participants and enforcement agents as well as generate public confidence in the state's commitment to the rule of law. In this regard, it is important to stress the interaction between effective market discipline and self-discipline. The role of policy-makers is not only to enforce current laws but to promote institutions that facilitate market discipline. Who could possibly argue with all of this, if one accepts the desirability of the global corporate governance regime? But who is to pay for it?

WHO IS RESPONSIBLE?

So who is, or ought to be, responsible for policing corporate governance? It certainly helps to establish firm and clear guidelines on who is responsible in the event of a breach of a law, a rule or a code. A guideline like this one, for instance:

> The SROs are responsible for enforcing compliance with the rule. The rule directs SROs to adopt a self reporting mechanism that would require a listed issuer to notify the SRO promptly after an executive officer of the issuer becomes aware of any material non-compliance with the rule.

Former Irish President and senior UN official Mary Robinson said that: 'Regulation is crucial to minimise abuses and to enforce compliance with minimum norms, but regulation alone won't establish the business case for making necessary changes.' But for the majority of observers, there is clearly a rationale for making the principle of criminal liability for legal entities more widespread: a concept which is already incorporated in various national legislation, and in a non-binding way, in the 2000 Convention of the United Nations against Transnational Organized Crime and in a binding manner in the 1999 European Penal Convention on Corruption. The principle of dual indictment could also become more widespread, that is to say that the legal entity can be sanctioned and so can the individuals concerned (leaders within the company) who take or consent to the decision which is being sanctioned. The very novelty of corporate governance initiatives, especially in jurisdictions such as China, ought to have worked in Asia's favour here: fresh legislation has a better chance of clarity than a concocted gathering of historical laws. However, in practice the CSRC has been the first to admit that laws have become contradictory, and responsibility in China has not always been adequately laid out even in the legal system (e.g. on intellectual property rights), without going further into enforcement. The CSRC also lacked independent enforcement authority; it must coordinate

259

any effort to penalize rule breakers with the Ministry of Public Security. But the legal loopholes in China especially, though, are gradually being closed, and the enthusiasm of the Chinese Peoples' Court to learn from Western practice is impressive. Stock exchanges have been empowered to issue public reprimands of listed companies for violations of their listing rules, and a Joint Bureau of Investigation for Securities Crime between CSRC and the Ministry of Public Security has been set up. By comparison – and this is an example of an area in which Asia remains 'two-speed' in the older sense – Malaysian allocation of responsibilities has been relatively clear for some years:

> The FSS' investigative function is limited, because direct investigative rights with respect to financial institutions are maintained by the Securities and Futures Commission operating under the control of the FSC. However, actual investigative rights may be exercised through business association with the Securities and Futures Commission. The punitive measures that may be taken by the FSS include the cancellation of business licences or registration for certain institutions, suspension of all or part of a business, closure of business, suspension of part or all of branch business, and the issuance of warnings. Judicial action may be taken by indicting related persons to face prosecution.

In case a violation is discovered during the process of examining trading or of monitoring members, the KSE may directly punish, or otherwise take other appropriate measures against, relevant members or related persons, pursuant to the KSE's Articles of Incorporation and service regulations. However, the punishment shall be limited to suspension of trading for a specific period, imposing fines in an amount not exceeding RM1 billion or instructing violators to be more careful in future. In general, KSE reports such cases to the Financial Supervisory Services instead of taking its own investigation and punitive actions.

IDENTIFYING CULPRITS

Asia has a long way to go in putting in place corporate systems to catch culprits. Hong Kong is among the leading jurisdictions for corporate governance in Asia, but the results of KPMG Forensic's 2003 Fraud and Misconduct Diagnostic Survey,[1] the first survey of its kind, which polled a total of 2,000 Hong Kong entities including all those listed on the Hong Kong Stock Exchange, demonstrated precisely this. Fifty-seven per cent of respondents claimed that managing the risks posed by fraud and other types of misconduct and unethical activity within their organizations was not adequately addressed or only partially addressed; 65 per cent of respondents felt that the responsibility for managing fraud risks within their organization was poorly defined or that the responsibilities needed better definition; among many interesting replies, 56 per cent of respondents thought that fraud risks had not been matched, or had only been partially matched, to controls; 58 per cent of respondents told KPMG that the overall responsibility for fraud prevention and detection fell on the CEO or CFO; only a third of respondents were completely satisfied that their recruitment screening would prevent fraudsters from joining their employment, with one in ten respondents being of the view that their recruitment process would let a fraudster into their organization; one in ten respondents told us that they believed that their regional or head office personnel didn't have the necessary experience and background to detect those red flags which may indicate the existence of fraud from a review of their organization's financial statements; 8 per cent of respondents did not have any communication channels for reporting suspicions of fraud and 12 per cent did not have fraud and ethics policies and principles in place. Responses from surveys of this kind are perhaps skewed to the negative and the sensational: and even so, for a third of those surveyed to have such confidence in their firm's screening policies is quite good news. But the identification of culprits within firms even in the US or Europe, especially when there is collusion with outside auditors, is notoriously difficult. There really is little reason to mark down Asia's scorecard on this part of the equation.

Part of the problem, as identified in Chapter 3, is that independent directors 'go native' with startling rapidity and depressing uniformity. The solution to the problem, which would appeal to Asian governments but not to the international investors who are driving the corporate governance agenda, would be to mandate genuinely independent directors, one from the Civil Service and one from the charity sector, to all listed companies and all private companies over a certain size. It is most unlikely that any Asian jurisdiction will adopt such a course of action, however: they are still trying to reduce the stakes taken in private companies by government, without trying to impose external monitoring directly onto a board. There would be severe resourcing problems, too, especially in finding suitable candidates from charities – and there would not even be total confidence that this measure would guarantee the active independence of these directors. This problem will remain severe.

MECHANISMS OF ENFORCEMENT

The OECD tells us that corporate governance frameworks employ a number of different enforcement mechanisms to hold directors accountable and to give shareholders redress for violations of their rights. Some mechanisms (administrative fines, sanctions and orders) require action by regulatory bodies; other mechanisms (civil and criminal penalties, injunctive relief) require a determination of wrongdoing by courts. A few mechanisms, however, such as appraisal rights and cumulative voting, are shareholder triggered, in the sense that the shareholder may invoke them without a prior finding by a state body (regulatory or judicial).

261

On the whole, as the OECD observes, Asian legal regimes favour regulatory over judicial redress. Until recently, Asian jurisdictions have lacked sufficient legal infrastructure to permit class action or (apart from common law jurisdictions) derivative suits. In addition, where infrastructure for class action or derivative action suits does exist, instigation of these suits can be hampered by high minimum share requirements, high court filing fees and other mechanisms that hinder litigation irrespective of the merits of the underlying claim. However, there appears to be an accelerating trend favouring greater availability and use of class action or derivative action suits. For example, Korea has liberalized its derivative action rules and has seen some litigation already; Taiwan has enacted rules permitting shareholder class action lawsuits; Chinese courts have permitted China's first common action by shareholder plaintiffs. The Malaysian Securities Commission is undertaking a study of class action suits, and may implement recommendations by the High Level Finance Committee on Corporate Governance of the Malaysian Ministry of Finance to make such derivative actions more 'user friendly' in terms of process and cost.

Thoughtful development of a corporate governance framework will take into account the capabilities of a particular legal system. In one case, a system with highly effective administrative enforcement may rely less on judicial and shareholder-triggered mechanisms. In another case, a system with strong courts may place less emphasis on regulatory and shareholder-triggered mechanisms. Where, in a third case, however, a system is still developing the effectiveness and capacity of its regulators and courts, shareholder-triggered mechanisms can become essential. As a consequence, where this third case obtains, local law or listing requirements should encourage cumulative voting for listed companies by making it the default rule, with individual opt-out by supermajority vote of the shareholders. Both Pakistan and another non-OECD member country, Russia, mandate cumulative voting. According to one Asian Roundtable expert with experience in Russia, the result in that country has been considerable diversification of board representation, as well as creation of a focal point for institutional-investor activism. China's Code of Corporate Governance lays out a middle ground by requiring cumulative voting for listed companies that are more than 30 per cent owned by controlling shareholders. The code further stipulates that this requirement be reflected in the company's articles of association. Of course, where a family or group controls a high percentage of the voting shares, not even cumulative voting can ensure a balance of interests at the board level. One OECD member country in Asia, Korea, has addressed this situation by partially restricting the voting rights of certain major shareholders in large corporations. Where a Korean company has more than KRW2 trillion (US$1.54 billion) in assets, shareholders with more than 3 per cent of all voting shares cannot exercise the voting rights of those shares that exceed 3 per cent when voting for non-executive directors who will serve on the audit committee. Insufficient evidence has yet been gleaned to draw a conclusion on the benefits of this rule.

SANCTIONS

Identifying those responsible for corporate governance and pinpointing breaches is of no use, as any policeman will tell you, if the sanctions for rule-breaking remain weak, easily evaded, poorly disseminated throughout the marketplace, ill-defined, corruptible, unjust, subject to endless revision, or brazenly defied. Corporate governance observers agree that major areas of corporate misconduct, such as asset stripping, improper transfer pricing and undervalued transfers to offshore companies related to company managers, break existing laws. A new code, by itself, will not deter this misconduct. It will only be prevented if there is a widely shared expectation, subsequently fulfilled, that regulators and the courts will vigorously enforce the law in a fair and balanced manner. A further deterrent would take effect when a company's independent auditors insist on full disclosure in financial statements and if non-compliance is treated as a breach of directors' duties to the company.[2] For example, the OECD has pointed out that although Asian legal systems have generally instituted laws and rules to prohibit insider trading, sanctions are often insufficient to deter wrongdoing. While jurisdictions generally appear to track trading electronically, enforcement in this area remains problematic due to capacity constraints and difficulties in identifying and proving wrongdoing.

So, for example, it is good to know that:

> Where a company fails to disclose the matters set out in para 4.1 in its annual report, it is open to the Exchange to take any action against the listed entity or its directors as set out in the listing requirements and section 11 of the Security Industry Act 1983.

However, what matters is whether in practice the KLSE has taken such action in the event of such a breach. In fact, during 2000 and 2001, there were only two cases of partial business suspension, four cases of reprimand and/or institutional warning, and nine cases of other punitive actions taken by the Financial Supervisory Services. This, it has been suggested, indicates the relatively minimal level of its practical enforcement activities. In China, securities companies are now being judged on how well they carry out due diligence. If abuses by the candidate are uncovered, the sponsor has points deducted from a 12-point total and their chances of lead managing further IPOs are hurt. They are also restricted as to the number of candidates they put forward, which should encourage them to pick the best ones. Since 2001 the CSRC has punished a number of listed companies, brokerages, accountants, and fund houses, which in turn has provided some credibility for the government's attempt to create a credible corporate governance regime in China.

Perhaps a small intrusion of the great debate about criminality is in order here. Is the policeman right? Does a strong rule powerfully enforced generate high standards of corporate governance? Or is a liberal view of the question correct – that a harsh regulatory regime of itself, rather like the draconian measures available to the Chinese courts for corruption by minor officialdom, seems to have limited if not negative effects. Korean and US academics researched how regulatory, industry, and economic factors affect firms' corporate governance practices. In their paper,[3] armed with a strong index,[4] they investigate the factors that predict a firm's score on CGI and the five subindices that comprise CGI (for shareholder rights, board structure, board procedure, disclosure to investors, and ownership parity). They explore the relative importance of firm growth, profitability, and other firm specific factors, industry factors, and regulatory factors. Regulatory factors are highly important. Industry factors are also important. Firm-specific factors are less important and have only a modest effect on governance, even when they are statistically significant. Among firm-specific factors, the most significant are size (larger firms are better governed), firm risk (riskier firms are better governed) and long-term profitability (more profitable firms are worse governed). Industry-level growth predicts CGI more strongly than firm growth. Need for external equity finance (a measure that combines growth and profitability) predicts better governance; this effect is driven by the negative correlation between profitability and CGI. Long-term averages of growth, profitability and equity finance need are stronger than short-term averages, suggesting that firms alter governance slowly in response to economic factors. Ownership by the largest shareholder is sometimes but not reliably significant.

CONCLUSION

Abuse of corporate governance remains a common problem in many Asian countries. Investors have still seen their shares diluted by insiders and major shareholders. Companies have still seen their assets stripped by various means of transfer pricing. The interests of creditors have still not been adequately protected and the mobilization of capital has been reduced as a result. The enforcement of corporate governance in Asia still seriously lags in its theoretical development and legislative and code provision. This is set to continue although efforts at unifying compliance and enforcement are being made throughout Asia, and there have been some demonstrably successful cases of compliance, such as SembCorp in Singapore, and enforcement, such as the CSRC's actions against banks and brokers.

264

The future

THINKING ABOUT THE FUTURE

It is possible to analyse the future of corporate governance under several key headings that represent trends that have shown every sign of persistence, acceleration and deepening, as Asian corporate governance systems copy and begin to make independent contributions to the emerging global corporate governance regime.

The OECD White Paper of June 2003 set out the following six main priorities for reform:

■ Public and private sector institutions should continue to raise awareness among companies, directors and shareholders of the value of good corporate governance.

■ All jurisdictions should strive for effective implementation and enforcement of corporate governance laws and regulations.

■ The Asian Roundtable countries should work towards full convergence with international standards and practices for accounting, audit and non-financial disclosure.

■ Boards of directors must improve their participation in strategic planning, monitoring of internal control systems and independent review of transactions involving managers, controlling shareholders and other insiders.

■ The legal and regulatory framework should ensure that non-controlling shareholders are protected from exploitation by insiders and controlling shareholders.

265

■ Governments should intensify their efforts to improve the regulation and corporate governance of banks.

What is likely to happen? Here is a partly alternative list of headings for a prognosis of developments in corporate governance in Asia over the next few years.

Awareness. There seems little doubt that awareness of corporate governance will continue to spread throughout all levels of society in Asia. Shares will be more widely held and the level of interest in corporate affairs seen in Singapore, where corporate matters have almost completely displaced politics at the centre of media attention, is likely to become pervasive, especially as internet use continues to spread and news programmes continue to concentrate ever more on business events. Corporate governance as the 'rules' or 'software' of business is moving into the mainstream of society, and certainly as much in Asia as Europe, if not yet to the same extent as in the US.

Banks and the financial sector. In Asia and Latin America corporate governance will focus on the way banks lend and the governance of banks, especially with the implementation of Basle II. As Asian banks are forced by the WTO into global competition – which has not yet happened properly even in Singapore, let alone China or Malaysia – effective governance will be necessary for smaller local banks even to survive. They will need to demonstrate an iron commitment to shareholder value to be able to attract the outside investment they will need to make in technology, marketing, human resources and even acquisitions to stay in the Asian financial services market. This will feed through into non-performing loan (NPL) analysis and the reform of the banking sector in countries such as Japan, China and Indonesia.

Board diversity. The New York Stock Exchange's requirement that listed companies have a majority of independent directors (rather than a fixed number or a percentage), if copied in Asia, presents an unprecedented opportunity to increase the number of women and ethnic minorities in Asian boardrooms, as only among these minorities can genuine independence even possibly be found. With hundreds of directorships possibly becoming vacant, there are real prospects for changing the character of Asia's corporate boards, where racial issues, in particular, are usually more multidimensional than in the West. Asian CEOs – if you are reading this – steal a march! Will rainbow boards be any better, though? Will such directors really be 'independent'? Some political powers are in favour of boards that are controlled or at least composed by independent managers in order to obtain a more effective monitoring of the executive managers' action. However, as CEOs play an important role in the selection, remuneration and

266

retention of outside directors, their power and monitoring capacity will perhaps always be limited, and perhaps – but not certainly – more so in Asia than in Europe or the US. Moreover, is there really any point in appointing a director so independent that they know nothing about the particular business concerned, or perhaps any business at all? How will they even recognize the very improprieties they are supposed to prevent? *Best practice must be to promote board diversity where it does not conflict with efficiency.*

Elsewhere in the world, especially in the US, there are now moreover real concerns about whether companies can get the people they need to serve as non-executive directors. Amid an avalanche of new rules and regulations and heightened fears of liability, chief executives are increasingly turning their backs on directorships at other companies, according to executive board recruitment agencies. In the UK likewise, non-executive directors are arguing that their fees are insufficiently high to reflect the increased level of personal financial responsibility associated with recent reforms, caused by the heightened risk of litigation for directors in the light of corporate reforms, most notably pending rules raising the responsibilities of board audit committee members. These problems have yet to reach Asia, as shareholder activism has not been sufficiently prominent to act as a deterrent. But the time may eventually come when it is as difficult to recruit a good non-executive director in Shanghai as it already is in Miami. Organizations will step forward to help (and perhaps provide insurance through collective schemes). The president and CEO of the Securities Investors Association of Singapore (SIAS) believes that 'SIAS can contribute to the appointment process by being an intermediary and helping to nominate independent directors, perhaps in collaboration with the Singapore Institute of Directors'.

Convergence. Convergence is especially important when considering the relative benefits that different corporate governance systems confer on particular states: if the EU experience is anything to go by, the rise of ASEAN, along with convergence of accounting standards, *will* erode comparative advantage in corporate governance systems, albeit very gradually. Convergence is already happening across a whole range of facets of corporate governance. Most obvious are the international accounting standards that have the beneficial side effect of rendering international valuation comparisons more meaningful. In recommending full accountancy standard convergence as a goal to be achieved over time, OECD Roundtable participants recognize the practical challenges imposed by local conditions. At the same time, however, OECD Roundtable participants have encouraged regional standards-setters to address analytical and policy concerns connected with standards through active participation in the international standards-setting process. In this respect, the Roundtable believes that regional standards-setters should focus on influencing international standards while they are being formulated, rather than justifying deviation from such standards after they have been issued. To this end, Asian countries, individually and as a group, need to ensure their full involvement with international standards-setting bodies, such as IASB and IFAC, as well as with international organizations that contribute data and policy analysis to the international standards-setting process. But does the OECD really think that the Philippines, or Indonesia, is going to have a significant impact on global accountancy standards? The only obvious area where Asia, and in particular Malaysia, ought to take a leading role is in the integration of Islamic banking and other Islamic financing instruments with global account-ancy standards, and indeed the global corporate governance regime as a whole. If Malaysia – and other Islamic jurisdictions such as Saudi Arabia – does not do this, there is a serious risk of financial as well as cultural divergence between the Islamic world and the West, something which the Malaysian government in particular is fully committed to prevent.

The OECD Roundtable's view is that while full convergence with international standards and practices may be challenging, Asian regimes should nonetheless establish it as a goal to be achieved over time. As a transitional measure, inter-national standards might be applied initially to listed companies, and the consolidated financial statements of corporate groups. In addition, jurisdictions that wish to establish standards that go beyond IAS and ISA may do so via supple-mentary disclosures. From country to country, of course, local conditions may require adoption of a set of standards, such as IAS, individually (rather than all at once) and/or at differing speeds. However, the OECD takes the view that such local conditions should be used neither to politicize the standards-setting process nor to encourage the adoption of standards that diverge from inter-nationally recognized benchmarks. ASEAN is likely to agree with this and the ADB is already committed to similar principles. In addition, the OECD believes that standards-setters should disclose where local standards and practices diverge from IAS (and the reasons for these divergences); company financial statements should reference specific disclosures where they apply to specific items and yield materially different results. This is likely to become the norm across Asia as it already is in countries such as Singapore. What is unlikely, however, is that stand-ards-setting bodies in Asia will be subject to oversight by a single, unified body that acts, and is seen to act, in the public interest, which is what the OECD believes is required: no one body, whether it be ASEAN, ADB or OECD itself, has the necessary authority. For that, the EU is a model but it is but a gleam in the eyes of the next generation of visionary Asian leaders.

Codes of corporate governance, standards of CSR, the extent of shareholder activism, and the role of government are further areas where convergence is happening very rapidly. The Secretary-General of the ACGA, Jamie Allen, observed in February 2003 that 'convergence does not herald complete unifor-mity in legal and economic systems. Companies and securities law, not to mention judicial systems, will continue to differ widely'. The concept of the corporation also varies, board structure too, and ultimately also the style of enforcement: dictat or recommendation, autocracy or consultation.

Corporate social responsibility. This is on the march in Asia. Even a recent report on the Indian IT industry included among its recommendations that 'Environmental, Sustainability and Social reporting should be increased to the proper level' and that 'Companies should form strategies based on triple bottom line concept (economic, social and environmental) for enhancing corporate performance'. The idea that proper CSR forms part of a well-governed company will spread in Asia, and it will happen that leading Asian corporations will start to produce CSR reports. The Ethical Corporation conference in 2003 held in Singapore was sufficiently well attended to attest to the burgeoning interest in this area in Asia, and more will follow as Asian governments start to withdraw from state direction and public provision of services.

Directors and their boards. The future is clearly pretty bright for independent directors of public companies in Asia, if they can be found and enticed onto boards. Their responsibilities will be increasingly well defined; for example, they will have the responsibility for supervising disclosure.

The OECD Roundtable recommendations comprised three basic categories. The first focused on director training, voluntary codes of conduct, expectations for professional behaviour and directors' resources and authority over management. These recommendations aimed to increase the pool of candidates who are willing and able to perform the tasks entrusted to directors and to give them the skills and authority to do their jobs. So directors would be more thoroughly trained – although whether that will make them better directors, or just better informed directors, will remain to be seen. Business judgement is more than just book learning. However, they will know their potential liabilities very well and while this may make tomorrow's directors more cautious, they may also avoid some of the mistakes of their predecessors, for example over-borrowing. Exactly how directors will be able to demonstrate that they have been adequately trained remains obscure, but this will no doubt resolve itself in due course, though most probably not at first in Asia. *Best practice must be for all directors to have independent confirmation from a reputable source, such as the national Institute of Directors, backed up by a training company, that they have received all necessary training and eventually – yes – continuous professional development (CPD) as well.*

A second set of recommendations sought to reduce or eliminate loopholes by tightening standards for director 'independence', by defining 'shadow' directors and rendering them liable for their actions, by increasing sanctions for violations of duties of loyalty and care, and by advocating delineation of a core set of related-party transactions (such as company loans to directors and officers) that should

269

be prohibited outright. In Thailand, for instance, the next step to further enhance the independence and effectiveness of the board structure may be a requirement for the two-tier board structure, which consists of the main board or supervisory board and the executive board. The supervisory board which should contain a sufficient number of independent non-executive directors will be responsible for selecting, evaluating and compensating the executive board and for formulating overall corporate strategy and monitoring corporate performance, while the executive board will execute corporate strategy and manage daily operations of the business.

The logic of corporate governance, with the demand that directors have no conflicts of interest, suggests that the trend must also eventually be towards the reduction of interlocking directorships overall. *Best practice must already be for directors to have no other directorships, except perhaps of companies within the same group*, however difficult this may be to achieve in practice. Finally, Roundtable participants recommended adequately empowering shareholders to seek redress for violations of their rights and to ensure director accountability. Policy options in this area include incorporating shareholder derivative or class action suits into national jurisprudence, permitting shareholders directly to nominate candidates for the board, and cumulative voting for directors for listed companies. Progressively more Asian companies will adopt remuneration and nomination committees as well as audit committees.

The OECD believes that Asian jurisdictions still have more work to do in clarifying and strengthening the fiduciary duty of directors to act in the interest of the company and all of its shareholders; for example they should prohibit indemnification of directors by companies for breaches of fiduciary duty; and they should provide shareholders who suffer financial losses with private and collective rights of action against controlling shareholders and directors. Bank directors should be able to pass 'fit and proper' tests for service, although there is as yet no international best practice on what these are. These directors should also assume responsibility for bank systems and procedures that ensure sound lending and monitoring practices, as well as the capacity to handle distressed debt. The OECD believes that a director should not be entitled to indemnification if that director cannot show that he or she acted in good faith and in a manner he or she reasonably believed to be in, or not opposed to, the best interests of the corporation. Typically, approval or ratification is only required for a transaction (or series of related or connected transactions) of a material size. Some Roundtable participants have expressed reservations over categorically prohibiting the company from executing transactions notwithstanding the approval of disinterested directors and/or disinterested shareholders. Such prohibitions, however, enjoy limited but growing application in OECD member countries as well as support in academic literature.

Disclosure. Chow[1] has said that best corporate governance practice is a moving target and even Hong Kong still has some way to go to match the highest standards worldwide, for example in areas such as the disclosure of remuneration policy for directors (including the breakdown between performance-based and non-performance-based pay, and other benefits) and details of individual directors' remuneration. More detailed disclosure, he argues, is also needed on the work carried out during the year by audit and other board committees, the number of board and committee meetings held and individual attendance records. Those public companies in Asia that do not report quarterly, and report on the internet, will gradually do so. With this weight of opinion, increased disclosure by Asian companies is a safe bet. What is interesting is whether, in the short to medium term at least, a 'disclosure gap' opens up between the best and the rest – certainly between listed companies and private ones, and maybe even between the large, global brand Asian companies which have international investors on the one hand, and all the other companies on the other. Asian jurisdictions ought to work hard to avoid this, but it may happen all the same.

The OECD believes – *of course* – that all Asian governments should introduce measures, or enhance existing measures, to provide minority shareholders with adequate protection from exploitation by controlling shareholders. These measures should *of course* include strengthening disclosure requirements (particularly of self-dealing/related-party transactions and insider trading). Notice and proxy materials should *of course* be sent out sufficiently far in advance that recipients have time to digest the information, to send documents to proxy holders and to solicit proxies from other shareholders. Information should *of course* include full details of the proposed meeting, text of agenda items and proposed resolutions, and a discussion of the pros and cons of items and resolutions sufficient for shareholders to make an informed decision. *Of course*, the meeting date and the record date should be announced at the same time, and the record date should be sufficiently in advance of the meeting to permit information to be sent to shareholders regarding the meeting and proxies and voting instructions to be obtained from beneficial owners. Setting a record date in advance of a meeting is a desirable practice that should *of course* be encouraged as long as the record date is not too early (e.g. before the announcement date of the meeting) or too late. Under Delaware law, for example, the record date may be set no fewer than 10 days and no more than 60 days before the meeting. (The OECD says that realistically, however, 30–45 days advance is usually necessary to obtain voting instructions from beneficial owners of a public corporation.) With respect to self-dealing/related-party transactions, insiders (and other interested persons, including 'controlling' and 'significant' shareholders) and the company should at least be required to disclose these transactions and to seek the approval of a majority of disinterested directors or approval or ratification by an appropriate

271

majority of disinterested shareholders. Furthermore, in some cases, it may be appropriate for companies to be prohibited altogether from engaging in certain kinds of related-party transactions. Directors' compensation needs increasingly to be accurately and promptly disclosed and it must be rated as highly probable that it will be. All these measures, the OECD believes – probably rightly – will strengthen corporate governance in Asia. Of course they *would*. It is even likely that eventually they *will*. The question is, how rapidly?

There is wide agreement at each national level that there ought to be system-ization and clarification of disclosure regulations. Some have suggested, for example in China, that because regulations on disclosure appear in many different acts, codes and rules, some of which are contradictory, the solution lies in a Corporate Disclosure Act, backed up by a Code of Conduct promulgated for example by the national Institute of Directors and approved by the relevant regulator. Such an act and code would answer questions such as who should disclose? What should be opened? How to disclose? What are the standards of disclosure? How to establish an internal balance mechanism in the listed corpor-ations? Which roles do CSRC and stock exchanges play in the disclosure system? What is the position and liabilities of media institution and specialists in the disclosure system? What is the position and liabilities of newspaper in the

---

Box 12.1 TITAN NATIONAL SECURITY SOLUTIONS SUPPLIER POLICY

Purchasing

Materials, supplies, consulting and other services will be purchased from qual-ified suppliers at the lowest cost but consistent with meeting performance, quality and delivery schedule requirements of Titan.

Purchasing activities will:

- Meet the highest ethical standards in all areas such as source selection, awards, and negotiation.
- Comply with applicable government regulations and contract provisions.
- Have proper internal controls and compliance monitoring.
- Accept for use only those goods that meet contract specifications and pass required inspection procedures.
- Maintain and encourage competition and comply with the rule of no gifts or gratuities to or from suppliers, consultants or subcontractors.
- All offers of gifts, gratuities, or favors from suppliers, must be reported immediately to one's supervisor. Our suppliers are also encouraged to report to us any solicitations by employees of such gifts, gratuities or favors.

> ## Box 12.2 CARLTON GROUP PAYMENT POLICY
>
> ### Creditor payment policy
>
> The Group does not follow any particular code on payment practice. Operating businesses are responsible for agreeing the terms and conditions under which business transactions with their suppliers are conducted and making those suppliers aware of the terms of payment. It is Group policy that payments to all suppliers are made in accordance with the agreed terms, provided that the supplier is also complying with all relevant terms and conditions.
>
> Trade creditor days of the Company for the year ended 30 September 2002 were 30 days, based on the ratio of Company trade creditors at the year-end to the amounts invoiced during the year by trade creditors.

disclosure system? What is the role of investment bank in the disclosure system? What are the legal liabilities of violator, especially civil liabilities? What are relevant judicial remedies, especially civil procedures?

Boxes 12.1 and 12.2 show two examples from the US of company policies disclosed. Asian company websites can expect be filled up with more of this in the future, with no detail spared, however insignificant or gruesome:

Many commentators suggest that increased disclosure will establish a virtuous circle. The OECD has suggested that the quality of information disclosure depends on the standards and practices under which it is prepared and presented. *Best practice is already the full adoption of international accounting, audit and financial disclosure standards and practices* which will facilitate transparency, as well as comparability, of information across different jurisdictions. Such features, in turn, strengthen market discipline as a means for improving corporate governance practices.

Disinterestedness. Some quarters in Malaysia and elsewhere have called for an additional independent review and certification on companies going for IPOs. The intention apparently would be to provide some measure of independent evaluation for the benefit of the typical public investor who will become a minority shareholder of these companies. The argument put forward is that since the IPO market now is under a disclosure-based regime where the Securities Commission no longer evaluates the merits of each IPO applicant, the responsibility now shifts to investors to undertake such evaluations. The problem for the typical investor, according to this way of thinking, is that he or she does not have the necessary skills or sophistication to make a reliable analysis of an IPO prospectus. An independent review of the contents of IPO documents together with a commendation on corporate governance issues can probably, it is argued, go a long way in providing a perceived yet unspoken need in the current IPO market and provide a level of confidence to the share market, in general. The benefits to companies going for IPOs if such a corporate governance evaluation is done should be a tangible awareness of good corporate governance principles and a conscious effort in assimilating best practices – a representation of sorts at the outset of a company's life as a PLC on the KLSE. It is acknowledged that companies that collapse due to some form of wrong behaviour could have been caught much earlier because telltale signs of questionable corporate governance were apparent at specific points in time or may even have been latent, not having reached 'critical mess'. By minting IPO companies with evaluated good corporate governance practices from the outset, preventive action can be taken so that instances of companies getting into trouble just after their IPO can be minimized, if not eliminated completely.

While this does seem attractive and indeed logical, two reasons might be put forward as to why it is unlikely to happen. First, who is to pay for this? Independent scrutiny of IPOs would not come cheaply, especially if the auditors signing off the prospective public company would render themselves liable to prosecution by shareholders if they got it wrong. If the answer is to be a levy on the securities industry, there would be complaints that existing public companies are being taxed for the benefit of their competitors. If the taxpayer, then there would be complaints that shareholders are benefiting at the expense of other less fortunate members of society – especially in countries in Asia which are far from being shareholder democracies. That leaves those who will actually benefit, the prospective shareholders themselves, and the best way of organizing such an independent review and the only way it might happen is for the cost to be levied *retrospectively* on the new shareholders in proportion to their shareholding. The cost might put some off, though. The second objection is more wide-ranging. Why should the benefits of an independent review like this be limited to IPOs? Why not existing public companies and even those soliciting outside private capital? This would then go to the heart of the problem: that the piper paying the auditor's tune is the company, whereas it ought to be the shareholders. Only when auditing is completely removed from the control of the company itself will this conflict of interest be removed. It is just conceivable that in the future, when Asian countries feel more confident about taking the lead in corporate governance initiatives, their dual concern with independence of auditors and lack of scruple about introducing regulations may prompt an Asian country to be the first to introduce a regulation of this kind.

Enforcement.   Enforcement will gradually become *the* subject for corporate governance. The revised OECD principles may also include guidelines on how to ensure the suggestions are put in practice and how to enforce them, as it has become too painfully obvious to be ignored that further pious principles are superfluous. Contrary to 1999, the principles are intended to be formally endorsed by OECD member governments at the organization's annual meeting rather than just published – although that itself is still far from enforcement. The OECD has already said that 'The next phase of the OECD Asia Roundtable will focus on implementation and enforcement issues and culminate in two years' time (2005) with a stock-taking of developments and progress.' That will make interesting reading. How is progress to be measured, once every country has the 'right' legislation, codes and superficial practice? Debates about sanctions and methods of enforcement, policing methods and deterrence, statistics on numbers of scandals, offence rates, clear-up rates, and penalties, are the very essence of future research about corporate governance in Asia – as elsewhere.

Institutions. The OECD will surely go on producing reports, as will the Asian Development Bank and numerous other institutions. The OECD is upgrading its principles for good corporate governance in response to the new challenges posed by a wave of global corporate scandals. Draft revised principles on corporate governance were put to public consultation by the OECD, with the draft text strengthening the original 12 principles on several points: it detailed the right of investors to nominate directors; it maintained that shareholders should be able to have input on director/executive pay and to question auditors; it called for enhanced transparency from analysts, rating agencies and brokers in disclosing conflicts. The revised OECD principles continue to emphasize the need for transparency and equal treatment of shareholders, but they are likely as eventually agreed to include guidelines on issues such as how to strengthen the independence of non-executive directors sitting on a company's board and committees, how to get institutional investors more involved in the companies they invest in and how to deal with executive pay packages. Watch out too for the developing role of ASEAN, which sees itself ultimately as an Asian EU and which therefore will want a key role in the evolution of regional corporate governance. The OECD has already staked out a role for itself and the ADB in claiming that:

> Transitioning will also involve significant training, as well as financial and human resource commitments at the company, professional firm, standards-setting and regulatory levels. In such cases, the support and involvement of international technical-assistance bodies may be particularly important to successful convergence.[2]

One day, there will be turf war between institutions in respect to corporate governance in Asia – but that is quite a long way off yet.

Annual Corporate Governance Awards at an international level from CLSA, *Euromoney* and numerous other bodies at an international and national level will no doubt continue. It is likely that they will become more detailed and widespread, if not competitive.

275

Institutions at a national level will become more proactive. In the UK for instance, the Financial Reporting Review Panel (FRRP) which until now investigated company accounts only on receipt of specific complaints or when integrity was questioned, will review some 300 company accounts annually. Such proactivity can be expected in future from Asian regulators – China's CSRC currently investigates only on the scale of the FRRP in a market which stands potentially to dwarf that of the UK.

Where the practices noted in Chapter 8 as prejudicial to active shareholder democracy can be corrected through simple changes in laws, regulations or listing requirements, Asian policy-makers and regulators will gradually effect these changes. In addition, company officers and directors will be made directly responsible to shareholders for full and detailed compliance with the rules governing meetings. But this too will be a gradual process with plenty of loopholes for the unscrupulous. Regulators (whether governmental or stock exchange) are already authorized (but not obliged) to oversee company compliance, including attending shareholder meetings as observers (at company expense, if appropriate), with the power to sanction conduct that either violates the letter of norms or abuses their spirit, and as the example of China shows, this is happening in practice too. Liberalizing proxy voting and voting *in absentia* are both likely to be permitted and encouraged. The provision of formal instructions by shareholders on the use of proxies should be facilitated. Listed companies will be encouraged, at their expense, to hire independent and reputable professionals to collect proxies and organise proxy procedures in a predictable manner, and the more far-sighted of them actually will. Moreover, shareholder protection groups will be encouraged by government to assist minority shareholders in consolidating their votes at general shareholder meetings, including by way of proxy. Regulations will be drafted to allow custodians and nominees to split or apportion their votes to carry out the instructions of the beneficial owners for whom they act. Regulators and shareholder protection groups together will develop a set of rules and practices to ensure integrity and transparency in the proxy process – probably at a national level for the immediate future. Such rules will try to assign clear responsibilities for reaching beneficial owners in the dissemination of information and in facilitating their participation in the corporate decision-making process. With respect to American Depository Receipts (ADR) and Global Depository Receipts (GDR), voting rights will increasingly be used in the best interest of holders instead of being automatically transferred to management. Regional regulators will try, to the extent it is within their jurisdiction, to see that depositories and custodians notify beneficial owners and exercise voting rights in accordance with these owners' instructions. Listed companies of the better sort will be seen to cooperate with custodians and depositaries to facilitate timely receipt of voting instructions from beneficial owners of their shares, including holders of depositary receipts. Subject to reimbursement, regional custodians or depositaries will be required to contract with reputable agents in relevant countries to distribute information and to collect proxies or ballots. All this is very much achievable within a medium-term perspective of a decade or so. Roundtable participants have emphasized that in applying this provision, institutional investors' and nominee shareholders' fiduciary obligations should militate in favour of exercise of voting and other rights. Participants noted that assertion of rights by institutional investors and nominees encourages other shareholders to assert their own rights and fosters a culture of shareholder activism that benefits equity markets generally. The Roundtable has therefore concluded that regulators, shareholder associations, institutes of directors and other public and private sector bodies should encourage all shareholders to exercise their rights vis-à-vis shareholder meetings.

Arguably, in the short to medium term all these measures will further widen the already extensive gap between the exemplary corporate governance of many Asian listed companies and the grey anonymity of Asia's numerous private companies.

Louder shareholders. Aided by this multiplicity of helpful and encouraging regulation, institutional shareholders, even in Asia, will gradually become more active. The unleashed power of the Chinese fund management industry, once it starts managing private pensions for a billion people – and the Indian fund management industry likewise – will be bound to become a powerful force for good corporate governance in Asia. Statutory derivative actions, class actions, cumulative and secret voting will all become part and parcel of the life of companies with external finance in Asia. In the shorter term, past experience suggests that Chinese companies already opened up to foreign investors are likely to be the first ones to make the most progressive strides toward better government standards. Looking forward, as China's capital markets open up more to international investors and the general public's awareness of corporate governance increases, shareholders should eventually become more actively focused on protecting their own interests and ownership rights. In Korea, shareholder activists believe that, for example, as shareholder derivative suits against publicly held companies still require 0.01 per cent of the outstanding stock, and awards from a shareholder derivative action are paid to the corporation, to allow shareholders to press claims against managers for their malfeasance it is critical that Korea permits class action litigation, as approved by the National Assembly's Committee on Judiciary Affairs. Shareholders will eventually also be able to terminate improper directors with only a standard voting quorum and not through a special supermajority requirement. Another option that should be considered, in their view of shareholder activists, is to reduce the terms of directors from three years to one year to allow shareholders to easily replace those who harm their interests. Echoing these views, the OECD Roundtable's participants in 2003 recommended

277

adequately empowering shareholders to seek redress for violations of their rights and to ensure director accountability. Policy options in this area (taking into account the conceptual and practical concerns discussed in the annotations) include incorporating shareholder derivative or class action suits into national jurisprudence, permitting shareholders directly to nominate candidates for the board, and cumulative voting for directors for listed companies. Gradually, these views are gaining acceptance and will eventually become the norm.

More measurement. Asia is keen on measurement, and corporate governance is no exception. A good example of where change can be expected is the Philippines. A rating scheme, which will apply to banks' boards of directors, is being pushed by the Institute of Corporate Directors (ICD), which has an exclusive mandate from the Bangko Sentral ng Pilipinas (BSP) to push corporate governance programmes to the country's universal and commercial banks. Under the plan, the ICD will conduct a periodic review of banks' directors and their compliance with international standards of good governance, with particular emphasis on the elimination of corporate malfeasance. The rating results will then be disclosed to the public to allow them to make informed decisions about the way each bank makes important corporate decisions, especially with regard to their deposits. ICD president and CEO, Jesus P. Estanislao had hoped to have the scheme in operation by the end of 2003 after a couple of false starts in 2001 and 2002. Estanislao noted that most bank failures were caused by flagrant violations of prudential guidelines since the processes that lead to these were shielded from public scrutiny. Thus, a public ranking of banks' corporate practices would allow depositors and borrowers to choose their banks based on their risk appetite: banks would have no choice but comply with the scheme since the central bank has mandated that all banks undergo corporate governance programmes in line with international best practices. 'This is a BSP requirement', he said, adding that the reforms are required under Phase II of the Bank of International Settlements' Basle Accord. In addition, Estanislao said that banks that fail to subscribe to corporate governance codes would find themselves increasingly isolated from the rest of the financial and business communities that are becoming increasingly intolerant of corporate practices that are susceptible to malfeasance. 'They may find that they won't be able to conduct correspondent banking with foreign firms if they don't have the scorecard', he warned. For his part, BSP Governor Rafael B. Buenaventura expressed support for the scheme but hinted at reservations at an accelerated implementation timeframe. 'It might take some time, because we have to make sure that everyone is ready', he said. Buenaventura said the local banking system spans a whole range of firms from the very large and sophisticated to the smaller operations that may be unfamiliar with international corporate governance standards. 'Eventually, we'll get there but we have to make sure that everyone knows how to use [the manual] first.' Such measures under discussion are typical of the efforts being made in countries such as Indonesia and the Philippines to catch up with the rest of Asia, especially with Singapore and Hong Kong, and thereby reduce the element of 'two speed' about the region. *Best practice must already be, for a listed company, to seek to obtain a good corporate governance rating and to improve those areas criticised by a rating agency.*

New instruments. Examples abound. Tenev and Zhang[3] suggested that the Chinese state's current equity stake in SOEs should be replaced by an interest akin to non-voting preferred stock. Supporters of corporate governance respond that the problem of continuing state ownership of enterprises cannot be finessed so easily. Non-voting preferred stock might be a good investment in the right circumstances, Clarke argues,[4] but it is hard to see why a policy-maker who believes that state ownership ought to mean something would be satisfied with it, or why the state should commit itself never to sell it. Indeed, in replacing its equity stake with non-voting preferred stock, the state would be giving up its ability to use control not just to pursue non-economic goals, but also to defend itself from exploitation by management or controlling shareholders, or even to exploit other shareholders for its own economic benefit. Cass's Wang and the World Bank's Zhang believe that listed companies should replace stock issuances with bond issuances as primary sources of capital. Maybe this will not happen, but it is an example of the way that corporate finance in Asia will continue to evolve, as it did through the rapid growth of private equity during the 1990s. The key corporate governance issues of the next decade are lurking below the surface – perhaps in an innovative academic article, or in the mind's eye of a radical company CFO. They cannot be predicted in advance.

Political independence. The writing is on the wall for corporate political donations as disclosure will increasingly show them to the outside world. *Best practice is not to make them at all.*

Speed. David Webb argues:

> When people find security loopholes in Microsoft's operating systems, the firm publishes software 'patches' in a matter of days or weeks, in a race against time with hackers who can and will write viruses that will exploit the weakness. The Listing Rules are the 'software' of the market, and SEHK should act with the same speed, to avoid exploitation of loopholes by listed companies, who may hack away at shareholder wealth.

His pro-shareholder position seems to be gaining ground everywhere, and such a rapid response process may well be what the future holds for companies in Asia and elsewhere.

279

It is a similar argument to that which he has put regarding information disclosure to shareholders, for example about the status of investments by listed companies which may change significantly in a month. The problem here is that of a potential conflict between legitimate commercial advantage and the discipline of shareholder disclosure. What is the international practice? How will it be for Asian firms in the future? ST Assembly Test Services (Stats) and Chartered Semiconductor Manufacturing (Chartered), both with a listing on the Nasdaq, know what it is like to conform with the SEC rules. The SEC demands that Nasdaq works on a quarterly platform and stipulates that domestic companies have to release their quarterly results on Form 6-K within 45 days of the end of the period in question. Chartered and Stats, being foreign issuers, have no such obligation but to satisfy the appetite of their US investors they voluntarily released such reports by mid-August. As well as imposing stringent time constraints, the SEC-mandated disclosure requirements for Nasdaq companies are substantial.

A six-week time limit to release interims does not seem too onerous, especially given that companies with highly complex operations appear to be capable of meeting this deadline. If major firms such as SingTel can release within six weeks, then smaller companies can also do it. In time, as journalists in Singapore have argued, the exploitation of the internet for financial reporting purposes will render the above argument irrelevant. The internet offers the potential for real-time reporting where periodic statements, possibly even monthly, will hit cyberspace almost as soon as the period has ended.

Strategy.   Shareholders cannot expect to be forever silent when management undertake value-destroying activity such as M&A. The last major M&A boom occurred before the rapid expansion of shareholder activism, certainly in Asia. If the objective of corporate governance is the preservation of shareholder value, then given that M&A has been demonstrated time and again to be a major destroyer of shareholder value, why not start a proper process of linkage and start controlling the way in which corporations spend accumulated cash reserves? Fund managers may well already be looking to control the aspirations of some Asian companies in this direction.

Structures.   Commentators on Chinese corporate governance suggest that there is still room for further legislation. Some academics' recommendations are clearly receiving consideration by PRC lawmakers, but 'It will still be some time before minority interests can be adequately defended in China's courts'. That makes indispensable the strengthening of external independent regulators and agencies, together with the discipline of competition. To achieve this, an antitrust or competition law should be enacted and corresponding institutions established. Among other things, these institutions should be given the power to address banking and finance issues. The power of the China Securities and Regulatory Commission to protect minority shareholders should be increased. Also, the power of the China Banking Regulatory Commission will be expanded and the salaries of supervisors increased to reduce the risk of graft. Finally, to facilitate effective competition in the banking sector, other elements of the financial markets need to be developed. Wu Jinglian, chief economist with the State Council's Development Research Center (DRC), has criticized excessive intervention from the government and parent SOEs and proposed that listed companies drop their state-owned stakes. Zhang Weiying, Professor at Beijing University, has recommended that the government allow company shareholders to select corporate managers and that China privatize its state banks. Dai Yuanchen, an economist at the China Academy of Social Sciences (CASS), believes that more state industries should be opened to private investors. Wu and CSRC Chairman Zhou Xiaochuan have stated that a crucial obstacle to successful corporate governance of listed companies is 'insider control'. Wang Guogang, vice director of CASS's Financial Research Institute, has recommended that companies move toward an institutionalized management system to alleviate undue influence by individuals. Wu and Dai proposed the introduction of independent board directorships to monitor the management of listed companies. And Zhang Chunlin, an economist at the World Bank, believes China should set up financial institutions to replace government agencies to monitor enterprise management. The core of effective corporate governance lies in the creation of a fair and efficient competitive market environment, according to Lin Yifu, professor at Beijing University.

Meanwhile, in Japan, where change has recently been enacted, now that options beyond the conventional institutional structure, which has traditionally been the only legal option for all corporations without distinction, have been made available to Japanese companies, it is difficult to predict which of the three new structures they will choose, or whether these revisions will bring substantial corporate changes to Japan. The final assessment of these three corporate structures will be left to the verdict of the stock market. With a fairly well-developed stock market and the fundamental impact this mechanism is beginning to have on socioeconomic factors in Japan, today's investors use corporate structure as one of their considerations in determining whether or not they will invest in a company. The definitive factor in surviving today's global competition is likely to rest with whether these companies make choices that are acceptable to investors.

The Singapore government has stated that the end goal for the country is not meeting corporate governance norms, but building lasting competitive strengths and improving the chances of superior business performance. To do this, quality matters more than form. For instance, the quality of independent directors matters more than their numerical representation on the board. Better to have directors with the force of character to challenge management when necessary, and with enough substantive knowledge about the business to be able

281

to spot risks and advise on strategies, than directors who are independent only because the rules define them such. The government has identified the need for public sector institutions (including governments) to understand the role good corporate governance plays in promoting national competitiveness, economic/ financial stability, growth, job creation, poverty alleviation and higher living standards. Private sector institutions need to understand how good corporate governance facilitates better corporate performance, management succession (particularly intergenerational succession within family-run firms), access to (and lower cost of) capital, diversification of wealth and informed entrepreneurial risk-taking. In China, the CSRC says that the biggest challenge in improving corporate governance is the extensive involvement of government in business. A single agency, the State Asset Management Commission is to be established to represent the state as the owner of state assets. CSRC currently stresses three separations – the separation of personnel, assets and finance between a controlling shareholder and a listed company. Would-be reformers of FBS in the Hong Kong context, like Khan, argue that the need for further FBS corporate governance reform is led by concern that such companies are not value maximizing.

The OECD says that across the region, priorities include further developing the human and monetary resources of regulatory institutions, as well as training and exposure to effective policies and practices from other countries. The range of sanctions available for deterring and punishing wrongdoing will gradually be broadened. Legislators, and securities and exchange regulators, will be promoting effective shareholder participation in shareholder meetings. In particular, rules on proxy and *in absentia* voting will be liberalized, and the integrity of the voting process will be strengthened as a result. None of this will happen overnight, and the risk of it applying only to listed companies is serious.

Eventually, something will have to be done about Asia's family companies. How this will happen is still a matter of conjecture. A generation ago, the supposition was that on the whole the controlling families' shareholdings would be progressively reduced, and that the competition for the influx of external capital would bring its own pressure for reform of corporate governance. This rosy vision looks increasingly unlikely now.

Technology. Looking forward, we can see enterprise resource planning (ERP) systems being used for corporate governance purposes – corporate portals, web-based tools to use transactional information to deliver personalized views of the company, configured on a need-to-know basis, produced by companies such as Peoplesoft and Oracle, and shareholders recording shareholder meetings with handheld electronic devices and communicating there and then with international offices for voting and other measures. In addition, although trading in listed shares is already tracked electronically in Asian jurisdictions, it can be expected that technology will be employed more readily, more promptly and more effectively

282

in bringing insider trading cases to court. Another example: there have been an increasing number of businesses who have set up a network system exclusively for their board members to browse and communicate using confidential board materials and documents.[5]

Whistleblowing.   Observers say that it is necessary for companies to reconsider their form of corporate governance and rebuild their organization and business management to include, among others, (1) the thorough protection of whistle-blowers who are the source of information, as recommended by the OECD; (2) the elimination of ambiguous decision-making; and (3) the investigation of cases in which people engage in illegal and unethical acts to further their own individual interests as breaches of trust. The UK Combined Code now suggests that the audit committee should 'review arrangements by which staff of the company may, in confidence, raise concerns about possible improprieties in matters of financial reporting or other matters'. Although whether this ever happens in practice remains to be seen, it is highly likely that such whistleblowing provisions will be dutifully copied by Asian jurisdictions in due course. Among other potential changes discussed at a meeting of OECD experts were a relaxation of libel laws that have inhibited journalists from investigating corporate and government wrongdoing, protection for whistleblowers, and a substantial expansion in disclosure requirements. No doubt all these would be useful from the point of view of corporate governance, but they trespass on political practice and some Asian governments may see them as threatening. It is surely unlikely that in the short to medium term these laws will be relaxed as they ought to be.

THE LIMITS TO CORPORATE GOVERNANCE

As Vice Chairman of the Board of Councillors, Nippon Keidanren, Chairman and Chief Executive Officer of the Sony Corporation, rightly said:

> Ultimately, there is no end to the discussion on corporate governance. We must continue to examine and explore how companies can eliminate the occurrence of deplorable events, reward all their stakeholders, and enhance their corporate value through a sound corporate governance system.

But will all these changes make Asian companies more responsive to the interests of their shareholders, especially their minority shareholders? Yes, probably. But 'So long as politicians have an important effect on the market, there will be an incentive for businessmen to attempt to influence the political process for their own ends'.[6] Observers agree that even if individual companies, the government, and business circles put systems in place, it will be difficult to discover and eliminate scandals. The Singapore government recognizes this very well:

283

'good corporate governance goes beyond meeting the statutory requirements. It is not difficult for boards and executives to comply with regulatory requirements without fundamentally changing the way they run their companies'. After all, observers point out, even TEPCO, which had an internal report system, had to wait for a whistleblowing charge to an outside organization, the Nuclear and Industrial Safety Agency. But the point of a well-run company is not just to permit or even encourage whistleblowing, but to put in place systems which prevent the development of such practices in the first place.

Corporate governance can only ever go part of the way to stopping such practices. As Edward Chow has rightly said:

> I would stress that good corporate governance is not just about transparency, it is also very much about personal honesty and integrity. No system can ever be 100% foolproof against those who are determined to abuse it. Therefore, good individual and corporate ethics and clear sense of corporate responsibility are fundamental to good governance.

The OECD said in 2003 that Asian regimes must further strengthen cultures of integrity, professionalism and even-handedness. Can Asia cut the mustard on this last, vital ingredient to high standards of corporate governance? With the rise of international investment and shareholder activism, and greater disclosure and a role for whistleblowers, time really will tell.

Appendix

Tables on corporate governance in Asia

I. / II. Shareholders' rights and equitable treatment[45]

1. Shareholders' Information

1.1. What periodic information are listed companies required to provide?

	Bangladesh	China	HK China	India	Indonesia	Malaysia	Pakistan	Philippines	Singapore	South Korea	Ch. Taipei	Thailand	Vietnam
Annual reports	Yes	Yes	Yes	Yes	Yes	Yes	Yes	Yes	Yes	Yes	Yes	Yes	Yes
Unaudited semi-annual reports	Yes	Yes	Yes	Yes	Yes	Yes	Yes (subject to limited audit)	Yes (cumulative quarterly statements)	Yes	NP	Yes (Audited financial reports)	Yes (for financial institutions)	Yes
Quarterly financial statements	No	Yes	Y/N: yes for Growth Enterprise Market; no for Main Board listed companies	Yes	Yes (for listed companies)	Yes	Yes (for listed companies)	Yes	Yes (if market capitalisation n > S$75 million)	Yes	Yes	Yes (audited statements for listed companies)	Yes

Yes
1.2. What information must be contained in the company's annual report?
Yes

	Bangladesh	China	HK China	India	Indonesia	Malaysia	Pakistan	Philippines	Singapore	South Korea	Ch. Taipei	Thailand	Vietnam
General information on the company	Yes	Yes	Yes	Yes	Yes	Yes	Yes	Yes	Yes	Yes	Yes	Yes	Yes
Audited annual accounts	Yes	Yes	Yes	Yes	Yes	Yes	Yes	Yes	Yes	Yes	Yes	Yes	Yes

---

[45] Based on information provided to the OECD Secretariat by Roundtable participants.

White Paper on Corporate Governance in Asia

	Bangladesh	China	HK China	India	Indonesia	Malaysia	Pakistan	Philippines	Singapore	South Korea	Ch. Taipei	Thailand	Vietnam
Personal details of company's directors	Yes	Simple introduction	Yes	Yes	Yes	Yes	Names and meetings attended	Yes	Yes	Yes	Yes	Yes	No
Directors' report on past and future operations	Yes	Yes	Yes	Yes	Yes	Yes	Yes	Yes, submitted by management with board approval	Yes	Yes	Yes	Yes	Yes
Financial status of the company	Yes	Yes	Yes	Yes	Yes	Yes	Yes	Yes	Yes	Yes	Yes	Yes	Yes
Consolidated financial reports	Non-compliance with existing provisions	Yes (if company is up to disclosure standards)	Yes	Yes	Yes	Yes	Yes	Yes	Yes	Yes	Yes	Yes	No, but MinFin regulations are expected
Information on Corporate Governance	No	Yes	Yes	Yes	NP	Yes	Yes	Yes	Yes	Yes	Yes	Yes	No

2. Shareholders' Participation

2.1. Convening of shareholder meetings

	Bangladesh	China	HK China	India	Indonesia	Malaysia	Pakistan	Philippines	Singapore	South Korea	Ch. Taipei	Thailand	Vietnam
Time of notice (days before meeting)	- AGM: 14 days - EGM: 21 days	30 days	- AGM: 21 days - EGM: 14/21 days	21 days for AGM, EGM	28 days for announcement, 14 days for invitations	- AGM: 21 days - EGM: 14/21 days.	21 days for AGM, EGM	15 business days for AGM, EGM	14 / 21 days	14 days	- AGM: 20/30 days - EGM: 10/15 days	7 days, 14 days for certain EGM matters	7 days
Information contained in the notice	Agenda items, audited accounts for AGM, intentions to propose extraordinary and special resolutions	Agenda, relevant company documents, accounts, details on auditors, directors	Agenda items, reports and audited accounts, statement explaining rationale of proposed resolutions	Agenda. Reports and accounts, draft resolutions, proxy form, explanatory note on special business	Agenda items, substance/ need for EGM	Agenda, material facts, statements regarding effect of proposed resolutions	Agenda items, statement of material facts in case of special business	Agenda, financial statements, major transactions, plan of operation, details on officers, directors, auditors	Agenda items, details of proposed resolutions or other business	Agenda, details on directors, candidates for the board and auditors	Agenda items, proxy form	Agenda items, background information, opinions of the board	Agenda, discussion documents for proposed resolutions

White Paper on Corporate Governance in Asia

	Bangladesh	China	HK China	India	Indonesia	Malaysia	Pakistan	Philippines	Singapore	South Korea	Ch. Taipei	Thailand	Vietnam
Thresholds for requesting or convening an extraordinary shareholder meeting	10% to request directors to convene EGM	10% of voting rights to request directors to convene EGM	5% to request directors to convene EGM; if directors refuse, then >½ of the aggregate voting rights of all the requisitionists	10 % of the paid-off share capital carrying voting rights to request EGM	10 % to request EGM	10 % of voting rights or issued and paid up capital	10% of voting rights	None, unless otherwise provided in by-laws approved by shareholders	10% of paid up capital	3% of voting rights to request directors to convene an EGMNP	3% of outstanding shares	20% of issued shares or 25 shareholders holding 10%	10% of ordinary shares hold for more then 6 month (default-rule)
Legal minimum quorum requirements	5 persons for public companies (default rule)	None	2 persons	2 persons	50 % of voting shares (67% for special resolution)	2 persons	For listed companies, 10 persons representing 25% of voting rights; (proxies possible)	>50 % of outstanding capital stock	2 members	50% of voting rights	50% of voting shares (67% for special resolution)	1st call: 25 persons or 50% of shareholders holding 33 %; 2nd call: none	1st call: 51 % of voting shares, 2nd: 30 %, 3rd none

2.2. What kinds of voting rights may shares have?

	Bangladesh	China	HK China	India	Indonesia	Malaysia	Pakistan	Philippines	Singapore	South Korea	Ch. Taipei	Thailand	Vietnam
Non-voting common	Yes	No	No	No	No	No	No	No	No	Yes	No	No (non-voting depositary receipts possible)	No
Multiple voting rights	Yes	No	No, except for existing companies qualifying under limited grandfathering provisions in the listing rules	No	No	No	No	No	Not for publicly listed companies	No	No	Not for common shares	Yes

White Paper on Corporate Governance in Asia

	Bangladesh	China	HK China	India	Indonesia	Malaysia	Pakistan	Philippines	Singapore	South Korea	Ch. Taipei	Thailand	Vietnam
Removable voting rights	Yes	No	No	No		No	No, but subscribed but unpaid shares may lose right to vote	No	No	Yes	No	No	NP

2.3. Can shareholders vote Yes

	Bangladesh	China	HK China	India	Indonesia	Malaysia	Pakistan	Philippines	Singapore	South Korea	Ch. Taipei	Thailand	Vietnam
by proxy	Yes	Yes	Yes	Yes	Yes	Yes	Yes	Yes	Yes	Yes	Yes	Yes	Yes
by mail	No	No	Yes	Yes	No	No	No	No	Yes	Yes	No	No	Yes
by telephone / videoconference	No	No	No	No	No	No	No	No	Yes	No	No	No	Yes, if charter provides
by other means?	No	No	No	No	No	No	No	No	Yes	No	No	No	Yes, if charter provides

2.4. Do shareholders have the right to vote on: Yes, if charter provides

	Bangladesh	China	HK China	India	Indonesia	Malaysia	Pakistan	Philippines	Singapore	South Korea	Ch. Taipei	Thailand	Vietnam
Appointment of directors	Yes Ordinary resolution (>50%)	Yes Ordinary resolution (>50%)	Yes Ordinary resolution (>50%)	Yes Ordinary resolution (>50%)	Yes	Yes Ordinary resolution (>50%)	Yes	Yes Ordinary resolution (>50%)	Yes Ordinary resolution (>50%)	Yes Ordinary resolution (>50%)	Yes	Yes	Yes Ordinary resolution (51% majority)
Removal of directors	Yes Special resolution (75% majority)	Yes	Yes Special resolution (75% majority), to be amended to ordinary resolution	Yes Ordinary resolution (>50%)	Yes	Yes Ordinary resolution (>50%)	Yes	Yes, ≥2/3 of outstanding capital stock entitled to vote	Yes Ordinary resolution (>50%)	Yes Special resolution (67% majority)	Yes (67 % of attending shares for public companies)	Yes Special resolution (75% majority)	Yes Ordinary resolution (51% majority)

White Paper on Corporate Governance in Asia

	Bangladesh	China	HK China by >50%	India	Indonesia	Malaysia	Pakistan	Philippines	Singapore	South Korea	Ch. Taipei	Thailand	Vietnam
Appointment and removal of auditors	Yes Ordinary resolution (>50%)	Yes	Yes Ordinary resolution (>50%)	Yes Ordinary resolution; Special resolution for state-controlled companies	Yes	Yes (>50%; 75% if not proposed in notice)	Yes	Appointment ratified at AGM. Removal: 2/3 of outstanding capital stock	Yes Ordinary resolution (>50%)	Yes Ordinary resolution (>50%)	Yes	Yes Ordinary resolution (>50%)	No (Unless prescribed by company's charter)
Authorising share capital	Yes Special resolution (amendment of articles)	Yes	Yes Ordinary resolution (>50%)	Yes Special resolution (75% majority)	Yes	Yes Ordinary resolution (>50%)	Yes Ordinary resolution (75% majority)	Yes, 2/3 of outstanding capital stock entitled to vote	Yes Special resolution (75% majority)	Yes Ordinary resolution (>50%)	Yes (67 % of attending shares for public companies)	Yes Special resolution (75% majority)	Yes Special resolution (65% majority)
Issuing share capital	No (if issuance within authorised capital)	Yes	Yes Ordinary resolution (>50%)	Yes Special resolution (75% majority)	Yes	Yes Ordinary resolution (>50%)	Yes	Yes, 2/3 of outstanding capital stock entitled to vote, where pre-emptive rights are not denied and where there is declaration of a stock dividend	Yes Ordinary resolution (>50%)	Yes Ordinary resolution (>50%)	No	Yes Special resolution (75% majority)	Yes Special resolution (65% majority)
Dissapplication of pre-emption rights	Yes Special resolution	Yes	Yes, under the listing rules.	Yes Special resolution (75% majority)		NP	Yes Special resolution	Yes, by >50% vote of the board and 2/3 of outstanding capital stock entitled to vote	No pre-emption rights for public listed companies	NP	No (pre-emptive rights not always applicable, cf. 4.3)	No pre-emptive rights	No (unless prescribed by company's charter)
Amendments to company articles or statute	Yes Special resolution (75%)	Yes Special resolution (66%)	Yes Special resolution (75%)	Yes Special resolution (75%)	Yes	Yes Special resolution (75%)	Yes Special resolution	Yes, by >50% vote of the board and	Yes Special resolution (75%	Yes Special resolution (67%)	Yes (67% of attending shares for public	Yes Special resolution (75%)	Yes Special resolution (65%

White Paper on Corporate Governance in Asia

	Bangladesh	China	HK China	India	Indonesia	Malaysia	Pakistan	Philippines	Singapore	South Korea	Ch. Taipei	Thailand	Vietnam
				majority)				≥2/3 of outstanding capital stock entitled to vote	majority)	majority)	companies)	majority)	majority)
Remuneration of board members	Yes Ordinary resolution at AGM	Yes	Yes Ordinary resolution (>50%) at AGM	Yes Ordinary resolution (>50%)		No	Yes, unless articles empower directors	Yes, by >50% vote of the board and ≥2/3 of outstanding capital stock entitled to vote	Yes Ordinary Resolution (>50%)	Yes Ordinary Resolution (>50%)	Yes (>50%)	Yes Ordinary resolution (>50%)	Yes
Major corporate transactions (acquisitions, disposals, mergers, takeovers)	Yes For sale or disposal of undertaking remitting debt due to a director (Ordinary resolution)	Special resolution (>66%)	Yes, ordinary resolution	Yes Special resolution (75% majority)	Yes	Yes, if transaction > 25% of net tangible assets (Ordinary resolution)	Yes Special resolution	Yes, by >50% vote of the board and ≥2/3 of outstanding capital stock entitled to vote	Yes	Yes Special resolution (67% majority)	Yes (67 % of attending shares for public companies)	Yes, if transaction > 50% of net tangible assets Special resolution (75% majority)	Yes Special Resolution (65% majority)
Transactions with related parties	Only direct contracts between company and director	Y/N some do not require approval	Yes, if the transaction is above the de minimis limits	Yes	Yes (interested person shall abstain from voting)	Yes Ordinary resolution (>50%); interested person shall abstain from voting	Yes, in case of investment in associated companies (Special resolution)	Ratification when interested director counted in quorum or vote of the board (2/3 majority)	Yes Ordinary resolution (>50%); interested person shall abstain from voting	Disclosed in annual report	No	Yes, if transaction > 10 mil. Baht or 3% of net tangible assets Special resolution	Yes, if contract valued at > 20% of the total value of assets
Changes to company business or objectives	Yes Special resolution (75 %)	Yes If change to articles is required	Yes (75 %), if it requires amendment of the articles	Yes Special resolution (75% majority)	Yes	Yes Special resolution (75% majority)	Yes Special resolution	Yes, by >50% vote of the board and ≥2/3 of outstanding capital stock entitled to	Yes Special resolution (75% majority)	Yes Ordinary Resolution (>50%)	Yes, if this requires an amendment of the articles.	Yes Special resolution (75% majority)	Yes, if this requires an amendment of the articles

White Paper on Corporate Governance in Asia

	Bangladesh	China	HK China	India	Indonesia	Malaysia	Pakistan	Philippines	Singapore	South Korea	Ch. Taipei	Thailand	Vietnam
2.5 How are votes counted and by whom?	Show off hands or poll, by Chairman of the meeting	Poll, counted by at least two shareholders and one supervisor under monitoring of notary public	Show of hands, the Chairman of the meeting is obliged to demand a poll if the results of the vote of hands is different from the proxies in his hands (representing 5% or more of the voting rights). Further, shareholders can request a poll. Counted by share registrar or auditor	Show of hands counted by Chairman. Shareholders (10% of shares or Rp. 50,000) can request a poll		Show of hands, but shareholders (10%) can request a poll counted by the Chairman	Show of hands, but shareholders can request a poll. Counted by Chairman/ nominee.	vote — Show of hands, poll or other means provided in the by-laws	Show of hands, but shareholders can request a poll	Show off hand or poll counted by Chairman of the meeting	Show of hands or poll Board may recommend but not nominate a monitoring person.	Show of hands or poll, by a person appointed by the Chairman	Depends company charter
2.6 Does law provide for the disclosure of voting-agreements?	No	No	No	No		No	No	Voting trust agreements are filed with the SEC	No	No	Yes	Material agreements disclosed in annual report	No
2.7 How may shareholders directly nominate candidates for the board of directors?	No special procedure required	1% of shares for independent directors, >5% of shares for	5% or 100 members may request appointment of a	No special procedure required		Yes, ≥25% of voting rights, or not less than 100 members	Nominations submitted by candidates (shareholders)No	No special procedure required	Shareholders holding over 5%	Shareholders holding > 1% of shares over 6 months	No special procedure required	No special procedure required	Shareholders holding > 10 % of shares over 6 months

White Paper on Corporate Governance in Asia

	Bangladesh	China	HK China	India	Indonesia	Malaysia	Pakistan	Philippines	Singapore	South Korea	Ch. Taipei	Thailand	Vietnam
		other directors	director			holding shares in company with average sum per member not less than RM500 (approx. US$ 130	special procedure required						
2.8. To what extent and how does the board of directors nominate candidates for the board?	No nominations by board of directors	Board of directors can nominate candidates at AGM	Candidates nominated by board of directors	Candidates nominated by board of directors		Nominations usually made by the nomination committee of the board of directors	No nominations by board of directors	Board nominates candidates through Nomination Committee, which must include an independent director	Nominating Committees are usual for public listed companies	Nominating Committees are usual for large companies	Since 5/2003, board of directors can make recommendations	Nominations are usually made by the board of directors	No right to nominate candidates, unless provided in company's charter
2.9. Can shareholders place items on the shareholders' meeting agenda?	Yes, 10% of issued shares required for an EGM	Yes, 5% of shares required	Yes, 5% shares or 100 members may request a resolution	Yes, if application is made by at least 100 shareholders	Yes, 10 % of shares required	Yes, ≥25% of voting rights, or not less than 100 members holding shares in company with average sum per member not less than RM500 (approx. US$ 130	Yes (circulation shall be made before the meeting)	Yes	Yes	Yes, but must have held 1% of shares for six months	Shareholders may only propose contemporaneous motions at meetings	Yes, 1/3 of issued share capital required	Yes, 10% of shares held for six months required

3. Share in the Profits of the Corporation

White Paper on Corporate Governance in Asia

	Bangladesh	China	HK China	India	Indonesia	Malaysia	Pakistan	Philippines	Singapore	South Korea	Ch. Taipei	Thailand	Vietnam
3.1. Does law or regulations provide for timely payment of dividends to the shareholders?	Dividends payable within 2 months after declaration	Dividends payable within two months after declaration	No Date fixed by board	Dividends payable within 30 days after declaration		Payable within 1 month after book closure, 3 months after declaration	Payable within 45 days after declaration	Cash and stock dividends payable within 18 trading days after record date	No	Dividends payable within one month after their declaration	No Date fixed by board, based on shareholder resolution	Payable within 1 month after declaration	No Date fixed by board
3.2. Body responsible for declaring, approving and issuing dividends:	Declaration and issue: board; Approval: shareholders	Declaration and issue: board; Approval: shareholders	Interim: by board; Final dividends proposed by board must be approved by shareholders. Shareholders can only approve or reject the proposal and cannot set own dividend	Interim: board; Final dividend: shareholders		Declaration and issue by company; approval by shareholders	Shareholders	Cash and property dividend: board; Stock dividend: board declares at ≥2/3 shareholders approve	Shareholders	Shareholders	Shareholders	Interim: board; Final dividend: shareholders	Declaration and issue: board; Approval: shareholders

4. Corporate Control

	Bangladesh	China	HK China	India	Indonesia	Malaysia	Pakistan	Philippines	Singapore	South Korea	Ch. Taipei	Thailand	Vietnam
4.1. Thresholds for notification in case of substantial acquisition of shares:	None (rules in process of being issued)	5%	5	5%		5%	10%	5% and 10% for non-directors; no threshold for directors	5%	5%	10%	5%	5%
4.2. Thresholds requiring a mandatory offer for all shares at a particular price:	None	30%	30%	15% (mandatory offer to an extra 20%)	25%	33%	25%	35% interim	30%; or 1% in any 6-month period if shareholder already owns ≥30%	NP	Acquisition of 20% within 50 days	25%, 50%, 75%	25%

	Bangladesh	China	HK China	India	Indonesia	Malaysia	Pakistan	Philippines	Singapore	South Korea	Ch. Taipei	Thailand	Vietnam
4.3. Under which circumstances do shareholders have pre-emptive rights to purchase company shares?	Increase in share capital	Options on SPO	Issuance of new shares, under the listing rules	Issuance of new shares		Issuance of new shares offered pro rata to existing shareholders	Issuance of new shares and issuance or disposition of authorised but previously unissued shares belonging to the original stock of the company (offers in proportion to existing shareholders)	Issuance of new or un-issued shares	Approval by shareholders for issue of shares, convertible securities or options		Issuance of new shares, except for qualified acquisitions / warrants, private placement, merger, stock options, public offerings	None	Issuance of new shares (offers in proportion to existing shareholders)

5. Shareholders' Redress

5.1. How can shareholders seek redress if their rights are violated?

	Bangladesh	China	HK China	India	Indonesia	Malaysia	Pakistan	Philippines	Singapore	South Korea	Ch. Taipei	Thailand	Vietnam
Derivative Action	No	No	Yes	Yes (100 shareholders holding 10 % of voting rights)		Yes	No	Yes	Yes	Yes, for shareholders who own more than 1% of outstanding shares	Yes (shareholders holding 3% of shares within 1 year)	Yes (Minimum 5 shareholders or 20 % of shares)	Yes
Direct individual action	Yes	Yes	Yes	Yes (Company Law Board and Tribunal)		Yes	Yes	Yes	Yes	Yes	Yes	NP	Yes

White Paper on Corporate Governance in Asia

	Bangladesh	China	HK China	India	Indonesia	Malaysia	Pakistan	Philippines	Singapore	South Korea	Ch. Taipei	Thailand	Vietnam
Class action/ Minority action	No	No	Yes	Yes (Company Law Board)		Yes, with procedural limitations	Yes	Yes	Yes	No	Yes	In progress (draft bill reviewed by State Council)	No
5.2. Are lawyer contingency fees allowed?	No	No	No	With the permission of the court		No	No	Yes	No	NP	Yes	No	No
5.3. Who pays the legal fees of the prevailing party?	The prevailing party	The losing party	The losing party	The prevailing party		Decided by the court	Decided by court	Decided by court	NP	NP	The prevailing party	The losing party	The losing party

6. Insider Trading

6.1. Penalties attached to the offence of insider trading:

	Bangladesh	China	HK China	India	Indonesia	Malaysia	Pakistan	Philippines	Singapore	South Korea	Ch. Taipei	Thailand	Vietnam
Civil liability	NP	Yes, but no detailed regulations	Yes	Yes Penalty up to 3 times of the made profit		Yes Penalty up to RM 500,000 or 3 times made profit	Yes Up to the amount of gain/loss avoided	Yes Up to 3 times the transaction value plus actual damages	Yes, up to 3 times profits obtained or loss avoided, subject to minimum penalties	Yes, up to the value of the shares purchased or sold	Yes Up to 3 times of the amount of the damage	Yes	Yes
Fines	Up to Tk. 5,000 or Tk. 100 per day of breach	Up to the value of the shares purchased or sold	Up to HK$ 10 million	Determined by adjudicating officer	Up to Rp 15 billion	Minimum fine of RM 1,000,000	Up to 3 times of the gain/loss avoided	Min. fine of P50,000; max. fine of P5 million	Up to S$ 250,000 for individuals, S$500,000 for companies	Up to Won 20 million	Up to NT$ 3 million	Min. Baht 500,000, Max. 2 times of the made profit	From 20-50 million VMD (US$ 1,250-3,125))
Imprisonment	NP	Up to 10 years	Up to 10 years	Up to 3 years	Up to 5 years	Up to 10 years	Up to 3 years	7-21 years	Up to 7 years	Up to 10 years	Up to 7 years	Up to 2 years	NP

White Paper on Corporate Governance in Asia

	Bangladesh	China	HK China	India	Indonesia	Malaysia	Pakistan	Philippines	Singapore	South Korea	Ch. Taipei	Thailand	Vietnam
Others	Cancellation of licenses/ certificates	Restriction on exercise of profession	Restriction on exercise of profession	Restriction on exercise of profession		Actions for recovery and civil penalties by SC		Suspension of registration, Disqualifications	Restriction on exercise of profession	NP	Restriction on exercise of profession	Disqualification	Restriction on exercise of profession
6.2. Bodies or institutions tracking stock-market activity using statistical or computer-based methods:	Stock Exchanges, Electronic Trading System	Stock Exchange Surveillance department	Stock Exchange and Securities & Futures Commission	Stock Exchange/ Securities Exchange and Board of India		KLSE and the SC	SECP, Stock Exchanges	Market Regulation Department of SEC, PSE Market Surveillance Department	Singapore Exchange (SGX)	KSE, KSDA, FSC	SFC, TSE and GTSM	Stock Exchange and the SEC	State Securities Commission, Securities Trading Centre

7. Related party-transactions

	Bangladesh	China	HK China	India	Indonesia	Malaysia	Pakistan	Philippines	Singapore	South Korea	Ch. Taipei	Thailand	Vietnam
7.1. Does the legal and regulatory framework provide for the disclosure of related-party transactions?	Yes	Yes	Yes	Yes	Yes	Yes	Yes	Yes	Yes	Yes	Yes	Yes	Yes
7.2. Must related-party transactions be approved by the shareholders?	No, except direct contracts between companies and their directors	Yes, if value of transaction is >5% of net tangible assets or >30 million RMB	Yes, if above de minimis limits	Yes (with exceptions)	Yes	Yes, if value of transaction ≥5% of net tangible assets	Yes, in case of investment in associated companies	Yes, if interested director counted in quorum or majority vote of the board	Yes, if value of transaction > 5% of net tangible assets	NP	No (only major corporate transactions)	Yes, if transaction > 10 M Baht or 3 % of net tangible assets	Yes, if contract valued at + 20 % of the total value of assets
7.3. Are related persons required to abstain from voting on the transactions?	Yes	Yes	Yes	Yes	Yes	Yes	Yes	No (in practice abstention is common)	Yes	Yes	Yes	Yes	Yes

White Paper on Corporate Governance in Asia

III. The Role of Stakeholders

1. Codes of conduct

	Bangladesh	China	HK China	India	Indonesia	Malaysia	Pakistan	Philippines	Singapore	South Korea	Ch. Taipei	Thailand	Vietnam
1.1. Self-binding instruments applied by companies to protect stakeholder rights:	None	Codes of corporate governance for listed companies in China	Codes of conduct may be issued by companies (no statutory provision)	Recommendations of the Kumar Mangalam Committee Report on Corporate Governance, voluntary code of conducts	By agreement, or per company's articles or code of conduct	Codes of conduct may be issued by companies	Statements of ethics and business practices required by Code of Corporate Governance	Company policies, Manuals of corporate governance and self-rating following SEC policies	Memorandum and articles of association	NP	Corporate Governance Best Practice Principles, Internal company rules following SFC Guidelines	Stock Exchange Guidelines, codes of conduct issued by companies	Working manuals, internal rules

2. Employees' rights

2.1. What are the rights of employees regarding

	Bangladesh	China	HK China	India	Indonesia	Malaysia	Pakistan	Philippines	Singapore	South Korea	Ch. Taipei	Thailand	Vietnam
Information on the company	No special rights (public information only)	No special rights (public information only)	No special rights (public information only)	No special rights (public information only)	No special rights (public information only)	No special rights (public information only)	No special rights (public information only)	No special rights (public information only)	No special rights (public information only)	NP	No special rights (public information only)	No special rights (public information only)	No special rights, except annual meeting of employees for state owned enterprises
Collective bargaining	Through registered trade unions or collective bargaining agents	No specific regulations	Through labour unions	Right to collective bargaining	Through labour unions	Through trade unions	No special right	Through labour unions and labour-management councils/committees	No restrictions	Yes	Through employee unions	Through employee committees and unions	Right to collective bargaining
Participation in the board of directors	None	None	None	None	None	None	None	None	None	None	None	None	None

White Paper on Corporate Governance in Asia

	Bangladesh	China	HK China	India	Indonesia	Malaysia	Pakistan	Philippines	Singapore	South Korea	Ch. Taipei	Thailand	Vietnam
Consultation	None	Prescribed by Labour Code	None	No special rights	None	Prescribed by the Code of Conduct on Industrial Harmony issued by the Ministry of Human Resources	None	Prescribed by Labour Code	No restrictions	Yes	None	None	None (only in case of divestment of SOEs)
2.2. Can employees participate in the company's profits by													
Share ownership	Yes, but no statutory right	Yes	Yes	Yes	Yes	Yes, but no statutory rights	Yes, but no statutory rights	Yes, but no statutory rights	Yes	Yes	Yes	Yes	Yes
Share options	Yes, but no statutory right	No	Yes	Yes	Yes	Yes, but no statutory rights	Yes, through a scheme approved by SECP	Yes, but no statutory rights	Yes	Yes	Yes	Yes	Yes, available to shareholding employees
Profit sharing schemes	Yes, but no statutory right	No	May be included in employment contract	Yes	Yes	Yes, but no statutory rights	Yes (Companies Profit Participation Act)	Yes, but no statutory right	Yes	NP	Yes	Depends on contractual provisions	Productivity-based bonuses
2.3. Who manages employee pension funds?	Trustees	Social Security Administration	Fund managers/ trustees	Government trustees, Regional Provident Fund Commissioner	State-owned fund, private insurance company or company itself	Employee Provident Fund Board, other governmental pension funds and approved private schemes	Board of Trustees	Either managed in-house or by a third party	The Central Provident Fund (CPF) Board	National Pension Fund and employer	Central Trust Bureau of China	Asset management companies	Vietnam Social Insurance Agency (government-initiated funds)
2.4. What priority do employee wages and benefits have in the event of insolvency	Fourth (after administration on costs, receiver's fees, government dues)	Second, after fees and costs of bankruptcy proceeding	Employees' claims come after the costs of insolvency administration	None	Second, after government	Second, after costs and expenses of winding up, including the taxed	Second (after debts owed to government)	Second (after national government taxes)	Before secured creditors	First priority for last three-months wages, accumulated severance	Second (after expenses and debts pertaining to the estate in insolvency)	Among the priority claims under Section 130 of Bankruptcy Code	Second (after fees and costs of bankruptcy proceeding)

White Paper on Corporate Governance in Asia

	Bangladesh	China	HK China	India	Indonesia	Malaysia	Pakistan	Philippines	Singapore	South Korea	Ch. Taipei	Thailand	Vietnam
						costs of petitioner, remuneration of liquidator and costs of audit, (after all other secured debts)				payments for last three years and compensation for work related injuries			
2.5. Do employees have access to internal redress mechanisms (mediation/arbitration) in case of violation of their rights?	May be prescribed by statutes or contract	Depends on the company	NP	Yes, Trade Unions / Board of Conciliation	Yes, Labour Unions / Board of Conciliation, or court	May be prescribed by contract	May be prescribed by contract	Yes, HDR, grievance machinery (collective bargaining agreement)	Yes, representation of workers' rights through unions	Arbitration Committee, collective contract with employer	Yes, Labour Dispute Mediation Office, Labour Relations Committee	Depends on the company	Yes, Labour conciliatory councils of companies, Labour office's labour conciliators

3. Creditors' rights

	Bangladesh	China	HK China	India	Indonesia	Malaysia	Pakistan	Philippines	Singapore	South Korea	Ch. Taipei	Thailand	Vietnam
3.1. Are creditors involved in governance in the context of insolvency?	No	Yes (application to court for appointment of insolvency committee members)	Yes (participation in creditors' meetings, membership in committee of inspection possible)	Y/N (right to initiate process of winding-up of the company)	Yes, through creditors' meeting	Yes (consent of creditors required for arrangement scheme under appropriate company law provisions)	Y/N (courts shall have regard to wishes of creditors or contributories)	Yes (by proper representation or with prior approval in selection of a receiver committee/restructuring)	Y/N (creditors can initiate proceedings to wind up company)	NP	Yes (Creditors meeting may decide on procedure, administration, continuation and discontinuation of bankruptcy)	Yes (vote on composition or reorganisation plan, Creditors Committee monitors performance of plan administrator or and receiver)	Yes (meeting of creditors proposes restructuring solutions and motions on the distribution of assets to the judge)
3.2. How are creditors protected against fraudulent conveyance / insolvent trading in the context of insolvency?	Statutory prohibitions of fraudulent preferences	Statutory prohibitions and insolvency committee	Personal liability of directors and management	Any transfer done within 6 months before winding-up shall be deemed a	Internal control and insolvency committee (curator)	Personal liability of parties to fraudulent conveyances, application to court by	Statutory protection available	Court takes jurisdiction over properties and assets during insolvency proceeding	Protected by criminal sanctions	NP	The trustee in bankruptcy shall apply to the court in cases of insolvent trading	Application to the court, insolvent-trading legislation	Insolvent trading laws prohibit disposals and certain transactions during

White Paper on Corporate Governance in Asia

	Bangladesh	China	HK China	India	Indonesia	Malaysia	Pakistan	Philippines	Singapore	South Korea	Ch. Taipei	Thailand	Vietnam
				fraudulent preference		liquidator or creditor							insolvency
3.3. How can creditors seek redress if their rights are violated?	Judicial redress	Judicial redress	Personal liability of officers, promoters, receivers or liquidators towards the company	Criminal prosecution	Judicial redress or arbitration	Judicial redress	Judicial redress	Judicial redress	Seek redress from insolvency administrator and courts	Civil and insolvency law	Trustee may avoid acts done within 6 months after adjudication of bankruptcy	Through Creditors' Committee, Judicial redress	NP

IV. Disclosure and Transparency

	Bangladesh	China	HK China	India	Indonesia	Malaysia	Pakistan	Philippines	Singapore	South Korea	Ch. Taipei	Thailand	Vietnam
1. Consolidated financial reporting													
1.1. Does law or regulations provide for consolidated financial reporting?	Y/N (only for holding companies)	Yes	Yes	Yes	Yes	Yes	Yes	Yes	Yes	Yes	Yes	Yes	No, but MinFin regulations are expected
2. Non-financial information													
2.1. Are companies required to disclose information on:													
Corporate governance structures and practices	No	Yes (annual report)	Yes (compliance with Code of best practices)	Yes (quarterly compliance /annual report)	Yes (JSX listing rules)	Yes, compliance with code on corporate governance	Yes	Yes (submit Corporate Governance Manual to SEC)	Yes (annual report)	Yes	Yes (annual report)	Yes (annual report)	No
Education and professional experience of directors and key	No	Simple introduction in annual report	No	Yes (annual report)	Yes, in prospectus and per JSX listing	Yes (profile of directors)	No	Yes (annual report)	Yes (annual report)	Yes	Yes (annual reports and prospectus)	Yes (annual report)	Yes (listed companies)

White Paper on Corporate Governance in Asia

	Bangladesh	China	HK China	India	Indonesia	Malaysia	Pakistan	Philippines	Singapore	South Korea	Ch. Taipei	Thailand	Vietnam
executives													
Remuneration of directors and key executives	No	Yes (salary brackets)	Yes	Yes (annual report)	Yes, per JSX listing rules	Yes (range of remuneration of directors)	Yes	Yes (annual report)	Yes (annual report)	Yes	Yes (annual report, financial statements, prospectus)	Yes (annual report)	Yes (listed companies)
Deviations from corporate governance codes	No	No	Yes	Yes (annual report)	Yes, per JSX listing rules	Yes	Yes	Yes, in annual report and evaluation system in Manual	Yes (annual report)	No	Yes (annual reports)	Yes (annual report)	No
Management discussion and analysis (MD&A)	No	Yes	Yes	Yes (annual report)	Yes (annual reports, prospectus)	Yes (chairman, CEO and management)	Yes (directors' report)	Yes (annual and quarterly report)	Yes (annual report)	No	Yes (annual reports, prospectus)	Yes (annual report, quarterly statements)	No
Forward looking statements of the company	No	Yes	Yes (included in MD&A)	Yes (director's report)	Yes (annual report)	Yes (chairman's statement)	Yes (directors' report)	Yes (annual and quarterly reports)	Yes (annual report)	Yes	Yes (in certain cases)	Yes (part of the MD&A)	No
3. Audit/Accounting													
3.1. Are companies required to have their financial statements externally audited?	Yes	Yes	Yes	Yes	Yes	Yes	Yes	Yes	Yes	Yes	Yes	Yes	Yes (listed, insurance, credit and foreign invested companies)
3.2. How and by whom are external auditors appointed?	By shareholders at AGM	By shareholders at AGM	Nominated by management and approved by shareholders at AGM	By shareholders	By shareholders or delegated to board	Appointed by shareholders, nominated by the board	By shareholders at AGM	By shareholders at AGM	By shareholders at AGM	By Audit Committee or External Auditor Appointment Committee	By a resolution of the board of directors	By shareholders at AGM upon proposition by board	N/A (special regulations for banks and state-owned companies)

White Paper on Corporate Governance in Asia

	Bangladesh	China	HK China	India	Indonesia	Malaysia	Pakistan	Philippines	Singapore	South Korea	Ch. Taipei	Thailand	Vietnam
3.3. To whom do the internal auditors report?	Depends on terms of engagement	Board of directors	NP	Management	Audit Committee (if any), board of directors	Audit Committee	CEO, access to chair of audit committee	To the Board of directors or to the Audit Committee	Audit Committee	Board of directors, shareholders (AGM)	Board of directors and supervisors	Board of directors	Board of Management
3.4. Which rules regulate the audit profession?	Bangladesh Chartered Accountants Order 1973 and following rules and regulations; Bylaws of the Institute of Chartered Accountants (ICAB)	Audit law	Professional Accountants Ordinance (Chap. 50)	Institute of Chartered Accountants of India Act 1949, Companies Act 1956	Directorate General of Financial Institutions under MinFin and Indonesian Inst. of Accountants	By-laws issued by the Council of the Malaysian Institute of Accountants (MIA)	Chartered Accountant Ordinance, 1961; Chartered Accountant By-laws, 1983; Companies Ordinance, 1984	Professional Regulation Laws by the Professional Regulation Commission (PRC) and the Board of Accountancy; SEC Guidelines on Accreditation of External Auditors (effective 6/30/03)	Companies Act, Accountants Act	Act on External Audit of Stock Companies, Act on Public Accountants	Accountant Law, Securities and Exchange Law, and rulings issued accordingly to these laws	Auditing Act, Securities and Exchange Act	1988 Ordinance on Accounting and Statistics, new Law on Accounting and Audit expected by the end of 2003
3.5. Is certification or training of auditors mandatory?	Yes	Yes	Yes	Yes	Yes	Yes	Yes	Yes	Yes	Yes	Yes	Yes	Yes
3.6. Is there a code of ethics relating to the audit profession?	Yes	Yes	Yes (Hong Kong Society of Accountants)	Yes	Yes	Yes (Practice Review Committee)	Yes	Yes	Yes	Yes	Yes	Yes	No
3.8. Which authorities ensure the review, quality and independence of auditors?	Institute of Chartered Accountants (ICAB) through its committees	CSRC and MOF		Institute of Chartered Accountants through Accounting Standard Rules	Directorate General of Financial Institutions under MinFin and BAPEPAM (for accountants registered with BAPEPAM)		Institute of Chartered Accountants Pakistan (ICAP)	Board of Accountancy, Institute of Certified Public Accountants (PICPA)	Public Accountants Board and SGX	Financial Supervisory Board	Yes (CPA Association, ROC, SFC)	Board of Auditing Practices, SEC, Auditing Ethic Sub-committee	Ministry of Finance, Vietnam Association of Accountants, National Accounting Council

White Paper on Corporate Governance in Asia

	Bangladesh	China	HK China	India	Indonesia	Malaysia	Pakistan	Philippines	Singapore	South Korea	Ch. Taipei	Thailand	Vietnam
3.9. Is a rotation of audit firms and auditors mandatory?	No (only for bank companies: every 3 years)	CSRC is preparing a regulation to mandate rotation of auditors, but not of audit firms	No	NP	Yes	No	Yes (every 5 years for listed companies)	Yes (every 5 years, required by corporate governance code)	Yes (every 5 years)	Yes (audit partner may not direct the audit for a listed company for more than four consecutive years)	No (recommended by Best Practice Principles)	No (only for bank companies: every 5 years)	No
3.10. To what extent are national auditing and accounting norms materially divergent from international standards?	23 out of 41 the IAS	Basic principles are similar to IAS; divergence exists in areas like measurement based on fair market value	Policy of convergence. Remaining areas of divergence currently being addressed	NP	No material divergence	Not materially divergent, national standards follow IAS and GAAP	Conformity (IAS has become part of the law upon notification by SECP)	25 areas of differences, 2003: 11 differences (programmed for adoption in 2005)	Closely aligned	Mixture of IAS and US GAAP	No material divergence	Not materially divergent	Goal of conformity by 2004
3.11. Which body is responsible for development of accounting standards and oversight of accountants?	ICAB (self-regulatory body)	Standards: MOF; Oversight: MOF and CSRC	HKSA (self-regulatory body)	Institute of Chartered Accountants of India (self-regulatory body)	Directorate General of Financial Institutions under MinFin and Indonesian Inst. of Accountants	Standards: Malaysia Accounting Standards Board (MASB), Oversight: Malaysian Institute of Accountants (MIA)	Institute of Chartered Accountants Pakistan (self-regulatory body)	PRC, Board of Accountancy, SEC, PICPA, Accounting Standards Council, Auditing Standards Council	Standards: Council on corporate disclosure and governance Committee, Oversight: Public Accountants Board	Standards: FSC, Korean Accounting Standard Board (KASB), Oversight: SFC	Standards: Financial Accounting Standards Committee (self-regulatory body); Oversight: SFC, CPA Association	Standards: Thai Institute of Certified Accountants and Auditors; Oversight: Board of auditing Practices	Ministry of Finance, Vietnam Association of Accountants (self-regulatory body)

4. Reporting Requirements

4.1. To what extent do Stock Exchanges require

	Bangladesh	China	HK China	India	Indonesia	Malaysia	Pakistan	Philippines	Singapore	South Korea	Ch. Taipei	Thailand	Vietnam
Semi-annual reporting	Yes (financial statements)	Yes	Yes	Yes	Yes	Yes	Yes	Yes (cumulative quarterly reports)	Yes	Yes	Yes (audited financial statements)	Yes (financial institutions)	Yes

	Bangladesh	China	HK China	India	Indonesia	Malaysia	Pakistan	Philippines	Singapore	South Korea	Ch. Taipei	Thailand	Vietnam
Quarterly reporting	None	Yes	Yes, only for companies listed on Growth Enterprise Market	Yes	Yes	Yes	Yes	Yes	Yes (if market capitalisation exceeds S$75 million)	Yes	Yes	Yes	Yes
Publication of audited annual reports	Yes (at AGM)	Yes	Yes (4 months after year end for Main Board companies (3 months for Growth Enterprise Market companies) or 21 days before AGM, whichever is earlier)	Yes (6 months after end of fiscal year and 21 days prior to AGM)	Yes	Yes (6 months after the end of the financial year)	Yes	Yes (105 days after the end of the financial year)	Yes (120 days after the end of the financial year)	Yes	Yes (4 months after the end of the financial year)	Yes (120 days after end of year, 60 days for financial statements)	Yes (90 days after the end of the financial year)
Immediate reporting of price-sensitive information?	Yes (within ½ hour)	Yes (within two days)	Yes (as soon as reasonably possible)	Yes	Yes	Yes (immediate reporting)	Yes	Yes (within 10 minutes, confirmed within 1 day)	Yes (immediate reporting)	Yes	Yes (before trading hours of next day)	Yes (the day on which the event occurs)	Yes (on a real time basis)
4.2. What penalties are attached to the non-compliance with the above-cited prescriptions?	Tk.500.00 per day, de-listing or suspension of trading possible	Criticism by relevant media, temporary suspension of trading	Temporary suspension of dealings	Show Cause notice to the company, suspension or delisting possible	Stock exchange policy	Caution letter, reprimand, fine not exceeding RM 1 million, directions for rectification, conditions for compliance, suspension, de-listing	Reprimand/delisting by Stock Exchanges, Fine up to Rs100,000 and Rs.1,000 per day	Fines from P50,000 - P500,000, daily fines, suspension and delisting for repeated violations	Reprimand, Fine up to S$250,000, imprisonment up to 7 years, civil penalties	Caution or warning; imprisonment ≤1 year or fine ≤5 million won. False statements: imprisonment <5 years or fine <30 million won	Fine of NT$ 120,000 - NT$ 600,000, suspension of trading or delisting possible	Fine up to 100,000 Baht + 3,000 Baht per day of contravention	Fine from 20-50 million VMD (US$ 1,250-3,125))

White Paper on Corporate Governance in Asia

	Bangladesh	China	HK China	India	Indonesia	Malaysia	Pakistan	Philippines	Singapore	South Korea	Ch. Taipei	Thailand	Vietnam
4.3. Is there a central registry for financial and non-financial corporate information, which is readily accessible to shareholders?	Yes (Registrar of Joint Stock Companies and Firms)	No (information kept by company and on SSE website)	Yes, Companies Registry and HKEx website	Yes (Electronic Data Information Filing and Retrieval System)	Yes, under Company registration Law and Capital Market Reference Center and per stock exchange rules	Yes (Companies Commission in Malaysia)	Yes, Registrar of Companies	Yes (both in PSE and SEC)	Yes (Registry of Companies and Business, RCB)	Yes (Financial Supervisory Services & Stock Exchange)	Yes (Market Observation System Post System)	No (information kept on SEC and SET websites)	No
4.4. To what extent new technological developments are integrated into the existing disclosure regimes?	None	Electronic filing of disclosure reports	Electronic filings of disclosure reports to HKEx	Electronic Data Information Filing and Retrieval System	Capital market electronic reporting system (in progress)	Posting of corporate announcements on KLSE website	In progress	Electronic corporate disclosure rules for electronic filing approved by SEC	Electronic filings with RCB	Electronic filing of disclosure reports for listed companies	MOPS website, electronic filing	Electronic filing at SEC and SET, documents on SEC and SET websites	Electronic filing for business registration or disclosure of reports

V. The responsibilities of the board

	Bangladesh	China	HK China	India	Indonesia	Malaysia	Pakistan	Philippines	Singapore	South Korea	Ch. Taipei	Thailand	Vietnam
1. Members of the board													
1.1. Prescribed board structure (unitary/dual board structure):	Unitary	Dual board structure	Unitary	Unitary	Dual board structure	Unitary	Unitary	Unitary	Unitary	Unitary	Modified dual structure	Unitary	Unitary
1.2. Can a dual board structure be established in the articles of association?	Yes (Option not used)	N/A	Yes	NP	N/A	Yes (Option not used)	No	No	Yes (Option not used)	No	N/A	NP	NP
1.3. Minimum/maximum number of directors for listed companies:	Min: 3; Max: None	Min: 5; Max: 19	Min: 2; Max: None	Min: 3; Max: None	Min: 2; Max: None	Min: 2; Max: None	Min: 7; Max: None	Min: 7; Max: 15	Min: 2; Max: None	Min: 3 if total capital ≥500 million Won Max: None	Min: 5 Max: None	Min: 5; Max: None	Min: None; Max: 11

White Paper on Corporate Governance in Asia

	Bangladesh	China	HK China	India	Indonesia	Malaysia	Pakistan	Philippines	Singapore	South Korea	Ch. Taipei	Thailand	Vietnam
1.4. Does law require representation of labour unions on the board?	No	No	No	No	No	No	No	No	No	No	No	No	No
1.5. Is cumulative voting for the election of board members permitted?	Yes, if provided for by articles of association	Yes, mandatory of a shareholder owns more than 30% of shares	No	No	Yes, if provided for by articles of association	No	Yes, mandatory	Yes	Yes, if provided for by articles of association	Yes	Yes (default rule)	Yes (default-rule)	NP
1.6. Maximum election term for members of the board:	None	3 years (re-election possible)	None	None	None	3 years	3 years	1 year, unlimited re-election	None	3 years, unlimited re-election	3 years (re-election possible)	3 years (1 year for cumulative voting)	3 years
1.7. Does the regulatory framework permit staggered election terms for board members?	No	No current specific regulation	No	No	NP	Yes, once in every 3 years	No	Not for stock/profit corporations	Yes	Yes	No	Yes, except in case of cumulative voting	Depends on company charter
1.8. Is there a limit to the number of boards on which an individual may serve?	No	No, but max. 6 years service for independent directors on any one board	No	Yes (Max: 15)	No	Yes (listed companies: 10; others: 15)	Yes (Max. 10)	No	No	Max. 2 for non-executive directors	Y/N, maximum of 5 boards for independent directors	No, except for bank directors: 5	No
1.9. Are companies required to disclose the attendance records of board meetings?	No	No	No	Yes	No	No	Yes	Yes	No (recommended best practice)	Yes	No	No (included in SEC guidelines)	No
1.10. What is the minimum number of board meetings to be held per year?	4 (one every quarter)	4	4	4 (one every quarter)	None	None	4 (one every quarter)	12 (monthly, default rule)	None	None	None (6 meetings suggested)	4	4
1.11. Limitations to the appointment of non-residents or foreigners to the board of listed companies:	None	None	None	Approval by Reserve Bank and Department Company of Affairs required	None	None	None	Foreign representation must be in proportion to foreign equity ownership	None	None	None	Yes ½ of board members shall be residents	Yes, only residents are allowed to establish or manage companies

White Paper on Corporate Governance in Asia

1.12. What are the rule and procedures for

	Bangladesh	China	HK China	India	Indonesia	Malaysia	Pakistan	Philippines	Singapore	South Korea	Ch. Taipei	Thailand	Vietnam
Nominating	Not prescribed by law	Nominated by board of directors, shareholders or supervisory board	Nominated by board of directors or shareholder through resolution in AGM	Application to be filed by candidates 14 days prior to AGM	NP	By nomination committee, if any, or the board of directors, or by shareholder having ≥5% of voting rights, or not less than 100 members holding shares in company with average sum per member not less than RM500 (approx. US$ 130	Creditors and specified institutions may nominate directors to the board	Through the nomination committee, which should include an independent director	NP	Nominated by Nomination Committee (including candidates recommended by major shareholders)	Nomination made at shareholder meetings	Nominated by Nomination Committee or major shareholders	Shareholders holding >10% of shares over 6 month (default rule)
Electing	Elected by shareholders	Elected by shareholders	Elected by shareholders	Elected by ordinary shareholder resolution	Elected by shareholders	Elected by shareholders	Elected by shareholders	Elected by shareholders	Individually elected by shareholders	Elected by shareholders	Elected by shareholders (cumulative voting)	Elected by shareholders (cumulative or ordinary voting)	Elected by shareholders
Removing board members?	Extraordinary shareholder resolution (3/4 majority)	No specific regulation	Removal by special shareholder resolution	Removal by ordinary shareholder resolution	Removal by shareholder resolution	Removal by ordinary shareholder resolution	Removal by shareholder resolution	Removal by shareholders (2/3 majority)	Removal by ordinary shareholder resolution (special notice requirement: 28 days)	Removal by shareholders	Removal by special shareholder resolution (2/3 majority)	Removal by special shareholder resolution (75% majority- 50% quorum)	Removal by ordinary shareholder resolution (51% majority)

White Paper on Corporate Governance in Asia

	Bangladesh	China	HK China	India	Indonesia	Malaysia	Pakistan	Philippines	Singapore	South Korea	Ch. Taipei	Thailand	Vietnam
1.13. Does law require the separation of Chairman and CEO?	No	No	No (except Monetary Authority's rules on Authorised Institution)	No	No	No (recommended by corporate governance code)	No (code of corporate governance requires separate terms of reference)	No	No (recommended best practice)	No	No (recommended Best Practice)	No	No

2. Powers of the board

2.1. Does the board of directors decide on:

	Bangladesh	China	HK China	India	Indonesia	Malaysia	Pakistan	Philippines	Singapore	South Korea	Ch. Taipei	Thailand	Vietnam
Appointment and compensation of senior management	No, unless required by articles of association	Yes	Yes	No	Yes	Yes	Yes	Yes	Yes	Yes	Yes	Yes	Yes
Review and adoption of budgets and financial statements	Review of annual audited financial statements	Yes	Yes	Yes	Yes	Yes	Yes	Yes	Yes	Yes	Prepared by board (reviewed by supervisor)	Yes	No
Review and adoption of strategic plans	No, unless required by articles of association	Yes	Yes	Yes	Yes	Yes	Yes	Yes	Yes	Yes	Yes	Yes	Yes
Major transactions outside the ordinary course of business	No, unless required by articles of association	Depends on the articles of association	Yes, plus shareholder approval	Yes	Yes, plus shareholder approval	Yes, for substantial transactions	Yes	Yes, plus shareholder approval if > 25%	Yes	Yes	Yes	Yes	Yes
Changes to the capital structure	No, unless required by articles of association	Yes, plus shareholder approval	Yes, plus shareholder approval	Yes	Yes, plus shareholder approval	Yes, with shareholder approval	Yes	Yes, plus shareholder approval	Yes, plus shareholder approval/ court order	Yes	Yes (within the authorised capital)	Yes	NP
Organisation and running of shareholder meetings	No, unless required by articles of association	Yes	Yes	Yes	Yes	Yes	Yes	Yes	Yes	Yes	Yes	Yes	Yes
Process of disclosure and communications?	No, unless required by articles of association	Yes	Yes	Yes	Yes	Yes	Yes	No (decided by management)	Yes	Yes	Yes	Yes	NP

White Paper on Corporate Governance in Asia

	Bangladesh	China	HK China	India	Indonesia	Malaysia	Pakistan	Philippines	Singapore	South Korea	Ch. Taipei	Thailand	Vietnam
The company's risk policy	No, unless required by articles of association	No specific regulations	Yes	Yes	Yes	Yes	Yes	Yes	Yes	Yes	Yes	Yes	NP
Transactions with related parties?	Yes	Yes, if transaction ≤5% of net tangible assets or ≤30 million RMB	Yes, shareholder approval might be required	Yes	Yes, plus independent shareholder approval	Yes, with shareholder approval also required if ≥5% of net assets	Yes	Yes, plus shareholders approve	Yes, plus shareholders approval	Yes	Yes, for acquisition of real properties	Yes	Yes, if > 20% of total assets

3. Board Committees

3.1. Which board committees must be established under current law or regulations?

	Bangladesh	China	HK China	India	Indonesia	Malaysia	Pakistan	Philippines	Singapore	South Korea	Ch. Taipei	Thailand	Vietnam
Audit committees	No	No	Yes	Yes	Yes, per JSX requirements	Yes	Yes	Yes	Yes	Yes (if assets>2 trillion won)	No	Yes	No
Remuneration committees	No	No	No	Yes	No, but recommended by National Committee on Corporate Governance	No, but recommended by Code of Corporate Governance	No	Yes	No, but recommended best practice	No	No	No (recommended)	No
Nomination committee	No	No	No	No	No, but recommended by National Committee on Corporate Governance	No, but recommended by Code of Corporate Governance	No	Yes	No, but recommended best practice	Yes (if assets>2 trillion won)	No	No (recommended)	No
Other committees	None	None	None	Shareholders and Investor Grievance Committee	No, but recommended by National Committee on	As of 6/30/03, banks are required to set up Risk Manageme	None	Stock Exchange: governance committee	None	None	None	Risk management committee (recommended)	Inspection committee in companies with > 11 shareholde

White Paper on Corporate Governance in Asia

	Bangladesh	China	HK China	India	Indonesia	Malaysia	Pakistan	Philippines	Singapore	South Korea	Ch. Taipei	Thailand	Vietnam
					Corporate Governance	nt, Remuneration and Nomination Committees							rs

4. Directors' qualification

	Bangladesh	China	HK China	India	Indonesia	Malaysia	Pakistan	Philippines	Singapore	South Korea	Ch. Taipei	Thailand	Vietnam
4.1. May legal entities serve as directors?	No	No	No	No	No	No	No	No	No	No	Yes	No	NP
4.2. Prescribed minimum/maximum age for directors.	Min: None; Max: None	Min: None; Max: None	Min: 18; Max: None	25-70 (for managing directors)	None	Min: 21; Max: 70 (default rule)	Min: Majority; Max: None	Min: 18 (banks:25); Max: None	Min: 21; Max: None	Min: None; Max: None	Min: 20; Max: None	Min: None; Max: None	Min: Majority; Max: None

4.3. What other requirements must members of the board fulfill?

	Bangladesh	China	HK China	India	Indonesia	Malaysia	Pakistan	Philippines	Singapore	South Korea	Ch. Taipei	Thailand	Vietnam
"fit and proper test" (i.e. no criminal convictions or prior bankruptcies)	Yes	Yes	Yes	Yes	Yes	Yes	Yes	Yes (financial sector)	Yes	Yes (financial sector)	Yes	Yes	Yes
Minimum education and training	No	No	No	No	No	Yes, KLSE listing rules require mandatory training (which may take place after election to board)	No	Yes (financial sector)	Yes	No	No	No	NP
Professional experience	No	Yes	Yes	Yes	No	Yes	Yes	Yes (financial sector)	Yes	No	Yes	No	Yes (specific industries)
4.4. Does law or regulations require continuing training for board directors?	No	No	No	No	No	Yes (KLSE listing rules)	No	Only in banking sector	No, but recommended best practice	No	No	No	No
4.5. Does law or regulations provide for certification procedure of board directors?	No	No	No	No	No	Yes, accreditation	No	No	No	No	No	No	No

White Paper on Corporate Governance in Asia

	Bangladesh	China	HK China	India	Indonesia	Malaysia	Pakistan	Philippines	Singapore	South Korea	Ch. Taipei	Thailand	Vietnam
4.6. Does the institutional framework provide for voluntary training possibilities for board directors?	No	Yes (Stock Exchange)	Yes (Hong Kong Institute of Directors)	No	Yes	Yes, compulsory and voluntary training by KLSE and SC (via SIDC)	Code of corporate governance requires Orientation Courses for directors	Yes	Yes (Singapore Institute of Directors)	No	Yes (Securities and Futures Institute)	Yes, (Thai Institute of Directors Association)	No
5. Independent directors													
5.1. Does law, regulations or listing rules require the election of independent directors to the board?	No	Yes (SEC Guidelines)	Yes (listing rules)	Yes (1/3 if non-executive chairman, ½ if executive chairman)	Yes, JSX (listing rules)	Yes (2 directors or 1/3 of the board)	No (recommended)	Yes (2 directors or 20% of the board, whichever is lower)	No (1/3 recommended)	Yes (25% of board for listed companies; for companies, at least 3 directors and a majority of the board for banks or companies with assets > 2 trillion won)	Y/N, (listing rules; since 2/2002 for new listing applicants only)	Yes	Yes
5.2. Does the definition of "independence" exclude persons who are													
Related to management (by blood or marriage)	NP	Yes	Yes	No	No, unless director has interest in company	Yes	Yes	Yes	Yes	Yes	Yes	Yes	N/A
Related to major shareholders	NP	Yes	Yes	No	No, unless director has interest in company	Yes	Yes	Yes	Yes	Yes	Yes	Yes	N/A
Employees of affiliated companies	NP	Yes	Yes	Yes	Yes	Yes	Yes	Yes	Yes	Yes	Yes	Yes	N/A

White Paper on Corporate Governance in Asia

	Bangladesh	China	HK China	India	Indonesia	Malaysia	Pakistan	Philippines	Singapore	South Korea	Ch. Taipei	Thailand	Vietnam
Representatives of companies having significant dealings with the company in question	NP	Yes	Yes	Yes	Yes	Yes	Yes	Yes	Yes	Yes	Yes	Yes	N/A

6. Directors' liability

6.1. May breaches of duty by members of the board generate their individual

	Bangladesh	China	HK China	India	Indonesia	Malaysia	Pakistan	Philippines	Singapore	South Korea	Ch. Taipei	Thailand	Vietnam
Civil	Yes	Yes	Yes	No	Yes (possible)	Yes	Yes	Yes	Yes	Yes	Yes	Yes	Yes
Administrative	No	Yes	NP	No	Yes (possible)	Yes	No	Yes	Yes	Yes	Yes	Yes	Yes
Criminal liability?	Yes	Yes	Yes	Yes	Yes (possible)	Yes	Yes	Yes	Yes	Yes	Yes	Yes	Yes

6.2. Does law or regulations provide for

	Bangladesh	China	HK China	India	Indonesia	Malaysia	Pakistan	Philippines	Singapore	South Korea	Ch. Taipei	Thailand	Vietnam
Individual shareholder suits against the board and management	Yes	Yes	Yes	Yes	Yes	Yes	No	Yes	Yes	Yes	Yes	Yes (5% of outstanding shares required)	Yes
Class action suits against the board and management	No	No	Yes, Order 15, rule 12 of the Rules of the High Court allows representative actions	Yes	Yes	Yes, though subjected to procedural requirements	Yes	Yes	Yes	No	Yes	In progress	Yes
Derivative suits against the board and management	No	No	Yes, under common law	Yes	Yes, ≥10% of shares are required	Yes	No	Yes	Yes	Yes	Yes	Yes (5% of outstanding shares required)	Yes
Ombudsman suits on behalf of shareholders?	No	No	No	No	No	Yes, (in limited cases) by relevant	No	Yes	No	No	Yes (Investor Protection Institute)	Yes (Corporate Registrar)	No

White Paper on Corporate Governance in Asia

	Bangladesh	China	HK China	India	Indonesia	Malaysia	Pakistan	Philippines	Singapore	South Korea	Ch. Taipei	Thailand	Vietnam
6.3. To what extent is the board responsible for the financial statements included in the company's annual report?	Responsible for timely submission to general meeting	Criminal liability	Fully responsible	Fully responsible	Fully responsible	regulatory authorities Collectively responsible	Fully responsible	Collectively responsible	Certification by directors required	Joint responsibility; Fine of up to 30 million won or up to 3 years imprisonment	Discharged by shareholders, unless unlawful conduct	Liable as far as statement made wilfully or knowingly	Responsible for timely submission to general meeting
6.4. Do insolvent-trading laws apply to directors?	No	No specific regulations	Yes	No specific regulations	Yes	Yes	Yes	NP	Yes	NP	Yes	No	NP
6.5. Is directors/officers liability insurance commonly obtained?	No	No	Yes (for listed companies)	Yes	No	Yes	No	Gaining acceptance	Yes	Yes (for listed companies)	Tendency rising	Yes	No
6.6. In what circumstances is the company prohibited from indemnifying a director?	Breach of duty, breach of trust, negligence, default	In cases of breach of duty prescribed by law, regulation, or article of association	In cases of breach of duty, negligence or default	Actions outside course of employment and director's powers	In cases of negligence, default, breach of duty, breach of trust	In cases of negligence, default, breach of duty, breach of trust	In case of final judgement against the director	When found liable for unlawful acts	In cases of negligence, default, breach of duty, breach of trust	NP	In case of final judgement against the director	None	NP
7. Remuneration of board members													
7.1. Is there a trend towards the use of stock options for directors' remuneration?	No	No	Yes	Yes	Yes	No	No	No	Yes (limitations on the number of options a company can grant)	Yes	Yes (but limited to directors who also act as employees)	Yes (used by 3-5% of listed companies in 2001)	No (only 3 of 20 listed companies use stock-options in 2003)
7.2. Does law or regulations provide for the approval of executive directors' compensation by shareholders?	No	No	Yes	Yes, for Managing Director / Manager, Fulltime Director	Yes	No	No	Yes	Yes	Yes, aggregate amount of compensation, grant of stock options	Yes	Yes	No

White Paper on Corporate Governance in Asia

	Bangladesh	China	HK China	India	Indonesia	Malaysia	Pakistan	Philippines	Singapore	South Korea	Ch. Taipei	Thailand	Vietnam
7.3. Does law or regulations require directors to take a portion of their remuneration in company shares?	No	No	No	No	No	No	No	No	No	No	No	No	No

8. Self-dealing transactions

8.1. Under which circumstances self-dealing transactions must be disclosed to

	Bangladesh	China	HK China	India	Indonesia	Malaysia	Pakistan	Philippines	Singapore	South Korea	Ch. Taipei	Thailand	Vietnam
The board of directors	Any contract or arrangement in which a director is interested	In case of director's direct or indirect interest in a contract or proposed contract	In case of directors' direct or indirect interest in a contract or proposed contract	All transactions by board members, relatives or major shareholders	All related-party and conflicts of interest transactions	All related-party transactions (as recommended by Code on Corporate Governance)	All related party transactions	All related party transactions	NP	Transactions > 1% of total sales or assets, cumulated transaction s > 5 % with same person	In case of personal interest in a matter under discussion at board meeting	Varies from company to company	NP
The shareholders	Loans, guarantees or securities to a director or a company in which a director is interested	In case of director's direct or indirect interest in a contract or proposed contract	If above: (a) HK$ 1M (approx. US$0.125 M); (b) 0.03% of net tangible assets; or (c) 0.01% of total assets (depending on which criterion is adopted)	Transactions by board members, relatives, major shareholders	All related-party and conflicts of interest transactions	All related-party transaction s ≥5% of net tangible assets	Investment (including loans, advances, equity....) in an associated company	All related party transactions	Transaction value (or aggregated annual value) >3% of net tangible assets and above S$100,000	Transactions >1% of total sales or assets, cumulated transaction s >5 % with same person	NP	Transactions exceeding 10 mil Baht or 3% of net tangible assets	Transactions valued at > 20% of total value of assets
The Stock Exchange or Securities Commission?	Any contract or arrangement in which a director is interested	All related party transactions	Transactions disclosed to shareholders disclosed to regulators	No specific regulations	All related-party and conflicts of interest transactions	All related-party transactions	Quarterly returns must be filed with the SECP	All related party transactions	Transaction value (or aggregated annual value) >3% of net tangible assets and above	NP	Disclosure through financial statements and through MOPS for public reporting	Transactions exceeding 1 mil Baht or 0.03% of net tangible assets	Changes in the ownership of related-parties

White Paper on Corporate Governance in Asia

8.5. Under which circumstances self-dealing transactions must be approved by

	Bangladesh	China	HK China	India	Indonesia	Malaysia	Pakistan	Philippines	Singapore	South Korea	Ch. Taipei	Thailand	Vietnam
									S$100,000		companies		
The board of directors	Any contract or arrangement in which a director is interested	All related party transactions	NP	Transactions exceeding a quantified price limit	No specific regulations	Not prescribed	All related party transactions	All related party transactions	NP	Transactions >1% of total sales or assets, cumulated transactions >5 % with same person	NP	All direct or indirect transactions between a director and its company	Related party transactions valued up to 20% of the total value of assets
The shareholders	Loan, guarantee or security to a director or company in which a director is interested	Transactions above 5% of net tangible assets or 30 million RMB	Yes, if the value of the transactions is above: (a) HK$10 M (approx. US$1.25); (b) 3% of net tangible assets; or (c) 1% of total assets (depending on which criterion is adopted)	None	No specific regulations	Transactions ≥25% net tangible assets plus annual shareholders mandate for recurring transactions	Investment (including loans, advances, equity,...) in an associated company	In case the presence of self-dealing director was needed to obtain quorum or vote on the board	Transaction value (or aggregated annual value) >5% of net tangible assets	Grant of stock options	NP	Transactions exceeding 10 mil Baht or 3% of net tangible assets	Transactions valued at > 20% of total value of assets
The Stock Exchange or Securities Commission?	Any contract or arrangement in which a director is interested	Some acquisitions and dispositions (before notification to shareholders)	No, only shareholder approval is required	None	No specific regulations	Announcements as required in KLSE listing requirements	None	None	None	NP	NP	None	NP

Notes

1 THE BACKGROUND

1 Berle and Means, 1932.
2 I will use Western to mean OECD countries, excluding Japan.
3 Berle and Means, ibid.
4 Berle and Means, ibid.
5 Berle and Means, 1932; Jensen and Meckling, 1976.
6 Fama and Jensen, 1983b.
7 Jensen and Ruback, 1983.
8 La Porta, Lopez-de-Silanes and Shleifer, around 1999.
9 'The Business Roundtable is urging boards of directors to designate management responsibility for business resiliency and to periodically review management's plans as part of their oversight function. Business resiliency can include risk assessment and management, business continuity, physical and cyber security, and emergency communications' (April 2003).
10 Apreda, 1999.
11 Gedajlovic and Shapiro, 2002.
12 Davis and Useem, 2000.
13 OECD, 2003. *White Paper on Corporate Governance in Asia*, Paris: OECD.
14 See e.g. Gourevitch and Shinn.
15 Gourevitch, interview.
16 Kagono Tadao, Professor at the Graduate School of Business Administration, Kobe University, Japan.
17 Wu Xun, 2002.
18 Sylvia Ostry, University of Toronto.
19 Davis and Useem, 2000.
20 Babic and Janosevic, 2001.
21 INSEAD, 2003. www.insead.fr/projects/cgep/Public/Objectives.htm (accessed 10 December 2004).
22 OECD, ibid.
23 Claessens, Djankov and Lang, 1999.
24 La Porta, Lopez-de-Silanes and Shleifer, 1998.
25 Claessens *et al.*, 2000.
26 This provides an interesting sidelight on the measurement of corporate governance – should Asian companies receive good marks for this omission?

27 OECD, 2003.
28 Ibid.
29 Ibid.
30 China poses a problem here because of huge regional disparities in per capita GDP.
31 Monks, 2002.
32 Babic, 2001.
33 Boot and Macey, 2002.
34 Carati and Tourani Rad, 2000.
35 Donnelly *et al.*, 2001.
36 OECD, 2001.
37 Becht, 1997.
38 Khan, 2003.
39 E.g. requirements that chief executive and chief financial officers personally certify periodic reports to the SEC, which have had important implications for audit committees.
40 The Asian Corporate Governance Association (ACGA) is an independent, non-profit membership organization working on behalf of all investors and other interested parties for the improvement of corporate governance in Asia. ACGA is funded by a growing network of sponsors and corporate members, including investment funds, financial institutions and other institutions. ACGA advocates the competitive benefits of better corporate governance and works closely with institutional investors, regulators and companies to achieve concrete improvements. It is one of the few organizations systematically researching corporate governance developments around Asia, tracking 11 markets and producing independent analyses of new laws and regulations, investor action and corporate initiatives. ACGA is incorporated under the laws of Hong Kong and is managed by a secretariat based there. Its governing council comprises directors from around Asia.
41 OECD, ibid.
42 Martin, 2002.
43 Ibid.
44 Yeager, 1999.

2 CATCHING UP AND COPYING

1 See Mekong Capital, *Recommendations on Good Corporate Governance Practices in Vietnam*, January 2003.
2 Paul Krugman, 'What happened to Asia?', draft paper, Department of Economics, Massachusetts Institute of Technology, 1998.
3 See Kang, forthcoming.
4 Kang, ibid.
5 S. Nestor, *International Corporate Governance Convergence*, in Nestor and Yasui, 2001.
6 Corporate Governance Forum of Japan 1998.
7 Solomon, *et al.*
8 Edward Chow Kwong-fei, Chairman of the HKSA's Corporate Governance Committee.

9   G. N. Bajpa, Chairman, Securities and Exchange Board of India (Sebi).
10 OECD White Paper, 2003.
11 Andrew Sheng, Chairman, Securities and Futures Commission, Hong Kong.
12 Ken Rushton, director of the UK Listing Authority at the Financial Services Authority (FSA).
13 Including emerging groups, such as the Bank of Communications, China International Trust and Investment Corporation, China Merchants Bank, China Everbright Bank and China Minsheng Banking Corporation, as well as several city commercial banks, especially those in Beijing and Shanghai.
14 Khan, 2003b.
15 Tharman Shanmugaratnam, Singapore Minister of State for Trade and Industry, 2003.
16 OECD, 2003.
17 Christina Ahmadjian, 2001.
18 *Chinese News Weekly* magazine.
19 ACGA first annual conference, November 2001, Hong Kong.
20 Clarke, 2003.
21 Khan, ibid.
22 Christina Ahmadjian, ibid.

3   THE BOARD OF DIRECTORS

1   BIS, *Enhancing Corporate Governance for Banking Organisations*, Basel 1999.
2   MAS Banking Guidelines, 2003.
3   OECD, 2003.
4   Edward Chow Kwong-fei, Chairman of the HKSA's Corporate Governance Committee.
5   Low, 2003.
6   Tokyo Stock Exchange, *Survey on Listed Companies' Corporate Governance*. Tokyo, 2000.
7   MAS, Insurance Company Guidelines, 2003.
8   MAS Guidelines for Bank Corporate Governance, 2003.
9   These rules were established by CSRC in Zhengjianfa [2001] No. 102 issued in August 2001.
10 ACCA, *Responsibility in Business: Governance in China and South East Asia*, 2002.
11 MAS Guidelines for Bank Corporate Governance, 2003.
12 Finance Committee on Corporate Governance, *Code of Corporate Governance*, March 2000.
13 MAS, ibid.
14 Edward Chow Kwong-fei, Chairman of the HKSA's Corporate Governance Committee.
15 MAS, ibid.
16 MAS, ibid.

4 ACCOUNTING STANDARDS AND PROCEDURES

1 If you were a prospective shareholder, though, would you not rather see the order book than the accounts? And you can't see that because of commercial confidentiality – you might after all be a shareholder of a competitor.
2 OECD, 2003.
3 Ibid.
4 Fritz Bolkestein to Harvey Pitt, 29 August 2002.
5 MAS Corporate Governance Guidelines for Banks, February 2003.
6 Discussion of this Board Committee has been deferred from Chapter 3.
7 MAS, ibid.

5 CORPORATE GOVERNANCE AND CORPORATE STRATEGY

1 Chartered Institute of Management Accountants (CIMA).
2 Jesus P. Estanislao, President and CEO, Institute of Corporate Directors, Philippines.
3 Burwell and Mankins, 2002.
4 *Pursuing a Corporate Strategy to Support Future Growth*, Yamaha Motors, 2003.
5 Clarke, 2003.
6 I can vouch for this as a Singapore Permanent Resident myself from the 'heartlands'.
7 Donaldson earned a salary of $18.7 million as chairman of Aetna Inc.
8 Aon Consulting FORUM November 2003.
9 Mak Yuen Teen, 'Performance shares: what's fair, what's not' *Business Times, Singapore*, 28 August 2003.
10 Good governance obliges the author to point out that he is a Vice-President of MHCi.
11 *Asian Advertising & Marketing*, 1991.
12 Aman Mehta, 'Good corporate governance crucial for competitive edge' *Hindu Business Line*, 5 November 2003.
13 Claessens and Fan, 2003.

8 THE ROLE OF ACTIVE SHAREHOLDING IN ASIA

1 The resignation of Rana Talwar from Standard Chartered was very much an exception, but one which is expected to be repeated.
2 Kang, 2003.
3 See OECD tables 2, *Shareholder Participation* for a full comparative list.
4 The OECD tables themselves show that there are clear rules for the timing and agenda of shareholder meetings throughout Asia.
5 Minoo Shroff, Vice-Chairman, Raymond Ltd, July 2002.
6 Jayanthi Iyengar, *Vigilant Shareholders, Vigilante Groups*, Business Line, June 24, 2003.
7 Low, 2003.

9 MEASURING CORPORATE GOVERNANCE

1   CLSA Emerging Markets (CLSA) is a leading provider of brokerage, investment banking and direct investment services in the Asia-Pacific markets with 700 staff spread internationally. Founded in 1986 and headquartered in Hong Kong, CLSA is a unit of France's Credit Lyonnais banking group with substantial staff ownership.
2   CLSA/ACGA fourth annual Corporate Governance report, *CG Watch*: Fakin'it – Board Games in Asia.
3   Amar Gill, CLSA's head of research for Hong Kong and one of the authors of CG Watch.

10 CORPORATE GOVERNANCE AND COMPANY PERFORMANCE

1   E.g. Shelton, Deputy-Secretary General of OECD.
2   Brickley, Coles and Terry, *Journal of Financial Economics*, 1994.
3   Dechow, Sloan and Sweeney, *Contemporary Accounting Research*, 1996.
4   Klein, *Journal of Accounting and Economics*, 2002.
5   Carcello, Hermanson, Neal and Riley, *Contemporary Accounting Research*, 2002.
6   Dechow, Sloan and Sweeney, ibid.
7   Klein, *Journal of Accounting and Economics*, 2002.
8   Beasley, Carcello and Hermanson *Internal Auditing*, 2002.
9   Carcello and Neal, *Accounting Review*, 2002.
10 Raghunandan, Read and Rama, *Accounting Horizons*, 2001.
11 Black, Jang and Kim, 2002.
12 By E. Han Kim.
13 Professor Larry Lang, The Chinese University of Hong Kong.
14 Chen, Chen and Wei, 2003.
15 Claessens and Fan, 2003.
16 Yoser Gadhoum, *Corporate Governance and Top Managers : Potential Sources of Sustainable Competitive Advantage,* Université du Québec à Hull, Research Center SORCIIER, Université Laval.
17 Wiwattanakantang, 2001. See also his contribution to J. P. H. Fan, M. Hanazaki and J. Teranishi (eds), *Designing Financial Systems in East Asia and Japan – Toward a Twenty-First Century Paradigm*, Routledge.
18 Newell and Wilson, 2002.
19 CLSA, 2001.
20 CLSA, 2001.
21 Gugler, Mueller and Yurtoglu, 2001.
22 Klapper and Love, 2002.
23 Claessens and J. Fan, 2003.

11 POLICING CORPORATE GOVERNANCE: COMPLIANCE AND ENFORCEMENT

1   The KPMG 2003 Fraud and Misconduct Diagnostic Survey could be downloaded in pdf format as of January 2004.

321

2 Donald Beskine, Managing Director, ICAR.
3 Black, Jang and Kim, 2003.
4 Derived from their earlier, 2002 paper cited in Chapter 10.

12 THE FUTURE

1 Edward Chow Kwong-fei, Chairman of the HKSA's Corporate Governance Committee.
2 OECD, 2003.
3 Tenev and Zhang, 2002.
4 Clarke, 2003.
5 Companies such as Intel and Hewlett-Packard have built their own in-house networks, but many companies such as Motorola and Tiffany are starting to use a smart network system provided by BoardVantage. The cost for the BoardVantage system depends on which optional functions are selected, and is between $25 and $100K per year.
6 Edward Chow Kwong-fei, Chairman of the HKSA's Corporate Governance Committee.

Selected bibliography

The volume of articles and books on corporate governance in general, and even on Asia in particular, is now so huge that it is essential to point out that this bibliography is a guide to publications found useful, not a comprehensive list. Those marked (*) are now standard reference works. Most have substantial bibliographies of their own.

ACCA (2002) *Responsibility in Business: Governance in China and South East Asia,* ACCA (UK).

Ahmadjian, C. (2001) *Changing Japanese Corporate Governance,* Tokyo: Columbia University Business School.

Apreda, R. (1999) 'Corporate Governance in Argentina – New Developments through 1991–2000', *CEMA Working Papers 154,* Universidad del CEMA.

Audit Committees – Combined Code Guidance (known as the Smith Report), report and proposed guidance by a group sponsored by the UK Financial Reporting Council, January 2003 – see www.frc.org.uk.

Babic, V. (2001) 'The Key Aspects of the Corporate Governance Restructuring in the Transition Process', *Ekonomist,* vol. 33, no. 2, pp. 133–43.

—— and S. Janosevic (2001) 'How to Improve the Process of Strategic Change Management in Transition Economy Enterprises', Strategic Management Society, *21st Annual International Conference,* San Francisco, 21–4 October, p. 10.

Ball, R., A. Robin and S. P. Kothari (2000) 'The Effect of International Insitutional Factors on Properties of Accounting Earnings', *Journal of Accounting and Economics,* vol. 29, no. 1, pp. 1–51.

Becht, M. (1997) *Strong Blockholders, Weak Owners and the Need for European Mandatory Disclosure,* Executive Report. *The Separation of Ownership and Control: A Survey of 7 European Countries,* Preliminary Report to the European Commission, vol. 1, Brussels: European Corporate Governance Network.

Berle, A. and G. Means (1932) (revised edn 1968) *The Modern Corporation and Private Property,* New York: Harcourt, Brace & World. (*)

Black, B. S., H. Jang and W. Kim (2002) *Does Corporate Governance Matter? Evidence from the Korean Market,* Working Paper, Stanford Law School, CA, Korea University, and KDI School of Public Policy and Management.

——, —— and —— (2003) *Does Corporate Governance Affect Firm Value?: Evidence from Korea,* Working Paper 327, Stanford Law School, CA.

Blair, M. M. (1995) *Ownership and Control: Rethinking Corporate Governance for the Twenty-First Century,* Washington, DC: Brookings.

Boot, A. and J. R. Macey (2002) *The Trade-off between Objectivity and Proximity in Corporate Governance*, University of Amsterdam/Cornell University, November.

Burwell, B. and M. C. Mankins (2002) *Improving Corporate Governance from the Inside*, Marakon Associates – see www.marakon.com.

Cadbury Committee (1992) *Report of the Cadbury Committee on the Financial Aspects of Corporate Governance*, London.

Carati, G. and A. Tourani Rad (2000) 'Convergence of Corporate Governance Systems', *Managerial Finance*, vol. 26, no. 10, pp. 66–86.

Chen, J. (2001) 'Ownership Structure as Corporate Governance Mechanism: Evidence from Chinese Listed Companies', *Economics of Planning*, 34, pp. 53–71.

Chen, K. C. W., Z. Chen and K. C. John Wei (2003) *Disclosure, Corporate Governance, and the Cost of Equity Capital: Evidence from Asia's Emerging Markets*, Hong Kong University of Science and Technology.

China Securities Regulatory Commission (CSRC) (2001) *Guidance Opinion on the Establishment of an Independent Director System in Listed Companies*, issued 16 August.

Cho, Jang-yeon, Byung-min Kang and Kyung-soon Kim (2002) *Position Report on Korean Accounting Standards*, 6 September.

Claessens, S. and J. P. H. Fan (2003) 'Corporate Governance in Asia: A Survey', *International Review of Finance*, vol. 3, no. 2, pp. 71–113.

—— , S. Djankov and L. H. P. Lang (1999) 'Who Controls East Asian Corporations?', World Bank Working Paper. (*)

—— , —— , —— , *et al.* (1999) 'Expropriation of Minority Shareholders in East Asia', unpublished Working Paper, Washington, DC: The World Bank.

—— , —— , —— (2000) 'The Separation of Ownership and Control in East Asian Corporation', *Journal of Financial Economics*, vol. 58, pp. 81–112. (*)

Clarke, D. C. (2003) 'Corporate Governance in China: An Overview', Working Paper, University of Washington School of Law, July.

Dahya, J., Y. Yusuf Karbhari, J. Z. Xiao *et al.* (2003) 'The Usefulness of the Supervisory Board Report in China', *Corporate Governance*, vol. 11, no. 4, p. 308, October.

Davis, F. G. and M. Useem (2001) 'Top Management, Company Directors, and Corporate Control', in A. Pettigrew, H. Thomas and Whittington (eds) *Handbook of Strategy and Management*, London: Sage.

Donnelly, S., A. Gamble, G. Jackson and J. Parkinson (2001) *The Public Interest and the Company in Britain and Germany*, Anglo-German Society for the Study of Industrial Society.

Economist Intelligence Unit (2002) *Corporate Governance – The New Strategic Imperative*, sponsored by KPMG – see www.us.kpmg.com.

Fama, E. F. and M. C. Jensen (1983a) 'Agency Problems and Residual Claims', *Journal of Law and Economics*, 26, pp. 327–49. (*)

—— and —— (1983b) 'The Separation between Ownership and Control', *Journal of Law and Economics*, 26, p. 45. (*)

Gadhoum, Y. (1998) *Corporate Governance and Top Managers: Potential Sources of Sustainable Competitive Advantage*, Université du Québec à Hull, Research Center SORCIIER, Université Laval.

Gedajlovic, E. and D. M. Shapiro (2002) 'Ownership Structure and Firm Profitability in Japan', *Academy of Management Journal*, vol. 45, no. 2, pp. 565–7.

Gourevitch, P. and J. Shinn (2002) *How Shareholder Reforms can pay Foreign Policy Dividends*, Washington, DC: Council on Foreign Relations.

Greenbury Committee (1995) *Directors' Remuneration: Report of a Study Group Chaired by Sir Richard Greenbury*, Gee: London.

Gregory, Holly J. (1999) 'Comparison of Board "Best Practices" in Developing and Emerging Markets – Key Issues', August. Weil, Gotshal & Manges, LLP, 2000 edition, www.exgi.org/codes/countrydocuments/comparatives/international_comparison_emerging-markets.pdf (accessed 10 December 2004).

Gugler, K., D. C. Mueller and B. B. Yurtoglu (2001) *Corporate Governance, Capital Market Discipline and the Returns on Investment*, CIC Working Papers FS IV 01–25/Wissenschaftszentrum Berlin.

Hampel Committee (1997) *Final Report of the Committee on Corporate Governance*, Gee: London. (*)

Hart, O. (1995) *Firms, Contracts and Financial Structure*, Oxford: Oxford University Press. (*)

Higgs, D. (2003) *Review of the Role and Effectiveness of Non-executive Directors* (known as the Higgs Report), January 2003 (review sponsored by the UK Department of Trade and Industry and HM Treasury) – see www.dti.gov.uk/cld/non_exec_review/index.htm. (*)

Jensen, M. C. (2000) *A Theory of the Firm: Governance, Residual Claims, and Organizational Forms*, Cambridge, MA: Harvard University Press. (*)

—— and W. H. Meckling (1976) 'Theory of the Firm: Managerial Behavior, Agency Costs and Ownership Structure', *Journal of Financial Economics,* 3, pp. 305–60.

—— and R. Ruback (1983) 'The Market for Corporate Control', *Journal of Financial Economics*, 11, no. 1–4, pp. 5–50. (*)

Kang, D. (2002) *Crony Capitalism: Corruption and Development in South Korea and the Philippines*, Cambridge: Cambridge University Press.

—— (forthcoming) 'The Impact of Enron on Corporate Governance in Asia', *Vermont Law Review*.

Khan, H. A. (2003a) *Corporate Governance: The Limits of the Principal-Agent Approach in Light of the Family-Based Corporate Governance System in Asia*, University of Denver/CIJRE, July.

—— (2003b) *Corporate Governance in Singapore and Hong Kong: What Can the Other Asian Economies Learn?*, University of Denver/CIJRE, July.

Klapper, L. and I. Love (2002) *Corporate Governance, Investor Protection, and Performance in Emerging Markets*, Washington, DC: World Bank.

La Porta, R., F. Lopez-de-Silanes and A. Shleifer (1999) 'Corporate Ownership around the World', *Journal of Finance*, vol. 54, no. 2, April, pp. 471–517. (*)

—— , —— , —— , *et al.* (1998) 'Law and Finance', *Journal of Political Economy*, vol. 106, no. 6, pp. 1113–55.

Learmount, S. (2002) *Corporate Governance: What Can be Learned from Japan?*, Oxford, New York: Oxford University Press.

Loh, C. (2001) 'CEO Civic Exchange', ASIA Inaugural Conference, Hong Kong, www.oecd.org/dataoecd/6/12/1873066.pdf (accessed 10 December 2004).

Low, Chee Keong (2003) *A Roadmap for Corporate Governance in East Asia*, Chinese University of Hong Kong.

Mak Yuen Teen (2003a) 'Performance Shares: What's Fair, What's Not', *Business Times, Singapore*, 28 August.

—— (2003b) *The New U.K. Combined Code vs the Singapore Code of Corporate Governance*, Singapore: NUS.

Martin, R. (2002) 'Politicized Managerial Capitalism: Enterprise Structures in Post-Socialist Central and Eastern Europe', *Journal of Management Studies*, vol. 39, no. 6, pp. 823–39, September.

Mitton, T. A. (2002) 'Cross-Firm Analysis of the Impact of Corporate Governance on the East Asian Financial Crisis', *Journal of Financial Economics*, 64, pp. 215–41.

Monetary Authority of Singapore (2003) *Corporate Governance: Consultation on Guidelines and Regulations*, Singapore, 24 February.

Monks, R. A. G. (2001) *The New Global Investors: How Shareholders Can Unlock Sustainable Prosperity Worldwide*, Oxford: Capstone Publishing.

—— and N. Minow (2001) *Corporate Governance* (2nd edn), Oxford: Blackwell Publishing. (*)

Nestor, S. and J. Thompson (2001) 'Corporate Patterns in OECD Economies: Is Convergence Under Way?', in Stilpon Nestor and Takahiro Yasui (eds), *Corporate Governance in Asia: A Comparative Perspective*, Paris: OECD.

—— and Takahiro Yasui (eds) (2001) *Corporate Governance in Asia: A Comparative Perspective*, Paris: OECD.

Newell, R. and G. Wilson (2002) 'A Premium for Good Governance', *The McKinsey Quarterly*.

OECD (1999) *Principles of Corporate Governance*, www.oecd.org. (*)

—— (2001) 'Corporate Governance and National Development', *Technical Papers No. 180*, www.oecd.org.

—— (2003) *White Paper on Corporate Governance in Asia,* Paris: OECD.

Qi, D., W. Wu and H. Zhang (2000) 'Shareholding Structure and Corporate Performance of Partially Privatized Firms: Evidence from Listed Chinese Companies', *Pacific-Basin Finance Journal*, pp. 587–610.

Rose-Ackerman, S. (1978) *Corruption: A Study in Political Economy*, New York: Academic Press.

Sarkar, J. and S. Sarkar (2000) 'Large Shareholder Activism in Corporate Governance in Developing Countries: Evidence from India', *International Review of Finance*, 1, pp. 161–94.

Shinn, J. and P. Gourevitch (2002) *How ShareholderReforms Can Pay Foreign Policy Dividends*, Washington, DC: Council on Foreign Relations.

Shleifer, A. and R. Vishny (1997) 'A Survey of Corporate Governance', *Journal of Finance*, 52, 737–83. (*)

Solomon, J. F., W. L. Shih, S. D. Norton *et al.* 'Corporate Governance in Taiwan: Empirical Evidence from Taiwanese Company Directors', *Corporate Governance*, vol. 11, no. 3, pp. 235–48.

Tenev, S. and C. Zhang (2002) *Corporate Governance and Enterprise Reform in China: Building the Institutions of Modern Markets*, Washington, DC: World Bank/International Finance Corporation.

Tokyo Stock Exchange (2000) *Survey on Listed Companies' Corporate Governance*, Tokyo.

Tricker, B. (1999) 'Corporate Governance: The Ideological Imperative', in H. Thomas and D. O'Neal *Strategic Integration*, Chichester: Wiley.

Williamson, Oliver E. (1975) *Markets and Hierarchies: Analysis and Antitrust Implications*, New York: Free Press. (*)

326

Wiwattanakantang, Y. (2001) 'Controlling Shareholders and Corporate Value: Evidence from Thailand', *Pacific-Basin Finance Journal*. *See also* his contribution to J. P. H. Fan, M. Hanazaki and J. Teranishi (eds) *Designing Financial Systems for East Asia and Japan – Toward a Twenty-First Century Paradigm*, New York: RoutledgeCurzon.

World Bank (1999) *Corporate Governance: Framework for Implementation*, overview, see www.worldbank.org.

Wu Xun (2002) *Corporate Governance and Corruption: A Cross-Country Analysis* Singapore: National University of Singapore.

Yeager, T. J. (1999) *Institutions, Transition Economies, and Economic Development*, Boulder, CO: Westview Press.

Zhu, J., E. C. Chang and J. M. Pinegar (2002) *Insider Trading in Hong Kong: Concentrated Ownership versus the Legal Environment*, Working Paper: The University of Hong Kong and Brigham Young University.

Index